Prayer in Islamic Thought and Practice

The five daily prayers (*ṣalāt*) that constitute the second pillar of Islam deeply pervade the everyday life of observant Muslims. Until now, however, no general study has analyzed the rules governing *ṣalāt*, the historical dimensions of its practice, and the rich variety of ways that it has been interpreted within the Islamic tradition. Marion Holmes Katz's richly textured book offers a broad historical survey of the rules, values, and interpretations relating to *ṣalāt*. This innovative study on the subject examines the different ways in which prayer has been understood in Islamic law, Sufi mysticism, and Islamic philosophy. Katz's book also goes beyond the spiritual realm to analyze the political dimensions of prayer, including scholars' concerns about the righteousness and piety of rulers. The last chapter raises significant issues around gender roles, including the question of women's participating in and leading public worship. Katz persuasively describes *ṣalāt* as both an egalitarian practice and one that can lead to extraordinary religious experience and spiritual distinction. This book will resonate with students of Islamic history and comparative religion.

MARION HOLMES KATZ is Associate Professor of Middle Eastern and Islamic Studies at New York University. Her publications include *Body of Text: The Emergence of the Sunni Law of Ritual Purity* (2002) and *The Birth of the Prophet Muhammad: Devotional Piety in Sunni Islam* (2007).

Themes in Islamic History 6

THEMES IN ISLAMIC HISTORY comprises a range of titles exploring different aspects of Islamic history, society, and culture by leading scholars in the field. Books are thematic in approach, offering a comprehensive and accessible overview of the subject. Generally, surveys treat Islamic history from its origins to the demise of the Ottoman Empire, although some offer a more developed analysis of a particular period or project into the present, depending on the subject matter. All the books are written to interpret and illuminate the past, as gateways to a deeper understanding of Islamic civilization and its peoples.

Editorial adviser:
Patricia Crone, *Institute for Advanced Study, Princeton University*

Already published:
1. Chase F. Robinson, *Islamic Historiography*
2. Jonathan P. Berkey, *The Formation of Islam: Religion and Society in the Near East, 600–1800*
3. Michael Cook, *Forbidding Wrong in Islam: An Introduction*
4. David Cook, *Martyrdom in Islam*
5. Amy Singer, *Charity in Islamic Societies*

Prayer in Islamic Thought and Practice

Marion Holmes Katz

New York University

CAMBRIDGE
UNIVERSITY PRESS

CAMBRIDGE
UNIVERSITY PRESS

University Printing House, Cambridge CB2 8BS, United Kingdom

One Liberty Plaza, 20th Floor, New York, NY 10006, USA

477 Williamstown Road, Port Melbourne, VIC 3207, Australia

314-321, 3rd Floor, Plot 3, Splendor Forum, Jasola District Centre, New Delhi - 110025, India

79 Anson Road, #06-04/06, Singapore 079906

Cambridge University Press is part of the University of Cambridge.

It furthers the University's mission by disseminating knowledge in the pursuit of education, learning and research at the highest international levels of excellence.

www.cambridge.org
Information on this title: www.cambridge.org/9780521716291

First published 2013

A catalogue record for this publication is available from the British Library

Library of Congress Cataloging in Publication data
Katz, Marion Holmes, 1967–
Prayer in Islamic thought and practice / Marion Holmes Katz.
p. cm. – (Themes in Islamic history)
Includes bibliographical references and index.
ISBN 978-0-521-88788-5 (hardback) – ISBN 978-0-521-71629-1 (pbk.)
1. Prayer – Islam. 2. Salat. I. Title.
BP178.K35 2013
297.3′822–dc23 2012030009

ISBN 978-0-521-88788-5 Hardback
ISBN 978-0-521-71629-1 Paperback

Contents

Acknowledgments

I am grateful to Marigold Acland of Cambridge University Press and to Patricia Crone for proposing this book to me and seeing it through to completion. Their patience, and Professor Crone's inexhaustible erudition, made it a better work than it would otherwise have been. The fifth chapter draws on research done on a grant from the Carnegie Foundation for my project "Contesting the Mosque: Debates over Muslim Women's Ritual Access." Part of the third chapter was presented at the conference "Performing Religion: Actors, Contexts, and Texts" at the Orient-Institut Beirut, November 17, 2011; I thank Ines Weinrich for the opportunity to take part in the conference and the other participants for their feedback. I thank Iftikhar Zaman and Justin Stearns for their generosity in reading drafts and for their thoughtful comments. All errors of fact and interpretation are completely my own.

Working on this book has been a joy to me. My ever-patient husband, Bradley McCormick, humored my enthusiasms and soothed my frustrations. It would not have been possible without him. I dedicate it to Bill and Sue McCormick, who by their example have taught me a lot about faith.

Introduction

Over a number of years teaching a course on comparative religion early in my career, I found that students had differential expectations of the subject areas we would cover when studying specific traditions. Although (for instance) discussion of Buddhism evoked immediate interest in meditative practices, the subject of Islam reliably elicited questions about gender relations and politics. Both of these, of course, are important areas of inquiry (and both will be discussed at various points in this book). However, over time I began to wonder both whether Buddhist meditation and monasticism were actually as innocent of gendered and political connotations as my students seemed to assume, and whether it was possible to direct more attention to aspects of Islam that were more constitutive of Islamic faith and identity. Although Sufi contemplative practices did garner interest, they are not prevalent in all Muslim communities, and American students often perceived them in generic "spiritual" terms scarcely identifiable as Islamic. Hence this work on prayer, which focuses primarily on *ṣalāt*[1] (the canonical prayers ideally performed five times daily), but also on the more free-form *du'ā'*, or supplication. It hopes to direct needed attention to the practice most central both to personal faith and to the public constitution of Muslim communities, while showing that the spiritual and theological concerns inherent to prayer are not disembodied matters isolated from the issues of knowledge and authority that have exercised thinkers in other areas of Islamic law and thought.

This study is primarily a historical one, based on premodern sources (the majority of them dating from the ninth through sixteenth centuries C.E.). Because of this, it is framed largely in the past tense, although many of the practices and ideas described continue to be current. Many of the major sources, although centuries old, are still in print due to demand among contemporary believers, rather than primarily among historians; they are "classical" in the sense of retrospectively forming lasting points of reference for later communities of Muslims (although individual authorities are differently evaluated by

[1] The final "t" in this transliteration represents the Arabic *tā' marbūṭa*; the word can also be rendered as *ṣalāh*.

various sectarian or ideological groupings). Because it is hoped that this book will also be of some use to those whose interests focus on more recent times, in cases where modern developments have introduced major changes in practice or interpretation these have been briefly discussed. This study is based primarily on Arabic-language sources from the Middle East and North Africa, although the underlying issues examined are of broader interest and examples from other areas have been cited where possible.

The subject of prayer is also a useful entry point to the study of Islam because prayer, although certainly not practiced by all individuals, is ubiquitous enough to be familiar to almost everyone. Unlike many other aspects of life in Muslim societies, which were often regarded by Western observers with incomprehension and contempt, historically Islamic prayer practices were often perceived with some degree of sympathy and admiration. For the many devout travelers who wrote of their experiences in centuries past (including many members of the clergy, both Catholic and Protestant), prayer held an uncontested place of honor in their value system, and many of the criteria that Muslims used to evaluate it – including regularity, concentration, and humility – were familiar and shared. If (for instance) marriage in Muslim societies often failed to fulfill evolving European ideals of companionate marriage and female domesticity, and indigenous forms of governance were increasingly decried as "despotic" as Europeans developed (if not necessarily achieved) ideals of egalitarianism and democracy, European and American travelers were often frankly impressed by Islamic worship. Whatever their contempt for the beliefs of Muslims, Westerners often found the devotion of their prayer to be a reproach to the comparative laxity of Christians.

In a very early example, Riccold de Monte Croce, a Dominican missionary from Florence who set out for the Middle East in 1288, wrote, "What shall I say of their prayer? For they pray with such concentration and devotion that I was astonished when I was able to see it personally and observe it with my own eyes."[2] Two centuries later another Dominican, Felix Fabri, sadly observed the contrast between the "gravity and seriousness" of the daily prayers of his Muslim guides and those of his fellow Christian pilgrims to the Holy Land, who pray "with levity and wantonness, with unspeakable lukewarmness at all times, with wandering thoughts and weariness." What is more, many Christians let the entire day pass without engaging in prayer, while this could never occur among Muslims or Jews, "for all these heathens have even a fixed attitude and fashion wherein to pray, which they do not depart from in any case unless compelled by force."[3] A later sixteenth-century Catholic traveler, Guillaume

[2] Riccold de Monte Croce, *Pérégrination en Terre Sainte et au Proche Orient, Texte latin et traduction*, ed. and trans. René Kappler (Paris: Honoré Champion Éditeur, 1997), p. 161.

[3] Felix Fabri, *The Wanderings of Felix Fabri*, The library of the Palestine Pilgrims' Text Society, vol. VII (New York: AMS Press, 1971, reprinted from London edition of 1887–97), pp. 262–3.

Postel, wrote that "whoever saw the modesty, silence, and reverence that the Turks have in their mosques, would be extremely ashamed to see that the churches here are used for chatting, strolling, [and] doing business."[4]

Other Christian observers of the sixteenth to eighteenth centuries similarly praised the "fervor and earnestness," the concentration and the regularity displayed by Muslims in their prayers, which they regarded as a humbling example to their fellow Christians.[5] Typical sentiments were expressed by the late seventeenth-century French Protestant traveler Jean Chardin, who wrote:

> I cannot prevent myself from saying once more that the prayer of the Mahometans [*sic*] is made with an unimaginable reverence, and that one cannot observe the concentration that they bring to it, the zeal and humility with which they accompany it, without admiration. They do not move their eyes; all the movements of their bodies are made most precisely. . . . All of this is so composed, so exact, so considered that they surely put us Christians completely to shame.[6]

Even in the nineteenth century, at the apex of European imperialism, travelers continued to write of Islamic prayer with envy and respect. Edward William Lane, a devoted observer of Egyptian life in the 1830s, affirmed that "the utmost solemnity and decorum are observed in the public worship of the Muslims. . . . Never are they guilty of a designedly irregular word or action during their prayers."[7] Interestingly, one of the themes that gains new prominence in nineteenth-century travelers' descriptions is the egalitarianism of Muslim congregational prayer and of the public space of the mosque. They often regretfully concluded that Muslims were more successful in effacing markers of rank in the unity of prayer than their own Christian communities. Julia Pardoe, who made an extended visit to Istanbul in the 1830s, wrote that an upper-class Ottoman Turk "carries no pomp with him into the presence of his God," unlike the Christian who may "pass into the house of God to tenant a crimson-lined and well-wadded pew, and to listen to the words of inspiration

[4] Guillaume Postel, *Des Histoires Orientales, text modernisé, introduction et notes par Jacques Rollet* (Istanbul: Les Editions Isis, 1999), p. 115.

[5] See Karl H. Dannenfeldt, *Leonhard Rauwolf, Sixteenth-Century Physician, Botanist, and Traveler* (Cambridge, Mass.: Harvard University Press, 1968), p. 182; Antonius Gonzales, *Le Voyage en Egypte du Père Antonius Gonzales, 1665–1666*, ed., trans. from the Dutch, and annotated by Charles Libois, S. J. (Cairo: Institut Français d'Archéologie Orientale du Caire, 1977), 1:213; Joseph Pitts, *A True and Faithful Account of the Religion and Manners of the Mohammetans, with an Account of the Author's Being Taken Captive* (Exon, 1704), pp. 35, 42; Paul Lucas, *Troisieme voyage du Sieur Paul Lucas, fait en MDCCXIV, &c. par ordre de Louis XIV dans la Turquie . . .* (Rouen: Robert Machuel le jeune, 1719), 1:90–1.

[6] Sir John Chardin, *Voyages du chevalier Chardin en Perse, et autres lieux de l'orient, enrichis d'un grand nombre de belles figures en taille-douce, représentant les antiquités et les choses remarquables du pays*, new ed., rev. L. Langlès (Paris: Le Normant, Imprimeur-Libraire, 1811), 7:30–1.

[7] Edward William Lane, *An Account of the Manners and Customs of the Modern Egyptians*, introduced by Jason Thompson (Cairo: American University in Cairo Press, 2003), pp. 83–4.

beside a comfortable stove, in dreamy indifference."[8] The Reverend J. A. Spencer wrote in the mid-nineteenth century of the mosques of Cairo:

> Mats are spread over the entire space, and the worshippers go through with their devotions, high and low, rich and poor, all together, without distinction of classes – a feature of Mohammedanism, which reminded me rather painfully of the different notion of things, which Protestant Christians are apt to entertain in arranging their houses of prayer.[9]

The British traveler Harriet Martineau concurred, writing around the same time:

> We are accustomed to say that there is no respect of persons, and that all men are equal, within the walls of our churches: but I never felt this so strongly in any Christian place of worship as in this Mohammedan one, with its air of freedom, peace, and welcome to all the faithful.[10]

Even missionaries who sought to convert Muslims sometimes found the devotion and humility of their prayers to be a tacit rebuke of Christian failings. In the early twentieth century, Paul Harrison wrote of his observations in the Arabian Peninsula:

> Line behind line, they stand and kneel and prostrate themselves together. The master is there with his slave. The man who has spent twenty years in the schools stands next to a Bedouin who can neither read nor write. The richest man of the community stands next to one who is just out of jail for debt. No one is surprised, for it is the ordinary thing. It would surprise them to be told that there are places in this world where men persist in their conceits and divisions even when standing in the presence of the omnipotent God.[11]

The admiration expressed by nineteenth-century Western commentators for the egalitarianism and inclusiveness of Islamic prayer was balanced (usually by different observers) by a more critical theme, the condemnation of its "formal" and "external" qualities. If some observers were struck by the humble sincerity of Islamic worship, others took the set content of the prayers and the prominent role played in them by bodily postures as indicators that they were merely a matter of exterior show. As we have seen, Felix Fabri – a Catholic who himself performed the liturgy of the hours – had been positively impressed by the fact that Muslims and Jews had "a fixed attitude and fashion wherein to pray." The seventeenth-century Swedish diplomat Ignatius Mouradgea d'Ohsson, a Christian of the Armenian rite who wrote a description of the Ottoman Empire, credited the

[8] Miss Pardoe [Julia Pardoe], *The City of the Sultan; and Domestic Manners of the Turks, in 1836*, 2nd ed. (London: Henry Colburn, Publisher, 1838), 1:95.

[9] Rev. J. A. Spencer, *The East: Sketches of Travel in Egypt and the Holy Land* (New York: George G. Putnam, 1850), p. 193.

[10] Harriet Martineau, *Eastern Life, Past and Present* (London: Edward Moxon, 1848), 2:122.

[11] Cited in Eleanor Abdella Doumato, *Getting God's Ear: Women, Islam, and Healing in Saudi Arabia and the Gulf* (New York: Columbia University Press, 2000), pp. 96–7.

physical discipline of Islamic prayer with creating dispositions with a broad effect on Muslim personal comportment and social life.[12] In contrast, later Protestants – whose own denominations generally eschewed such physical gestures as genuflection in prayer – were often openly disdainful of the physical and rule-bound quality of Muslim canonical worship.

Richard Pococke, a Protestant Irish bishop, wrote sneeringly in the eighteenth century of Egyptian Muslims that "the outward appearance of religion is in fashion among them, and it is looked on as genteel to say their prayers in any place at the usual hours."[13] In the middle of the nineteenth century, Sarah Barclay Johnson acknowledged that Palestinian women assiduously performed their five daily prayers, "thus setting us an example" that would be beneficial if emulated, but dismissed their worship as a mere "bodily exercise" reflecting a theologically incorrect "reliance upon form alone." She is contemptuous of the "numberless kneelings, bowings, prostrations, and unmeaning gesticulations" of Muslim prayer.[14] Mary R. S. Bird, a Protestant missionary working in Iran in the late nineteenth century, notes the "gravity and devoutness" with which Muslims perform their prayers but concludes:

> Yet they are but "vain repetitions"; the greater proportion of the Muslims (at least, in Persia) not understanding Arabic, the "language of God and paradise," in which all their prayers are repeated. They are taught that a mistake in form or position renders the prayer valueless.[15]

In Bird's view, the prayers of Iranian Muslims reflect not only a mistaken attitude towards the importance and efficacy of ritual performance, but a wrong way of addressing themselves to God. The result is, in her view, that their prayers must fail to be morally transformative (as, she implied, were the prayers of Protestant Christians):

> To a Mohammedan prayer is all *duty*; not the happy communing of a child with its Father, nor the child's cry of sorrow or need to the One Who it knows is always able and willing to help. The result is that no power to change the life is gained, no fresh lesson as to how to gain the victory over besetting sin learnt.[16]

Such views were influential in the development of Western scholarship on Islam. William St. Clair Tisdall, another missionary to Iran and the author of a number of studies on Islam, wrote at the beginning of the twentieth century that

[12] d'Ohsson [Mouradgea d'Ohsson, Ignatius], *Tableau Général de l'Empire Othoman* (Paris, 1788), 2:95–6.

[13] Richard Pococke, *A Description of the East, and Some Other Countries* (London: W. Bowyer, 1743), 1:181.

[14] Sarah Barclay Johnson, *Hadji in Syria, or Three Years in Jerusalem* (Philadelphia: James Challen & Sons, 1858; repr. New York: Arno Press, 1977), pp. 222–3, 236, 237.

[15] Mary R. S. Bird, *Persian Women and Their Creed* (London: Church Missionary Society, 1899), p. 7.

[16] Ibid.

"the stress which [Islam] lays upon ceremonial observances, such as fasting, . . . the recitation of fixed prayers at stated hours, the proper mode of prostration, etc., *tends* to make the great mass of Muḥammadans mere formalists."[17] In the mid-twentieth century, the distinguished Islamicist Gustave von Grunebaum similarly wrote that Islamic prayer was characterized by a "peculiar formalism" that "left the believer satisfied with an arid, if physically exacting liturgy."[18]

In part, the devaluation of the set liturgy and prescribed physical postures involved in Islamic prayer reflected an internecine Christian dispute that had been in progress for centuries. Controversies over the recitation of set prayers, the use of a liturgical language incomprehensible to the majority of the faithful, and the appropriateness of bodily acts of devotion such as genuflection were central to the Reformation; as Mary Douglas put it in another context, "Shades of the Reformation and its complaint against meaningless rituals, mechanical religion, Latin as the language of cult, mindless recitation of litanies."[19] However, even within the domain of Christianity these issues cannot be reduced to a binary distinction between ritualist Catholics and anti-ritualist Protestants. Particularly among Protestants, they continued to be debated long after the Reformation. On the one hand, the prescription of liturgy raised complex questions about the relationship between external actions and subjective sentiments. Did ritualized bowing or kneeling constitute an exterior show of piety and submission that might belie the worshiper's true interior attitude, raising the specter of hypocrisy (or at least of futility)? Or, alternatively, did the repetition of appropriate physical postures contribute to the cultivation of proper interior dispositions, fundamentally shaping the person of faith? Did the prescription of specific words preclude the spontaneous expression of genuine religious feeling, or did appropriate, authoritative, and beautiful words alone guarantee the orthodoxy, communality, and effectiveness of prayer?

These questions were vigorously debated even among Christian thinkers working within a single Church, as the expediency of introducing uniform prayer books and the appropriateness of specific liturgical postures came under consideration. Eloquent voices were raised in support of a range of views. Responding to denial of communion on the grounds of his failure to kneel, the seventeenth-century English Puritan William Prynne wrote that God left all "corporal gestures" in prayer at the discretion of worshipers,

> not particularly or precisely commanding in the Old or New Testament, either the gestures of Kneeling, Sitting, Standing, Bowing, or Prostration in Publick or Private

[17] Cited in Paul R. Powers, "Interiors, Intentions, and the 'Spirituality' of Islamic Ritual Practice," *Journal of the American Academy of Religion* 72 (2004), p. 426.

[18] Cited in ibid., p. 427.

[19] Mary Douglas, *Natural Symbols: Explorations in Cosmology* (New York: Pantheon Books, 1982), p. 1.

Prayer. ... The reason is apparent, because those Gestures are in themselves things merely indifferent, and one Gesture may be more decent, expedient to stir up affection, devotion, attention, upon several emergent occasions, in relation to the same, or different persons.[20]

In contrast, another seventeenth-century English divine argued for the "correspondency, and sympathy between the soul and the body," asking rhetorically, "And do we not perceive plainly that when we betake ourselves to our knees for prayer; the soul is humbled within us, by this very gesture?"[21] On the recitation of set prayers, John Milton argued: "This is evident, that they *who use no set forms of prayer*, have words from their affections." In contrast, to impose set prayer formula was "to imprison and confine by force ... those two most unimprisonable things, our Prayers and that Divine Spirit of utterance that moves them."[22]

It is interesting that, although derogatory comments about Islamic prayer were of course not completely new in the nineteenth century, there seems to be a sharp rise in dismissive allusions to its supposedly exterior and formalistic qualities at that time. Since this issue was far from freshly raised among Christians in that period, it is unclear whether the doctrinal convictions of the individuals who expressed these views differed from those of Protestants who had expressed more complimentary views in the past, or (perhaps more likely) if this trend reflects a generally harsher attitude towards Muslims at the high tide of European colonialism.

The idea that *ṣalāt* is mechanical or formalistic is closely related to the notion that it is legalistic. Wael Hallaq has illuminatingly described how modern Western assumptions about the nature and scope of law have distorted perceptions of the sharia, in which rules of ritual performance play a central role.[23] Although the rules of ritual purification and prayer enjoy pride of place in traditional legal compilations, where they usually appear at the beginning and occupy a significant portion of the total space, they have been marginalized in the Western study of the sharia.[24] Very few of the issues addressed here are "legal" in the sense that they could be adjudicated in a court of law. However,

[20] William Prynne, *A moderate, seasonable apology for indulging just Christian liberty to truly tender consciences, conforming to the publike liturgy* ... (London: Printed for the author by T.C. and L.P., 1662) [electronic resource], image 4.

[21] Cited in Ramie Targoff, *Common Prayer: The Language of Public Devotion in Early Modern England* (Chicago: University of Chicago Press, 2001), p. 10.

[22] Cited in ibid., p. 36.

[23] Wael B. Hallaq, *Sharīʿa: Theory, Practice, Transformations* (Cambridge: Cambridge University Press, 2009), pp. 1–3.

[24] In a typical example, Joseph Schacht's classic survey of the sharia simply omits the entire category of ritual law (Joseph Schacht, *An Introduction to Islamic Law* [London: Oxford University Press, 1964], p. 112). Hallaq's survey, while it restores ritual to its rightful place, offers only two pages on prayer (*Sharīʿa*, pp. 230–1).

they are recognizably legal, even by modern Western standards, in the sense that they are analyzed in light of concepts of obligation and validity. Muslim legal scholars (*fuqahāʾ*) ask who is competent to bear the obligation of prayer and under what conditions it is validly discharged or rendered void. Rather than being a purely technical matter, for these thinkers the recognition and fulfillment of a relationship of obligation towards God is a central religious value.

This study thus aims in part to help in restoring ritual to its proper place in the study of the sharia, and legal analysis to its proper place in our understanding of this category of ritual. However, legal analysis has never been the exclusive frame of reference for the interpretation of *ṣalāt*. The Sufi tradition, with its focus on the cultivation of subjective states of intimacy with God and on the interior meaning of religious texts and ritual actions, has offered a powerful alternative approach. Although historically there have sometimes been tensions between Islamic legal scholars and Sufi mystics, overall these two tendencies should not be imagined as reflecting separate and antagonistic groups of Muslims. Neither were introspective or esoteric concerns the exclusive purview of Sufism. Rather, legal analysis, affective engagement, and mystical speculation have been complementary components of the piety of vast numbers of individual Muslims, including scholars.

For centuries, prayer was an arena where European and (later) American observers of Islamic practice could identify more closely with Muslims than in most other areas of life. Coming from backgrounds where congregational prayer was a regular (and often mandatory) feature of public life and individual devotion was often an important personal value, they recognized Muslim prayer as exemplifying many of the religious virtues that they themselves held dear. Regularity of worship, concentration, humility, and the abandonment of pretensions towards one's fellow man were all qualities that required no translation for Christian observers. It is for this reason that they were able to evoke admiration and, in many cases, uncharacteristic moments of self-criticism. Islamic prayer practices also, of course, evoked the issues and conflicts that divided Christians among themselves.

More recently, the decline of organized religion in broad sectors of Western societies has made the language of formal prayer less universally intelligible. This development has been localized and uneven, with (for instance) many more Americans reporting regular attendance at religious services than Europeans. However, even in the United States, where public prayer and congregational life are still enormously prevalent (although not equally so in all regions and social milieus), formal prayer has become a culturally and politically polarizing issue. Organized prayer in public schools and governmental bodies has been the subject of bitter litigation. Even in private life there is an increasing predominance of (particularly younger) Americans who identify themselves as "spiritual" rather than "religious," eschewing many of the trappings of official religion. A 2010 survey by the Pew Forum found that "less than half of adults under age 30 say they pray every day (48%), compared with . . . more than two-thirds of those 65 and older (68%)."[25] Perhaps even more indicative is the fact that the Pew survey apparently does not define "prayer"; the category of "daily prayer" seemingly subsumes anything from the laying of phylacteries to saying grace before meals or taking a moment of meditation before going to sleep. Particularly given the high proportion of Evangelical Christians identified by the survey, it seems likely that a dwindling proportion of Americans (particularly of the younger generation) directly identify with formal prayer as a personal practice or an ideal value.

In this context, non-Muslim readers of this book are less likely to react to the practices described with the admiration and envy recorded by so many premodern observers, or even with the theologically laden criticisms of the more recent past. However, the book's argument is that unfolding the ideals and implications of prayer has been an occasion for the examination of broader issues – regarding the ethically formative powers of human behavior, the individual's ability to discipline the psyche, and the ways in which human interactions with the divine mirror and shape this-worldly relationships and hierarchies – that are of abiding interest even for people who will never engage in the specific rituals under discussion.

[25] www.pewforum.org/Age/Religion-Among-the-Millennials.aspx#practices (accessed June 27, 2011).

1 Canonical prayer (*ṣalāt*) and supplication (*duʿāʾ*)

Development and rules

What did the word *ṣalāt* mean in Arabic before the revelation of the Qurʾān, and was it in origin Arabic at all? Was the ritual (or its components) already familiar in pre-Islamic Arabia? What might it have meant to contemporary observers? As noted by Gerhard Böwering, the Qurʾān appears to assume that the word requires no explanation.[1] The Qurʾān also gives *ṣalāt* an ancient pedigree, using the word to refer to the forms of prayer that were performed and commanded by previous prophets. Prayer – including physical prostration – is represented as a prophetic heritage going back to the beginnings of the human race. Verses 19:58–9 associate prostration and *ṣalāt* with the descendants of Adam, Noah, and Abraham. In some passages it is particularly associated with the line of Abraham, who beseeches in verse 14:40, "O Lord! Make me one who establishes regular prayer (*yuqīm al-ṣalāt*), and also [raise such] among my offspring."[2] Ishmael is described (verse 19:55) as one "who used to enjoin on his people prayer and charity," and Isaac and Jacob were inspired by God "to do good deeds, to establish regular prayers, and to practice regular charity" (21:73). Ritual prayer is also associated with the Jewish and Christian communities; verse 98:5 affirms of the People of the Book, "They have been commanded no more than this: To worship God, offering Him sincere devotion, being true [in faith]; to establish regular prayer, and to practice regular charity." Despite the strong thematic connection between *ṣalāt* and Abrahamic monotheism, however, in the Qurʾān ritual prayer is not associated exclusively with Abrahamic figures; in verse 31:17 the Arabian sage Luqmān counsels his son to "establish regular prayer, enjoin what is just, and forbid what is wrong."

The Abrahamic (or even Adamic) origin of Islamic practices is of course theologically central to Islamic self-definition; like the rites of the *ḥajj*, Arabian practices can be understood to have their ultimate origins in a pristine monotheistic dispensation obscured by local custom. This normative narrative of

1 *Encyclopaedia of the Qurʾān*, ed. Jane Dammen McAuliffe (Georgetown University, Washington D.C.: Brill, 2011), art. "Prayer" (by Gerhard Böwering), 4:218.

2 Quotations from the Qurʾān are based, with modifications, on the translation of Abdullah Yusuf Ali, *The Holy Qurʾan: English Translation of the Meanings with Notes* (Indianapolis: H&C International, 1992).

Islamic origins emphasizes its Arabian roots; although Islam sustains and revives a monotheistic tradition stretching to the beginnings of human history, it is reconstructed in pristine form in the relative cultural isolation of the Arabian Peninsula, where the purity of its divine origin is ensured. One of the central theses of many contemporary secular scholars, in contrast (including many who are to varying degrees revisionist, in the sense of challenging the basic narrative of Islamic origins), is that the Qurʾān and Islam are deeply embedded in the linguistic, theological, and liturgical traditions of the wider Late Antique Near East, particularly of its Jewish and Christian communities.[3]

The word *ṣalāt* itself, whose origins were disputed by classical Islamic scholars, suggests the complexity of the search for precedents. On the one hand, Muslim philologists were at pains to discover authentic Arabic linguistic origins for the term. According to al-Zamakhsharī (d. 538/1144), the literal meaning (*ḥaqīqa*) of the verb *ṣallā* is "to move the parts to the two sides of the tail-bone (*al-ṣalwayn*), because a person performing *ṣalāt* does this while bowing and prostrating."[4] The association of the root ṣ-l-w with the area below or to the sides of the tail of a horse or other animal appears well documented among Arabic lexicographers; derivations from it include the noun *al-muṣallī*, meaning the runner-up in a horse race (because its head is at the hindquarters of the winning steed).[5]

Other derivations suggested by classical scholars reflect the religious content of prayer, rather than its physical postures. The lexicographer al-Fayrūzābādī suggests that *ṣalāt* means "invocation (*duʿāʾ*), mercy (*raḥma*), the seeking of forgiveness (*istighfār*), and the goodly praise of God Most High upon His Prophet" as well as designating the canonical prayers. Although these interpretations skillfully summarize the implications of the various Qurʾanic usages of the term (clearly, the "*ṣalāt*" of God upon human beings [e.g., verse 2:157] cannot mean "invocation" or "prayer," and may well refer to His mercy), they reflect inferences from Qurʾānic diction rather than evidence for the preexisting semantic range of the Arabic root.[6] More fanciful etymologies include the

[3] See, for instance, John Wansbrough, *The Sectarian Milieu: Content and Composition of Islamic Salvation History* (Oxford: Oxford University Press, 1978); Patricia Crone and Michael Cook, *Hagarism: The Making of the Islamic World* (Cambridge: Cambridge University Press, 1977); G. R. Hawting, *The Idea of Idolatry and the Emergence of Islam: From Polemic to History* (Cambridge: Cambridge University Press, 1999). For a discussion of these and more recent contributions to the debate see Gabriel Said Reynolds, *The Qurʾān in Its Historical Context* (London and New York: Routledge, 2008).

[4] Mahmūd ibn ʿUmar al-Zamakhsharī, *al-Kashshāf ʿan ḥaqāʾiq al-tanzīl wa-ʿuyūn al-aqāwīl fī wujūd al-taʾwīl* (Cairo: Muṣṭafā al-Bābī al-Ḥalabī, 1388/1966), 1:131 (commentary on verse 2:3).

[5] Cf. Edward William Lane, *Arabic–English Lexicon* (Beirut: Librairie du Liban, 1980; reprint of London, 1872), 4:1720, s.v. ṣ-l-w; Ismāʿīl ibn Ḥammād al-Jawharī, *al-Ṣiḥāḥ*, ed. Aḥmad ʿAbd al-Ghafūr ʿAṭṭār (Beirut: Dār al-ʿIlm li'l-Malāyīn, 1399/1979), 6:2402, 2403.

[6] See Murtaḍā al-Zabīdī, *Tāj al-ʿarūs min jawāhir al-Qāmūs* (Beirut: Dār al-Kutub al-ʿIlmīya, 1428/2007), 38:240–1 (s.v. ṣ-l-w).

derivation of ṣalāt from *muṣallī*, "runner up," because it is the second religious duty in importance (after faith, *īmān*, itself). Al-Zajjāj (d. 310/923) derives *ṣalāt* from s-l-y, which he argues (based on Qurʾānic usage referring to the abiding of the unbelievers in the Fire) means "to adhere to, stay in permanently"; "it was called this because [prayer] is adherence to what was made obligatory by God."[7] The tenth-century lexicographer Ibn Fāris cites an anonymous (and perhaps Sufi-inflected) etymology that, again deriving *ṣalāt* from the root ṣ-l-y rather than ṣ-l-w, piously likens *ṣalāt* to the process of softening and straightening a reed by exposing it to fire; prayer, in this view, is so called because it rectifies and humbles the believer.[8]

Most of this seems to reflect speculation based on the verbal root of the word *ṣalāt* and its various plausible connections to the phenomenon of Islamic prayer. Only for the meaning of *ṣalāt* as *duʿāʾ* (invocation) was concrete evidence supplied from pre-Islamic Arabic sources. The most widely cited primary evidence for the use of a verbal form in this sense is a rather ambiguous verse from the poet al-Aʿshā, a pagan contemporary of the Prophet Muḥammad.[9] The Qurʾān commentator al-Qurṭubī (d. 671/1272) adds another, more convincing, verse from al-Aʿshā. In it the poet, describing his preparations to depart on a journey, recounts how his daughter exclaims, "O Lord, spare my father hardships and pain!" In return, he fondly wishes her "the same as you have prayed for [for me]" (*ʿalayki mithl al-ladhī ṣallayti*).[10] Here the verb *ṣallā* clearly refers to a pious supplication addressed to God, that is, precisely to *duʿāʾ*.

Thus, the search for Arabic semantic origins – or documented pre-Islamic usages – for the term *ṣalāt* yielded limited results. Even for scholars who accepted that the word was linguistically derived from an Arabic root already used to mean "invocation," it was necessary to propose that its Islamic usage reflected the figurative convention of using the name of a part for the whole, since for them *ṣalāt* – which involved bodily postures as well as spoken prayers – was far more than *duʿāʾ*. The other obvious alternative was that the term was of foreign origin. For some Islamic thinkers, this was religiously

7 Ibid., 38:240.

8 Abū al-Ḥusayn Aḥmad Ibn Fāris, *Mujmal al-lugha*, ed. Hādī Ḥasan al-Ḥammūdī (Kuwait: al-Munaẓẓama al-ʿArabīya li'l-Tarbīya wa'l-Thaqāfa wa'l-ʿUlūm, 1405/1985), 3:234; see also Muḥammad ibn Aḥmad al-Qurṭubī, *Tafsīr al-Qurṭubī (al-Jāmiʿ li-aḥkām al-qurʾān)*, ed. Sālim Muṣṭafā al-Badrī (Beirut: Dār al-Kutub al-ʿIlmīya, 1424/2004), 1:119 (commentary on verse 2:3).

9 The line itself is disputed (an alternative transmitted by another narrator does not use the relevant verb), and the meaning of the verb is unclear; the verse speaks of the wind having "ṣallā ʿalā" and sealed a wine jug, which is glossed (perhaps plausibly, but certainly not inevitably) as meaning that it "prayed that it [that is, the wine] would not turn to vinegar or spoil" (Rudolf Geyer, ed., *Gedichte von ʾAbû Baṣîr Maimûn ibn Qais al-ʾAʿšâ* [London: E. J. W. Gibb Memorial, 1928], p. 29 (poem 4, line 11); for gloss of *ṣallā* in this context see Zabīdī, *Tāj al-ʿarūs*, 38:240.) On the poet see *EI*^{2}, art."al-Aʿshā, Maymūn ibn Ḳays" (by W. Caskel).

10 Geyer, *Gedichte*, p. 73 (poem 13, line 12); Qurṭubī, *Tafsīr*, 1:118.

problematic; the Qurʾānic exegete al-Rāzī (d. 606/1209) held in this connection that every word in the Qurʾān must be authentically Arabic, as indicated by verse 12:2 ("We have sent it down as an Arabic Qurʾān").[11] However, the issue of whether this Qurʾānic statement actually precluded the possibility of foreign words appearing in the Qurʾān was debated by classical scholars; both early and medieval exegetes often suggested non-Arabic derivations for puzzling Qurʾānic terms, and some authorities simply required a loan word to have been incorporated into Arabic usage early enough to have been comprehensible to the first Arabian listeners of the revelation.[12] With respect to the closely related Qurʾanic term *ṣalawāt* (verse 22:40), which is understood to refer to synagogues, a series of alternative spellings transmitted in non-canonical readings (*qirāʾāt*) of the Qurʾān strongly suggests efforts to render a Syriac or Hebrew word phonetically in Arabic. Some Arabic lexicographers made this explicit; others found it troubling.[13] (Yet a third option was to hypothesize that the word *ṣālāt* was a new Qurʾānic coinage corresponding to a religious practice newly legislated by God, although this solution did not necessarily satisfy thinkers who insisted that the Qurʾān was in pure Arabic.[14])

Other instances of early Arabic usage suggest an association between the verb ṣ-l-w and the religious practices of Christians and Jews that may have predated (at least somewhat) the rise of Islam. The poet Labīd (a contemporary of al-Aʿshā – and of the Prophet Muḥammad – who is said to have become a Muslim late in life) speaks of a traveler arising in the early morning and groping in the gloom for his saddle blankets, "like a Jew praying" (*kaʾl-yahūdī*

[11] Al-Fakhr al-Rāzī, *al-Tafsīr al-kabīr* (Beirut: Dār Iḥyāʾ al-Turāth al-ʿArabī, n.d.), 3:44.

[12] See, for instance, ʿAbd al-Ḥaqq ibn ʿAṭīya al-Gharnāṭī, *al-Muḥarrar al-wajīz fī tafsīr al-kitāb al-ʿazīz*, ed. Aḥmad Ṣādiq al-Mallāḥ (Cairo: al-Majlis al-Aʿlā li'l-Shuʾūn al-Islāmīya, 1394/1974), 1:70.

[13] Majd al-Dīn Muḥammad ibn Yaʿqūb al-Fayrūzābādī, *al-Qāmūs al-muḥīṭ* (Cairo: Muṣṭafā al-Bābī al-Ḥalabī, 1371/1952), 4:355; Zabīdī, *Tāj al-ʿarūs*, 38:242. See also Arthur Jeffery, *The Foreign Vocabulary of the Qurʾan* (Baroda: Oriental Institute, 1938), p. 197.

[14] This is the option chosen by the tenth-century Arabic linguist Ibn Fāris and, following him, by the great late medieval scholar al-Suyūṭī (d. 911/1505). Among his examples, Ibn Fāris cites the word *kufr* (unbelief), which in the pre-Islamic period meant only "to cover or conceal," and *fisq* (iniquity, sin), which (so Ibn Fāris) originally referred to a date's emergence from its skin, but was repurposed in the Islamic dispensation to refer to a person's casting off obedience to God. As for the term *ṣalāt*, he states that before its meaning was revised and expanded by the divine law it simply meant "invocation." (Cited in Jalāl al-Dīn al-Suyūṭī, *al-Muzhir fī ʿulūm al-lugha wa-anwāʿihā*, ed. Muḥammad Aḥmad Jād al-Mawlā et al. [Cairo: ʿĪsā al-Bābī al-Ḥalabī wa-Shurakāʾuhu, n.d.], 1:294–5.) The Muʿtazilīs also held *ṣalāt* to be a technical term that originated with Islam, arguing that since prayer as defined by divine law was a new phenomenon instituted by revelation, the name designating it could not rationally have pre-dated the thing designated; their argument was later adopted by scholars beyond the school. See Zabīdī, *Tāj al-ʿarūs*, 38:241; Mohamed Mohamed Yunis Ali, *Medieval Islamic Pragmatics: Sunni Legal Theorists' Models of Textual Communication* (Richmond: Curzon Press, 2000), pp. 16–17, 108; David R. Vishanoff, *The Formation of Islamic Hermaneutics: How Sunni Legal Theorists Imagined a Revealed Law* (New Haven, Conn.: American Oriental Society, 2011), p. 24.

al-muṣallī); Arabic commentators interpret this as a reference to a Jewish mode of prostration in prayer.[15] Here the verb seems to mean "to pray" in the more expansive sense of physical as well as verbal worship. Another example occurs in a poem of the Christian poet ʿAdī ibn Zayd, who lived in the second half of the sixth century. ʿAdī declares, "Indeed I am, by God – accept my oath! – a monk, who moans[16] every time he prays."[17] It is perhaps also worth noting that al-Aʿshā, the source of the other two relevant uses of the verb noted in the Islamic sources, was (like ʿAdī) also a Christian whose training as a poet occurred in the Northern Arabian Christian center of al-Ḥīra.[18] Another pre- (or at least non-) Islamic usage of the active participle similarly refers to the context of Christian Ḥīra.[19] Overall, these examples suggest that the *ṣallā* in the sense of "pray" was distinctively associated at the time of the rise of Islam with Jewish and Christian practices.

The current academic consensus is that *ṣalāt* is, indeed, in origin a foreign term.[20] Beyond issues of linguistic roots, the combination of standing, recitation of scripture, and repeated prostration characteristic of *ṣalāt* (as well as the emphasis on nighttime prayer vigils that, as we shall see, features in early passages of the Qurʾān as well as later Islamic piety) appears to most closely parallel the documented practices of contemporary Eastern Christians. Michael Morony points out that "Monophysite [Christian] monks in Amid [in Iraq] in the sixth century were described as performing nightly vigils while prostrate on their faces in tearful prayer or while arranged in rows, supported by standing posts or tied to the walls or to the ceiling to keep them on their feet all night."[21] In contrast, whereas prostration is characteristic of Israelite Temple worship as described in the Hebrew Bible, the formal daily prayers prescribed by rabbinic Judaism involve only standing, bowing, and recitation.[22] Within the Qurʾān,

15 Labīd ibn Rabīʿa, *Sharḥ Dīwān Labīd ibn Rabīʿa al-ʿĀmirī*, ed. Iḥsān ʿAbbās (Kuwait: Wizārat al-Irshād wa'l-Inbāʾ, 1962), p. 183 (qaṣīda 26, line 32). For the poet's identity see *EI*², art. "Labīd b. Rabīʿa, Abū ʿAḳīl" (by C. Brockelmann).

16 The verb *jaʾara* means "to low, moo" (like a cow), and (consequently) "to supplicate, pray fervently." See Hans Wehr, *Arabic–English Dictionary*, ed. J. M. Cowan (Ithaca: Spoken Language Services, 1976), s.v. j-ʾ-r.

17 Abū'l-Faraj al-Iṣfahānī, *Kitāb al-Aghānī* (Cairo: al-Muʾassasa al-Miṣrīya al-ʿĀmma li'l-Taʾlīf wa'l-Tarjama wa'l-Ṭabāʿa wa'l-Nashr, n.d.), 2:113.

18 Caskel,"al-Aʿshā, Maymūn b. Ḳays."

19 See M. M. Bravmann, *The Spiritual Background of Early Islam: Studies in Ancient Arab Concepts* (Leiden and Boston: Brill, 2009), pp. 271–2 (reference to *muṣallūn* in a poem by al-Nābigha al-Dhubyānī).

20 Böwering,"Prayer," 4:217; Jeffery, *Foreign Vocabulary*, pp. 198–9. Here the verb *ṣallā* ("to pray") is understood to be derived from the noun *ṣalāt* (rather than vice versa, which would be the norm in the Semitic system of verbal roots); see ibid., p. 198.

21 Michael Morony, *Iraq after the Muslim Conquest* (Princeton: Princeton University Press, 1984), pp. 446–7.

22 See Uri Ehrlich, *The Nonverbal Language of Prayer: A New Approach to Jewish Liturgy*, trans. Dena Ordan (Tübingen: Mohr Siebeck, 2004), pp. 29–30.

nighttime prayer vigils involving standing, recitation, and prostration are associated with unspecified groups among the People of the Book (3:113); both bowing and prostration are enjoined on the Virgin Mary (3:43), and bowing is explicitly asociated with the Children of Israel (2:43). More broadly, Jews and Christians performed prayers repeatedly at set times of day; a specific spatial orientation (for Jews, Jerusalem, and for Christians, East) was also customary. Although Zoroastrians did not have a prayer ritual comparable to *ṣalāt*, they performed a purification rite similar to *wuḍūʾ* (the minor ritual ablution) repeatedly over the course of the day, standing and facing in a prescribed direction (either toward a light or sacred fire or toward the south).[23]

However, none of this means that either the term *ṣalāt* or the practices associated with it were exclusively Judeo-Christian. Angelika Neuwirth notes that early passages of the Qurʾān make no apparent distinction between the *ṣalāt* of Muslims and pagans except in terms of quality (as suggested by verses 107:3–5, non-believers are negligent and hypocritical in their devotions).[24] Uri Rubin infers, based on early reports that "the [pagan] Quraysh did not find any fault" with the morning (*ḍuḥā*) prayer and that it was first performed by Bedouin in thanksgiving for successful trade, that it may have been "a pre-Islamic Arab practice."[25] Although it is certainly possible that a form of prayer referred to as *ṣalāt* and involving prostration had already become customary among some Arabs in the Prophet's immediate environment before the rise of Islam, however, evidence is slim; if this is in fact the case, the lack of data may reflect the Islamic tradition's lack of interest in tracing the genealogy of this practice into the pagan Arabian past, even understood (like the *ḥajj*) as a relic of the Abrahamic legacy.

The overall evidence suggests that the term *ṣalāt*, and its major components, were known in Arabia at the time of the Prophet but that it was fundamentally reconfigured by the Islamic dispensation and achieved a salience that was totally new for pagan Arabs. To judge by the Qurʾānic evidence, the heart and essence of *ṣalāt* is the act of prostration (*sujūd*). The Qurʾān describes this posture as being the fundamental stance of the cosmos towards its Creator. God asks of the unbelievers, "Have they not looked at all the things God has created, how their shadows turn round to the right and the left, prostrating themselves to God in the humblest manner? And to God prostrates itself (*yasjudu*) all that is in the heavens and on earth, whether moving creatures or angels; they are not arrogant" (16:48–9; see also verses 13:15, 22:18, 55:6). As emerges from these

[23] Jamsheed K. Choksy, *Purity and Pollution in Zoroastrianism: Triumph over Evil* (Austin: University of Texas Press, 1989), pp. 53–62.

[24] Angelika Neuwirth, "Du texte de récitation au canon en passant par la liturgie," *Arabica* 47 (2000), pp. 210–11.

[25] Uri Rubin,"Morning and Evening Prayers in Early Islam," *Jerusalem Studies in Arabic and Islam* 10 (1987), p. 44.

verses, prostration is quintessentially an expression of humility and the opposite of arrogance (*istikbār*).

Toshihiko Izutsu has argued that, in the rhetorical structure of the Qurʾān, the foundational concept of *īmān* (faith) is opposed not primarily to "unbelief" in the sense of cognitive ignorance or rejection of the ideas of monotheism and prophecy, but to *kufr* in the sense of "ingratitude" – a stance of haughty disregard for God's innumerable favors, despite their manifest presence in the surrounding world.[26] Although this inner stance of arrogance toward the Creator can be expressed in many acts of disobedience and disregard, such as failure to show compassion to the weak and needy, the refusal to humble oneself in worshipful prostration is its ultimate emblem. The paradigmatic instance of refusal to prostrate in the Qurʾān is, strikingly, not toward God but toward the newly created first human, Adam. In verse 2:34 God declares, "And behold, We said to the angels: 'Bow down before Adam,' and they bowed down, all but Satan, who refused and was haughty; he was of those who reject faith." The number of times that this incident is invoked in the Qurʾān (see also 7:11, 15:28–33, 17:61, 18:50, 20:116) emphasizes its symbolic centrality. Satan refuses to prostrate himself out of pride (*istikbār*) and a sense of superiority to Adam (cf. verses 7:12, 17:61, 15:33). God responds to Satan's haughtiness (*takabbur*, literally "making himself big") by making him humble (*min al-ṣāghirīn*, literally "one of the small": verse 7:13). Prostration is a form of voluntary self-humiliation that reflects created beings' inherent subordination to God; when Satan refuses to do it out of an inflated sense of self-worth, God (so to speak) "cuts him down to size."

In the Qurʾānic story of Joseph, his brothers are initially estranged by a dream predicting that they will one day prostrate themselves before him. At the denouement of the story, they fulfill the dream by doing so (verse 12:100). Here again, prostration does not appear to be an act of worship reserved exclusively for God, but a more general expression of subordination toward a person of higher rank; Joseph is a high official in the Egyptian court, his brothers' benefactor, and their moral superior. Like Satan, Joseph's brothers are (initially) repelled by the act of prostration because it establishes a hierarchical relationship between the prone subordinate and the recipient of his obeisance. Within the text of the Qurʾān, read in isolation from the commentarial tradition, the performance of *sujūd* toward a human superior does not appear to be problematic; although God is at the apex of all hierarchies, and is thus the ultimate object of all appropriate deference, it appears that prostration in prayer is just one instance of a gesture that may also be performed in some contexts toward human superiors.

[26] Toshihiko Izutsu, *Ethico-Religious Concepts in the Qurʾān* (Montreal and Kingston: McGill–Queen's University Press, 2002), p. 120.

Evidence from pre-Islamic poetry suggests that prostration was familiar in Arabia both as a gesture of submission or deference to a high-status individual and as an act of religious devotion particularly associated with Christians and Jews.[27] Roberto Tottoli concludes that "Poetry and historical reports indicate that, at the time of Muḥammad, Arabs were acquainted with the *sujūd*, but that they considered it a foreign practice which could be appreciated as a poetic device for giving praise or performed to certain extent before kings when abroad, but which was essentially alien to their pre-Islamic pagan customs."[28]

The introduction of *sujūd* as a mandatory physical expression of subordination to God is represented by early Islamic sources as having offended the sensibilities of pagan Arabs, particularly those who (like Quraysh) traditionally enjoyed high status. The powerful and prestigious tribe of Thaqīf, negotiating the terms of its conversion, is said to have vainly demanded to be relieved of the obligation to prostrate themselves in prayer (which they characterized as "humiliation"). M. J. Kister observes:

> According to Arab concepts of honor prostration was deemed demeaning. This is well reflected in the reply of Abū Ṭālib, when invited by the Prophet to follow him in prayer: "I know that you are on the right path, but I do not like to prostrate so that my hindquarter is higher than (the rest of) me." . . . It is indeed instructive to find that [the self-styled prophet] Musaylima, when praying in front of Arabs, ordered them to perform the prayer upright, in the manner of noblemen.[29]

Beyond a general sense of "honor," it is unclear whether this distaste for prostration reflected indigenous Arabian egalitarianism or an indigenous Arabian sense of social hierarchy. Both the tribe of Thaqīf and the Prophet's uncle Abū Ṭālib enjoyed high rank in the order of pre-Islamic Arabia, and their reluctance to prostrate may be interpreted as an expression of their sense of social standing; Musaylima's followers may not have been "noblemen," but they apparently aspired to this rank.

Although both the Qur'ān and Arabic poetry appear to represent *sujūd* as a gesture performed both toward God and toward human superiors, *sīra* (Prophetic biography) and *ḥadīth* radically sever the two customs and assume a blanket prohibition on prostration to human beings. This principle was pointedly contrasted with the customs of other communities with which the nascent Muslim *umma* came into contact, including both pagans and Christians. A report in the *Musnad* of Aḥmad ibn Ḥanbal (d. 241/855) recounts an incident set at the court of the Christian monarch of Ethiopia, where persecuted Muslims

[27] Roberto Tottoli, "Muslim Attitudes Towards Prostration (*sujūd*): I. Arabs and Prostration at the Beginning of Islam and in the Qur'ān," *Studia Islamica* 88 (1998), pp. 9–12.

[28] Ibid., pp. 14–15.

[29] M. J. Kister, "Some Reports Concerning al-Ṭā'if," *Jerusalem Studies in Arabic and Islam* 1 (1979), pp. 3–4.

took refuge before the Hijra to Medina. When two emissaries of the pagan Meccans come in pursuit of them, the anecdote relates, they prostrate themselves (*sajadā*) in greeting. When the Muslims are summoned at their request, however, they merely give the Islamic salutation of peace. Challenged, their spokesperson replies, "We prostrate ourselves only to God Most High."[30] Here the refusal to prostrate oneself to a fellow human is constitutive of Islamic identity. It implies a sense of egalitarianism among human beings that is explicitly expressed in other early Islamic texts. For instance, in a report about the conquest of Persia recorded by al-Ṭabarī, the Muslim emissary commits a series of blatant violations of Persian etiquette before declaring to the commander, "God has sent us and brought us here so that we may extricate those who so desire from servitude to the people [here on earth] and make them servants of God."[31]

In another report recorded in the third Islamic century, Ibn Māja transmits:

> When Muʿādh returned from Syria, he prostrated himself to the Prophet. [The Prophet] said, "What is this, Muʿādh?!" He said, "I came to Syria and found that they prostrated themselves to their bishops and commanders;[32] I wished in my heart that we could do that to you." The Messenger of God said, "Don't do that! If I were to command anyone to prostrate to someone other than God, I would command a woman to prostrate herself to her husband."[33]

Although this report underlines the repudiation of prostration to a human being (despite a woman's subordination to her husband, she should not in fact bow down before him), it also suggests the continuing vitality of the connection between prostration as an act of submission to God and as an expression of deference within the human social hierarchy.

Narratives report that the Prophet Muḥammad was instructed in *ṣalāt* by the angel Gabriel himself, who modeled the correct performance of ablution and prayer immediately after the beginning of his prophetic mission.[34] Muslim scholars generally accept that the obligation of *ṣalāt* was imposed on the Islamic community at large on the occasion of the Prophet's ascension to heaven (*miʿrāj*). In a report recorded by al-Bukhārī (d. 256/870) the Prophet recounts how he rose to a level where the scratching of the pens of the heavenly scribes was audible to him. God initially imposes fifty daily prayers upon his

30 Aḥmad ibn Ḥanbal, *Musnad al-imām Aḥmad ibn Ḥanbal*, supervised by ʿAbd Allāh ibn ʿAbd al-Muḥsin al-Turkī, ed. Shuʿayb al-Arnaʾūṭ (Beirut: Muʾassasat al-Risāla, 1416/1996–), 7:408.

31 Muḥammad ibn Jarīr al-Ṭabarī, *The History of al-Ṭabarī, vol. XII: The Battle of al-Qādisiyya and the Conquest of Syria and Palestine*, trans. Yohanan Friedman (Albany: SUNY Press, 1992), p. 67.

32 For the meaning of *biṭrīq* see Zabīdī, *Tāj al-ʿarūs*, 25:49.

33 Ibn Māja, *Sunan, Kitāb al-Nikāḥ, Bāb Ḥaqq al-zawj ʿalā al-marʾa.*

34 See, for instance, A. Guillaume, *The Life of Muhammad: A Translation of Ibn Ishaq's Sirat Rasul Allah* (Karachi: Oxford University Press, 1967), pp. 112–13.

community; following the counsel of Moses, Muḥammad negotiates until the number is reduced to a manageable five, which will yield the reward of the original fifty.[35]

Although some narratives imply that the prayers were instituted on a single occasion very early in the Prophet's mission, both the Qurʾān and other *ḥadīth* suggest a longer process of development (or, from a religious point of view, of divine promulgation) of different aspects of *ṣalāt.* Angelika Neuwirth has argued that a number of Meccan chapters of the Qurʾān have structural and thematic features that suggest that they were originally intended for liturgical use, reflecting a prayer ritual that involved prostration and recitation of the salvation history of the emerging community.[36] This is a plausible hypothesis, but such a prehistory is not explicity reflected in the sources. Various Qurʾānic passages suggest that the daily prayers were originally performed twice, in the morning and the evening (verses 6:52, 7:205, 11:114, 18:28, 20:130).[37] In addition to prayers at the beginning and end of the daylight hours, the Qurʾān refers to nighttime vigils, involving prayer and recitation of the Qurʾān, as a central form of worship. Verses 17:78–9 declare: "Establish regular prayers – at the sun's decline to the darkness of the night, and the morning prayer and recitation . . . And pray in the small watches of the morning" (see also 20:130, 25:64, 76:26). Verse 73:20 eases the expectations for lengthy nocturnal devotions, encouraging the believers to "recite as much of the Qurʾān as may be easy" rather than holding vigil for a specific portion of the night. Passages of the Qurʾān traditionally regarded as later (revealed after the Hijra) reflect additions to the times of the daily prayers, particularly one performed in the middle of the day (cf. verses 2:238, 30:17–18).[38]

Although it is possible (at least tentatively) to identify each of the five daily prayer times in the text of the Qurʾān, the Qurʾān itself does not explicitly enumerate them. As the great early jurist al-Shāfiʿī (d. 204/820) himself noted, for this we are dependent upon *ḥadīth*.[39] As al-Shāfiʿī also observed, the Qurʾān also does not specify the exact components or number of repetitions in each prayer. Once again, *ḥadīth* suggest some development; in a report presented by al-Bukhārī, ʿĀʾisha states that each prayer originally comprised two prostration cycles.[40] The many *ḥadīth* reflecting details of the prayer ritual were

[35] al-Bukhārī, *Ṣaḥīḥ*, *Kitāb al-ṣalāt*, *Bāb kayfa furiḍat al-ṣalawāt fīʾl-isrāʾ*; see also Guillaume, *Life of Muhammad*, pp. 186–7.

[36] Neuwirth, "Du texte de récitation."

[37] Böwering, "Prayer," 4:223. See also Rubin, "Morning and Evening Prayers," p. 41 (citing al-Balādhurī).

[38] Böwering, "Prayer," 4:222, 224.

[39] Muḥammad ibn Idrīs al-Shāfiʿī, *al-Risāla*, ed. Aḥmad Muḥammad Shākir (Beirut: Dār al-Kutub al-ʿIlmīya, n.d.), pp. 176–7.

[40] Bukhārī, *Ṣaḥīḥ*, *Kitāb al-ṣalāt*, *Bāb kayfa furiḍat al-ṣalawāt fīʾl-isrāʾ*; see also Guillaume, *Life of Muhammad*, p. 112.

synthesized into clear and comprehensive rules by the early Islamic jurists, as well as being based on the continuous practice of the community. There follows an outline of the conditions and requirements of *ṣalāt* as laid out in classical Islamic legal sources.

Ṣalāt: conditions and components

Ṣalāt must be performed five times a day by every sane person who has reached the age of legal responsibility.[41] The timing of these five daily prayers is established by a report (*ḥadīth*) recounting that the angel Gabriel came to the Prophet and said, "Arise and pray," then performed the noon (*ẓuhr*) prayer when the sun began to decline from the zenith. Gabriel returned and instructed the Prophet to pray in the mid-afternoon (*ʿaṣr*) when the shadow of an object was equal to its height, at sundown (*maghrib*) when the disc of the sun disappeared beneath the horizon, in the evening (*ʿishāʾ*) when the glow of sunset had disappeared, and at sunrise (*fajr*) when the first rays of dawn arose. On the following day, Gabriel instructed the Prophet to pray *ẓuhr* when an object's shadow was equal to its height, *ʿaṣr* when its shadow was twice its height, *maghrib* again when the sun set, *ʿishāʾ* halfway through the night, and *fajr* when the sun had fully dawned. In closing, he instructed the Prophet that the time of each prayer was between those two times.[42]

Shīʿite sources preserve somewhat divergent reports about the timing of the prayers, with the stipulated time for the *ʿaṣr* prayer beginning as soon as it is possible to complete the noon prayer. The two prayers may thus form a continuous sequence. Since the time of the *ʿishāʾ* prayer is also defined as beginning as soon as it is possible to complete *maghrib*, Shīʿites also traditionally perform these two prayers as a continuous bloc, or separated by a short interval. As a result, although they observe the same five prayers as Sunnīs, because they combine two pairs of prayers Shīʿites in effect have three daily prayer times rather than five.[43]

[41] The obligation to pray is contingent on reaching puberty (*al-bulūgh*), which is identified by its physical signs (for instance, the growth of pubic hair or the onset of menstruation) rather than being set at a specific age. Although a child who has not reached biological puberty is not obligated to pray, his or her prayer will be valid (as a supererogatory act) if the child is mature enough to understand what he or she is doing (*al-tamyīz*). A *ḥadīth* of the Prophet states that a child should be told to pray at seven, and disciplined for failure to do so at ten (see, for instance, Abū Dāwūd, *Sunan*, *Kitāb al-Ṣalāt*, *Bāb Matā yuʾmaru al-ghulām bi'l-ṣalāt*).

[42] Wahba al-Zuḥaylī, *al-Fiqh al-islāmī wa-adillatuhu* (Damascus: Dār al-Fikr, 1425/2005), 1:663 (the *ḥadīth* is transmitted by Ibn Ḥanbal and al-Nasāʾī).

[43] See Zayn al-Dīn al-ʿĀmilī (al-Shahīd al-Thānī), *al-Rawḍa al-bahīya fī sharḥ al-Lumʿa al-dimashqīya* (Qum: Majmaʿ al-Fikr al-Islāmī, 1429), 1:150–2 (Imāmī/"Twelver" Shīʿite); David Thurfjell, *Living Shiʾism: Instances of Ritualisation among Islamist Men in Contemporary Iran* (Leiden: Brill, 2006), p. 30; al-Qāḍī Abū Ḥanīfa al-Nuʿmān ibn Muḥammad, *Daʿāʾim al-islām*, ed. Āṣif ibn ʿAlī Aṣghar Fayẓi (Cairo: Dār al-Maʿārif; bi-Miṣr, 1389/1969), 1:138–9 (Ismāʿīlī/"Sevener" Shīʿite).

In general, scholars hold that it is preferable to perform the prayer at the beginning of the stipulated time period, although it can be validly performed until the end. The exception to this rule is the *ʿishāʾ* (evening) prayer; rather than preferring that it be performed as soon as possible after darkness falls, it is held to be particularly meritorious to delay it until the middle of the night. If one fails for any reason to perform a prayer within the specified time period, one can (and should) make it up later (*qaḍāʾ*). However, one must not willfully delay prayers after their designated time; some scholars even questioned whether voluntarily omitted prayers could be made up (aside from the ever-present possibility of divine forgiveness).[44] One is not obligated to perform prayers that were missed because one was at the time incapable of performing them validly (for instance, a woman need not make up the prayers missed when she was menstruating) or in a state that exempted one from legal responsibility altogether (such as insanity or fainting). However, if the state in question was incurred through one's own intention and fault (for instance, if one willfully got drunk), one is obligated to make up any prayers missed. Disbelief, like drunkenness, is regarded by most scholars as a status that renders one incapable of performing valid prayer but culpable for one's failure to rectify the situation (in this case, by embracing Islam). Nevertheless, a non-believer who embraces Islam is not obligated to perform the prayers missed since he or she reached puberty (which for a mature convert could be a significant burden, and thus a significant

[44] See Ibn Qayyim al-Jawzīya, *Kitāb al-ṣalāt wa-ḥukm tārikihā* (Amman: Dār al-Furqān, 1423/2003), pp. 72–80. However, since most affirmed the obligation to make up missed prayers, believers who repented after a misspent youth or an adult turn to religiosity could devote significant time to making up the deficit. See Pitts, *A True and Faithful Account*, p. 35. In Imāmī Shīʿism there is the possibility that missed prayers (particularly those that could not be performed during one's final illness) may be made up after death by the eldest son of the deceased or by a person who is hired with money from a bequest for that purpose. See al-Shahīd al-Thānī, *Rawḍa*, 1:261, 290–1 (note the opinion that willfully omitted prayers may not be made up in this way); for a modern example see Lara Deeb, *An Enchanted Modern: Gender and Public Piety in Shiʾi Lebanon* (Princeton and Oxford: Princeton University Press, 2006), p. 104. Sunnīs generally hold that "physical" acts of worship such as *ṣalāt* (unlike "financial" ones such as *zakāt*) cannot be performed on someone else's behalf (see Zuḥaylī, *Fiqh*, 3:1094–5). However, such practices have been known among Sunnīs in some times and places; the Syrian Ḥanafī Muḥammad ibn Muḥammad ibn ʿĀbidīn (d. 1306/1889) has an epistle on the use of bequests to pay for makeup prayers, and even advises that one have the prayers of one's entire adult lifetime repeated in case they were unintentially invalid ("Minnat al-jalīl li-bayān isqāṭ mā ʿalā al-dhimma min kathīr wa-qalīl," in *Majmūʿat rasāʾil Ibn ʿĀbidīn* [n.p., n.d.], 1:207–30, esp. pp. 211–12). Ṭāhā Ḥusayn movingly describes how as a youth he took it upon himself to make up the prayers ommitted by his more secular older brother, who had died in a cholera epidemic (Ṭāhā Ḥusayn, al-Ayyām [[Cairo]: Dār al-Maʿārif bi-Miṣr, n.d.], 1:136; trans. in Taha Hussein, *The Days*, trans. E.H. Paxton, Hilary Wayment, and Kenneth Cragg [Cairo: American University in Cairo Press, 1997], p. 79). On this issue, emphasis on the absolute and individual nature of the obligation to pray was balanced, for some believers, by belief in the transferrability of merit and affirmation of the ties of obligation and love among human beings.

disincentive to conversion), based on *ḥadīth*s stating that Islam erases the sins committed before conversion.[45]

The validity of *ṣalāt* depends on several conditions (*shurūṭ*) that must pertain prior to the ritual and/or for its duration in order for the prayer to be legally valid. The obligatory components (*arkān*) of the prayer, in contrast, are the basic actions and utterances that comprise the *ṣalāt* itself. None of the *arkān* can be omitted in a valid prayer, whether intentionally or out of inadvertence or ignorance (although the postures can be modified, even to the point of performing the entire process lying down or through gestures or eye movements, in cases of illness or physical disability[46]). The conditions include the knowledge that the specified time for the prayer in question has arrived, the state of ritual purity (*ṭahāra*), the covering of one's private parts (*ʿawra*), the orientation of the body towards the *qibla* (i.e., towards the Kaʿba in Mecca), and the framing of the conscious intent (*nīya*) to perform a specific prayer (an issue that will be examined in detail in Chaper 2).

Although individuals may sometimes be left to their own judgment (*ijtihād*) in determining the time and direction of prayer, in most Muslim-majority communities the call to prayer (*ādhān*) is performed from the minarets of mosques and is audible from streets and private homes; in modern times broadcast of the *ādhān* may punctuate television or radio programming. In a mosque, a special niche (*miḥrāb*) indicates the direction of the *qibla*. Like the determination of the precise direction of prayer, the calculation of prayer times for different locations became a sophisticated discipline among medieval Muslim scientists.[47] On a much broader level, the division of the day and night into five unequal prayer-times creates an overall daily cadence that continues to regulate some aspects of life in some Muslim-majority regions. In modern times electronic alarm clocks or mobile-phone apps may sound the *ādhān*.

In order to perform a valid prayer, one must be in a state of ritual purity. If one has urinated, defecated, passed gas, or (according to various schools of law) had a nosebleed or directly touched a member of the opposite sex, one must perform the minor ablution (*wuḍūʾ*). This involves washing the face, hands, and feet and wiping the head with water (cf. Qurʾān 5:6). If one has had sexual intercourse or experienced ejaculation, or (as a woman) if one comes to the end of a menstrual period or of postpartum bleeding (*nifās*), one must perform a complete ablution (*ghusl*) that involves passing water over the skin and hair of the entire body. The

45 See, for instance, Muslim, *Ṣaḥīḥ*, *Kitāb al-Īmān*, *Bāb Kawn al-islām yahdim mā qablahu*.

46 For a survey of the rules relating to ablution and prayer for people with physical disabilities see Vardit Rispler-Chaim, *Disability in Islamic Law* (Dordrecht: Springer, 2007), pp. 19–25.

47 For a discussion of the calculation of prayer times and examples of premodern astronomical tables see *EI*², art. "Mīqāt" (by D. A. King).

requirement of ritual purity means that one may not pray while experiencing an ongoing polluting bodily function, such as menstruation or postpartum bleeding.[48] However, for both sexes there is a dispensation allowing prayer while suffering from a bodily flux that is chronic and uncontrollable.

One's garments and the place of prayer must also be ritually pure, or at least free of any significant quantities of polluting substances. It is for this reason that, particularly among Sunnīs, it is a common practice to spread a small carpet (*sajjāda*) in the place where one intends to pray. (Some authorities, such as Ibn Taymīya (d. 728/1328), regard this as a form of excessive scrupulosity that contrasts with the relaxed attitude to matters of ritual purity modeled by the Prophet's Companions.[49]) In contrast, Shīʿites require that the place of prostration (that is, the spot where the forehead is pressed to the floor) be either earth or some direct product of the earth that is not customarily eaten or worn as clothing (with the possible exceptions of cotton and linen). The ideal substance on which to perform the prostration is earth from Karbala, the site of the martyrdom of Imām Ḥusayn; this ordinarily takes the form of a small disk of clay positioned so that the forehead is pressed upon it in *sujūd*.[50]

The requirement to cover one's private parts applies whether or not one is in the presence of other people. (Scholars pondered the case of someone who lacks an appropriate covering, with proposed solutions ranging from smearing oneself with mud to taking refuge in darkness.) For a man, the area of the body that must be covered (*ʿawra*) extends from the navel to the knees. (In practice, of course, most men pray more modestly dressed than the minimum required by the sharia.) A woman's *ʿawra* comprises her entire body, with the exception of

48 Kevin Reinhart and Ze'ev Maghen have argued that the Islamic law of *ṭahāra* (here rendered "ritual purity") should not be described in English with the terms "purity" and "pollution," because the states conventionally designated in the secondary literature by the English term "pollution" are in fact ethically and symbolically neutral, and carry none of the stigma associated with the English terminology. (See A. Kevin Reinhart, "Impurity/No Danger," *History of Religions* 30 [1990], p. 15; Ze'ev Maghen, *Virtues of the Flesh: Passion and Purity in Early Islamic Jurisprudence* [Leiden and Boston: Brill, 2005], p. 35.) I have argued elsewhere that, while this may be true of the rules of *ṭahāra* as an abstract system conceptually isolated from concrete forms of Islamic piety, historically Muslim jurists, mystics, and others pervasively associated the negation of *ṭahāra* with themes of sin and mortality and ablution with purification (in the sense of physical cleansing, moral redemption, and otherworldly salvation). (See Marion H. Katz, "The Study of Islamic Ritual and the Meaning of *Wuḍūʾ*," *Der Islam* 82 [2005], pp. 106–45.) For these reasons, I believe that the connotations of the English words "purity" and "pollution" are appropriate to the description of the law of *ṭahāra* as it was elaborated by classical Islamic thinkers.

49 Taqī al-Dīn Aḥmad ibn ʿAbd al-Ḥalīm Ibn Taymīya, *Majmūʿ al-fatāwā*, ed. Muṣṭafā ʿAbd al-Qādir ʿAṭā (Beirut: Dār al-Kutub al-ʿIlmīya, 1421/2000), 22:86–102.

50 See al-Shahīd al-Thānī, *Rawḍa*, 1:181–3; Zayn al-Dīn al-ʿĀmilī (al-Shahīd al-Thānī), *al-Fawāʾid al-malīya li-sharḥ al-Risāla al-naflīya* (Qum: Markaz Intishārāt-i Daftar-i Tablīghāt-i Islāmī, 1420/2000), pp. 210–11.

her face, palms, and feet, although some scholars hold that she must cover the tops or the entirety of her feet. However, it is undesirable for her to cover her face in prayer; even women who customarily veil their faces will remove their veils to perform *ṣalāt*.

Although the basic outlines of the prayer ritual are the object of broad consensus among Muslims, groups have differed on various issues of detail. The most influential groupings in this regard have been, among Sunnīs, the schools of law (*madhāhib*) that began to crystallize in the second century of the Islamic era (the eighth century C.E.) and reached their classical form around the fifth century A.H./eleventh century C.E. By the twelfth century C.E. all but four of these schools (which were more numerous in the early period) had become obsolete; the remaining *madhāhib* came to recognize each other mutually as valid expressions of Islamic normativity, even while sometimes polemicizing sharply against each other's positions. These schools, the Ḥanafīs, Mālikīs, Shāfiʿīs, and Ḥanbalīs, were known by the names of the scholars retrospectively regarded as their founders: Abū Ḥanīfa (d. 150/767), Mālik ibn Anas (d. 179/796), al-Shāfiʿī (d. 204/820), and Aḥmad ibn Ḥanbal (d. 241/855). Each school came to be prevalent in specific parts of the Islamic world, with the Mālikīs dominating in North Africa and Muslim Spain, the Ḥanafīs in Central and South Asia, the Shāfiʿīs in much of the Middle East and Southeast Asia, and the Ḥanbalīs scattered widely (but eventually supplying the legal identity of the Saudi Arabian state). Among Imāmī ("Twelver") Shīʿites, legal doctrines were based on the teachings of infallible imāms descended from ʿAlī ibn Abī Ṭālib, particularly the Sixth Imām, Jaʿfar al-Ṣādiq (d. 148/765). Ismāʿīlī Shīʿites have historically followed a number of different lines of living imāms. The following description provides the basic rules that are accepted by most Muslims, noting significant divergences where appropriate.

One begins the prayer by standing upright and saying *Allāhu akbar* ("God is most great") in Arabic, loudly enough to be audible to oneself. It is desirable to hold one's hands up at shoulder height (or, according to the Ḥanafīs, with a man's thumbs at the level of his earlobes and a woman's hands at the level of her shoulders) with the palms facing the *qibla*. One then places one's right hand over the left, at waist level if one is a man and at chest level if one is a woman. According to the Shīʿites and most Mālikīs, in contrast, the hands dangle at one's sides. Gazing downward toward the spot where one will soon place one's forehead in prostration, one then recites the first chapter of the Qurʾān (the Fātiḥa), followed by another chapter or passage of one's choice. Once again saying *Allāhu akbar*, one then bows at the waist so that the back and head are level and parallel to the ground, placing the hands on the knees with the fingers separated (*rukūʿ*). Some schools hold that the hands are raised when lowering oneself into the *rukūʿ* and again when rising from the bowed position; the Ḥanafīs hold that the hands are raised only when pronouncing the *takbīr* that opens the the prayer sequence.[51] While in the bowed position, one repeats *Subḥāna rabbī al-ʿaẓīm* ("Glory to my mighty Lord") at least three times (some scholars prefer five or seven repetitions).[52] Returning to an upright position and allowing the hands to dangle at one's sides, one recites *Samiʿa Allāhu li-man ḥamidah* ("God hears the one who praises Him"). One then prostrates oneself in a kneeling position with the forehead touching the floor, the hands placed flat to either side of the head. In this position one repeats at least three times *Subḥāna rabbī al-aʿlā* ("Glory to my Lord Most High"). Once again saying *Allāhu akbar*, one sits upright with the hands on the knees. The seat is placed on the folded left leg; the right foot is upright, with the toes flat on the floor facing the *qibla*. (Alternatively, the posture favored by the Shāfiʿīs places the seat directly on the floor with the left leg crossing to the right.)[53] One then repeats *Allāhu akbar* and returns to prostration, once again pronouncing *Subḥāna rabbī al-aʿlā* three times with the forehead pressed to the floor. Finally, one repeats *Allāhu akbar* while returning to a standing position.

This entire sequence constitutes a single *rakʿa* (prostration cycle). Each *ṣalāt* is constituted by a set number of *rakʿa*s, which varies depending on the time and type of prayer. Only in the first two *rakʿa*s of a given prayer is a second recitation added after the Fātiḥa. Every second *rakʿa*, one remains seated after the second prostration and recites the *tashahhud*, an extended form of the confession of faith (*shahāda*). At the end of the final *rakʿa* one remains seated, invokes prayers upon the Prophet (*al-ṣalāt ʿalā al-nabī*), and usually adds additional *duʿāʾ*. The prayer closes by invoking peace (*salām*) to one's right and left sides.

There is a prescribed number of required (*farḍ*) prostration cycles for each of the five daily prayers. The dawn prayer comprises two *rakʿa*s, the noon prayer four, the mid-afternoon four, the sunset three, and the evening four. The obligatory prayers for different times of day also vary with respect to the manner in which the Qurʾānic recitation is performed; it is recited out loud in the dawn prayer and in the first two *rakʿa*s of the sunset and evening prayers, and silently in the noon prayer, the third *rakʿa* of the sunset prayer, and the final two *rakʿa*s of the evening prayer. In general, the preference is for silent prayer during the daylight hours and voiced prayer during the hours of darkness; thus, supererogatory prayers (*nafl*) are recommended to be performed out loud only if they occur at night.

Beyond the obligatory *ṣalāt*, it is recommended to perform a set number of additional *rakʿa*s before or after each of the five daily prayers based on the precedents set by the Prophet Muḥammad (*sunna*). This recommendation is

[51] See Muḥammad ibn Aḥmad Ibn Rushd al-Qurṭubī, *Bidāyat al-mujtahid wa-nihāyat al-muqtaṣid* (Beirut: Dār Ibn Ḥazm, 1424/2003), 1:124–5.

[52] See Muwaffaq al-Dīn Ibn Qudāma, *al-Mughnī* (Beirut: Dār al-Kutub al-ʿIlmīya, n.d.), 1:542.

[53] See Ibn Rushd, *Bidāyat al-mujtahid*, 1:126.

more binding in cases where he added *rakʿa*s regularly than in those where he did so only sporadically. In addition, one may perform supererogatory prayers (*nafl*) on a voluntary basis. Other supererogatory prayers are performed separately from the obligatory five, such as the highly recommended *tahajjud* (nighttime) prayer, which consists of two to eight *rakʿa*s and can be performed any time between the *'ishā'* and the dawn.[54] Other recommended prayers are performed in particular situations. For instance, it is *sunna* to perform two *rakʿa*s in greeting upon entering a mosque. It is also desirable to perform two *rakʿa*s following the minor ablutions (*wuḍūʾ*). A person facing a difficult or momentous decision, such as the choice of a career or a spouse, may perform the *ṣalāt al-istikhāra* to seek God's guidance. A two-*rakʿa* prayer with a special invocation is also recommended in situations of great need (*ṣalāt al-ḥāja*) or to express penitence (*ṣalāt al-tawba*).[55]

It is most meritorious to perform the five daily prayers in congregation (*ṣalāt al-jamāʿa*) rather than alone. The same is not true of supererogatory prayers, which according to many authorities are best performed in solitude; the Prophet is said to have stated that "the best prayer is one that a person performs at home, except for the obligatory prayers."[56] This tradition reflects the concern that public performance of supererogatory prayers could involve hypocrisy and public display, as well as that regular performance of such prayers in congregation might lead to the misconception that they were obligatory. *Ṣalāt al-jamā'a* is any prayer performed by two or more people, with one of them leading the other(s) as *imām*. Although he (or, in some situations to be discussed later, she) should be proficient in Qurʾānic recitation and in the prayer ritual, an *imām* requires no specific formal training, official appointment, or religious ordination. His primary function is to synchronize everyone's performance of *ṣalāt* and to perform the Qurʾānic recitations on behalf of the group. Although the most meritorious venue for congregational prayer is the mosque, in general it is possible to perform either individual or communal prayer in any location that fulfills the basic requirements of ritual purity and the absence of images of humans or animals. The only congregational prayer that must be performed in an officially designated, publicly accessible mosque is the Friday midday prayer (*jumʿa*), which is accompanied by two sermons (*khuṭba*s) and is obligatory for post-adolescent males. Additional congregational prayers include the funeral prayer (*ṣalāt al-janāza*); the eclipse prayer (*ṣalāt al-kusūf*), performed on the occasion of an eclipse of the sun or moon; the "prayer of seeking rain" (*ṣalāt*

[54] For a survey of the supererogatory prayers and their categorizations and level of recommendation according to the various schools see Zuḥaylī, *Fiqh*, 2:1055–96.

[55] Ibn Qudāma, *al-Mughnī*, 1:769.

[56] See, for instance, Muslim, *Ṣaḥīḥ*, *Kitāb Ṣalāt al-musāfirīn wa-qaṣrihā*, *Bāb Istiḥbāb ṣalāt al-nāfila fī baytihi wa-jawāzihā fī al-masjid.*

al-istisqāʾ), performed in times of drought;[57] and the *ṣalāt al-tarāwīḥ*, which Sunnīs perform during the nights of the Ramaḍān fast. Each of these has its own prescribed form, discussed in detail in legal manuals. The rules and significance of *ṣalāt al-jamāʿa* and of *jumʿa* prayers will be discussed in detail in Chapter 4.

Although all schools of law and sectarian groupings agreed on the most basic components of the *ṣalāt* ritual, they sometimes advanced divergent interpretations of the details. In principle, all Muslim parties sought to reproduce the Prophet's mode of prayer with maximum accuracy. Because of the conflicting content and contested authenticity of the many relevant *ḥadīth*, though, scholars were far from unanimity even on some rather basic points. For instance, it was disputed whether the *basmala* ("In the name of God, the Compassionate, the Merciful") was the first verse of the Fātiḥa or whether it was simply an invocation inserted at the beginning of each chapter of the Qurʾān. If the *basmala* was, in fact, the first verse of the Fātiḥa there was no question both that it should be recited in prayer and that it should be recited in the same way (audibly or silently) as the rest of the chapter. If it was not an integral part of the Fātiḥa, on the other hand, it was debatable whether it should be recited at all or, if so, whether it should be recited identically with the rest of the chapter.[58] In another case, that of the position of the hands during the "standing" portion of the prayer, the debate centered on different approaches to the Prophet's *sunna*: Mālikīs emphasized the authority of Medinian community practice as a repository of the authentic practices of the Prophet, whereas the Shāfiʿīs and other Sunnī schools argued that textual reports (*ḥadīth*) about the Prophet's words and actions were the ultimate arbiters of the *sunna*.[59]

In addition to debating the sources on which the details of the *ṣalāt* ritual were based, scholars occasionally debated more fundamental issues regarding the ritual's parameters and significance. For instance, all groups agreed that the prayer should be initiated by the *takbīr* (*Allāhu akbar*, "God is most great"). However, they differed on whether an alternative invocation (including one in a language other than Arabic) could validly be substituted. Abū Ḥanīfa and one of his two most influential disciples, Muḥammad al-Shaybānī, are said to have permitted opening prayer with any expression semantically equivalent to *Allāhu akbar*. Thus, one might say *Allāhu ajall* ("God is most glorious"), *al-Raḥmān*

57 For a discussion of the practices and symbolism associated with *ṣalāt al-istisqāʾ* see Nadia Abu-Zahra, "The Rain Rituals as Rites of Spiritual Passage," *International Journal of Middle East Studies* 20 (1988), pp. 507–29.

58 For a thorough analysis of the positions of the various schools on this issue see Najam Haider, *The Origins of the Shīʿa: Identity, Ritual, and Sacred Space in Eighth-Century Kūfa* (Cambridge: Cambridge University Press, 2011), pp. 57–77. I thank Professor Haider for providing me with the manuscript of his book before its publication.

59 See Yasin Dutton, "ʿAmal v. Ḥadīth in Islamic Law: The Case of Sadl al-Yadayn (Holding One's Hands by One's Sides) When Doing the Prayer," *Islamic Law and Society* 3 (1996), pp. 13–40.

aʿẓam ("The Compassionate One is most great"), or the like. In contrast, if one begins by exclaiming "O God, forgive me" this is not permissible, because the glorification of God is contaminated with one's own need. As Ibn Rushd pithily observed, the issue was whether the obligation was associated with the words, or with the meaning.[60] Abū Ḥanīfa also allowed a person to make the opening invocation in other languages, on the basis that verse 87:15 of the Qurʾān (which speaks of people who "glorify their Lord, and lift their hands in prayer") specifies only its content, rather than its form. Reportedly Abū Yūsuf and Muḥammad al-Shaybānī agreed on this point with al-Shāfiʿī, who held that pronouncing the *takbīr* in another language is valid only if the individual does not know Arabic.[61]

The debate between the Ḥanafīs and their opponents over the language of prayer applied to the recitation of the Qurʾān, as well as to the *takbīr* and other prescribed invocations. Most scholars held that only the original Arabic text was genuinely the Qurʾān, whose miraculous inimitability was located in its incomparable style as well as in its meaning. Thus, al-Shāfiʿī held that it was invalid to perform the Qurʾānic recitation in another language under any circumstances, regardless of the linguistic skills of the person in question; if he or she was incapable of reciting in Arabic, the only solution was to perform the prayer without recitation (which under these circumstances would be valid) until the Arabic words could be mastered. Based on al-Shāfiʿī's position, since recitation in Persian is not actually recitation of the Qurʾān, it is human – that is, profane – speech (*kalām al-nās*); the intrusion of human speech invalidates prayer, just as if one were to interject a conversation with another person into one's *ṣalāt*.

In contrast, Abū Ḥanīfa is said to have held that it was valid (although undesirable) to recite in Persian even if one is capable of doing so in Arabic. (His two disciples are said to have allowed recitation in a foreign tongue only in cases of inability to recite in Arabic.) In addition to citing the precedent of the Prophet's Companion Salmān, who is said to have translated the Fātiḥa into Persian for the use of new converts, Ḥanafīs also argued that the miracle of the Qurʾān was constituted by its meaning, not by its linguistic form. The Qurʾān is a proof against all people, and the Qurʾānic challenge to compose verses like it (cf. verses 2:23, 10:38, 1:13) applies to all people. Thus, the Persians were challenged to compose verses like it in Persian. Furthermore, the Qurʾān is the uncreated word of God, and all languages are created in time; thus (so the Ḥanafī authority al-Sarakhsī) it is not possible to say that the Qurʾān is in a specific language.[62]

[60] Ibn Rushd, *Bidāyat al-mujtahid*, 1:115.
[61] Zuḥaylī, *Fiqh*, 2:817–18.
[62] Muḥammad ibn Aḥmad al-Sarakhsī, *al-Mabsūṭ*, ed. Muḥammad Ḥasan Muḥammad Ḥasan al-Shāfiʿī (Beirut: Dār al-Kutub al-ʿIlmīya, 1421/2001), 1:137–8.

In practice Ḥanafīs, like followers of other schools, seek to follow the Prophet's example by pronouncing the conventional *takbīr* and reciting the Qurʾān in Arabic. However, in addition to raising important theoretical questions about form and meaning, their approach is particularly sensitive to the needs of non-Arab converts. The debate over the language of prayer, although effectively moot in the sense that almost all Muslims have historically prayed in Arabic, addresses the significant investment in learning required for proficient prayer (and the challenges it might raise for new or non-Arab Muslims).

Supplication: *Duʿāʾ*

The word *duʿāʾ* simply refers to the act of "calling out" (in this case, to God), and thus it can apply to any invocation. Scholars analyzing *ṣalāt* may refer to all of the utterances prescribed or recommended at different points in the ritual as *duʿāʾ*. However, the word is more specifically used to designate petitionary prayer or supplication, that is, appeals for divine aid or favor. It is defined in classical sources as "seeking from God the good things that He possesses and imploring Him with requests" or "the servant's petitioning God for help and appealing to Him for aid."[63] Unlike *ṣalāt*, *duʿāʾ* is analyzed by Muslim thinkers as a verbal phenomenon (although certain physical postures, such as holding the hands out with the palms facing up or standing with one's face to the *qibla*, may be recommended). The essence of *duʿāʾ* is to address God, and the content of that address is ordinarily human need and distress (although it can and should also contain elements of celebration and praise). The most spontaneous and mundane appeal that a human can direct to God ("Please let me pass this test!") is a *duʿāʾ*.[64]

Indeed, the Qurʾān represents *duʿāʾ* as something that even pagans engage in instinctively in moments of uncertainty and distress. Verses 10:22–3 describe how, in peril on the high seas, unbelievers "call out to God . . . saying, 'If You deliver us from this, we shall truly show our gratitude!'" As soon as God delivers them, however, they forget their promise and live as heedlessly as before. Verse 10:12 treats this human tendency more generally, declaring, "When trouble touches a person, he cries unto Us lying down on his side, or sitting, or standing. But when We have solved his trouble, he passes on his way as if he had never cried out to Us for a trouble that touched him" (see also verse 30:33).

However, crying out to God in life's predicaments is not merely the craven habit of nonbelievers. The Qurʾān also presents petitionary prayers by exemplary figures (although they are less given to bargaining with the deity). When

[63] See Zabīdī, *Tāj al-ʿarūs*, 38:25 (s.v. d-ʿ-w); Rāzī, *Tafsīr*, 5:97 (commentary on verse 2:186).
[64] For an overall discussion of *duʿāʾ* see *Encyclopaedia Iranica*, s.v. "Doʿā," (by Hamid Algar).

Job is overcome by his afflictions, "he cried out to his Lord, 'Truly distress has seized me, but You are the most merciful of those who have mercy.'" The passage continues, "So We listened to him: We removed the distress that was on him" (verses 21:83–4). When Jonah has attempted to evade God's command and been devoured by the whale, he calls out from the darkness of the beast's interior, "There is no god but You. Glory to You; I was indeed wrong!" Again God affirms, "So We listened to him and delivered him from distress; thus do We deliver those who have faith" (verses 21:87–8). The prayer of Jonah is considered a particularly powerful *duʿāʾ*, widely used by Muslims of later generations.[65] Also paradigmatic is the supplication of Zakarīyā, who in verses 19:2–11 asks God for a son in his old age and has his apparently improbable wish fulfilled.[66] In verse 19:4 he expresses his confidence in God's responsiveness to his appeals: he has reached old age, "but never yet, O my Lord, has my prayer to You remained unanswered." Zakarīyā's faith in the fulfillment of his prayer reflects affirmations made elsewhere in the Qurʾān. Verse 2:186 represents human supplication and the intimate responsiveness of God as a fundamental part of the human–divine relationship: "When my servants ask you [, Muḥammad,] concerning Me, I am indeed close; I answer the prayer of every suppliant when he calls me." The value of *du'ā'* is also emphasized in *ḥadīth*; the Prophet is reported to have declared that "supplication is the marrow of prayer (*al-duʿāʾ mukhkh al-ʿibāda*)" – that is, its essential or choicest part.[67]

Although *duʿāʾ* may be a spontaneous personal cry from the heart, scholars emphasize the merits of prayers drawn directly from the Qurʾān or from the words of the Prophet.[68] Popular manuals offer recommended *duʿāʾ* texts to be performed in conjunction with routine daily activities and mundane personal concerns, as well as for more fraught or perilous circumstances. Al-Ghazālī, like many scholars, presents standard invocations for acts as lowly as entering and leaving the outhouse, as well as for going out to the mosque and other more noble acts.[69] In this respect *duʿāʾ* closely resembles *dhikr*, the remembrance of God that should accompany all human activities; however, *duʿāʾ* is distinguished by the inclusion of some appeal or request. The Sufi tradition, although

[65] See Regula Burkhardt Qureshi, "Transcending Space: Recitation and Community among South Asian Muslims in Canada," in Barbara Daly Metcalf, ed., *Making Muslim Space in North America and Europe* (Berkeley: University of California Press, 1996), p. 58.

[66] Cf. Constance E. Padwick, *Muslim Devotions: A Study of Prayer Manuals in Common Use* (Oxford: Oneworld, 1996), p. 262.

[67] al-Muḥammad ibn ʿĪsā al-Tirmidhī, *Sunan al-Tirmidhī, Kitāb al-Daʿawāt, Bāb mā jāʾa fī faḍl al-duʿāʾ*. (Al-Tirmidhī considers this *ḥadīth gharīb*, and others deem it *ḍaʿīf*; however, see also the other *ḥadīth* in this chapter.)

[68] See, for instance, Yaḥyā ibn Sharaf al-Nawawī, *Kitāb al-Adhkār al-muntakhab min kalām sayyid al-abrār* (Cairo: al-Dār al-Miṣrīya al-Lubnānīya, 1408/1988), p. 105. This entire work is devoted to invocations transmitted from the Prophet from reliable sources.

[69] Abū Ḥāmid al-Ghazālī, *Iḥyāʾ ʿulūm al-dīn* (Beirut: Dār al-Fikr, 1414/1994), 1:156, 384.

it often valorizes *dhikr* over *du'ā'*, is nevertheless the source of a rich body of petitionary prayers.[70] Shī'ites cultivate a rich tradition of petitionary prayers – often lengthy and elaborate – transmitted from the imāms; Hamid Algar notes that "these prayers constitute, for the mass of the believers, both the chief textual legacy of the imams and the principal means by which they commune with them."[71] The "Prayer of Kumayl," said to have been revealed to the Imām 'Alī ibn Abī Ṭālib from the immortal sage Khiḍr and passed on to his follower Kumayl ibn Ziyād al-Nakha'ī, is among the most important Shī'ite invocations; it is traditionally recited in special gatherings on Thursday nights.[72] An entire manual of petitionary prayer, the *Ṣaḥīfa al-Sajjādīya*, is attributed to the Fourth Imām, 'Alī Zayn al-'Ābidīn.

Du'ā' is also an integral element of *ṣalāt*. The Fātiḥa, recited in every *rak'a* of prayer, affirms that "It is from You alone that we seek help," and supplications are incorporated at several points in the ritual. Their centrality is such that the prominent jurist and Sufi Ibn 'Abd al-Salām al-Sulamī (d. 660/1262) writes that the benefits accruing to the person who performs the canonical prayers include "what they contain of prayers (*du'ā'*) for this-worldly and other-worldly well-being (*maṣlaḥa*)."[73] In addition to the standard invocations (*takbīr*, *tasbīḥ*, etc.) that are integral to the prayer rite, it is traditional to include several more extensive interludes of *du'ā'*.

All of the Sunnī schools except the Mālikīs (who consider it preferable to proceed directly from the first *takbīr* to the recitation of the Fātiḥa) hold it desirable to recite an invocation before the first Qur'ānic recitation in *ṣalāt*. The Shāfi'īs prefer a prayer transmitted from the Prophet, and closely based on verses 6:79 and 6:162–3 of the Qur'ān:

> I have turned my face towards the One who created the heavens and the earth as a pure monotheist and a submitter to God [*ḥanīfan musliman*], and I am not one of the polytheists. Indeed, my prayer and my devotion, my life and my death belong to God, the Lord of the worlds, to Him who has no partner. And thus I am commanded, being one of the submitters to God (*muslimīn*).[74]

Based on some versions of the relevant *ḥadīth*, this invocation may continue with a petition for the forgiveness of sins:

70 Algar, "Do'ā."
71 Ibid.
72 See Thurfjell, *Living Shi'ism*, pp. 34–5.
73 al-'Izz ibn 'Abd al-Salām al-Sulamī, *Maqāṣid al-ṣalāt*, ed. Iyād Khālid al-Ṭabbā' (Beirut: Dār al-Fikr al-Mu'āṣir/Damascus: Dār al-Fikr, 1413/1992), p. 11.
74 See Padwick, *Muslim Devotions*, p. 60. The speaker in verse 6:79 is Abraham. Verses 6:162–3 are an invocation that the Qur'ān instructs the Prophet Muḥammad to pronounce; in verse 6:163 the Qur'ānic text is "I am the *first* of those who submit to God," which is modified for ordinary believers to "I am *one* of those who submit to God" (emphases added).

You are the King; there is no deity but You. I am Your servant and have wronged myself and confess my sin, so forgive me all of my sins; no one forgives sins but You! Guide me to the best of moral characteristics; no one guides to the best of them but You![75]

Based on the Prophet's practice as recorded in another *ḥadīth*, one may also say:

O God, separate me from my sins as far as You have separated the eastern and western horizons! O God, cleanse me of my sins as a white garment is cleansed from dirt! O God! Wash away my sins with water, ice and hail![76]

The most important and open-ended opportunity for invocation and supplication within the *ṣalāt* ritual, however, is the final "sitting" at the end of the closing prostration cycle. It is recommended to begin one's prayers on that occasion by invoking blessings upon the Prophet Muḥammad, usually a form transmitted from the Prophet in the best-authenticated collections of *ḥadīth*:

O God, send prayers upon (*ṣalli ʿalā*) Muḥammad and the family of Muḥammad as You sent prayers upon Abraham and the family of Abraham; indeed, You are most praised, glorious. O God, bless Muḥammad and the family of Muḥammad as You blessed Abraham and the family of Abraham; indeed, You are most praised, glorious.[77]

This invocation can be followed by personal prayers of the worshiper's own selection.

A more controversial supplication that some groups consider desirable or even obligatory in the context of ṣalāt is the *qunūt*, a supplicatory prayer inserted into the *ṣalāt* ritual whose content and rules differ widely among the schools of law. (The term *qunūt* has a number of meanings; in this context the reference appears to be to "standing" in prayer.[78]) The *qunūt* is said to be rooted in a traumatic event during the Prophet's lifetime, when he cursed the clans responsible for the slaughter of a party of Muslims daily in his dawn prayers for a month.[79] Ultimately the angel Gabriel himself came to declare, "O Muḥammad, God did not send you to revile people or to curse them; He sent you as a mercy to the worlds [cf. Qurʾān 21:107]." He then taught him another *qunūt*:

O God, we seek Your help and Your guidance; we seek Your forgiveness and turn towards You in repentance; we have faith in You and depend upon You; we praise you for all good things; we thank You and are not ungrateful to You, and we cast off and abandon those who disobey You. O God, it is You Whom we worship, and to You that we pray and

[75] Ibn Qudāma, *al-Mughnī*, 1:516–17.
[76] Ibn Rushd, *Bidāyat al-mujtahid*, 1:116; Ibn Qudāma, *al-Mughnī*, 1:517.
[77] See Padwick, *Muslim Devotions*, p. 167.
[78] See *EI*², art. "Ḳunūt" (by A. J. Wensinck).
[79] The disputed details of this event, the expedition of Biʾr Maʿūna (4 A.H.), are analyzed by M. J. Kister in his article "The Expedition of Biʾr Maʿūna," in George Makdisi, ed., *Arabic and Islamic Studies in Honor of Hamilton A. R. Gibb* (Leiden: E. J. Brill, 1965), pp. 337–57.

prostrate; to You we strive and hasten. We hope for Your mercy and fear Your punishment; indeed, Your grave punishment will be inflicted on the non-believers.[80]

Various schools of law differed over the rules regulating the *qunūt* invocation, its text, and in which of the daily prayers it could or should be performed. Sunnī jurists (with the exception of Mālikīs) also envisioned that the *qunūt* should be performed in situations of public peril or distress (such as war, drought, or plague). The Imāmī Shīʿites endorsed the performance of *qunūt* in all prayers, which rendered it a distinctively Shīʿite practice on most occasions.[81]

Despite the inclusion of *duʿāʾ* in every *ṣalāt*, scholars pondered the parameters of the more personal petitionary prayers that might be performed in the context of the ritual. On the one hand, the *ṣalāt* ritual offered a context of heightened intimacy with God, and one in which the worshiper's actions were presumably pleasing to Him. Thus, *ṣalāt* presented itself as a privileged and propitious context for personal *duʿāʾ*. However, some concrete requests might appear too self-interested to be appropriate for *ṣalāt*, or simply so mundane and extraneous that they amounted to profane speech. In fact, some scholars pondered whether such supplications might be so incompatible with the spirit of *ṣalāt* that they would invalidate the prayer itself. The early Ḥanafī scholar Muḥammad al-Shaybānī recounts the following exchange, probably intended to be with his teacher Abū Ḥanīfa:

I said, "What do you think about a man who performs *ṣalāt* and prays to God (*daʿā Allāh*), asking him for his daily bread and asking him for good health; does that rupture his prayer (*ṣalāt*)?" He said, "No." I said, "Is the same true for every invocation that is from the Qurʾān or resembles the Qurʾān (*shabaha al-qurʾān*), that it does not rupture prayer?" He said, "Yes!" I said, "What if he were to say, "O God, give me a garment to wear! O God, give me so-and-so in marriage!"?" He said, "That ruptures prayer; any invocation that resembles this is [worldly] speech and ruptures prayer."[82]

Both the source of the invocation (whether it had to be drawn from the Qurʾān or *ḥadīth*, or could be freely improvised by the worshiper) and its content were debated by other early authorities as well. In one report Aḥmad ibn Ḥanbal is consulted by a follower about the opinion (being advanced by unnamed persons) that it is not permissible to perform any non-Qurʾānic invocations in the context of canonical prayer. Ibn Ḥanbal waves his hand in exasperation and asks how anyone could hold this view, given that reports to the contrary were incontrovertibly transmitted from the Prophet himself. However, he goes on

80 See Zuḥaylī, *Fiqh*, 2:1002.
81 For a thorough survey of the opinions on this point see Haider, *Origins*, pp. 95–118. The summary here is based on this source and on Zuḥaylī, *Fiqh*, 2:1000–9.
82 Muḥammad al-Shaybānī, *Kitāb al-Aṣl al-maʿrūf bi'l-Mabsūṭ*, ed. Abū'l-Wafāʾ al-Afghānī (Beirut: ʿĀlam al-Kutub, 1410/1990), 1:193.

to state that a person "should supplicate as is known and as is transmitted."[83] Some later members of his school inferred that his statement limited legitimate prayers to those that were textually "transmitted" and "known." In another early report, in contrast, Ibn Ḥanbal is said to have declared, "There is no harm in a man's supplicating (*an yadʿuwa*) for all of his needs relating to this world and the next."[84] The great Ḥanbalī scholar Ibn Qudāma endorsed the latter view but cautioned that "it is not permissible for him to make a prayer in his *ṣalāt* by which he aims at the indulgences and pleasures of this world, and that resembles the speech and wishes of human beings, such as 'O God, give me a pretty slave girl, a spacious house, good food, and a pretty garden.'" In contrast, al-Shāfiʿī is supposed to have emphasized that one could pray however, and for whatever, one liked.[85]

Even outside of the context of *ṣalāt*, however, there were possible reservations even about appeals that were neither selfish nor materialistic. Insofar as a given *duʿāʾ* involved a request, asking God for the alleviation of misfortunes or the bestowal of advantages, it implicitly expressed dissatisfaction with the present situation; there was a fine line between supplication and complaining. Phrased more theologically, an appeal for the alteration of the current (and divinely decreed) state of things might suggest discontent with God's will. It also implied the petitioner's belief that he could judge his own needs and welfare better than the divine Providence; in the Qurʾānic commentator al-Rāzī's words, it could imply "preferring one's own objective (*murād*) over God's."[86] In fact, however, this sentiment was balanced by a keen appreciation of the raw sincerity of the human's cry to God and its potential to create a vital connection to the divine. *Ḥadīth* reports state that "Whoever does not make requests of God, He becomes angry with him," and urge, "Ask God for His bounty; God loves those who ask Him."[87] (However, it is also reported that the Prophet said [in a first-person report from God], "Whoever is preoccupied by My remembrance from making requests from Me, I will give him better than what I give those who make requests."[88])

It was perhaps in the Sufi tradition that the theme of complete trust in God (*tawakkul*) was most fully developed (although it is a universal Islamic value),

83 Ibn Qudāma, *al-Mughnī*, 1:583–4.

84 Ibid., 1:586.

85 Ibid., 1:585.

86 Rāzī, *Tafsīr*, 5:98.

87 See Ibn Ḥajar al-ʿAsqalānī, *Fatḥ al-bārī bi-sharḥ Ṣaḥīḥ al-Bukhārī*, ed. Ṭāhā ʿAbd al-Raʾūf Saʿd and Muṣṭafā Muḥammad al-Hawārī (Cairo: Maktabat al-Kullīyāt al-Azharīya, 1398/1978), 23:111.

88 Ibn Abī Shayba, *Muṣannaf Ibn Abī Shayba fī al-aḥādīth wa 'l-āthār*, ed. Saʿīd al-Laḥḥām (Beirut: Dār al-Fikr, 1428–9/2008), 7:40; Muḥammad ibn ʿAbd al-Qādir al-Fāsī, *Tuḥfat al-mukhliṣīn bi-sharḥ ʿUddat al-ḥiṣn al-ḥaṣīn min kalām sayyid al-mursalīn*, ed. Muḥammad ibn ʿAzzūz (Casablanca: Markaz al-Turāth al-Thaqāfī al- Maghribī, 1428/2007), 1:165.

and one might expect that Sufis would deprecate supplication in favor of unquestioning acceptance of God's decree and willing abandonment of any benefits – whether material or spiritual – that God might choose to withhold. However, Sufis were also particularly sensitive to the value of heartfelt cries to God in creating a spontaneous and sincere intimacy with the divine. A particularly searching and influential examination of this interrelationship is provided by Abū'l-Qāsim al-Qushayrī (d. 465/1072) in his foundational handbook of Sufi terminology and teachings. Al-Qushayrī particularly favors the irrepressible cries for help that express genuine and immediate need. He cites Sahl ibn ʿAbd Allāh (al-Tustarī, d. 283/896) as declaring, "The prayer that is most likely to be answered is the prayer of one's spiritual state (*duʿāʾ al-ḥāl*), and the prayer of one's spiritual state is the one someone makes when he is hard pressed and cannot do without the thing he is praying for." This point is illustrated by an anecdote about a woman who comes to the Baghdādī mystic al-Junayd and asks him to pray for her, because her son is lost. Each time he tells her to go and practice fortitude (*uṣburī*). Finally she comes and cries out, "My fortitude has run out, and I have none left!" He then tells her to go home, because her son has returned. Returning to al-Junayd, the grateful and astonished woman asks how he could have known. He answers by reciting verse 27:62 of the Qurʾān: "Who listens to the one hard pressed when he calls out to Him, and relieves his suffering?"[89]

As the preceding anecdote suggests, there is a tension between supplication and acceptance, exemplified by the religious virtue of steadfast fortitude (*ṣabr*). Al-Qushayrī observes that there is a difference of opinion on whether it is preferable to engage in petitionary prayer or to remain silent in contentment with God's decree (*al-sukūt wa'l-riḍā*). Those who prefer *duʿāʾ* point out that calling out to God in prayer is a form of worship (*ʿibāda*), and it is better to engage in worship than to eschew it. In any case, even if one's prayer is not answered, *duʿāʾ* also expresses the appropriate creaturely posture of neediness towards God. Here al-Qushayrī cites a Sufi master who declared, "It would be harder for me to be deprived of supplication than to be deprived of [God's] answering [my supplication]." On the other, some argued that it was best mutely to accept God's decree and predestination. Yet a third opinion, according to al-Qushayrī, held that it was best to combine supplication by the tongue with contentment in the heart. Al-Qushayrī's summary of the relative merits of *duʿāʾ* and silent acceptance was particularly influential; among other places, it is reproduced in al-Nawawī's (d. 677/1278) popular handbook of invocations.[90]

[89] Abū'l-Qāsim ʿAbd al-Karīm ibn Hawāzin al-Qushayrī, *al-Risāla al-qushayrīya fī ʿilm al-taṣawwuf*, ed. Maʿrūf Zurayq and ʿAlī ʿAbd al-Ḥamīd al-Balṭajī (Beirut: Dār al-Jīl, n.d.), p. 264.

[90] Nawawī, *Adhkār*, p. 496.

If al-Qushayrī's overriding concern is with the texture of the individual's relationship to the divine, he nevertheless quite strikingly affirms the concrete efficacy of *duʿāʾ*. He initiates a series of anecdotes about the power of petitionary prayer with a story about a merchant who is threatened by a highway robber and recites a *duʿāʾ* so powerful that it instantly summons an angel on horseback who dispatches the bandit with a spear of light.[91] In general, classical Muslim scholars were sanguine about the practical efficacy of prayer. This confidence was founded in the divine assurances that "I answer the prayer of the suppliant when he calls me" (Qurʾān 2:186) and "Call on Me; I will answer you" (Qurʾān 40:60). Commenting on God's promise in verse 40:60, Ibn Ḥajar al-ʿAsqalānī (d. 852/1449) acknowledges the objection that, empirically, "many people pray and do not have their prayers answered." However, he affirms that all prayers are answered, even if their fulfillment is not immediately obvious to the human observer. He states, "The response to that is that every supplicant has his prayer answered, but the answer may be of various kinds. Sometimes it is answered by the specific thing that the person prayed for, and sometimes by a substitute (*ʿiwaḍ*) for it." The person may be compensated, for instance, by being spared an equivalent ill that would otherwise have befallen him. Alternatively, God may save it up for him in the form of otherworldly reward. Ibn Ḥajar supports all of these options with *ḥadīth*.[92] He also, however, cites verse 40:65, which instructs, "Call upon [God], giving Him sincere devotion." This demonstrates, he argues, that God's promise to answer people's prayers is conditioned on their *ikhlāṣ*, the purity and exclusivity of their devotion to God – an exacting standard that surely would exclude the half-hearted or self-interested prayers of many people.[93]

The Qurʾān commentator Fakhr al-Dīn al-Rāzī (d. 606/1209) also addresses the verses apparently affirming the unqualified efficacy of prayer. He argues that these general statements are modified by the more restrictive statement in verse 6:41, which states, "On Him you would call, and He would remove [the distress] which occasioned your call upon Him *if He wills*" (emphasis added). Like Ibn Ḥajar, al-Rāzī also argues, however, that *duʿāʾ* always has a reward of some kind. It may be that what the person is asking for corresponds to the divine decree, in which case his prayer will be fulfilled as requested. It may be that his petition is not destined to be fulfilled, but in that case his prayer will be answered with serenity (*sakīna*), emotional relief, and inner fortitude to help him in his affliction. Furthermore, he points out that God did not promise to respond to prayer immediately; even if the response comes in the life to come, He has thus kept His promise.[94]

91 Qushayrī, *Risāla*, pp. 266–8.
92 Ibn Ḥajar al-ʿAsqalānī, *Fatḥ al-bārī*, 23:112 (see also 23:166).
93 Ibid., 23:111.
94 Rāzī, *Tafsīr*, 5:100.

Some thinkers particularly emphasized that the efficacy of petitionary prayer lies primarily (or, in some cases, exclusively) in its effect on the inner state and spiritual attitude of the person praying. Al-Ghazālī (d. 505/1111), despite his general affirmation of the effectiveness of prayer, ultimately sees it as a spiritual good in its own right:

The usual way with [human] creatures is that their hearts do not turn to the remembrance of God until need befalls them and calamity afflicts them. When evil befalls a person, he is expansive in his prayers; need causes people to be in need of prayer, and prayer turns the heart back to God in entreaty and submission, and by this means the remembrance (*dhikr*) [of God] occurs, which is the noblest of acts of worship. It is for this reason that affliction was given free rein over the prophets.[95]

The traditionist Abū Bakr al-Khaffāf (d. 543/1148) comments on a *ḥadīth* stating that "supplication is effective against what befalls [a person] and what does not befall [him or her]":

It is possible that supplication makes it easier for the supplicant to bear the afflictions and calamities that befall him, and [so] the reward of what befell [him] is multiplied, because he attains the reward for the calamity and affliction, the reward of neediness and want toward [God], and the honor of supplicating Him. Supplicating after affliction has befallen him is a cause of fortitude and contentment and a cause of immunity from despair, which deprives one of reward.[96]

In the words of the North African Sufi master Zarrūq, *ṣalāt* results in "the matter becoming easy for the soul, so that the burning of need is cooled, which is the objective of the request."[97]

Despite the recognition that supplication might be met with the alleviation of one's feelings rather than of one's troubles, overall *duʿāʾ* was (and is) considered a central and efficacious means of addressing predicaments and catastrophes, whether communal or personal. A famous example is recounted in the introduction to a manual on the Prophet's sayings about prayer composed by the scholar Ibn al-Jazarī (d. 833/1429), which he finished just as Timur Lank (Tamerlane) besieged Damascus in 791/1389. He had a vision of the Prophet, whom he beseeched to pray for him and for the Muslims:

So he raised his noble hands as I watched, and he prayed and then passed them over his noble face. This happened on the eve of Thursday, and on the eve of Sunday the enemy fled, and God gave relief to me and to the Muslims by means of the *baraka* of what is in this book.[98]

95 al-Ghazālī, *Iḥyāʾ*, 1:390.
96 Cited in Fāsī, *Tuḥfat al-mukhliṣīn*, 1:173.
97 Ibid., 1:171.
98 Cited in Padwick, *Muslim Devotions*, p. xxvii. Ibn al-Jazarī's deliverance was not permanent, as he was taken prisoner by Timur in 805/140 and sent to Samarqand. See *EI*^{2}, art. "Ibn al-Jazarī" (by M. Bencheneb).

Great public catastrophes naturally created a demand for petitionary prayer. Tarif Khalidi writes that "faith in the effectiveness of prayer permeates many of the chronicles of the period" of the Crusades and the Mongol invasions.[99] The depredations of the Black Death evoked extensive reflections about the form, the religious propriety, and the effectiveness of *duʿāʾ* against the disease. In the fourteenth and fifteenth centuries it became customary to perform formal congregational prayers in times of plague modeled on the prayer for rain.[100]

Ibn Qayyim al-Jawzīya (d. 751/1350) composed an entire monograph in response an anguished question about

> a man who has been beset with an affliction, and knows that if it continues to affect him it will ruin his life in this world and the next. He has striven to avert it from himself by every means, but it only becomes more aggravated and severe. What stratagem can be used to avert it? And what is the way to alleviate it?[101]

Ibn al-Qayyim's answer revolves primarily around the importance and effectiveness of *duʿāʾ*. He writes, "*Du'ā'* is one of the most salutary medicines; it is the foe of affliction, averts and heals it, prevents it from descending [upon a person], and eliminates or alleviates it if it descends; it is the weapon of the believer."[102]

Ibn al-Qayyim acknowledges that the efficacy of prayer is not absolute, however.

> It is one of the strongest means of averting detestable things and attaining desired ones. However, it may fail to have its effect either because of its inherent weakness – in that it is a *duʿāʾ* that God does not like, because of the hostility (*ʿudwān*) in it – or because of the weakness of the [petitioner's] heart and its lack of attentiveness to God and concentration on Him at the time when the *duʿāʾ* is made . . ., or because something occurs that prevents it from being answered, such as [the petitioner's having] eaten something forbidden, the prevalence of sins over the hearts and the domination and control of heedlessness, desire, and frivolity over them.[103]

The efficacy of petitionary prayer also depends on the relative strength of the prayer and the affliction in question; if the prayer is stronger, the affliction will be averted; if it is less strong, the affliction will still befall the person, but its strength will be diminished; and if the prayer and the affliction are equally

[99] Tarif Khalidi, *Arabic Historical Thought in the Classical Period* (Cambridge: Cambridge University Press, 1994), p. 212.

[100] Michael W. Dols, *The Black Death in the Middle East* (Princeton: Princeton University Press, 1977), p. 120.

[101] Ibn Qayyim al-Jawzīya, *al-Jawāb al-kāfī li-man saʾala ʿan al-dawāʾ al-shāfī*, ed. Ḥusayn ʿAbd al-Ḥamīd (al-Manṣūra: Dār al-Yaqīm, 1420/2000), p. 9.

[102] Ibid., p. 14.

[103] Ibid., pp. 12–13.

strong, they will cancel each other out. (It is unclear exactly what this means in practice.)[104]

Ibn al-Qayyim takes a pragmatic and empirical approach to the efficacy of prayer. However, he concedes that experiential data can be misleading, because various factors can contribute to the effectiveness or ineffectiveness of a prayer. For instance, the prayer can be accompanied by favorable circumstances such as the petitioner's sincere need, wholehearted concentration on God, or recent acts of benevolence, or it can happen to fall at a particularly propitious and holy time. An observer may assume, based on the fulfillment of the prayer, that the secret lies in the prayer formula itself. This is like someone whose malady responds well to a medication because he takes it in the right way and at the right time; someone might inaccurately assume that the medicine itself sufficed to yield the favorable result. (Despite Ibn al-Qayyim's reservations, the texts of "answered prayers" of proven efficacy – *al-duʿāʾ al-mustajāb* – were and are in wide circulation.) Similarly, a person may wrongly infer that the success of a prayer resulted from its being made at the grave of a holy person, when in fact it was the petitioner's genuine need and sincere reliance on God that led to its fulfillment.[105] Like any good empiricist, Ibn al-Qayyim realizes that it is difficult to hold one's variables constant; based on his own religious concerns (such as his belief in the religious illegitimacy of worship at tombs), he is concerned to emphasize that the data may be misleading.

Classical sources suggest a range of factors potentially affecting the efficacy of prayer. It is advisable to select a propitious time, such as the time of the Friday congregational prayers (sometimes known as the "hour of answering," *sāʿat al-ijāba*), the last watch of the night, the "Night of Power" (*laylat al-qadr*) in the last ten days of the month of Ramaḍān, or the day of ʿArafa during the *ḥajj* pilgrimage.[106] Al-Ghazālī also suggests as auspicious such occasions as the act of prostration, the falling of rain, and the meeting of armies. (He relates their propitious qualities to their inherent holiness, to their conduciveness to the tranquility and focus of the heart, and to the collective power of hearts united in seeking God's mercy on occasions of communal worship.)[107] Certain holy places, such as the mosques of Mecca and Medina and (according to some scholars) the tombs of holy persons, are also conducive to the fulfillment of supplications.[108] The effectiveness of one's prayers may be limited by the consumption of illicit food or drink, the possession of ill-gotten wealth, ritual impurity, lack of sincerity, or other moral infractions.[109] Thus, one should

[104] Ibid., p. 14.
[105] Ibid., p. 22.
[106] See al-Fāsī, *Tuḥfat al-mukhliṣīn*, 1:277–309; Padwick, *Muslim Devotions*, pp. 259–60.
[107] al-Ghazālī, *Iḥyāʾ*, 1:361–2.
[108] See al-Fāsī, *Tuḥfat al-mukhliṣīn*, 1:309–17; Padwick, *Muslim Devotions*, p. 259.
[109] See al-Fāsī, *Tuḥfat al-mukhliṣīn*, 1:227–9; Qushayrī, *Risāla*, pp. 267–8.

precede *du'ā'* with repentance and the redress of any wrongs one has committed. The efficacy of one's prayers may also be improved by observation of the proper etiquette, including facing the *qibla* and holding one's hands out with the palms facing upward; at the end of the prayer one should wipe one's face with one's palms. One should open the prayer by mentioning God and invoking blessings upon the Prophet Muḥammad. (This is because God would not deny the first request honoring the Prophet, who is said to have instructed, "If you ask God Most High for a need, begin by invoking blessings upon me; God is too gracious to be asked for two things and fulfill one and refuse the other.") One should pray with humility and awe, yet in confident hopes of being answered. One should persist in one's petition by repeating it three times, yet not be impatient in awaiting its fulfillment.[110]

Even granted the ideal content and performance of a *du'ā'*, however, the question remained whether God's preeternal decree could be altered in response to human supplication. If, like most Sunnīs, one accepted divine predestination of all acts and events, it was unclear whether or how prayer had a role in determining their unfolding. Scholars sought to give a theological account of petitionary prayer (which they recognized to be not only condoned but encouraged by the Qur'ān and the *ḥadīth*) that acknowledged both the supremacy of God's insight into human welfare and the immutability of His decree. They recognized that petitionary prayer might seem frivolous in light of the belief that "the pens had dried," that is, that divine predestination (or at least foreknowledge) already stipulated all that was to come. Ibn al-Qayyim sees the effectiveness of prayer as merely a subcategory of the larger problem of cause and effect. Those who object that what is predestined will occur whether or not one prays for it (and that *du'ā'* is thus in vain), he argues, do not realize that their logic applies to all instances of causation. Carried to its logical conclusion, their argument implies that satiety will occur if it is divinely decreed whether or not one eats, or that one will have the offspring that are destined for one whether or not one has intercourse with one's spouse.

Misgivings with respect to causation were particularly prevalent in the Ash'arī school, which historically favored an occasionalist doctrine positing that God directly created and caused all things and events at every instant; there was thus no causal nexus between the state of things at one moment and that at the next, but simply an endless series of instantaneous acts of divine creation. Without identifying the Ash'arīs by name, Ibn al-Qayyim describes their doctrine that there are no actual causal connections between (for instance) fire and being burned; there are only customary conjunctions. He briskly dismisses this idea as conflicting with sensory data, rational thought, divine revelation, and

110 al-Ghazālī, *Iḥyā'*, 1:362–5.

innate common sense. He also presents (but rejects) the idea that petitionary prayer is an arbitrary act of obedience commanded by God (*taʿabbud maḥḍ*) for which one will earn a reward, but which bears no functional relation to the fulfillment of one's request. He also cites and dispatches the belief (probably also Ashʿarī) that *duʿāʾ* is simply a sign (*ʿalāma*) that God has established in order to indicate the fulfillment of the wish (rather than a case of its fulfillment).[111]

Al-Ghazālī, an Ashʿarī who nevertheless affirmed secondary causation,[112] writes of the efficacy of *duʿāʾ*:

> If you were to say, "What is the use of petitionary prayer, when there is no way of averting the [divine] decree?" Know that the [divine] decree includes the averting of affliction by means of prayer; prayer is a means of warding off affliction and obtaining [divine] mercy, just as a shield is a means of warding off an arrow and water is a means of growing plants from the earth. . . . Acknowledging the decree of God Most High does not require that one not carry weapons – [indeed], God has said, "take your precautions" [verse 4:71] – or not water the earth after scattering the seed.

He concludes that "connecting causes with effects is the first [divine] decree."[113]

Although Ibn al-Qayyim vehemently rejected Ashʿarism, his own proposed solution does not differ dramatically from al-Ghazālī's. He argues that God decrees something only in conjunction with its causes; God decrees both the prayer and the response to the prayer that is its (actual, but predestined) effect. He concludes:

> Thus, prayer (*duʿāʾ*) is one of the strongest causes. If the thing prayed for is decreed to occur by means of the prayer, it is not correct to say that there is no benefit in praying, just as it is not said that there is no benefit in eating, drinking, and all other movements and acts. There is no means more beneficial than *duʿāʾ*, or more effective in achieving what is desired.[114]

Al-Rāzī, another Ashʿarī, writes of the first objection to *duʿāʾ* – that it is a vain activity in light of divine predestination – that it is contradictory as a rationale for discouraging *duʿāʾ*, because prayer itself by that logic is a predestined activity that will occur willy-nilly if it has been decreed by God. (In other words, if everything is preordained it is frivolous to argue about whether one

[111] Ibn al-Qayyim, *al-Jawāb al-kāfī*, pp. 23–4. For a discussion of the Ashʿarī al-Rāzī's views on causation see Justin K. Stearns, *Infectious Ideas: Contagion in Premodern Islamic and Christian Thought in the Western Mediterranean* (Baltimore: Johns Hopkins University Press, 2011), p. 74.

[112] See R. M. Frank, *al-Ghazālī and the Ashʿarite School* (Durham and London: Duke University Press, 1994), pp. 15–22, 36–9.

[113] al-Ghazālī, *Iḥyāʾ*, 1:390.

[114] Ibn al-Qayyim, *al-Jawāb al-kāfī*, p. 24.

"should" do anything.) Divine foreknowledge and predestination, he argues, are beyond human comprehension; the affirmation of human responsibility in the face of these facts serves to maintain human beings in that state of fear and hope that is necessary for true servanthood toward God. To the objection that God already knows what is best for us better than we ever could (and that presenting our wishes to Him in prayer is thus unnecessary) he responds that the point of *duʿāʾ* is not to inform God of our needs; rather, it is to manifest servanthood, abasement, brokenness, and complete dependence on God. This logic also responds to the objection that *duʿāʾ* expresses a lack of contentment with God's decree; if the prayer is not a demand but a display of humility and need, it leads smoothly into resignation toward God's decision.[115]

Ibn Ḥajar al-ʿAsqalānī takes on one of the most theologically problematic issues relating to prayer: how it could be permissible or effective to pray for long life. Given that one's lifespan (*ajal*) is Qurʾānically attested to be predetermined by God (cf. verses 6:60, 39:42), this would appear to be one of the most obviously futile petitions. Ibn Ḥajar writes:

> The scholars have said: the destined lifespan neither increases nor decreases, but the benefit of praying [for long life] can be imagined (*tataṣawwar*) to be that it is possible that God predestined that Zayd's life will be thirty years, and if someone prays [for his long life] forty, so that one of the two things [actually] occurs. The same applies to all varieties of petitionary prayer; otherwise it would have no benefit, because all things occur by God's predestination.[116]

Overall, even in the obviously problematic case of an issue (length of life) that is unambiguously described in the Qurʾān and *ḥadīth* as being predetermined by God, scholars were at pains to affirm the efficacy of prayer.

Of course, expectations of efficacy – even if they could in theory be deferred to the afterlife – were likely to give rise to evaluations of effectiveness. Outcomes could influence the perceived religious legitimacy of specific kinds of supplication. In one of the most influential "plague treatises," Ibn Ḥajar al-ʿAsqalānī writes that public congregational prayers for relief from the plague, modeled on the prayer for rain, were a new practice that had been introduced in Damascus in the year 749/1348 (i.e., the first year of the epidemic). After they were first performed the plague became much more severe than it had been before. He proceeds to observe that when the plague afflicted Cairo in his own time, a three-day fast was announced, as in the case of the prayer for rain; the people gathered to perform *duʿāʾ*, and by the end of the month more than a thousand people were dying in the city per day. Implicit in these accounts is the judgment that an inappropriate ritual action has provoked divine displeasure

[115] Rāzī, *Tafsīr*, 5:99–100 (commentary on verse 2:186).
[116] Ibn Ḥajar al-ʿAsqalānī, *Badhl al-māʿūn fī faḍl al-ṭāʿūn*, ed. Aḥmad ʿIṣām ʿAbd al-Qādir al-Kātib (Riyadh: Dār al-ʿĀṣima, 1411), p. 325.

(and thus caused adverse effects). Others made different empirical judgments; according to Ibn Ḥajar, one scholar argued when consulted about public prayer against plague that it had been tried under a previous sultan and proved efficacious.[117]

In a modern and secular context it may be natural to conceive of answered prayers as divine interventions in an otherwise regular natural order, as breaches in the chain of cause and effect. For the classical Islamic scholars whose views are surveyed here, in contrast, divine responsiveness to prayer is an integral part of the natural order and of the chain of causality – however these are imagined or to whatever extent they are affirmed by the individual thinker. To affirm that prayer caused relief was no different from affirming that intercourse caused pregnancy or that nutritional imbalances caused disease. Whether a genuine secondary cause or merely another of God's "habits," the efficacy of prayer was analyzed in tandem with other instances of natural order. As Ibn Ḥajar al-ʿAsqalānī declares in his treatise on the Black Death, "There is no doubt that treatment with supplications is more effective than treatment with drugs."[118] Although it is difficult to gauge the extent to which prayer actually worked, it is certain that most contemporary medical treatments did not. Ibn Ḥajar's conviction was thus neither logically nor empirically irrational.

In the twentieth century, petitionary prayer came to appear to some Muslim thinkers less as a technology analogous to medicine than as a fatalistic expression of trust in God. In Iran around the time of the revolution of 1979, overt debate arose over the role of *duʿāʾ* and whether it promoted passivity in the face of personal and social problems. The fact that this debate arose specifically among Imāmī Shīʿites may reflect the prominent role of *duʿāʾ* in traditional Imāmī ritual life. In a series of lectures delivered soon after the fall of the Shah, Khomeini defended traditional invocations such as the "Prayer of Kumayl." "These prayers do not deter man from labor and activity," he argued. Rather, "it is precisely prayer and the like that make man become a true human being" by causing him "to turn toward the origin of his being in the unseen and to strengthen his attachment to it." He concludes, "Once a man has become a true human being, he will be the most active of men."[119]

117 Ibid., pp. 328–9.

118 Ibid., p. 318.

119 Rūḥ Allāh Khumaynī, *Islam and Revolution: Writings and Declarations of Imam Khomeini*, trans. Hamid Algar (Berkeley: Mizan Press, 1981), p. 399–400. On the debate over *duʿāʾ* see Algar, "Doʿā."

2 Valid prayer and ideal prayer

As described in the previous chapter, *ṣalāt* as constructed by the legal tradition is an activity governed by a fairly elaborate set of rules. Although Islamic law was never the only religious discourse shaping the ways in which Muslims practiced and understood ritual prayer (as we shall see, in the premodern period Sufism competed with law as the most influential tradition of piety in this respect), the vast majority of Muslims have historically accepted that the rules generated by legal thinkers set the parameters for valid prayer. Although these rules could be exacting – everything from the necessity of waking before sunrise, to the frequency of prayer, to the restrictions of ritual purity might demand effort and commitment – they were recognized as achievable by ordinary people, rather than requiring the special gifts of the spiritually adept. *Ṣalāt* may be demanding, but it is eminently doable for anyone determined to do it. Beyond the basic fulfillment of the rules, however, Muslim thinkers recognized that *ṣalāt* could be performed with varying degrees of attention, sincerity, and emotional intensity. It might merely discharge one's obligation toward God and thereby avert otherworldly punishment, or it might increase one's intimacy with the divine. Punctilious performance of the daily prayers might leave one's sinful nature otherwise untouched, or it could lead to fundamental ethical transformation. Various authors pondered the relationship between legally adequate and spiritually ideal prayer, and explored means to cultivate more profound *ṣalāt*.

Intent (*nīya*)

The schools of law are unanimous in requiring the proper intent (*nīya*) for prayer, although they differ in characterizing it as a mandatory component (*rukn*, *farḍ*) of *ṣalāt* or as a necessary condition (*sharṭ*).[1] One view conceptualizes proper intent as a state that accompanies the other actions of prayer (somewhat like facing the *qibla*), whereas the other frames it as a discrete action

[1] The Ḥanafīs, Ḥanbalīs, and some Mālikīs consider it a condition; the Shāfiʿīs and some Mālikīs hold that it is a component (*rukn*).

in itself. However, in some respects all schools of law conceptualize the framing of the *nīya* as an action, in that it occurs at a particular time (preferably immediately before beginning to pray, or as one pronounces the opening *takbīra*). Thus, it is not simply an attitude that underlies the physical actions of prayer. In content, scholars agree that *nīya* involves the framing of a resolve (*qaṣd*, *ʿazm*, *irāda*) to perform a specific prayer. It entails mentally declaring one's intent to pray and identifying the prayer in question, including whether it is mandatory or supererogatory and what kind of prayer (for instance, dawn, noon, or Friday) it is. It may also involve specifying whether one will pray alone, as a prayer leader, or following someone else.

Some jurists advocated that the *nīya* be articulated in words, although none held that the verbal utterance of the *nīya* was an actual condition for the validity of prayer. Ḥanafīs argued that it was desirable (*mustaḥabb*) to combine the framing of the *nīya* within the heart with its utterance with the tongue as an aid to concentration; Shāfiʿīs and Ḥanbalīs generally also considered it recommended. Mālikīs, in contrast, held that it was preferable not to verbalize the *nīya* unless one was suffering from a debilitating state of doubt (*waswās*, somewhat similar to obsessive-compulsive disorder in modern psychology), in which case one could use verbalization as a way of resolving one's mental struggle.[2] Even scholars who supported the practice admitted that there was no report, no matter how weak, attributing it to the Prophet or his Companions; it is not traced back even to the founding authorities of the four schools. Nevertheless, verbalization of the *nīya* had become a prevalent custom by the time of Ibn Taymīya (d. 728/1328), who briskly rejected it as an innovation (*bidʿa*).[3] It retained its popularity despite such objections; the nineteenth-century Ḥanafī Ibn ʿĀbidīn considered it to have been ubiquitous in many parts of the Islamic world over the course of many centuries.[4] Despite the lack of authoritative precedent, he argued that it was a "good innovation" (*bidʿa ḥasana*) if one's aim was to gather one's resolve, because it was human nature for one's thoughts to become scattered.[5]

The basic function of the *nīya* is to distinguish the ritual of prayer from other, merely routine activities: to identify it as *ʿibāda* (an act of worship) rather than *ʿāda* (a purely customary action).[6] Mālik ibn Anas (the eponymous founder of the Mālikī school) is said to have observed that someone who prostrates himself in worship of God is performing an action formally identical to that of someone

[2] al-Zuḥaylī, *Fiqh*, 1:774, 776, 777, 779.

[3] Ibn Taymīya, *Majmūʿ al-fatāwā*, 22:119–24.

[4] Muḥammad Amīn ibn ʿĀbidīn, *Ḥāshiyat Radd al-muḥtār ʿalā al-Durr al-mukhtār: sharḥ Tanwīr al-abṣār* (Cairo: Muḥammad Maḥmūd al-Ḥalabī wa-Shurakāʾhu, 1386/1966), 1:416.

[5] Ibid., 1:416. For a modern debate over the verbalization of the *nīya* see John R. Bowen, *Muslims through Discourse* (Princeton: Princeton University Press, 1993), pp. 301–6.

[6] See Paul R. Powers, *Intent in Islamic Law: Motive and Meaning in Medieval Sunnī Fiqh* (Leiden: Brill, 2006), pp. 44–5.

who prostrates himself to an idol; only the *nīya* renders one an act of worship and the other an act of disbelief.[7]

The Shāfiʿī Ibn ʿAbd al-Salām al-Sulamī (d. 660/1262) acknowledges that *ṣalāt* – here understood as a complex series of physical postures and verbal utterances – does not outwardly resemble any purely customary action. Indeed, it is difficult to imagine that anyone would perform the entire sequence purely coincidentally. However, he argues that *nīya* is nevertheless necessary to define *ṣalāt*. Since the validity of prayer is dependent on the validity of the entire sequence, the first act of the series must itself be identified not simply as an act of prayer, but as a prayer of a specific type and status. For instance, obligatory prayers are superior to supererogatory prayers, and supererogatory prayers that are to be performed at a specific time are superior to those that may be performed at any time. *Nīya* is necessary to establish at the outset the identity of the specific prayer being performed.[8]

Other scholars argue that *nīya* is necessary when the benefits of an act do not automatically accrue from its external performance; because the act's objectives are not achieved by its physical form, a subjective dimension (constituted by the *nīya*) is necessary to fulfill them. The Mālikī jurist Shihāb al-Dīn al-Qarāfī (d. c. 684/1285) observes:

> *Ṣalāt* was legislated for the purpose of glorifying (*taʿẓīm*) and exalting God Most High, and glorification occurs only by virtue of intention. Don't you see that if you prepared a banquet for a person and someone else ate it without your intending him to, you would [still] be glorifying the first person rather than the second, by virtue of your intent? Any [action] that is devoid of intent is devoid of glorification.[9]

In contrast,

> Any act whose [outward] form suffices to produce its benefits does not require *nīya*, for instance paying debts, returning stolen items, paying maintenance for wives and relatives, giving feed to beasts of burden, and the like. This category of actions requires no *nīya* as a matter of law; someone who pays his debt while oblivious of the intent of closeness to God (*al-taqarrub*) does so validly, and it need not be repeated.[10]

The earlier Mālikī authority Ibn Rushd puts the point more succinctly: "As for the *nīya*, the scholars are agreed that it is a condition for the validity of prayer,

[7] ʿAbd Allāh ibn Muḥammad ibn al-Ḥājj, *al-Madkhal ilā tanmiyat al-aʿmāl bi-taḥsīn al-nīyāt wa'l-tanbīh ʿalā baʿḍ al-bidaʿ wa'l-ʿawāʾid al-latī untuḥilat wa-bayān shanāʿatihā*, ed. Tawfīq Ḥamdān (Beirut: Dār al-Kutub al-ʿIlmīya, 1415/1995), 1:9. Similarly al-Marghīnānī, *al-Hidāya*, published with Muḥammad ibn Muḥammad al-Bābartī al-Ḥanafī, *al-ʿInāya sharḥ al-Hidāya*, ed. Abū Maḥrūs ʿAmr ibn Maḥrūs (Beirut: Dār al-Kutub al-ʿIlmīya, 1427/2007), 1:220.

[8] ʿIzz al-Dīn ʿAbd al-ʿAzīz ibn ʿAbd al-Salām al-Sulamī, *Qawāʿid al-aḥkām fī maṣāliḥ al-anām* (Beirut: Mu'assasat al-Rayyān, 1410/1990), 1:153–4.

[9] Aḥmad ibn Idrīs al-Ṣanhājī al-Qarāfī, *al-Furūq wa-Anwār al-burūq fī anwāʾ al-furūq* (Beirut: Dār al-Kutub al-ʿIlmīya, 1418/1998), 1:237.

[10] Ibid., 1:236.

because prayer is the chief one of the acts of worship that were mandated without a rationally comprehensible objective (I mean, in the realm of tangible benefits)."[11] In short, since prayer does not observably achieve anything on the material level, its work is understood to take place on the subjective level of interior intent and orientation toward the divine.

As is perhaps already suggested by the above quotations, *nīya* can be understood in either a minimalist or a maximalist sense. At the most basic legal level, and the one that most jurists would use as the technical criterion of the validity of prayer, *nīya* simply serves to constitute an otherwise disparate set of physical postures and verbal utterances as a coherent and consciously identified ritual act. Paul Powers has argued that "the overarching function of *niyya* in *fiqh al-ʿibādāt* [ritual law] is definitive and taxonomic, allowing actors to locate their actions on the map of ideal-typical actions laid out in the works of *fiqh*."[12] On this level, *nīya* does not involve any deep introspective scrutiny of one's degree of sincerity or level of absorption.

Furthermore, as long as no incompatible intention intervenes during the performance of the prayer, for purposes of technical validity the *nīya* need not be consciously maintained throughout all of the actions of the prayer sequence. Rather, it is understood to persist unchanged unless displaced by another intention, such as the intent to cut short one's prayer (which ruptures one's state of prayer even if it is accompanied by no outer action). In general, jurists hold that with respect to acts of worship involving multiple actions, the framing of the proper intent at the opening of the sequence is sufficient.[13] Thus, in principle *nīya* is not necessarily a mental state intensively experienced for the duration of the prayer sequence; as long as it is not actively ruptured, its de jure persistence is simply assumed once it is initially established.

From this minimalist legal point of view, *nīya* is not necessarily to be identified with sincerity (although, as we shall see below, the relationship between the two concepts was both complex and contested). The sixteenth-century Shāfiʿī scholar Ibn Ḥajar al-Haytamī was asked about someone who was guilty of hypocrisy (*rāʾā*, noun: *riyāʾ*) in the first phase of his *ṣalāt*, the pronunciation of the *takbīr* with the *nīya*. Is his or her prayer formally valid (*taṣiḥḥ ṣalātuhu ẓāhiran*) or not? He replied:

> As long as the *nīya* is definite and fulfills its conditions [i.e., of specifying the prayer and its level of obligation] . . ., the prayer is valid and soundly constituted, even if we assume that [the person] combined [his intent] with a worldly objective. It is for this reason that

11 Ibn Rushd, *Bidāyat al-mujtahid*, 1:113.
12 Powers, *Intent*, p. 73.
13 *al-Mawsūʿa al-fiqhīya*, 2nd printing (Kuwait: Wizārat al-Awqāf wa'l-Shuʾūn al-Islāmīya, 1406/1986), art. "insiḥāb," paragraph 5b (6:335).

our authorities have held that if someone were told, "Pray and I'll give you a dinar," and he prayed with that objective, his prayer would be valid.[14]

Indeed, the fourth/tenth-century scholar Abū'l-Layth al-Samarqandī is supposed to have approvingly cited the opinion that "hypocrisy does not affect any obligatory ritual" (*al-riyā' lā tadkhul fī shay' min al-farā'iḍ*), which he described as "the sound doctrine, [which is] that hypocrisy does not forfeit the basic reward [for performing the obligatory ritual], but merely forfeits the multiplication of the reward."[15] Here intent (*nīya*) is quite distinct from motive (*qaṣd*); a person may frame a correct *nīya* while being motivated by quite different considerations. Furthermore, legal validity is quite distinct from the degree of otherworldly merit or reward that the act of worship might yield. The fifteenth-century Ḥanafī scholar Ibn Bazzāz explicitly notes (in a formula widely quoted in his school) that "there is no hypocrisy in obligatory rituals with regard to the discharge of the obligation" (*fī ḥaqq suqūṭ al-wājib*).[16] Al-Marghīnānī makes the point more explicit: "If [someone] prays for the sake of hypocrisy and reputation, his prayer is valid in legal status (*tajūz ṣalātuhu fī'l-ḥukm*) because its conditions and components are present, but it does not merit reward."[17]

However, not all legal scholars were in agreement that the formal validity of prayer was independent of its subjective sincerity, or that it could discharge the legal obligation to pray without fulfilling at least a basic standard of spiritual wholeheartedness. The early nineteenth-century Ḥanafī scholar Ibn ʿĀbidīn outlined some of the complexity of the discussion over the history of his own school:

Know that dedicating one's worship exclusively to God (*ikhlāṣ al-ʿibāda li'llāh taʿālā*) is obligatory, and hypocrisy in it – which is doing it for the sake of something other than God Himself – is forbidden by consensus, on the basis of definitive textual proofs. [The Prophet] (peace be upon him!) called hypocrisy "the lesser polytheism." [The fourteenth-century Ḥanafī scholar] al-Zaylaʿī explicitly stated that someone who performs a prayer needs to have the intent of devoting his prayer exclusively [to God: *nīyat al-ikhlāṣ*]. The *Miʿrāj* [a commentary on al-Marghīnānī's *Hidāya* by the fourteenth-century Ḥanafī scholar Muḥammad ibn Muḥammad al-Kākī] states, "We have been commanded to worship [God], and worship does not exist without the exclusive devotion

14 Ibn Ḥajar al-Makkī al-Haytamī, *al-Fatāwā al-kubrā al-fiqhīya* (Beirut: Dār al-Kutub al-ʿIlmīya, 1417/1997), 1:212. See also Ibn ʿĀbidīn, *Ḥāshiyat Radd al-muḥtār*, 1:415; al-Ḥaṣkafī, *al-Durr al-mukhtār*, published with Ibn ʿĀbidīn, *Ḥāshiyat Radd al-muḥtār*, 1:438. Al-Ḥaṣkafī specifies that although the prayer is valid the person is not entitled to the dinar.

15 Cited in Ibn ʿĀbidīn, *Ḥāshiyat Radd al-muḥtār*, 6:426.

16 Ibn Nujaym al-Ḥanafī, *Sharḥ al-Ashbāh wa'l-naẓā'ir*, published with Aḥmad ibn Muḥammad al-Ḥamawī, *Ghamz ʿuyūn al-baṣā'ir fī sharḥ al-Ashbāh wa'l-naẓā'ir*, ed. Nuʿaym Ashraf Nūr Aḥmad (Karachi: Idārat al-Qur'ān wa'l-ʿUlūm al-Islāmīya, 1424/2004), 1:39.

17 Cited from al-Marghīnānī's *Mukhtārāt al-nawāzil* in Ibn ʿĀbidīn, *Ḥāshiyat Radd al-muḥtār*, 1:438.

(*ikhlāṣ*) that is commanded; *ikhlāṣ* is devoting one's actions [exclusively] to God, and that can only happen by means of intent (*nīya*)."

Ibn ʿĀbidīn comments:

This [intent of which al-Kākī speaks] is the intent [necessary] to earn merit, not [the intent necessary] for the validity of the action, because validity has to do with the conditions and components [of prayer], and the *nīya* which is a condition for the validity of prayer is, for instance, that [the person] know in his heart which prayer he is performing.

Citing an example from al-Marghīnānī in which a person inadvertently performs his ablutions with ritually impure water, resulting in a prayer that is technically invalid but yields merit because of its sound intent, Ibn ʿĀbidīn concludes, "From this one can conclude that there is no necessary connection between merit and validity; there may be merit without validity, as in the example, or vice versa."[18]

Other scholars took a harder line, asserting that corrupt motivations rendered prayer altogether null. Asked about someone who, when beginning to pray, prolonged his bowing in order to be seen by an approaching observer, Abū Ḥanīfa is supposed to have replied, "I fear something dreadful for him," meaning that it was "hidden polytheism," or hypocrisy.[19] The Shāfiʿī scholar (and Sufi mystic) Ibn ʿAbd al-Salām al-Sulamī declares:

Hypocrisy is displaying the act of worship so that the person who displays it can gain some impermanent thing of this world, either by obtaining a worldly benefit or by averting a worldly harm, or [for the sake of his own] glorification or aggrandizement. Whoever joins any of that to his worship nullifies it (*abṭalahu*), because he made the worship and obedience of God a means to gain lowly, despicable impermanent things.[20]

A quite similar, but more elaborate, analysis of this issue is provided by al-Qarāfī. In discussing *riyāʾ* (hypocrisy, or "doing something for show"; the word is derived from the verb "to see"), he defines it with respect to acts of worship as polytheism (*shirk*) and assigning a partner to God in obedience (*tashrīk maʿa Allāh taʿālā fī ṭāʿatihi*) and states:

It entails disobedience, sin, and invalidity in those acts of worship, as was explicitly stated by the Imām al-Muḥāsibī [an early mystic, d. 243/857] and others. This is supported by what is in the sound *ḥadīth* transmitted by Muslim and others, that God says: "I am less in need of partnership than any partner; whoever performs an action and gives someone other than Me a share in it, I abandon it to him or abandon it to My partner" – the clear meaning of this is that this action does not count with God.[21]

18 Ibid., 6:425.
19 Ibid., 1:438.
20 al-Sulamī, *Qawāʿid al-aḥkām*, 1:107.
21 Qarāfī, *Furūq*, 3:42.

Al-Qarāfī distinguishes between *riyā' al-shirk*, where one performs an act of worship both for the sake of God and for the sake of earning people's admiration and gaining benefits or averting harm from them, and *riyā' al-ikhlāṣ*, which involves performing the act purely from worldly motives. Although his discussion is somewhat ambiguous, it appears that al-Qarāfī regards both of these categories as invalidating prayer. In contrast, he asserts that there are subsidiary motivations that do not invalidate an act of worship because they are unavoidable concomitants of it and God accorded the benefits in question to the person performing the act of worship. For instance, if someone engages in jihad both in obedience to God and to gain a share of the booty, that does not harm him, because it was assigned to him by God. In contrast, if he engages in jihad so that people will think he is brave or so that the ruler will assign him moneys from the public treasury, it is forbidden *riyā'*. The distinction is that legitimate subsidiary benefits do not involve the exaltation of other human beings (*ta'ẓīm al-khalq*) by making their attitudes and actions the criterion and motive of one's worship, nor are they done to be observed by others. It is a defining element of *riyā'* that it be based on a desire for the regard of others, an interpretation rooted in the etymology of the term. Nevertheless, any ulterior motives may diminish the merit of an act of worship, even if they do not invalidate it or constitute sins.[22]

Ultimately, most scholars were reluctant to establish conditions for the validity of prayer that might be prohibitively difficult to fulfill (or impossible to confirm). The modern Shī'ite authority Ayatollah S. Mohammad Kazem Shariatmadari taught in regard to *nīya*:

> There are three reasons why people might pray: (a) for fear of hell, (b), for hope of heaven, (c) for love of God. Sayyid Ibn Ta'us issued a fatwa . . . that the first two reasons invalidate prayer and only the third makes prayer valid. But the fatwa is wrong for four reasons: (1) there are very few people who could live up to the fatwa, that is, pray only for love of God all the time.[23]

Even scholars who took an extremely dim view of the moral and legal implications of performing prayer out of mixed or corrupt motives maintained that the fear that such motives might contaminate one's prayers was in no way a valid excuse for failure to pray. The Ḥanafī al-Ḥaṣkafī (d. 1088/1677) states that someone "should not refrain [from praying] out of fear of the intrusion of hypocrisy, because it is merely something he is imagining" (*amr mawhūm*) – that is, the mere envisioned possibility of imperfect sincerity is not a legally relevant fact.[24] The fourteenth-century Shāfi'ī scholar Taqī al-Dīn al-Subkī

[22] Ibid., 3:43–4.
[23] Michael M. J. Fischer, *Iran: From Religious Dispute to Revolution* (Madison: University of Wisconsin Press, 1980), p. 65.
[24] al-Ḥaṣkafī, *al-Durr al-mukhtār*, base text published with Ibn 'Ābidīn, *Ḥāshiyat Radd al-muḥtār*, 1:438.

searchingly addressed the question of the mixed motives that might beset an aspiring worshiper. The lengthy enquiry that elicited his fatwa sets out the following scenario:

A person desires some act of worship, such as a nighttime vigil or the like, in the hopes of God's reward; he has a strong inclination/motivation (*bāʿith*) to do so, which is opposed within him by the obstacle of laziness and the love of ease. His soul (*nafs*) awakens the desire to do it from time to time; however, that inclination that repels the inclination of laziness does not prevail unless he adds to it the motivation of hypocrisy and good repute (*al-riyāʾ wa'l-sumʿa*). If he does not add it, he never performs that act of worship at all, while if the worldly motive is added to the otherworldly motive the act of worship is performed. Is it permissible for him to make it occur by virtue of the combination of the two motives, as a means of manifesting the effect of the religious motivation, or is it forbidden, or must one differentiate based on the strength of one of the motives as compared with the other . . .?[25]

Subkī begins by affirming that it is halal (licit) to use hypocritical motivations as a temporary aid in fostering one's pious desire to engage in acts of worship. He holds that it is forbidden only if the worldly motivation predominates. He continues:

My opinion . . . is that one should not omit a [pious] action for fear of hypocrisy at all, because it constitutes the omission of a certain benefit for the sake of an imagined harm. Many acts are contaminated [by hypocrisy] and then become pure – nay, most things are like that! Whenever someone embarks on some activity, it is inevitable that the bad will be mixed with the good, and then it is cleansed and purified until it is pure.

Specifically, "it is difficult to make the body conform properly to *ṣalāt* and other similar bodily activities at the beginning; one must remain committed to it while working on the sincerity of the heart, and will achieve it, God willing, with [God's] help. If we were to cut off the one who embarks on this from anything but what is pure from the beginning, much good would be cut off."[26]

As suggested by al-Subkī's pragmatic analysis, the *nīya* necessary for valid prayer was not intended by most scholars to involve an open-ended and psychologically taxing quest for mental focus or spiritual single-mindedness, although both mental focus and spiritual single-mindedness were valued as dimensions of an ideal act of prayer. Overestimating the content of the *nīya* and consequently suffering a psychological block in achieving it – a problem that could inhibit the regular and successful performance of the obligatory prayers – was one form of the malady of *waswās*, or "scrupulosity," an obsessive condition that particularly afflicted the pious.[27] (The other area in

[25] Taqī al-Dīn ʿAlī ibn ʿAbd al-Kāfī al-Subkī, *Fatāwā al-Subkī* (Beirut: Dār al-Maʿrifa, n.d.), 1:160.
[26] Ibid., p. 162.
[27] On this subject see Megan Reid, *Ritual and Piety in Medieval Islam* (Cambridge: Cambridge University Press, forthcoming).

which the hazard of *waswās* loomed large was that of ritual purity, where nagging doubts could lead to compulsive washing.) With respect to the *nīya* of prayer, this was a particular problem for followers of the Shāfiʿī school, because Shāfiʿī authorities often held that the *nīya* (which involved awareness of several different aspects of the prayer in question, such as its time of day and degree of obligation) must be sustained for the duration of the pronunciation of the *takbīr*. (Others questioned this requirement, such as al-Qaffāl, who staunchly declared that "the *nīya* occurs in a single instant, and its extension is unimaginable."[28])

Nevertheless, the great Shāfiʿī jurist and mystic al-Ghazālī (d. 505/1111) asserted that difficulty or obsessive doubts (*waswasa*) with respect to the *nīya* of prayer could result only from a mental disorder or from ignorance of the law, because achieving the legally required intent was in truth not problematic at all:

> The real meaning of *nīya* is the intent to perform the action (*al-qaṣd ilā al-fiʿl*); this is what makes the act voluntary. For instance, falling down to a prostrate position may sometimes be intentional and sometimes occur when a person falls onto his face because of a shock. This intentionality is the opposite of compulsion. The second intent is like a rationale (*kaʾl-ʿilla*) for this [first] intent. It involves taking action (*al-inbiʿāth*) to respond to a motivation, such as standing up when one sees a person [arriving]: if you intend to honor him, then you have the *nīya* of glorifying him (*taʿẓīmihi*), and if you intend to go out to the street, you have the *nīya* of going out. The intention (*qaṣd*) of standing up is not stimulated in the soul unless there is an objective in standing up; that objective is what is intended (*al-manwī*, the thing for which you have a *nīya*).[29]

Thus, if you act on your own initiative and know at the most basic level for what purpose you are acting, you necessarily have the appropriate *nīya*.

Despite al-Ghazālī's insistence that the *nīya* required for acts of worship was no more mysterious or problematic than the intentionality inherent to other voluntary actions, he clearly recognized that many serious believers regarded framing the *nīya* for prayer as a challenge. In another work he suggested the ridiculous quality of doubting one's own *nīya* by elaborating on the analogy between standing in prayer and standing in honor of another person. If someone stands up in honor of a scholar who is entering the room, his intent is clear unless there is some other explanation for his standing or he does so in an inappropriate way (for instance, with his back to the scholar). However, "if he were to say, 'I [hereby] intend to stand erect in glorification of the entrance of the honorable Zayd [i.e., the scholar], for the sake of his virtue, directing my face towards him,' this would indicate mental incompetence of his part." The intent of honoring the scholar would be manifest from the context, and no

[28] Cited in ʿAbd al-Malik ibn ʿAbd Allāh al-Juwaynī, *Nihāyat al-maṭlab fī dirāyat al-madhhab*, ed. ʿAbd al-ʿAẓīm Mahmūd al-Dīb (Jeddah: Dār al-Minhāj, 1428/2007), 2:112–15.

[29] Cited from the *Fatāwā* of al-Ghazālī in Badr al-Dīn Muḥammad ibn Bahādur al-Shāfiʿī, known as al-Zarkashī, *al-Manthūr fīʾl-qawāʿid* (Beirut: Dār al-Kutub al-ʿIlmīya, 1421/2000), 2:355.

sensible person would assume that it required mental scrutiny, let alone verbal proclamation.[30]

According to al-Ghazālī, the problem for the person afflicted with *waswās* is that he attempts simultaneously to focus on all of the defining features of the prayer (being a noon prayer, being performed at its original time rather than as a makeup, being obligatory) and to mentally articulate these multiple ideas in words, which he considers to be an impossible (and unnecessary) feat. Rather, the intentionality that invests prayer with its meaning (obedience to, and glorification of, God) is no more problematic than the intentionality that allows us to "mean" our ordinary social actions, and for other people to interpret them correctly. Even for the Sufi al-Ghazālī, for whom introspective interrogation of one's spiritual flaws was a central objective of the religious life, the legally necessary *nīya* for prayer was not a matter of mental gymnastics.

Al-Ghazālī's insistence that *nīya* was an unproblematic and inherent aspect of prayer, as of all mundane activities, was shared by a scholar otherwise as different as Ibn Taymīya. He similarly considered verbal utterance of the *nīya* an inherently nonsensical practice:

> The proclamation of intent is a defect in religion and in reason. It is a defect in religion as it is an innovation. It is a defect in reason because it is like someone who is about to eat and then proclaims: "By putting my hand into this vessel I intend to take a morsel, put it in my mouth, then chew upon it, then swallow it, so that I satiate my hunger." . . . If the person knows what is it he is about to do, by necessity he has the intention of doing it.[31]

Nevertheless, a more maximal view of *nīya* persisted in some circles, and sometimes gave rise to tormenting doubts about the validity of prayer. The Shāfiʿī Ibn al-Ṣalāḥ al-Shahrazūrī (d. 643/1245) was consulted about a man afflicted with a piteous inability to pray as a result of pathological doubts about his *nīya* (and responded with an explanation of the straightforward and minimal nature of the required intent).[32] In a polemic against the spiritual malady of *waswās*, the thirteenth-century Ḥanbalī scholar Ibn Qudāma writes about its victims:

> One of these people . . . utters the *takbīr* or recites something [of the Qurʾān] with his tongue that his ears hear and his heart knows . . . and despite this, he accepts Satan's word that he did not have the *nīya* for prayer or intend to do it, defying his own direct observation and denying the certainty of his soul, to the point that we see him pondering, perplexed, as if he were attending to something that was addressing him or trying to bring

[30] al-Ghazālī, *Iḥyāʾ*, 1:225.

[31] Yossef Rapoport, "Ibn Taymiyya's Radical Legal Thought: Rationalism, Pluralism and the Primacy of Intention," in Yossef Rapoport and Shahab Ahmed, eds., *Ibn Taymiyya and His Times* (Oxford: Oxford University Press, 2010), p. 210; see also Powers, *Intent*, pp. 38–9.

[32] Ibn al-Ṣalāḥ, *Fatāwā wa-masāʾil Ibn al-Ṣalāḥ fī'l-ḥadīth wa'l-uṣūl wa'l-fiqh*, ed. ʿAbd al-Muʿṭī Amīn Qalʿajī (Beirut: Dār al-Maʿrifa, 1406/1986), 1:257–8.

forth something from within him – all of this out of exaggerated obedience to Satan, and acceptance of his insinuation (*waswasa*).

Such a person might end up missing congregational prayers because he failed (in his own estimation) to frame the *nīya* in time. He might also require multiple tries to utter each syllable of the *takbīra*; Ibn Qudāma recounts that he heard someone stammering "Allāhu ak-k-kbar" as a result of his *waswās*.[33]

However, neither the clarifications nor the ridicule of scholars eliminated the problem, which was probably not widespread but certainly persistent. The Egyptian author Ṭāhā Ḥusayn, who attended the ancient university of al-Azhar at the turn of the twentieth century, describes in his autobiography the curious sounds he heard from the room adjoining his student lodgings. His neighbor recited, "al . . . al . . . al . . . Allāh, Allāh, Allāh ak . . . al . . . al . . . Allāhu ak. Allāhu ak. Allāhu akbar . . . " The voice went on on to recite the Fātiḥa, getting stuck on the "s" of *iyyāka nastaʿīn* then resuming its fitful efforts to utter the *takbīr*. These sounds first frightened the young Ṭāhā, then sent him into fits of suppressed laughter. His older brother later explained that their neighbor was a Shāfiʿī suffering from a case of *waswās*, and that he wanted to be sure of his *nīya* for prayer, and to focus his heart and mind exclusively on God when he began to pray and for the duration of his prayer. If he sensed that a worldly thought had intruded on his devotion, he would break off his prayer and begin again.[34] It is not difficult to imagine that such an exacting standard could make the five daily prayers a torturous process.

Hapless laypeople were not the only ones who sometimes attempted to pack more content into the framing of the *nīya*. The Mālikī theologian Abū Bakr al-Bāqillānī (d. 403/1013) is reported to have required that a person commencing *ṣalāt*

remember the createdness of the world and the proofs for it, the confirmation of accidents and the impossibility of substances being devoid of them, the refutation of created things that have no beginning, the proofs of the creator from the world, the affirmation of [divine] attributes, what is necessarily true of God, what is impossible, and what is possible, the proofs for miracles and the confirmation of prophethood, and finally the path by which legal responsibility reached him.

Al-Bāqillānī reportedly insisted that calling these matters to memory required only a small amount of time, unlike learning them in the first place. Nevertheless, the Mālikī scholar al-Māzirī reported that when he attempted to follow al-Bāqillānī's advice when beginning to pray, he had a dream in which he

[33] ʿAbd Allāh ibn Aḥmad Ibn Qudāma al-Maqdisī, *Dhamm al-waswās* (Damascus: Maktabat al-Fārūq, 1411/1990), pp. 20–1.
[34] Ḥusayn, *al-Ayyām*, 2:74–5; trans. in Hussein, *The Days*, pp. 154–5.

was plunging into a sea of darkness, which he recognized as an apt representation of al-Bāqillānī's doctrine.[35]

In order to take into account the multiple dimensions of *nīya*, some later legal scholars posited multiple kinds of intent. Some Shāfiʿīs distinguished *nīyat al-taqarrub* ("the intent of drawing near to God") from *nīyat al-tamyīz* ("the intent of differentiation," which distinguishes acts of worship from formally identical profane actions).[36] The Ḥanafī al-Zaylaʿī (d. 1342–3) stated that three intents were necessary for prayer: the intent to perform the specific prayer in question, the intent of *ikhlāṣ* (that is, of sincerely dedicating one's prayer exclusively to God), and the intent of facing the *qibla*.[37] Other scholars simply built the idea of devotion to God directly into their definitions of *nīya*; for instance, the Ḥanafīs al-Kāsānī and Zayn al-Dīn Ibn Nujaym defined it as "the will (*irāda*) to pray to God exclusively/sincerely (*ʿalā al-khulūṣ*)."[38] Some later legal scholars even incorporated expansive Sufi definitions of *ikhlāṣ* directly into the legal discussion of *nīya*. The early nineteenth-century Ḥanbalī Muṣṭafā ibn Saʿd al-Suyūṭī built on the comment of Marʾī ibn Yūsuf al-Karmī (d. 1623–4) that the *nīya* of prayer must include the intent of worshiping in order to draw near to God (*taqarruban ilā allāh*) by specifying that this is achieved

> by intending by his action God Most High to the exclusion of anything else such as ingratiating oneself to a created being, earning the good opinion of people, love for praise from them, or anything of the like; this is *ikhlāṣ*. One of them said: It is the purification of the act from attention to created beings.[39]

This passage, which continues for several more lines and is presented without attribution, is drawn directly from al-Qushayrī's manual of the mystical path.[40]

[35] Shihāb al-Dīn Aḥmad ibn Idrīs al-Qarāfī, *al-Dhakhīra* (Beirut: Dār al-Gharb al-Islāmī, 1994), 2:136. In contrast, Ibn al-Ḥājj al-ʿAbdarī approvingly cites a report attributing a similar opinion to al-Bāqillānī's commentator Imām al-Ḥaramayn al-Juwaynī, who remarked that teaching these facts to the ignorant required a long period of time, but recollecting them once acquired took only an instant. Ibn al-Ḥājj also provides his own expansive (although less theologically oriented) list of religious commitments involved in a complete *nīya* (Ibn al-Ḥājj, *Madkhal*, 1:44).

[36] *al-Mawsūʿa al-fiqhīya*, art. "Nīya," paragraph 36 (42:87–8), citing al-Zarkashī, *al-Manthūr*.

[37] ʿUthmān ibn ʿAlī al-Zaylaʿī, *Tabyīn al-ḥaqāʾiq sharḥ Kanz al-daqāʾiq* (Būlāq: al-Maṭbaʿa al-Kubrā al-Amīrīya, 1313–15 [1895/6–97/8]), 1:99.

[38] ʿAlāʾ al-Dīn Abū Bakr Ibn Masʿūd al-Kāsānī, *Badāʾiʿal-ṣanāʾiʿ fī tartīb al-sharāʾiʿ* (Cairo: Zakarīyā ʿAlī Yūsuf, n.d.), 1:362; Zayn al-Dīn Ibn Nujaym, *al-Baḥr al-rāʾiq sharḥ Kanz al-daqāʾiq* (Beirut: Dār al-Kutub al-ʿIlmīya, 1418/1997), 1:480.

[39] Muṣṭafā ibn Saʿd al-Suyūṭī, *Maṭālib ūlī al-nuhā fī sharḥ Ghāyat al-muntahā* (n.p.: Manshūrāt al-Maktab al-Islāmī, 1380/1961), 1:394.

[40] al-Qushayrī, *Risāla*, pp. 207–8.

Reverence (*khushūʿ*) and concentration (*ḥuḍūr al-qalb*)

Even the acceptance of a minimalist understanding of *nīya* does not limit *ṣalāt* to the mechanical reproduction of a set sequence of bodily positions and verbal utterances. Rather, concerns about the spiritual and emotional depth and moral efficacy of prayer have primarily revolved around other concepts, including *khushūʿ* (reverence), *ḥuḍūr al-qalb* ("presence of heart," or attentiveness), and emotional experience (designated by various terms relating to joy, love, and other affective states). In most cases, like that of *nīya*, scholars insisted that prayer was legally valid even in the absence of such ideal mental states; they were committed to a core model of prayer that is unproblematically achievable by an ordinary individual. Otherwise, the daily devotions of the majority of Muslims – who (like all other human beings) were beset by ordinary distractions and often failed to experience exalted spiritual states – would have been rendered invalid, and the salvation of the *umma* as a whole would have been placed in doubt. Nevertheless, Muslim thinkers believed that in its ideal form *ṣalāt* involved a deep and mutual relationship between spiritual and physical postures and dispositions.

The concept of *khushūʿ* (literally "reverence," "humility," or "submissiveness") is particularly revealing in the way that it links issues of interior sentiment and bodily composure. Muslim scholars write of the *khushūʿ* of both the heart and the limbs. The *khushūʿ* of the heart is that the worshiper focus his or her attention exclusively on God and be completely aware of standing before the King of Kings and engaging in intimate conversation with Him. It involves focusing on one's recitation and not being distracted by extraneous trains of thought. The *khushūʿ* of the limbs (sometimes known by the term *khuḍūʿ*) is that he or she refrain from fidgeting or playing with any part of the body or clothing. The Prophet's son-in-law ʿAlī is supposed to have summed up the ideal of *khushūʿ* by describing it as "the tenderness of the heart and the restraint of the limbs" (*layn al-qalb wa-kaff al-jawāriḥ*). The Prophet is said once to have seen a man fiddling with his beard while at prayer and declared, "If his heart were submissive (*khashiʿa*), then his limbs would be submissive." The Qurʾān commentator al-Rāzī writes:

> [The scholars] have differed with respect to [the definition of] reverence (*khushūʿ*). Someone of them considered it to be an act of the heart like fear and awe, and some of them considered it an act of the limbs like immobility and refraining from turning about. Some of them combined the two, which is more appropriate. The person who has reverence in his prayer will necessarily experience, with respect to the actions relating to the heart, the utmost degree of submission and self-abasement to the object of worship. In terms of actions he will refrain from (*turūk*), his thoughts will not turn to anything other than the glorification [of God]. With respect to the limbs, he [will necessarily] be immobile, with his head bowed, looking towards the place where

[he will place his head in] prostration. In terms of actions he will refrain from, he will not turn to the right or left.[41]

Some scholars have held that *khushūʿ* is actually a legal requirement of valid prayer. Ibn Taymīya cites Qurʾānic verses indicating divine approval of those who perform their prayers with *khushūʿ* and blame of those who do not (such as 2:45 and 23:1–2) to demonstrate its obligatoriness, since God only blames people who have omitted an obligatory action. His definition of *khushūʿ* includes both inner reverence and bodily composure.[42] Others have argued that a person's prayer may be technically valid without *khushūʿ*, although it is certainly far short of ideal. The *Risāla* of Ibn Abī Zayd al-Qayrawānī (d. 386/996), a foundational text of the Mālikī school, instructs that one must perform one's bowing and prostration in the belief that they express humility (*al-khuḍūʿ*); later commentators identified this attitude with *khushūʿ*. Al-Nafrāwī (d. 1125/1713) notes that there is a difference of opinion about the legal status of *khushūʿ* in *ṣalāt*: most jurists hold it to be merely commendable, because prayer is still valid if accompanied by worldly thoughts; others, such as al-Qāḍī ʿIyāḍ (d. 544/1149), consider it obligatory. Ibn Rushd is said to have split the difference by arguing that it was obligatory, but that its omission did not invalidate the prayer.[43]

Al-Qarāfī interestingly argues that *khushūʿ* is merely recommended (*mandūb*), and thus the person who fails to do it does not sin (*lā yaʾtham tārikuhu*). Nevertheless, he argues that (exceptionally) it may take precedence over actions that are themselves obligatory. He cites a well-authenticated *ḥadīth* in which the Prophet states, "When the call to [Friday] prayer is made, do not come hastily; come in a state of serenity and gravity; if you get there in time then pray, and whatever you miss [of the prayer], complete it (*atimmū*)" and remarks:

> Some scholars have said: He directed not to hurry excessively because if a person comes to prayer after hurrying intensely, he will be out of breath and in a state of discomposure that prevents the reverence (*khushūʿ*) that is appropriate for prayer; thus, [the Prophet] instructed him to [go with] serenity and gravity and to avoid anything that would lead him to lose his reverence, even if he misses Friday or congregational prayer.[44]

Affirmations of the validity of prayer without *khushūʿ* tended to be more explicit outside of the Mālikī school, particularly among the Ḥanafīs. The Ḥanafī Zayn al-Dīn Ibn Nujaym (d. 970/1563) remarks that "if [a person's] cares distract him from his reverence, this does not diminish his merit, unless it

[41] Rāzī, *Tafsīr*, 23:77.

[42] Ibn Taymīya, *Majmūʿ al-fatāwā*, 22:269.

[43] Aḥmad ibn Ghunaym al-Nafrāwī al-Azharī al-Mālikī, *al-Fawākih al-dawānī ʿalā Risālat Ibn Abī Zayd al-Qayrawānī* (Beirut: Dār al-Kutub al-ʿIlmīya, 1418/1997), 1:276–7.

[44] Qarāfī, *Furūq*, 2:232–3.

is the result of [his own] fault."[45] Overall, the assumption is that people do not have full control over their mental states and can fulfill their basic religious obligations by conscientiously going through the motions, but ultimately physical fulfillment of the requirements of prayer cultivates states of pious consciousness that in turn help one to perform the external forms of prayer more perfectly. Mind and body, heart and limbs, mutually contribute to the development of a holistic attitude of reverence before God, which is both produced and expressed by correct prayer.

In addition to inner feelings of humility and reverence, Muslim thinkers were concerned with the quality and exclusivity of the worshiper's concentration. All scholars agreed that it was desirable to focus single-mindedly on one's devotions; however, as in the case of *nīya*, most held that flagging attention diminished the otherworldly reward of one's prayer rather than canceling its legal validity. In a *ḥadīth* transmitted in several versions, the Prophet is reported to declare that a person may complete his prayer and be credited with only a fraction of it (such as a tenth, a sixth, a third, or a fourth); only that portion of the prayer that is performed with conscious awareness yields merit.[46] Nevertheless, the prayer need not be repeated; an inattentive prayer may be worthless as an offering to God, but it discharges one's obligation. Scholars accepted the reality that the human mind was given to wandering; Ibn Nujaym observed that "if someone who is praying thinks about something other than his prayer, such as his business or his studies, [his prayer] is not rendered void."[47] Although scholars certainly advocated cultivation of emotional and spiritual depth in the prayer experience, they firmly rejected any standard that would render basic fulfillment of the legal obligation to pray burdensome or uncertain. A legal requirement of full attention (or of sincere reverence) would make any act of prayer subject to scrutiny and doubt, and possibly to obsessive repetition.

The integral (indeed, definitive) role of attentiveness in prayer is most famously emphasized by al-Ghazālī, whose analysis is grounded on the idea (to be analyzed in Chapter 3) that *ṣalāt* is an act of intimate communication with God. Al-Ghazālī argues that because prayer is not physically onerous and does not inherently frustrate one's selfish desires (unlike other major religious obligations, such as almsgiving and fasting) it has value if and only if it focuses the mind and heart on the encounter with the divine. Relinquishing a portion of one's wealth as *zakāt* disciplines one's materialistic desires, however

[45] Zayn al-Dīn Ibn Nujaym al-Ḥanafī, *al-Ashbāh wa'l-naẓā'ir*, published with al-Ḥamawī, *Ghamz*, 1:433.

[46] The statement that one may be credited only with some fraction of one's prayer appears in Abū Dāwūd, *Sunan*, *Kitāb al-Ṣalāt*, *Bāb* 130 (*Mā jā'a fī nuqṣān al-ṣalāt*); the addition that one is credited only with what one has performed consciously or with understanding (*mā ʿaqala*) is not directly attributed to the Prophet.

[47] Ibn Nujaym, *Ashbāh*, 1:433.

offhandedly one performs the transaction; the *ḥajj* is rigorous and challenging even if one performs its rites absentmindedly. Because the actions of prayer are themselves not demanding, in contrast, it achieves its objectives only if it brings one into dialogue with God. "Speaking with inattention (*ghafla*) is not intimate conversation (*munājāt*) at all," so prayer – whose goal is to commune with God – is effective only if performed with whole-hearted attention.[48]

Al-Ghazālī addresses the objection that "if you hold that *ṣalāt* is nullified [by inattention] and make the presence of the heart a condition for its validity, you violate the consensus of the legal scholars; they made the presence of the heart a condition only while performing the *takbīr*" by replying that

> the legal scholars do not have any business with interior [states], nor do they penetrate into hearts or the path to the next world; rather, they base the rulings of the religion on the external actions of the limbs, and external actions suffice to avert the [penalty of] execution and punishment by the ruler [i.e., they maintain one's legal status as a believer]. As for whether [such a prayer] is beneficial in the next world, this is not a matter of law.

Even on a legal level, he continues, the claim of consensus (*ijmāʿ*) is unfounded. He cites the early Iraqi jurist Sufyān al-Thawrī (d. 161/778) as having declared, "Whoever does not feel reverence (*lam yakhshaʿ*), his prayer is defective (*fāsid*)," and similar statements from other preclassical authorities. In accordance with his general view of the true authority structure of the Islamic community, al-Ghazālī argues that the genuine scholars – the "scholars of the next world," roughly to be identified with the Sufis – and the relevant texts of scripture are in agreement that presence of mind and reverence are, indeed, conditions for valid prayer. However, legal judgments are based on the shortcomings of human beings, "and it is not possible to make the presence of the heart during the entire prayer a condition for people [in general], because most of humanity is incapable of this except for a small minority."[49] Thus, it appears that ultimately al-Ghazālī does not make concentration a condition for the technical validity of *ṣalāt* (although he sharply devalues the significance of legal validity as a standard of religious practice).

Al-Ghazālī is surely right in arguing that the legal model of prayer is based on the recognition that pure and continuous concentration is difficult for most people. Because religious authorities were not satisfied with merely externally adequate prayers, however, they explored a variety of means of enhancing concentration, some of them elementary and pragmatic and others involving a process of personal transformation. Most minimally, one should attend to one's basic bodily needs before turning to prayer; in a well-authenticated *ḥadīth* the

[48] al-Ghazālī, *Iḥyāʾ*, 1:189.
[49] Ibid., 1:190–1.

Prophet declares that one should not pray in the presence of the food one is planning to eat or when one needs to use the toilet.[50] One should cast one's gaze downward, towards the place where the forehead will rest in prostration, rather than letting it wander. One should also not pray facing people who are not praying or a wide-open and absorbing view; when praying alone, if one is not actually facing a wall, it is recommended to place an object before one that symbolically demarcates one's prayer space.

Not only was undivided concentration a universal human problem, but worship could be seen as an activity that particularly invited the insinuations of the devil and the cares of the world, precisely because of its spiritual importance. The Shīʿite scholar al-Shahīd al-Thānī (d. c. 965/1558) writes that prayer can be "one of the most powerful entrances for Satan" if one does not ward off demonic distractions:

> Observe your heart when you are at prayer [and see] how devils tug it to and fro among markets and gardens, paying workers, responding to opponents and others, and how they draw you along through the valleys and hazards of this world – to the point that you remember the vain things of this world that you had forgotten only when you are at prayer, and devils throng around your heart only when you pray. The mere form of prayer definitely will not drive Satan away from you, even if it satisfies your obligation and you discharge the responsibility of the divine decree.[51]

The most extensive and influential prescriptions for cultivating single-minded immersion in worship were probably those of al-Ghazālī himself; the Imāmī Shīʿite prayer manual of al-Shahīd al-Thānī, just cited, draws on it extensively. Al-Ghazālī begins by noting that there are two kinds of distractions that detract from prayer, those issuing from external stimuli and those originating in the psyche of the worshiper. As for the first category, they can be addressed by minimizing distracting sights or sounds in the place where one performs one's prayers. If necessary, one may choose to pray in a small and gloomy chamber where there is nothing to attract the eye. (Keeping the eyes closed during *ṣalāt* is in violation of the *sunna*, although Ibn ʿAbd al-Salām al-Sulamī made an exception if it was more conducive to concentration.[52])

"As for the internal causes," al-Ghazālī continues, "they are more severe." When a person's thoughts are internally agitated, "casting down his eyes does him no good, for what occurs in the heart suffices to occupy him. The correct

[50] Muslim, *Ṣaḥīḥ*, *Kitāb al-Ṣalāt*, *Karāhat al-ṣalāt bi-ḥaḍrat al-ṭaʿām*. A popular modern manual for women adds similarly pragmatic advice for the contemporary worshiper, including ensuring a comfortable temperature (if necessary by turning on the air conditioning) (Ruqayya bint Muḥammad al-Muḥārib, *Kayfa takhshaʿīna fī'l-ṣalāt*? [Riyadh: Dār al-Qāsim, 2000], pp. 20–1).

[51] al-Shahīd al-Thānī al-shaykh Zayn al-Dīn ibn ʿAlī ibn Aḥmad al-Jabʿī al-ʿĀmilī, *Asrār al-ṣalāt*, ed. Muḥsin ʿAqīl (Beirut: Dār al-Balāgha, 1410/1990), pp. 30, 31.

[52] See al-ʿIzz ibn ʿAbd al-Salām al-Sulamī, *al-Fatāwā al-miṣrīya*, ed. Iyād Khālid al-Ṭabbāʿ (Damascus: Dār al-Fikr, 1428/2007), p. 46.

way for such a person is to forcibly return his mind to understanding what he is reciting in prayer and occupy it with that to the exclusion of other things."[53] In order to prepare oneself mentally to focus on what one is saying in prayer, it is advisable to spend time before commencing prayer in reflection on the afterlife and the fact that one is about to have an intimate encounter with God, and try to empty one's thoughts of other concerns.

Al-Ghazālī proceeds:

This is the way of quieting the thoughts. If the agitation of his thoughts is not calmed by this tranquilizing medicine, nothing will save him but the purgative that will flush the substance of the malady from the depths of his veins, which is for him to consider the matters that are preoccupying him and diverting him from focusing his heart. No doubt they relate to his [worldly] affairs, and they became important [to him] only by virtue of his desires. Let him discipline himself by abstaining from those desires and severing those attachments. . . . This is the efficacious remedy for the disease itself, and nothing else is of use. . . .

An allegory for it is a man beneath a tree who wanted his thoughts to be undisturbed, but the voices of the birds were bothering him; he kept on driving them away with a piece of wood in his hand and returning to his thoughts, and then the birds would return, and he would go back to shooing them with the wood. [Finally] someone said to him, "If you want to be free of them, then uproot the tree!" Similarly, when the tree of desire grows tall and its boughs spread out, thoughts are attracted to it as birds are attracted to trees and flies are attracted to filth. It is weary work to drive them away; every time a fly is driven away it returns . . . and likewise thoughts. There are many desires, and rarely is a person devoid of them; they are united by one root, which is the love of this world, which is the source of all sin, the foundation of all deficiency, and the wellspring of all corruption.[54]

Al-Ghazālī argues that someone who is harboring love of this world cannot truly experience the pleasure (*ladhdha*) of communing with God in prayer. The remedy is to persist in compelling oneself to focus on prayer, even if this is initially a bitter medicine for one's ills. Thus prayer and inner virtue form a feedback loop: only the eradication of worldly desires can enable truly rapt and joyful prayer, and only the earnest cultivation of focus in prayer can help to eradicate one's worldly desires (or to develop the love of God that will gradually displace them).[55]

Despite his emphasis on the ideal of cultivating profound absorption in prayer, al-Ghazālī also pragmatically recognizes the inevitability of intrusive thoughts even for adepts of the mystical path. He notes that even the greatest spiritual masters have striven and failed to perform two prostration cycles

[53] al-Ghazālī, *Iḥyā'*, 1:194.
[54] Ibid., 1:194–5.
[55] Ibid., 1:195.

without distracting thoughts about the affairs of this world.[56] In another passage he writes with notable sensitivity about the human vulnerability to sexual thoughts, even at the most inopportune moments. Lust may be reined in by *taqwā* (consciousness of God) so that a person achieves external restraint; however:

> As for protecting the heart from insinuations (*waswās*) and thought, this is not subject to his will; rather, his lower self continues to tug at him and speak to him about matters relating to sex, and the Satan who whispers to him does not leave him alone most of the time. That may befall him during prayer, so that sexual matters come to his mind that he would be ashamed to speak openly about in front of the vilest person.[57]

Al-Ghazālī's typically pragmatic response to this problem is that the religious aspirant should simply satisfy his sexual urges (within the legitimate bounds of marriage, of course).

Al-Ghazālī even advises that one may resort to what might be characterized an imaginary form of *riyā'* – that is, attempting to make a good impression on a hypothetical human observer, if only immediately to identify and repudiate this effort:

> Imagine as you stand in prayer that you are watched and observed by the alert eye of a virtuous man of your family or by someone whom you wish to regard you as virtuous. Then your extremities will become quiet and your limbs will become reverent; every part of you will become calm for fear that that impotent, insignificant creature will consider you to be lacking in reverence. If you found yourself to become collected and composed when observed by an insignificant creature, upbraid yourself and tell yourself: "You claim to know and love God Most High; are you not ashamed of your impudence towards him in showing respect towards one of his servants? Do you fear people, and not fear Him . . .?"[58]

The cultivation of emotion

An emphasis on sentiments of reverence, humility, glorification, and awe was common among legal scholars who analyzed *ṣalāt*, and such sentiments were sometimes even held to be constitutive of the concept of worship (*ʿibāda*). Although most defined worship as obedience (*ṭāʿa*), or obedience combined

[56] Ibid. A *ḥadīth* transmitted by al-Bukhārī (*Ṣaḥīḥ*, *Kitāb al-Wuḍū'*, *Bāb al-Wuḍū' thalāthan thalāthan*) promises complete remission of sins for someone who performs *wuḍū'* with particular thoroughness and then completes two prostration cycles without having any extraneous thoughts.

[57] al-Ghazālī, *Iḥyā'*, 2:32. A similar point is made by ʿIzz al-Dīn al-Sulamī, who consoles a man who is tormented by doubts about the existence of God during his times of meditation with the assurance that *waswās* is the work of Satan, does not originate in his mind, and is not subject to his will; thus, he must simply persist in his acts of worship and trust in God (*al-Fatāwā al-miṣrīya*, pp. 74–5).

[58] Ibid., 1:196.

with the intent to draw close to God (*qurba*, *taqarrub*), some equated it with obedience combined with submissiveness (*khuḍūʿ*), self-abasement (*tadhallul*), or glorification (*taʿẓīm*).[59] As we have seen, these concepts could be interpreted in terms of the expressive intent of an action such as standing or prostration; one did these things with the objective of glorifying God, much as one might stand in honor of a distinguished human being. However, they were also understood as affective states; for instance, glorification of God was not simply an objective that distinguished one's action from other, formally similar motions (such as standing up to stretch one's legs or falling down in shock) and rendered it legible to an outside observer, but a subjectively experienced sentiment. Such feelings toward God were not merely expected to be present; they were understood to require cultivation and development as one's relationship with God was deepened by repeated acts of mindful worship. The analysis of the affective dimenstion of *ṣalāt* was often informed by Sufi attitudes and concepts.

Enumerating the "interior factors" that "enliven" prayer, al-Ghazālī establishes a hierarchy beginning with "presence of heart" (*ḥuḍūr al-qalb*), which leads to comprehension (*tafahhum*) of what one is saying and doing. Attentiveness and comprehension then lead to glorification (*taʿẓīm*), awe (*hayba*), hope (*rajāʾ*), and shame (*ḥayāʾ*). Each of these sentiments is, according to al-Ghazālī, both indispensable and distinct. Al-Ghazālī notes that it is possible for someone to address his slave with full awareness and understanding of his own words without respecting or glorifying his slave, so *taʿẓīm* is analytically separate from attentiveness and comprehension. Awe (*hayba*) is in turn distinct from glorification; it is a kind of fear (*khawf*) that arises from glorification. On the one hand, one cannot be said to experience awe without feeling fear. On the other, not all kinds of fear can be characterized as awe. For instance, one's fear of a scorpion cannot be termed "awe"; rather, the word is used to characterize the fear one feels for an exalted king. Hope is yet another element added to awe. One may be in awe of an earthly king or fear his power without entertaining any hope of his favor. In contrast, a person who prays should hope for God's reward as well as fearing God's punishment for his shortcomings. Finally, shame (*ḥayāʾ*) results from one's awareness of one's shortcomings and sins.[60]

Another emotion that features centrally in discussions of prayer is love. A widely cited *ḥadīth qudsī* (that is, a statement in the voice of God transmitted by

[59] See Yaḥyā ibn Sharaf al-Nawawī, *al-Majmūʿ sharḥ al-Muhadhdhab*, ed. ʿĀdil Aḥmad ʿAbd al-Mawjūd et al. (Beirut: Dār al-Kutub al-ʿIlmīya, 1423/2002), 2:322; the Ḥanafī scholar Abū'l-Baqāʾ al-Kafawī (d. 1683) argues that while all acts performed in compliance with the divine command constitute obedience, worship involves "glorifying God to the utmost extent" (*al-Kullīyāt*, ed. ʿAdnān Darwīsh and Muḥammad al-Miṣrī [Beirut: Mu'assasat al-Risāla, 1412/1992], p. 583).

[60] al-Ghazālī, *Iḥyāʾ*, 1:191.

the Prophet outside of the Qurʾān) states: "My servant continues to seek closeness to Me by supererogatory acts of worship until I love him. When I love him, I am his hearing with which he hears, his sight with which he sees, his hand with which he grasps, and his foot with which he walks."[61] This statement suggests that voluntary acts of worship (of which prayer is a paradigmatic case) not only result in love between the worshiper and God, but lead to some kind of identity between them – not surprisingly, an implication that was theologically challenging but attractive to thinkers of a mystical bent. This report is discussed by al-Ghazālī in an analysis of the love (*ḥubb*) that can exist between a human being and God. Unlike many other Islamic thinkers he accepts the idea that one basis of love between the human and the divine is resemblance or similarity (*munāsaba*, *mushākala*). He regards the special affinity that exists between beings of like character to be a basic rule that is empirically confirmed both by everyday experience and by the privileged insights of brethren on the mystical path. Al-Ghazālī states: "This correspondence (*munāsaba*) becomes manifest only by means of the regular performance of supererogatory [prayers or other acts of devotion] after proper performance of those that are obligatory, as God said, 'My servant continues to seek proximity to me by means of supererogatory acts until I love him.'" He quickly notes, however, that this is the point at which he must cease writing on this subject, which has lured some people into false claims of literal unification with the divine.[62]

Unsurprisingly, scholars less influenced by Sufism provide a wide range of interpretations of this *ḥadīth* that strive to avoid any hint of actual resemblance or identity (however abstract and rarified) between the human and the divine. One is that God becomes the person's "hearing and sight" in the sense that he comes to love obedience and service to God more than his most precious faculties. Another is that he becomes so preoccupied with God that he listens to nothing that is not satisfactory to Him and looks only at what He commands. A third is that God will come to his aid and help him to achieve his objectives, just as he uses his own faculties and limbs to achieve these ends. Other interpretations posit implied wording that eliminates altogether any implication of identification with the divine; for instance, proposing the amplification "I am *the guardian of* his hearing" or interpreting "his hearing" as "what he hears" (*masmūʿ*), that is, "he hears only the remembrance of Me, and takes pleasure only in the recitation of My Book, and is comforted only by intimate conversation with Me (*munājātī*)."[63]

Interestingly, some of the most profound reflection on the role in worship of emotion in general, and of love in particular, was produced by the stern reformer

[61] Bukhārī, *Ṣaḥīḥ*, *Kitāb al-Riqāq*, *Bāb al-Tawāḍuʿ*.
[62] al-Ghazālī, *Iḥyāʾ*, 4:324.
[63] al-ʿAsqalānī, *Fatḥ al-bārī*, 24:140.

Ibn Taymīya (d. 728/1328). Despite his fierce opposition to textually unfounded ritual practices (*bidaʿ*, or "innovations"), it has more recently been acknowledged that he was more sensitive to the spiritual and emotional needs of ordinary people than previously recognized, as well as being himself a moderate Sufi.[64] Furthermore, as Joseph Bell notes, "Love is far from an isolated or minor topic in the system of Ibn Taymīya."[65] With respect to *ṣalāt*, far from appearing a dry formalist, Ibn Taymīya devotes great attention to the affective dimensions of the experience of worship. In more than one place in his work he defines worship (*ʿibāda*) – for him, a very broad category including but not limited to formal rituals such as *ṣalāt* – as combining love with humility (*al-maḥabba maʿa al-dhull*).[66] For him, the two sentiments – although perhaps apparently in tension with each other – are inseparable components of the unique emotional stance that should distinguish a person's relationship to God:

> Someone who humbles himself before a person while hating him does not worship him; [conversely], if he were to love something but not humble himself before it, he would not be worshiping it, just as he may love his child or friend [without worshiping them]; for this reason, [just] one of them [i.e., either humility or love] does not suffice in the worship of God Most High.[67]

Underlying Ibn Taymīya's analysis of the love for God that is indispensable to the human stance of worship is his interpretation of the *fiṭra*, the fundamental human nature with which everyone is born (cf. Qurʾān 30:30). He states that God created (*faṭara*) human hearts in such a way that none of their loves short of love of God are ultimate sources of serenity and satisfaction. Whatever food, clothing, or beautiful sights or sounds we may love, we experience in our hearts a longing for something beyond them. It is only the love for God in which human hearts experience tranquility. Here he cites verse 13:28 of the Qurʾān, which declares, "Verily, in the remembrance of Allah do hearts find rest" (of course, *ṣalāt* is a paradigmatic instance of the "remembrance of God").[68]

Ibn Taymīya recognizes that not everyone finds relief or delight in prayer. In his view the emotional valence of prayer is diagnostic of the state of one's relationship with God. As he declares in one of his legal opinions, "Whoever does not find delight and relief in prayer is deficient in faith."[69] In another place

[64] See Raquel M. Ukeles, "The Sensitive Puritan? Revisiting Ibn Taymiyya's Approach to Law and Spirituality in Light of 20th-Century Debates on the Prophet's Birthday (*mawlid al-nabī*)," in Rapoport and Ahmed, eds., *Ibn Taymiyya and His Times*, pp. 319–27; George Makdisi, "Ibn Taymīya: A Ṣūfī of the Qādirīya Order," *American Journal of Arabic Studies* 1 (1973), pp. 118–29.

[65] Joseph Norment Bell, *Love Theory in Late Hanbalite Islam* (Albany: SUNY Press, 1979), p. 48.

[66] Ibn Taymīya, *Majmūʿ al-fatāwā*, 10:43, 86.

[67] Ibid., 10:87.

[68] Ibid., 10:43–4.

[69] Ibid., 11:250.

he writes, "When someone is standing to pray, he is conversing intimately with his Lord. . . . The more the servant tastes the sweetness of prayer, the stronger will be his attraction to it; and that is proportional to the strength of [his] faith." He then cites *ḥadīth* texts in which the Prophet asks the *mu'adhdhin* Bilāl to "relieve us with prayer" (*ariḥnā bi'l-ṣalāt*) and declares that "of the things of this world of yours, women and perfume were made dear to me, and prayer was made my delight."[70] Unlike some Islamic thinkers, Ibn Taymīya strongly affirmed that faith and unbelief were not merely binary qualities, but that faith could increase and decrease;[71] the experiential quality of prayer is a prime indicator of the magnitude and quality of one's faith.

Ibn Taymīya's disciple Ibn Qayyim al-Jawzīya (d. 751/1350) both elaborates on the emotional dimensions of ritual prayer and suggests one of the motives underlying this emphasis. His book *Asrār al-ṣalāt* (The secrets of prayer) opens (and is concerned throughout) with the issue of "comparing the experiential quality [*dhawq*, literally "taste"] of *samāʿ* with that of *ṣalāt* and Qur'ān[ic recitation]," asserting that "the two experiences (*al-dhawqayn*) are different in all respects, and that the more the strength and dominance of the *dhawq* of one of them increases, the more the strength and dominance of the *dhawq* of the other decreases."[72] By the thirteenth century Sufism was one of the predominant spiritual influences competing for the allegiance of ordinary Muslims in the Middle East. Sufis pursued immediate intimacy with the divine through distinctive ritual practices including *dhikr* (the ritualized "remembrance" of God, through the repetitive recitation of divine names and often the use of breath control and rhythmic motion) and *samāʿ* (mystical audition, which often involved the performance of devotional verses to legally suspect musical accompaniment). These practices had an experiential element, and a power to evoke heightened emotional and sensory states, that was accessible to many believers even in the absence of advanced mystical discipline. As an outside observer can easily attest, Sufi *dhikr* and *samāʿ* may have a hypnotic and compelling quality even if one has little personal investment in Sufi forms of ethical and spiritual self-refinement. As compared with the austere discipline of *ṣalāt*, music and chanting had obvious crowd appeal (as well as gaining many elite and pious followers), and aesthetic and emotional enjoyment must have been a large part of their attraction. In his work on the "secrets of prayer," Ibn al-Qayyim seeks to demonstrate both that *ṣalāt* is the source of profound pleasure and delight to the true faithful (in contrast to the deficient believer, who finds it burdensome and oppressive) and that the joys of prayer are fundamentally

[70] Ibid., 22:292 (see also ibid., 28:16–17).

[71] See Ibn Taymīya, *Kitāb al-Īmān* (Beirut: Dār al-Kutub al-ʿIlmīya, 1403/1983), pp. 195–204.

[72] Ibn Qayyim al-Jawzīya, *Asrār al-ṣalāt wa'l-farq wa'l-muwāzana bayna dhawq al-ṣalāt wa-'l-samāʿ*, ed. Iyād ibn ʿAbd al-Laṭīf ibn Ibrāhīm al-Qaysī (Beirut: Dār Ibn Ḥazm, 1424/2003), p. 55.

different from – and superior to – those evoked by Sufi *samāʿ*. The prevalence of affective language in his discussion is overwhelming.

Building on the reports (already cited by his teacher Ibn Taymīya) that the Prophet called prayer his "delight" and instructed the *mu'adhdhin* Bilāl to "relieve us with prayer," he likens the comforts of prayer for the pious to the relief of a weary person seeking release from his burdens. He contrasts this with the feelings of a person who prays grudgingly and unwillingly: "He is in torment as long as he is engaged in it, and when he finishes it he feels ease in his heart and soul. That is because his heart is full of other things; prayer cuts him off from his worldly concerns and predilections." Such a person's distaste for prayer is evident from the perfunctory way in which he performs it; he does it merely because he knows he must, "saying with his tongue what is not in his heart." Ibn al-Qayyim concludes, "So distinguish between someone for whose limbs prayer is a heavy fetter, for whose heart it is a narrow and oppressive prison, and for whose [lower] soul it is an obstacle, and someone for whose heart prayer is bliss, for whose eye it is coolness [i.e., to whom it is a delight], for whose limbs it is a relief, and for whose soul it is a garden and a pleasure."[73]

Ibn al-Qayyim appropriates the Sufi term *dhawq* (literally, "taste") to refer to the affective dimension of prayer. Sufis use this word to suggest the immediate, non-verbal, non-discursive nature of spiritual perception; Ibn al-Qayyim uses it to designate the subjective sweetness of prayer as experienced by the true believer. He asserts that genuine *dhawq* is that associated with *ṣalāt* and with the audition of the Qurʾān, not that associated with mystical poetry and instrumental music.[74] In fact, although he concedes that a person of genuine spiritual sensibilities may experience ecstasy while participating in Sufi *samāʿ*, he asserts that it will be followed by feelings of depression and alienation.[75] Thus, he accepts the Sufi assumption that the experience of comfort, joy, and ecstasy are true measures of spiritual elevation, but contests the nature of the practices by which they can be achieved in a genuine form. For Ibn al-Qayyim, true *dhawq* and *wajd* (ecstasy) are to be found only in the legally central obligations of *ṣalāt* and in the recitation of the Qurʾān (itself, of course, an integral component of *ṣalāt*).

As we have seen, the evocation of appropriate pious emotional states is an integral part of *ṣalāt* as understood by many classical Muslim authorities. However, the centrality of emotion also raised the question of the boundaries of its proper expression within prayer. Immersion in the contemplation of the majesty of God, one's own insignificance, and the inevitability of divine judgment could arouse strong and tempestuous feelings that had the potential to disrupt the prayer ritual itself. To what extent was it desirable to be swept away

73 Ibid., pp. 124–5.
74 Ibid., pp. 128–9.
75 Ibid., p. 135.

by these emotions, and at what point did the unbridled expression of love, fear, and awe interfere with correct performance of *ṣalāt*? The possibility that a worshiper might sigh, moan, or break into unrestrained weeping was one that scholars saw as both promising and problematic. In many ways the discussion of desirable and acceptable expressions of emotion in prayer paralleled that about the recitation of the Qurʾān; because Qurʾānic recitation is an integral part of *ṣalāt*, the two issues are closely related. Scholars saw the experience of powerful affective states as an effect of piety, and weeping as a proper or inevitable manifestation of such feelings.[76] However, they also recognized that emotional displays could be self-indulgent or forced, and that exaggerated or feigned weeping could be exhibitionistic. Precisely because weeping was an index of piety, it was subject to the suspicion of hypocrisy.

Several Qurʾānic passages suggest a positive evaluation of groaning or weeping, particularly when it is evoked by the recitation of the Qurʾān or accompanies the act of prostration. Verse 19:58 describes previous prophets as falling down "in prostration and tears" when God's revelations were recited to them (see also verse 17:109). The Prophet himself and some of his closest Companions are described in some reports as weeping during prayer. In one *ḥadīth* an eyewitness reports that he found the Prophet praying, and heard the sound of weeping in his chest like the simmering of a boiling cauldron.[77] In a report cited by Ibn Taymīya, ʿĀ'isha describes her father Abū Bakr as "a tender man who is overcome by weeping when he recites [the Qurʾān]" and the Prophet affirms that he should lead the prayers for the people. He also cites a report stating that ʿUmar's sobs could be heard from the back rows of worshipers when he recited verse 12:86 ("I only complain of my distraction and anguish to God").[78]

Despite the apparent authoritative precedents for the shedding of pious tears during prayer, however, jurists worried that excessive expressions of grief could constitute extraneous activities that would rupture the validity of one's prayers. Although they accepted that it was impossible completely to eliminate all extraneous motions or sounds during *ṣalāt* – after all, it is not always possible to avoid twitching or sneezing – they held that at a certain point intrusive actions or utterances constituted turning away from prayer to engage in another activity, which canceled one's state of prayer and required that one start again. For instance, most jurists agreed that if one uttered as little as two

[76] On "sadness" (*ḥuzn*) and weeping as a feature of the ideal recitation and audition of the Qurʾān see Kristina Nelson, *The Art of Reciting the Qurʾan* (Cairo and New York: American University in Cairo Press, 2001), pp. 89–100.

[77] See, for instance, Muḥammad ibn Isḥāq Ibn Khuzayma, *Ṣaḥīḥ Ibn Khuzayma*, ed. Muḥammad Muṣṭafā al-Aʿẓamī (Beirut: al-Maktab al-Islāmī, 1391/1971), 2:53 (*Jimāʿ abwāb al-afʿāl al-mubāḥa fī'l-ṣalāt*).

[78] Ibn Taymīya, *Majmūʿ al-fatāwā*, 22:299.

syllables (or, according to some, a single syllable) communicating a worldly matter (that is, outside of the standard and personal invocations that are appropriate to *ṣalāt*), one's prayer would be invalidated. At what point, therefore, did moaning or sobbing become an action sufficiently independent of prayer that it was inadmissible?

Of the eponymous authorities of the classical schools of law, Abū Ḥanīfa is said to have held that even if moaning or weeping led to the utterance of audible syllables (*ḥurūf*), it did not invalidate prayer if it was inspired by the remembrance of paradise and hell; this simply manifested an excess of humility and was tantamount to glorifying God, which is the essence of prayer. In contrast, if one's moaning or weeping arose from personal sorrow or distress, it did rupture one's prayer.[79] This was both because it then expressed sentiments incompatible with prayer (that is, discontent with God's decrees) and because it could be construed as a form of nonreligious communication; in the words of the Ḥanafī jurist al-Zaylaʿī, "It is as if he said, 'Help me, I'm in pain!'"[80] The most restrictive position is attributed to al-Shāfiʿī, who held that if a moan or sob constituted two syllables it canceled prayer regardless of other considerations (such as its origin in fear of God or physical pain, or the voluntary or uncontrollable nature of the utterance).[81] It is not completely clear whether the syllables were required to be linguistically meaningful, or whether prayer would be canceled by two syllables of inarticulate woe. Ibn Taymīya focuses not on the comprehensibility of the actual sounds uttered, but on their implicit communicative value; he points out that if sobs emitted from the fear of God were rendered into words, the content would involve seeking refuge from hell or pleading for heaven, either of which is permissible in prayer; if moans and groans respond to illness or misfortune, in contrast, the explicit statements that would correspond to their implicit content would be impermissible in prayer.[82]

In addition to the implied or overt semantic content of moans or weeping, jurists sometimes argued that even extraneous expressions of distress were compatible with prayer provided that they were beyond one's control. Abū Ḥanīfa's disciple Abū Yūsuf is said to have argued that if one involuntarily moaned or wept out of physical pain, it did not invalidate one's prayer; the younger discipline al-Shaybānī is supposed to have added the proviso that this applied only if one's ailment was severe.[83] In the thirteenth century Ibn Qudāma noted that he knew of no relevant statements from Aḥmad ibn Ḥanbal, but inferred from the principles of the school that weeping or moaning had no

[79] Abū Bakr ibn ʿAlī al-Ḥaddād al-Zabīdī, *al-Jawhara al-nayyira sharḥ Mukhtaṣar al-Qudūrī*, ed. Ilyās Qablān (Beirut: Dār al-Kutub al-ʿIlmīya, 1427/2006), 1:174.
[80] al-Zaylaʿī, *Tabyīn al-ḥaqāʾiq*, 1:156.
[81] Ibid., 1:156.
[82] Ibn Taymīya, *Majmūʿ al-fatāwā*, 22:299.
[83] Ḥaddād, *Jawhara*, 1:174.

effect if the person was overcome (*maghlūban ʿalayhi*); if it was under the worshiper's control, however, it invalidated prayer unless it issued from the fear of God.[84]

Ethical transformation

In the eyes of classical scholars, as we have seen, ideal prayer comprises both rule-bound correctness and emotional depth. However, even the most punctiliously accurate and spiritually profound act of *ṣalāt* does not constitute perfect prayer unless it transforms the life of the believer. In principle, to perform *ṣalāt* regularly is not merely to fill a divine commandment (thereby meriting otherworldly reward and avoiding punishment) but to form oneself ethically. However, Muslim thinkers also recognized it to be an empirically verifiable fact that people who prayed regularly and proficiently (at least on an external level) could also be morally corrupt; fulfillment of one's ritual duties is in itself no guarantee of good behavior in other areas of life. Reflections on this issue are often elicited by the interpretation of verse 29:45 of the Qurʾān, which declares, "establish regular prayer, for prayer restrains from [literally, "forbids"] shameful and unjust deeds." Al-Ṭabarī (d. 310/923) notes that some early exegetes interpreted "prayer" (*al-ṣalāt*) in this context to mean "the Qurʾān," specifically, the Qurʾān that is recited in prayer (or in mosques). This interpretation makes some sense, insofar as the Qurʾānic text literally "forbids" bad conduct. However, like most authorities, al-Ṭabarī himself concludes that it is the act of prayer itself that deters one from misbehavior. In response to the objection that prayer itself – as opposed to the commandments and prohibitions contained in the Qurʾān – cannot "forbid" someone from sin, al-Ṭabarī argues firstly that prayer occupies an individual so thoroughly that he cannot engage in bad actions (implicitly, for the duration of prayer), and secondly that the observation of the legal requirements of prayer is an act of obedience that will serve to discourage bad behavior (presumably because obedience and disobedience are incompatible).[85]

Al-Ṭabarī's interpretation, although it affirms the ethically efficacious nature of prayer, is still fairly minimal; it suggests only that the activity of *ṣalāt* precludes bad behavior while one is actually engaged in it (although it may also promote a general attitude of compliance to God's commands). Al-Rāzī is dissatisfied with this explanation. After all, he points out, if prayer "forbids" sin

[84] Ibn Qudāma, *al-Mughnī*, 1:707. The Mālikī al-Qurṭubī holds that weeping during prayer is permissible (and, implicitly, even praiseworthy) if it issues from fear of God or from awareness of disobedience to Him (Qurṭubī, *Tafsīr*, 10:221 [commentary on verse 17:109]).

[85] Muḥammad ibn Jarīr al-Ṭabarī, *Jāmiʿ al-bayān ʿan taʾwīl āy al-qurʾān* (Beirut: Dār al-Fikr, 1408/1988), 19:154, 155.

only in the sense that one cannot commit sins while busy performing it, the same can be said for many other occupations, including sleep. He proceeds to offer a series of more ambitious models for the role of prayer in the ethical and spiritual self-fashioning of the believer. Like al-Ṭabarī (and most other interpreters), al-Rāzī recognizes that not everyone who prays is free of sin. However, true prayer, he argues, prevents one from engaging in obscene or evil acts at any time. He states here that "legally valid prayer" (*al-ṣalāt al-ṣaḥīḥa sharʿan*) precludes shameful and unjust deeds; however – like many Sufis, but unlike most scholars – he holds that only prayer devoted exclusively to God is legally valid; insincere prayer is void and must be repeated. Unlike many legal thinkers al-Rāzī thus closes the gap between legally adequate prayer and spiritually pure prayer; only prayer that is single-hearted fulfills the legal obligation of *ṣalāt*, and prayer of this kind necessarily deters one from sinful behavior.[86]

The possibility that not all everyone's prayers are successful in this regard is expressed by al-Qurṭubī (d. 671/1272), another interpreter deeply influenced by Sufism. He states that the opinion preferred by the most accurate scholars and promoted by the Sufi masters is that regular and correct prayer deters one from sin

> by virtue of the Qur'ān[ic recitation] that it contains, which includes exhortation (*al-mawʿiẓa*); [furthermore], prayer occupies the entire body of the worshiper. When the worshiper enters his place of prayer, humbles and subjects himself to God, and remembers that he is standing before Him and that He observes and sees him, his spirit [or "lower self": *nafs*] will become sound and submissive and pervaded by [awareness of] God's scrutiny, and awe of Him will be manifest in his limbs; he will scarcely have slackened in that when another prayer shades him and returns him to the best of states.

Al-Qurṭubī cites the example of an early Muslim (*baʿḍ al-salaf*) who used to tremble and turn pale when he performed *ṣalāt*; asked about this he replied, "I am standing before God Most High; this would befit me with the kings of this world, so what of the King of Kings?!" Al-Qurṭubī continues:

> This is a [mode of] prayer that will inevitably "forbid shameful and unjust deeds." [However,] whoever's prayer is based on [mere legal] validity, and contains no reverence (*khushūʿ*), remembrance, or [other] virtues, like our prayer – if only it is valid! (*laytahā tujziʾ*) – this [kind of prayer] leaves the one who performs it in the same rank where he was; if he was on the path of sins that make him more distant from God Most High, it lets him continue in his distance.[87]

[86] Rāzī, *Tafsīr*, 25:72.

[87] Qurṭubī, *Tafsīr*, 13:230–1. Al-Qurṭubī goes on to a cite a (poorly authenticated) *ḥadīth* stating that "whoever's prayer does not restrain him from shameful and unjust deeds, it only increases his distance from God."

Unlike al-Rāzī, al-Qurṭubī distinguishes between the bare legal validity of prayer and its spiritual substance – although legal validity itself seems to be far from assured, even on the part of a distinguished scholar such as himself. His standard for the sincere prayer that will effect the moral reformation of the worshiper is idealistically high, referring his readers to the example of Sufi masters and pious early Muslims (whose standard of faith was widely assumed to be unattainable by later generations).

Striking a somewhat similar note, in his commentary on verse 29:45 al-Zamakhsharī (d. 538/1144) addresses the objection that prayer is observably not always accompanied by general good behavior:

> If you were to say, "How many a person who prays commits [sins], and his prayer does not deter him [from sinning]?" I would say: "The prayer that is [true] prayer in the sight of God, by means of which one merits reward, is the one that one commences after preceding it with sincere penitence (*al-tawba al-naṣūḥ*) and with awareness of God (*muttaqiyan*)."

Al-Zamakhsharī also specifies that the true prayer that forestalls sin is accompanied by reverence (*khushūʿ*) of the heart and the limbs. He cites the example of Ḥātim,[88] who declared, "It is as if my foot were upon the Bridge, with paradise to my right, hell to my left, and the Angel of Death above me; I pray between fear and hope." This evocation of the vivid and fervent awareness accompanying the *ṣalāt* of a paragon of piety, such as that cited by al-Qurṭubī, is as inspiring as it is difficult for the ordinary person to emulate (although it suggests a visualization technique that may help in evoking the appropriate emotions). On a more pragmatic note, al-Zamakhsharī states that if a person prays consistently, it will draw him to cease sinning eventually. In support of this he presents a *ḥadīth* in which a young man of the Anṣār performs his prayers regularly with the Prophet, yet continues to commit all sorts of shameful deeds. When this is reported to the Prophet, he declares, "His prayer will deter him"; and soon the youth indeed repents. Al-Zamakhsharī concludes philosophically:

> In any case, someone who prays regularly must surely be further from shameful and unjust acts than someone who does not pray regularly. Furthermore, how many people who pray are deterred by their prayer from shameful and unjust acts! The [Qurʾānic] statement does not require that not a single person who prays be excluded from its purview, just as you may say, "Zayd forbids unjust acts"; you do not intend that he forbids every [possible] unjust act, but that this attribute is present in him and is performed by him, without entailing that it be comprehensive.[89]

[88] Presumably the early mystic al-Ḥātim al-Aṣamm (d. 237 A.H.); see al-Qushayrī, *Risāla*, pp. 393–4.
[89] al-Zamakhsharī, *Kashshāf*, 3:207.

Conclusion

The reflections of classical Islamic scholars on *ṣalāt* illustrate both their rigorous pragmatism (which unsparingly recognized and tolerantly accommodated every kind of human weakness) and their idealistic belief in an open-ended human potential for spiritual growth. A broad and comprehensive underlying consensus confirmed that even the most ordinary person could perform an adequate prayer if he or she could find the time and resolve simply to follow the requisite steps. Even a tradesman preoccupied by worldly cares, a mother distracted by her baby, or an adolescent beset by sexual fantasies could fulfill his or her obligation to God by performing a formally correct prayer that would count both in this life and the next, providing this-worldly membership in the Muslim *umma* and freedom from punishment in the afterlife. At the most basic level, *ṣalāt* is something that everyone who has reached the age of responsibility is both obligated to do and capable of doing, regardless of the individual's degree of religious education or spiritual prowess.

However, the scholars' flinty realism about the inevitability – and the acceptability – of flawed prayer is balanced by their aspirations for prayer that is single-hearted, emotionally vivid, and ethically transformative. To a certain extent, the two extremes reflect the contrasting values and expertise of legal scholars and Sufi mystics, two distinct yet overlapping groups of religious authorities who pursued the divergent paths of legal technicality and spiritual aspiration. However, spiritual, affective, and ethical concerns are also integral to the discourse of *fiqh*, whereas external obedience is of inherent interest to Sufis. Furthermore, the sources cited here reflect the deep interpenetration of these two discourses, and the extent to which the personal piety and the scholarship of individual thinkers combined both frameworks and priorities.

In the predominant synthesis of classical scholarship, the spiritual, affective, and moral attributes that contribute to one's ability to achieve better and better approximations to ideal prayer are also the attributes that are fostered by prayer itself, in a potentially endless cycle of self-refinement and refinement of *ṣalāt*. The more and better one prays, the more prayer will shape and inform one's feelings and desires, and the more one will desire and enjoy prayer itself. Saba Mahmood has observed in an ethnographic study of participation in the modern Egyptian women's "mosque movement" that one of her informants "does not assume that the desire to pray is natural, but that it must *be created* through a set of disciplinary acts."[90] One does not simply happen to be a person with the will power and the motivation to get up for the dawn prayer, for instance; rather, one strives to become such a person. In turn, "ritual acts are the sole and

[90] Saba Mahmood, *Politics of Piety: The Islamic Revival and the Feminist Subject* (Princeton: Princeton University Press, 2005), p. 126 (see also pp. 123–5).

ineluctable means of forming pious dispositions."[91] Classical scholars as different as al-Ghazālī and Ibn Taymīya would have agreed; to crave prayer and experience it as pleasurable and joyous is, in their account, not simply a happy gift but a disposition that one can actively cultivate. Similarly, profound and joyful prayer will shape one's character beyond the purview of the ritual itself. Ritual prayer is thus both an end in itself (enabling the conscious and positive relationship of servantship to God that is, according to Islamic thinkers, the objective of human existence) and a tool for self-fashioning as a better human being.

[91] Ibid., p. 133.

3 Interpretive models

What is ṣalāt, *and what does it do?*

In general, the legal texts setting forth the components and conditions of valid prayer deal only with actions and their normative statuses (obligatory, recommended, permitted, repugnant, or forbidden). By virtue of their genre they rarely address broader issues of meaning and function. The implicit question to which they respond is "What must I do?" rather than "What kind of activity is this, what does it signify, and what does it achieve?" Of course, some of the questions raised by jurists are revealing in this regard; for instance, legal arguments addressing the actions conducive to concentration in *ṣalāt* imply the centrality of certain mental states to the objectives of prayer. However, such incidental forays into the interpretation of prayer do not provide an overall account of the role of *ṣalāt* within a religious worldview.

It is possible to interpret this omission as carrying an implicit interpretation of its own, one that posits adherence to the divine command (regardless of content) as a supreme value eclipsing – or even willfully denying – any appeal to the human meaningfulness of any given religious rite. If the rituals defined by Islamic law are pure exercises in obedience, then it is not only unnecessary but perhaps perverse to invest them with humanly defined significance or attempt to identify their underlying objectives. The idea of the intentional human incomprehensibility of acts of worship (or, indeed, of other provisions of the divine law) is expressed within the Islamic legal tradition by the expression *taʿabbud*, which designates a pure act of servanthood.[1] An action may be deemed *taʿabbudī* on the grounds that it is incomprehensible (*lā yuʿqalu maʿnāhu*, *ghayr maʿqūl al-maʿnā*) or lacks an identifiable rationale (*ʿilla*). The slippage between comprehensibility and function is reflected in Islamic jurists' usage of the word *maʿnā*, which may be used to refer both to "meaning" in the semantic

[1] On *taʿabbud* and the semantic emptiness of Islamic ritual see Ze'ev Maghen, "Much Ado about Wuḍūʾ," *Der Islam* 76 (1999), pp. 219–20, 238–9. However, it should be noted that Islamic jurists did not regard all rites as *taʿabbudī*; the category of *taʿabbud* is not coterminous with the category of ritual, and sometimes the *taʿabbudī* status of a specific ritual was disputed. There was some debate over whether God imposed intentionally arbitrary commandments as exercises in obedience, or whether *taʿabbudī* commandments actually had an underlying wisdom (*ḥikma*) that was simply inaccessible to human beings. See *al-Mawsūʿa al-fiqhīya*, art. "taʿabbudī" (12:201–14); Katz, "The Study of Islamic Ritual and the Meaning of *Wuḍūʾ*."

sense and to the motivating factor (*ʿilla*) identifiable as a rule's rationale. Although acts of *taʿabbud* are usually assumed to have some underlying purpose and meaning, these are known only to God.[2]

The concept of *taʿabbud* is articulated as early as the work of al-Shāfiʿī (d. 204/820), who emphasizes the obligation imposed by the revealed utterances of Qurʾān and *ḥadīth* and the impossibility of identifying or questioning the motivations behind the divine fiat beyond what is revealed in these texts.[3] Al-Shāfiʿī invokes the concept of *taʿabbud* particularly frequently in connection with issues of ritual purity.[4] Although the concept of *taʿabbud* is not uniquely associated with acts of worship, canonical rituals are associated with more concrete textual stipulations and fewer obvious pragmatic functions than most other provisions of the law. The Andalusian legal theorist Abū Isḥāq al-Shāṭibī (d. 790/1388) writes that in the Qurʾān any rule that is presented with precise parameters and qualifications is based on *taʿabbud* and its meaning cannot be discerned by the unaided intellect of the responsible believer. This applies to all ritual duties, "because there is no role for intellects in [understanding] acts of worship (*al-ʿibādāt*)," whether with respect to their fundamental existence or their specific details.[5]

However, not all early Islamic thinkers agreed that acts of worship primarily involved adherence to an inscrutable divine decree whose rationales were exempt from human scrutiny. Indeed, some argued that such an attitude robbed prayer and other rituals of their deeper significance and even of their basic coherence. For Muslim thinkers who believed *ṣalāt* to point to profound underlying truths, fulfilling its outer requirements without awareness of these inner meanings – even if one did so with sincere humility – was a mere husk lacking the essential kernel. The tenth-century C.E. Ismāʿīlī Abū Yaʿqūb al-Sijistānī, after expounding the esoteric meaning of *ṣalāt*, declares to an imagined non-Shīʿite interlocutor that someone who performs it without understanding its true meaning will have discharged the lesser obligation while neglecting the greater.[6] Many Sufis would have expressed similar sentiments, if in support of somewhat different readings of the ritual.

[2] Here the ideas of function and meaning blend into one another. The identification of a motive or rationale for a given ritual both specifies the benefit that it is intended to produce and allows the mind to grasp it. The (apparent or real) absence of function is a form of incomprehensibility, while the communication of meaning is in itself a function.

[3] See, for instance, al-Shāfiʿī, *Risāla*, pp. 217–18.

[4] See, for instance, Muḥammad ibn Idrīs al-Shāfiʿī, *al-Umm* (Beirut: Dār al-Maʿrifa, n.d.), 1:6, 8, 13 bottom (addition present in some MSS), 18.

[5] Abū Isḥāq al-Shāṭibī, *al-Muwāfaqāt fī uṣūl al-sharīʿa*, ed. Muḥammad al-Iskandarānī and ʿAdnān Darwīsh (Beirut: Dār al-Kitāb al-ʿArabī, 1423/2002), p. 480.

[6] Abū Yaʿqūb al-Sijistānī, *Kitāb al-Iftikhār*, ed. Muṣṭafā Ghālib (Beirut: Dār al-Andalus, 1980), p. 118.

Such arguments were not merely abstract or neutral theoretical matters; rather, they were embedded in hotly contested debates over religious authority. Al-Shāfiʿī's model placed knowledge of Islamic rituals firmly within the purview of textual scholars, particularly those who transmitted and interpreted *ḥadīth*. In contrast, models that posited deeper meanings not explicitly present in the texts of Qurʾān and *ḥadīth* assigned interpretive authority over the rites most central to Islamic identity to those who claimed access to those meanings, whether they claimed to do so through rational analysis, mystical insight, or privileged divine guidance such as that which Shīʿites attributed to their imāms. The authority of rational insight (and of those who wielded it) was emphasized by Muslim philosophers and by Muʿtazilī theologians; the centrality of mystical insight was promoted by Sufis. Ismāʿīlī Shīʿites, who posed one of the most potent intellectual and political challenges to the Sunnī establishment from the ninth through the eleventh centuries C.E., based their arguments both on analytic concepts borrowed from *falsafa* and on the ultimate need for the nondiscursive and divinely bestowed knowledge of the imām.

Both Sufis and Ismāʿīlīs were labeled by their detractors as *bāṭinīya*, "esotericists." The legal scholars whose professional expertise came to be institutionalized as the primary form of *ʿilm* (religious knowledge) specialized in the *ẓāhir*, the external aspect of things; to the extent that this manifest knowledge was subordinated to a privileged *bāṭin* (interior dimension), their status was correspondingly reduced. Ismāʿīlīs seem to have been particularly active in early debates about the inner significance of prayer, and their positions were met with a resistance reflecting the existential threat they represented to their opponents. Nevertheless, many of their views – like those of the Sufis, whose contributions often came in the form of personal example rather than of analytic debate – were eventually incorporated into influential strands of Sunnī thought.

For its proponents the identification of rational objectives behind *ṣalāt* served in part to refute the accusation that religiously mandated rituals were arbitrary and ridiculous. While few dared to make such allegations openly, the notorious skeptic Ibn al-Rāwandī (who lived in the third/ninth century) is quoted as declaring, "The Messenger [of God] brought things that are intellectually repugnant, like *ṣalāt*, the ablutions for sexual pollution, the stoning of the pillars, the circumambulation of a house that does not hear or see, and hastening between two stones that can neither benefit nor harm."[7] The fifth/tenth-century Ismāʿīlī missionary al-Muʾayyad al-Shīrāzī responded to this allegation by likening the Prophet to a parent training a child by taming its animalistic (*bahīmīya*) qualities and cultivating its human qualities, the foremost of these being reason. If the parent were to neglect this training (*riyāḍa*), the child would

[7] Cited in Paul Kraus, *Alchemie, Ketzerei, Apokryphen im frühen Islam: Gesammelte Aufsätze* (Hildesheim: Georg Olms Verlag, 1994), p. 115.

be no better than the beasts of the field. Similarly, a prophet educates and trains people by breaking their natural habits (*al-ʿādāt al-ṭabīʿīya*) and inculcating angelic ones. The discipline of repeated daily ablution and prayer is an integral part of this training, violating the pattern of natural habits and differentiating human beings from animals.[8]

From a theological standpoint the functional or symbolic interpretation of prayer was simply an instance of the independent human ability to discern the rationales for divine commands. The Muʿtazila, who argued that the goodness or badness of human acts was an inherent attribute discernible by the unaided intellect, regarded prayer as an instance of "thanking the benefactor," one of the categories of action whose goodness they believed to be axiomatic. Ashʿarīs, in contrast, held that actions had no inherent moral status; the good was simply that which was decreed by God, and could have been decreed otherwise by His inscrutable and sovereign will. From this point of view the rational analysis of acts of worship appeared as a form of misplaced intellectual hubris. The Ashʿarī al-Ghazālī argues in an implicit reference to prayer, "One who would seek intimacy with a Sulṭān merely by wiggling his fingertips from the corner of the room seems a fool in [the judgment of] his *ʿaql* [intellect]. Yet the bondsmen's acts of worship, when measured against the Majesty of God, are less in stature [than the wiggling of the fingers to the sultan]."[9] Here, even the apparent legibility of *ṣalāt* as a form of grateful self-abasement to the divine benefactor is placed in doubt by equating it with the absurd and trivial act of "wiggling the fingertips," on the grounds that both are equally inconsequential from the viewpoint of God.

In addition to raising troubling issues of religious authority, some thinkers feared that a belief in the rational functionality of *ṣalāt* might lead to the conclusion that it could be superseded altogether by more direct means to the same ends. Even if one still adhered to the external forms of Islamic worship, they might be devalued in favor of supposedly higher forms of discipline and insight. Al-Ghazālī cites the example of a hypothetical Muslim devotee of philosophy who acknowledges that the acts of worship prescribed by the divine law serve to preserve order and discipline among ordinary people, but claims that "I am not one of the ignorant common people that I should enter within the narrow confines of duty." Such a person may choose to attend Friday and congregational prayers, yet insist that he does so merely "to exercise my body, and because it is a custom in the place, and to keep my wealth and family."[10] For al-Ghazālī, of course, performance of *ṣalāt* on the basis of such pragmatic and prudential considerations

8 Ibid., pp. 115–16.

9 Cited in A. Kevin Reinhart, *Before Revelation: The Boundaries of Muslim Moral Thought* (Albany: SUNY Press, 1995), p. 116.

10 W. Montgomery Watt, trans., *The Faith and Practice of al-Ghazālī* (London: George Allen & Unwin Ltd., 1953), pp. 72, 73 (translation of al-Ghazālī, *al-Munqidh min al-ḍalāl*). I thank Patricia Crone for drawing my attention to this passage.

as the discipline of the body and the preservation of one's juridical status as a Muslim is far from realizing the ideal of genuine worship. He attributes similar views to the Ismāʿīlīs, who may claim to acknowledge the obligations of the divine law but (he alleges) actually believe that

> if they have comprehended the truth of things by means of the Imām and come to know the inner realities of these outer [rules], these bonds are taken off of them and physical obligations are removed from them, because the objective of the acts of the limbs is to rouse the heart to seek knowledge; once [a person] has achieved [knowledge] he is prepared for the ultimate felicity, and the obligations of the limbs no longer apply to him.[11]

Particularly in the case of the *falāsifa*, such fears were not without foundation. The sixth/twelfth-century philosopher Ibn Ṭufayl depicts a fictional hero, Ḥayy ibn Yaqẓān ("Alive the son of Awake"), who grows up alone on an island and deduces his religious faith from first principles. Significantly, he develops a mystico-philosophical form of worship more closely resembling Sufi spiritual exercises than canonical prayer. His objective is to emulate the heavenly bodies, which move in circular orbits in abstract contemplation of the Necessary Existent. The preliminary, physical form of Ḥayy's worship involves circling the island or his house (reminiscent of the circumambulation of the Kaʿba) or spinning around himself until he falls unconscious (reminiscent of the ecstatic dance of a Sufi). Although his twirling induces altered states of consciousness, his most refined form of worship simply involves sitting silently, eyes shut and senses withdrawn from the world, meditating devoutly on the First Cause. In Islamic terms this is surely *dhikr* rather than *ṣalāt*. Only when he encounters an emissary from a society with a prophet does he learn of the "Five Pillars," including canonical prayer. Although he commits himself to performing them, he regards their inner significance (*ḥikma*) as obscure and their requirements far short of the exacting standards of self-discipline that he has discovered by means of intellectual inquiry.[12]

[11] Abū Ḥāmid al-Ghazālī, *Faḍāʾiḥ al-bāṭinīya*, ed. ʿAbd al-Raḥmān Badawī (Cairo: al-Dār al-Qawmīya liʾl-Ṭibāʿa waʾl-Nashr, 1383/1964, pp. 46–7. For an Ismāʿīlī repudiation see Abū Yaʿqūb Isḥāq al-Sijistānī, *Kitāb Ithbāt al-nubūʾāt*, ed. ʿĀrif Tāmir (Beirut: al-Maṭbaʿa al-Kāthūlīkīya, 1966), p. 65. Al-Sijistānī responds to the objection of an imaginary interlocutor, who argues that if worship consists of inner secrets and external restraints, "then whoever comprehends the secrets that are beneath it and restrains himself from harming [other] people so that they are safe from him, is not obligated to worship God as stipulated by the divine law." Al-Sijistānī responds that this person has neglected a third factor, which is the cultivation of noble character traits, which is possible only by means of the divinely revealed laws (*al-sharāʾiʿ al-nāmūsīya*).

[12] Ibn Ṭufayl, *Qiṣṣat Ḥayy ibn Yaqẓān*, ed. ʿIṣām Fāris al-Ḥarastānī (Amman: Dār ʿAmmār, 1416/1995), pp. 79–82, 97–8; translation in Lenn Evan Goodman, trans., *Ibn Tufayl's Hayy Ibn Yaqzān: A Philosophical Tale*, updated ed. (Chicago: University of Chicago Press, 2009), pp. 146–8, 161. A similar point is made by the Jewish scholar Maimonides, who reflects a similar intellectual and religious background in Islamic Spain and North Africa. In his *Guide to the Perplexed* he implies that while external acts of worship are pedagogically necessary based on

The idea that the spiritual or pragmatic function of acts of worship could be rationally discerned also raised the possibility that humans could supplement or modify them. In this case the implied objects of the critique included Sufis, whose various devotional exercises often lacked a textual or legal basis. Al-Shāṭibī's categoric assertion that intellects have nothing to offer when it comes to matters of ritual is surely connected to his overwhelming concern, which dominates another of his major works, with his fellow believers' tendency to develop new forms of religious devotion. As far as al-Shāṭibī was concerned, illegitimate innovation (*bidʿa*) was a phenomenon exclusively associated with acts of worship (*ʿibādāt*); whereas creativity was possible in other areas of law (indeed, al-Shāṭibī encouraged it far more than many other Islamic jurists), legitimate ritual acts began and ended with the concrete stipulations of the revealed law.[13]

Nevertheless, thinkers who supported the rational and symbolic analysis of prayer often offered nuanced interpretations that carefully parsed the relationship between external obedience and symbolic or functional interpretation (whether or not their ideological positions actually inspired adherents to neglect the external duty of prayer). The Muʿtazilīs and Ismāʿīlīs made particularly significant contributions to this dialogue. In a passage polemicizing against the *bāṭinīya* (here the Ismāʿīlī Shīʿites), Muṭahhar ibn Ṭāhir al-Maqdisī (d. 355/966) complains of their tendency to adduce abstruse interpretations of such ritual details as the number and timing of the prayers, which he represents as part and parcel of their overall effort to undermine the Islamic religion and community. In response, al-Maqdisī (himself a Muʿtazilī) offers a carefully calibrated approach to the rational intelligibility of rites such as ablution and prayer. On the one hand, he affirms that the basic function and meaning of each ritual is apparent to the intellect, and none contradict its dictates. Ablutions cleanse the extremities, which are the parts of the body most often exposed to various kinds of filth (with the addition of the face, which may be sullied by the excretions that pass from its various orifices). Prayer displays humility before God and acknowledges His benefactions, which al-Maqdisī as a Muʿtazilī affirms to be necessitated by the intellect. Nevertheless, the details of these acts of worship – such as their timing, number, and precise mode of performance – are arbitrary divine decrees that are imposed in order to test (*ibtilāʾ*, *imtiḥān*) human fidelity. If God had designated a different number of *rakʿa*s for each prayer, a different number of daily prayers, or a different posture or direction for prayer, or if He

human cultural expectations, the ideal form of worship would be pure abstract contemplation (Moses Maimonides, *The Guide of the Perplexed*, trans. Shlomo Pines [Chicago: University of Chicago Press, 1963], p. 526).

13 See Abū Isḥāq al-Shāṭibī, *al-Iʿtiṣām* (Beirut: Dār al-Maʿrifa, n.d.), 1:37.

had directed that two bowings be performed for every prostration (rather than the other way around), all of this would be perfectly possible.[14]

One of the most extensive discussions of the meaningfulness of the law, with particular attention to rites of worship, is provided by Abū Yaʿqūb al-Sijistānī. In an exchange with an imagined interlocutor, his hypothetical opponent argues that there are only two possibilities: either the prophets have called humankind to what is in any case intellectually acceptable (in which case prophecy is superfluous), or they have called us to things that are intellectually repugnant (in which case prophecy is unacceptable). Al-Sijistānī responds that the laws revealed by prophets are not intellectually repugnant in all respects; rather, they appear so on the surface in some respects, but are intellectually attractive in others. The deeper wisdom (*ḥikma*) in this is that that people find it pleasurable and tempting to perform actions that are familiar and intellectually appealing, so that there is no true servanthood (*taʿabbud ḥaqīqī*) in adhering to them. In contrast, if the actions in question appear odd, difficult, and intellectually repugnant, true *taʿabbud* will be involved. Only after achieving this stage (i.e., of unquestioning obedience to the divine commandments, regardless of their rationality) should one seek the hidden truths underlying the acts in question, by which they contribute to the welfare of the world.[15]

Al-Sijistānī likens the modes of worship mandated by God through the Prophets to living beings. A person may be able to produce a likeness of such a being that is more attractive and elegant than the real thing, but it will not have the same attributes as a product of nature; a painted horse will not gallop, and a painted citron will not smell sweet. Like living organisms, the ritual and legal prescriptions produced by God and mediated by the prophets are not reproducible by human art, however great the skill and discernment of the artisan. It is in this light that al-Sijistānī interprets the *ḥadīth* texts condemning makers of images. Furthermore, the proper mode of worship of each human limb is known only to the one who comprehends the ultimate nature of that limb; thus, one must worship God as instructed by those who comprehend the secrets of the human constitution. In an extended simile, al-Sijistānī likens the worshiper to a sick person, worship to the discipline of medicine, the prophet to a doctor, and the object of medical knowledge (that is, nature) to the object of worship (that is, God). Just as a sick person should seek to be treated only by a skillful doctor with thorough knowledge of the human constitution, a person should perform acts of worship only as directed by the prophets.[16]

[14] Muṭahhar ibn Ṭāhir al-Maqdisī, *Kitāb al-badʾ waʾl-tārīkh*, ed. Clément Huart (Paris: Ernest Leroux, 1916), 5:46–52. I thank Patricia Crone for this reference.

[15] al-Sijistānī, *Ithbāt*, p. 62.

[16] Ibid., pp. 63–5.

Interestingly, al-Sijistānī's main points are reproduced in some detail (if in different words) by that inveterate opponent of the Ismāʿīlīs al-Ghazālī. In an unacknowledged echo of al-Sijistānī's argument that the satisfactions of intellectual comprehension are incompatible with pure *taʿabbud*, he writes of some of the component rites of the *ḥajj* pilgrimage:

> The soul has no share in them and is not comfortable with them, and intellects cannot discern their meanings. There is no motive for engaging in them but the [divine] command alone and the intention of obeying [God's] command purely on the basis of its being obligatory. ... One's nature inclines to some extent to everything whose meaning can be recognized by the intellect; this inclination aids the commandment and joins with it in motivating one to perform the action. Thus, [actions whose rationales are comprehensible] scarcely display the perfection of servanthood and submission.[17]

Al-Ghazālī also parallels al-Sijistānī's analogy between ritual and medicine. Likening prophets to "physicians of the heart," he argues that "formal worship, which is the medicine for the disease of the hearts, is compounded of acts differing in kind and amount; the prostration (*sujūd*) is the double of the bowing (*rukūʿ*) in amount, and the morning worship half of the afternoon worship." The components and proportions of this remedy, however, cannot be discovered or comprehended by the human faculties: "In the case of the medicines of formal worship, which have been fixed and determined by the prophets, the manner of their effectiveness is not apprehended by the intellectual explanations of the intellectuals; one must rather accept the statements (*taqlīd*) of the prophets who apprehended those properties by the light of prophecy."[18] Regardless of whether al-Sijistānī originated either of these arguments, motifs in the discussion of the meaningfulness of prayer crossed the lines of what was later defined as "orthodoxy."

Despite his emphasis on the humanly unfathomable wisdom of the forms of legally stipulated worship, however, al-Ghazālī himself does not always avoid interpretation of the meanings and functions of ritual acts.[19] Rather than thinking of *taʿabbud* as the sole and defining concept through which Muslim thinkers approached acts of worship such as *ṣalāt*, it is important to remember that it was always debatable whether a specific ritual (or a specific feature of a given ritual) was actually *taʿabbudī*. In a typical example, the fifteenth-century Ḥanafī jurist Mullā Khusraw writes of the double prostration performed in each cycle of *ṣalāt*:

[17] al-Ghazālī, *Iḥyāʾ*, 1:315. Interestingly, in this passage he contrasts the apparent meaninglessness of actions such as hastening between the hills of Ṣafā and Marwā with bowing and prostration in *ṣalāt*, which he characterizes as being fully legible as physical signs of humility toward God.

[18] Watt, *Faith and Practice*, p. 69.

[19] See Marion Katz, "The Hajj and the Study of Islamic Ritual," *Studia Islamica* 98/99 (2004), pp. 101–2.

As for the reason for its repetition, it is said that it is *taʿabbudī* and no meaning/rationale (*maʿnā*) is to be sought for it, as is the case with the number of *rakʿa*s [in each prayer]. It is also said that Satan was commanded to perform one prostration and did not do so, so we perform two prostrations to spite him. It is also said that the first [prostration] is an allusion to the fact that we were created from the earth, and the second to the fact that we will be returned to it.[20]

While one might certainly question whether the two interpretations offered explain the historical origin of this feature of the ritual, they demonstrate the ways in which concrete features of *ṣalāt* could be invested with meaning. In this case, Mullā Khusraw weaves the prayer ritual into the Islamic cosmic narrative, relating the double prostration both with its beginning (the creation of Adam) and its end (human death and resurrection).

Some modern secular scholars have taken the intentional meaninglessness designated by the concept of *taʿabbud* as a distinctive attribute of Islamic ritual. William Graham has argued that Islamic ritual is "fundamentally aniconic [and] amythical," and that its eschewal of condensed symbolism and of concepts of ritual efficacy reflect basic Islamic theological tenets.[21] Similarly, in a study of the Islamic law of ritual purity Kevin Reinhart concludes that "ritual cleansing is only a cleansing for ritual. It shapes no particular perspective on the course of life." It is this disconnect between ritual rules and religious worldview that has "helped Muslims accommodate to societies with markedly different personal cosmologies."[22] In this view, the legal texts define a formally stable but symbolically blank set of ritual forms that lend themselves to translation between culturally diverse societies, which may invest them with various meanings over time. According to the anthropologist John Bowen, the richness of debates over the ideal performance of *ṣalāt* in modern Indonesia is enabled by the fact that

the *salāt* is not structured around an intrinsic propositional or semantic core. It cannot be "decoded" semantically because it is not designed according to a single symbolic or iconic code. In particular times and places Muslims have construed the ṣalāt as conveying iconic or semantic meanings, but as part of particular spiritual, social, and political discourses.[23]

This view of *ṣalāt* has not gone unchallenged. Responding to Bowen, Heiko Henkel responds that the ritual "is ripe with references to fundamental concepts

[20] Mullā Khusraw, *Durar al-ḥukkām fī sharḥ Ghurar al-aḥkām* (Istanbul: n.p., 1329), 1:73. For a Shīʿite application of the last interpretation mentioned see Fischer, *Iran*, p. 18.

[21] William A. Graham, "Islam in the Mirror of Ritual," in Richard G. Hovanisian and Speros Vryonis, Jr., eds., *Islam's Understanding of Itself* (Malibu, Calif.: Undena Publications, 1983), pp. 65–6.

[22] Reinhart, "Impurity/No Danger," p. 21.

[23] John R. Bowen, "*Salat* in Indonesia: The Social Meanings of an Islamic Ritual," *Man* 24 (1989), p. 615.

of Islam, most centrally to God's unity, magnificence, and absolute authority."[24] While Henkel's point is undeniable, his interpretation of *ṣalāt* makes it refer to generic axioms of Islamic belief that are equally affirmed by any other Islamic ritual; it assigns no distinctive meaning or function to the individual components and gestures of *ṣalāt*. Indeed, Henkel (somewhat like Bowen) ultimately sees the utility of *ṣalāt* largely as a generically Islamic rite that unites Muslims of otherwise incompatible religious and political views.

It is certainly true that there is no single interpretive framework for the understanding of *ṣalāt* to which all Muslims must subscribe, or that is integrally incorporated into the ritual itself (as, for instance, the model of Jesus' Last Supper is inevitably referenced by the Christian rite of the Eucharist). However, while Bowen concedes that Muslims have invested prayer with specific meanings "in particular times and places" and "as part of particular spiritual, social, and political discourses," some of these discourses are just as long-lasting and pervasive as the legal discourse that defines the obligatory components of prayer. For instance, as we shall see below, several reports attributed to the Prophet Muḥammad define *ṣalāt* as an "intimate conversation" (*munājāt*) between the worshiper and God. While this idea may not yield the semantically defined "symbolic richness" described by Bowen, it is nevertheless a model of *ṣalāt* in which Islamic thinkers have discovered rich implications that go beyond mere external obedience to the formal requirements of prayer. Such master metaphors – which in many cases are far more than local meanings incidentally attached to the neutral structure of "orthodox" prayer, but deeply shaped the approach to prayer in the normative tradition – have always helped Muslim thinkers (and ordinary believers) to understand what *ṣalāt* is, what it says, and how it works.

The model of the royal audience

The most pervasive metaphor that informs discussions of *ṣalāt* across genres of Islamic thought is that of the royal audience. Jurists and mystics alike invoke the model of the reverent and fearful subject standing in the awesome and compassionate presence of a great king, both as a framework to analyze the function of *ṣalāt* and as a visualization to evoke appropriate sentiments and comportments from the worshiper. The model of the royal audience may have been suggested to Muslim thinkers by God's title of al-Malik, "the King," which appears in a number of different Qur'ānic verses (e.g., 20:114, 23:116, 59:23, 62:1, 114:2). Certainly the postures adopted in prayer suggested the physical expressions of human social hierarchy. As we have seen in the discussion of the origins of *ṣalāt*

[24] Heiko Henkel, "'Between Belief and Unbelief Lies the Performance of Salāt': Meaning and Efficacy of a Muslim Ritual," *Journal of the Royal Anthropological Institute* 11 (2005), p. 499.

in Chapter 1, the role of prostration as an expression of social deference to a human superior was very much present in the minds of Muslim thinkers who pondered the meaning of *ṣalāt*. While they rejected it as a gesture offered to anyone but God, the fact that human societies preceding and neighboring the Muslim *umma* used bowing and prostration to articulate human hierarchies was very relevant to their interpretations of prayer.

Although strict construal of the Prophet's *sunna* required more egalitarian forms of greeting (such as the exchanging of "peace" or the shaking of hands) even toward social and political superiors, over time physical gestures of subordination were reintroduced in Muslim contexts. Byzantine court ceremonial required prostration before the emperor, and an early Muslim emissary is said to have resorted to stratagems to avoid compliance. At least in the memory of later Muslims, early Islamic court ceremonial was sober and unpretentious; the fifth/eleventh-century courtier Hilāl al-Ṣābiʾ (d. 448/1056) states that in the good old days a person visiting a high official would make no physical obeisance, but simply offer the standard Islamic greeting. By his own time, however, people had reverted to the imperial practice of prostrating and kissing the ground.[25]

The known history of prostration as a form of human etiquette and the resurgence of related physical gestures in increasingly stratified medieval Islamic societies evoked both analysis and distress from some medieval scholars. Commenting on verse 12:100 of the Qurʾān, which recounts that Joseph's newly reunited family prostrated themselves to him, al-Qurṭubī (d. 671/1272) remarks that some early interpreters believed that this phrase refers not to actual prostration, but to an inclination of the head or a bow that was a customary greeting at the time. Others (including the early authorities al-Thawrī and al-Ḍaḥḥāk) insisted that "it was a prostration like the prostration that is known among us; that was what their greeting was." In any case, al-Qurṭubī concludes, "God abrogated all of that in our religious law, and substituted verbal utterances (*al-kalām*) for bowing." However, "This bowing and bending that was abrogated from our law has [once again] become a custom in the land of Egypt and among the Persians (*al-ʿajam*), as has standing up in honor of one another"; he laments, "They have deviated from the practices of the Prophet (*al-sunan*), and turned away from customary practice!"[26]

Envisioning *ṣalāt* as an encounter with a hierarchical superior made it intelligible as a series of gestures whose significance was seen as broadly human, even if their details were strictly Islamic. The early Shāfiʿī legal scholar

[25] Hilāl al-Ṣābiʾ, *Rusūm dār al-khilāfa*, cited in Nadia Maria El Cheikh, *Byzantium Viewed by the Arabs* (Cambridge, Mass.: Distributed for the Center for Middle Eastern Studies of Harvard University by Harvard University Press, 2004), p. 159.

[26] al-Qurṭubī, *Tafsīr*, 9:173–4.

Abū Bakr al-Qaffāl al-Shāshī (d. 365/976) analyzes *ṣalāt* through this framework in a work entitled *Maḥāsin al-sharīʿa fī furūʿ al-shāfiʿīya* (The virtues of the sharia in Shāfiʿī substantive law), which forms part of a minor genre emphasizing the coherent and beneficial nature of the provisions of the law.[27] In his analysis of ritual purification and *ṣalāt*, al-Qaffāl argues not only that these rites are rationally comprehensible, but that they conform to a logic of social interaction that is common to all human communities. Discussing the preparatory ablutions for prayer, al-Qaffāl states that some of the rules of *ṭahāra* correspond to "people's customs of washing to cleanse themselves for [other] people; it falls within the category of manifesting respect for those in authority (*li'l-ruʾasāʾ*)." Thus, when preparing for an audience with a social superior, a person cleans the parts of his body that are exposed to view, removes the smell of sweat from his body, and dons clean garments. Anyone who failed to do these things when visiting an august ruler would be considered foolish, ignorant, and ill-mannered. Al-Qaffāl concludes that ritual purification for prayer expresses reverence (*taʿẓīm*) for God, because prayer is tantamount to a private audience (*munājāt*) between the servant (*ʿabd*) and his divine Master (*sayyidihi*). Thus, people must cleanse their extremities and purify their clothes as if they were admitted to an audience with a human dignitary.[28] He continues:

> It is found in [all] human societies (*jamāʿāt al-nās*) that exaltation occurs by means of standing upright before the great king in such a way that the limbs are at rest and one hand is placed upon the other in order to quiet the body. This is something that indicates that the person who does it exalts his superior (*raʾīs*) . . . and is ready for a command that he wishes to execute. In addition to standing [in this way], praise and remembrance of the superior benefactor (*al-munʿim al-raʾīs*) may occur by means of the tongue. . . . Exaltation may also occur by means of bowing, then of prostration that involves rubbing the face – which is the noblest of the extremities – on the floor. Bowing refers to the fact that [the worshiper] is under [his superior's] command, so that he is dominated, not dominating. Then, this subordinate (*marʾūs*) may kneel before his superior, and that is [also] a form of exaltation, because sitting with one's legs crossed or stretching them out is something that one does only if his sovereignty has enlarged him and removed all feelings of awe and fear . . . So God brought together all of these things in *ṣalāt*.[29]

For al-Qaffāl, the legibility of the prayer ritual in terms of cross-culturally ubiquitous human customs serves to demonstrate its accessibility to human reason. The implication is that these Islamic rites, like their profane counterparts in human social interaction before and beyond the Islamic dispensation, have

[27] For a discussion of al-Qaffāl al-Shāshī, including the debate over his theological leanings, see Reinhart, *Before Revelation*, pp. 18–21.

[28] Abū Bakr Muḥammad ibn ʿAlī al-Shāshī, known as al-Qaffāl al-Kabīr, *Maḥāsin al-sharīʿa fī furūʿ al-shāfiʿīya* (Beirut: Dār al-Kutub al-ʿIlmīya 1428/2007), p. 48.

[29] Ibid., pp. 77–8.

pragmatic functions that should be recognizable to any sensible person. As he writes of the rites of ablution:

The books of the ancient philosophers, dealing with the ways in which a person should manage his body, state that he should wash his face when he arises from sleep to cleanse it for encountering people, and to avoid any appearance that would alienate them, isolate him, or be considered disgusting. To the same effect is what is commanded in the sunna, to wash oneself on Friday and on festivals; that is so that one encounters other people in a state that is not offensive to persons sitting nearby and no offensive odors are smelled on one. All of this falls into the category of good social behavior and fine comportment; the things that the sharia has established in this respect correspond to praiseworthy customs [in general] (*al-ʿādāt al-maḥmūda*) and are confirmed to be good and sound by intellects.[30]

Al-Qaffāl's contemporary, the Muslim philosopher Abūʾl-Ḥasan al-ʿĀmirī (d. 381/992), who was concerned to demonstrate the compatibility of the philosophical tradition with Islam, emphasizes both the universality of the gestures used in *ṣalāt* and the unparalleled comprehensiveness of their use in Islamic prayer. Al-ʿĀmirī argues that Islamic worship is uniquely perfect because it comprises more actions expressing humility than those of the other religions. "That is because the forms of self-abasement (*takhāḍuʿ*) before kings are divided into four categories. One is standing before them; the second is bending the back to them; the third is pressing the face in the dust on the ground; and the fourth is kneeling."[31] Al-ʿĀmirī interprets the sequence of the postures of *ṣalāt* in terms of the progression of a royal audience: a person engaged in prayer performs the actions "one after another, in a way similar to a servant who approached a great king and stood before him, sensing the awe of him and praising him; until, when [the king] called him to approach, he did obeisance[32] to him by bending his back; until, when he called him to approach closer, he pressed his face to the dust on the ground out of an excess of humility; until he gave him permission to sit, and he knelt before him" – all the while praising and glorifying him to the utmost extent. Although he clearly considers *ṣalāt* to manifest the logic of this comportment to a unique degree, he represents these basic components as being present (if imperfectly) in the prayer rites of other communities: "None of the prayers (*ṣalawāt*) of the people of the other religious possess this virtue: some of them were made to have bowing without prostration, and some of them were made to have prostration without bowing."[33]

Both al-Qaffāl and al-ʿĀmirī were interested in affirming the pragmatic function of *ṣalāt* in terms of a universal human logic of social interaction.

30 Ibid., p. 49.

31 Abūʾl-Ḥasan al-ʿĀmirī, *al-Iʿlām bi-manāqib al-islām*, ed. Aḥmad Sharīʿatī and Ḥusayn Manūchehrī (Tehran: Markaz-i Nashr-i Dāneshgāhī, 1347 H.Sh.), pp. 243–4.

32 *Kaffara*: to bow or incline the head in obeisance to a superior (see Ibn Manẓūr, *Lisān al-ʿarab*, [Beirut: Dār Ṣādir, 1410/1990], s.v. k-f-r, 5:150–1).

33 ʿĀmirī, *Iʿlām*, p. 244.

Most Islamic thinkers, in contrast, were less interested in the rational utility demonstrated by the model of *ṣalāt* as royal audience than by its capacity to elicit proper emotional and physical dispositions from the worshiper. Often the focus was on emotions of fear and awe, but the privilege of a private audience with the divine King could also evoke feelings of intimacy and honor. The early mystic al-Ḥārith al-Muḥāsibī (d. 243/857) describes *ṣalāt* as follows:

We have seen that kings do not permit all the people of their kingdoms to come in to see them or allow them to address them; only someone who possesses great honor in their eyes dares to request that from them. But by His gracious favor the Supreme King has permitted all of His servants, high and low, disobedient and obedient, to converse with Him in private; indeed, He has commanded them to do so, and made known that He is angry at anyone who does not do it. If the servant is a disobedient person the likes of whom despairs of speaking in private to subordinate kings, he should be aware of the magnitude of the boon that his Lord grants him when He permits him to converse with Him privately. . . . Some of the kings of this world allow someone who has honor in their eyes to converse with them privately, and [such a person] does so only with humility; so what if [such a king] gave permission to someone who had previously sinned, transgressed, and offended? What submissiveness and dread of punishment would [such a person] feel? . . . So let the servant [of God] be aware of the value of the private audience that God has moved him to; let him fear his sins, beware and humble himself, and approach Him with his heart and with the reverence (*khuḍū'*) of his limbs, in hopes that He may forgive him the length of his neglect of Him and his being busy with acts of disobedience to Him in his life before that time.[34]

In this passage al-Muḥāsibī relies on his audience's familiarity with the habits of human kings (or at least with received ideas about the habits of human kings) to emphasize both the similarity and the contrast between *ṣalāt* and a royal audience. On the one hand, he calls on the reader or listener's ability to imagine the awe that would overcome him if allowed to approach a great human monarch, particularly one whom he had not perfectly served. Picturing *ṣalāt* as a face-to-face encounter with the king serves as a humanly accessible means of concretizing the invisible presence and authority of God, increasing the worshiper's physical and emotional reverence. On the other hand, the very fact that every individual is admitted to a private audience with the divine King underlines the contrast between God's infinite (and egalitarian) mercy and the haughty practices of human dignitaries. It is useful to think of God as a king, but ultimately the parallel reminds one how little He is like a human king. Prayer is both very much like, and the opposite of, court ceremonial. Like the exclusive devotion of prostration to God, the overall scenario of the royal audience both references human hierarchies and rejects them. It precisely in their contrast with

[34] al-Ḥārith ibn Asad al-Muḥāsibī, *Fahm al-ṣalāt*, ed. Muḥammad ʿUthmān al-Khisht (Cairo: Maktabat al-Qurʾān, 1984), pp. 61–2.

the habits of human monarchs that God's grace and forgiveness are dramatized, and the only proper reaction is an awed gratitude.

The emotional dimension of prayer as royal audience continued to preoccupy Sufis of later centuries. Analyzing the challenges to concentration in prayer, al-Ghazālī argues that one's thoughts will necessarily linger on the objects of one's self-interest and concern; it is such considerations that focus the attention during an audience with a this-worldly grandee, even though a mere human being is incapable of benefiting or harming one in a lasting way.[35] Thus, only by pondering the omnipotence of God and reordering one's priorities will it be possible to achieve true attentiveness in prayer. For al-Ghazālī the human capacity for states of extreme concentration is demonstrated by familiarity with the awe and distraction that one experiences in the presence of a powerful superior. A person may have an audience with a king or vizier, speak with him about his concern, and leave his presence; if he were to be questioned about the people in the king's entourage or about the royal robes, he would be incapable of describing them because all of his attention was absorbed by the great man. Thus, accounts of the extreme absorption of spiritual adepts in prayer, who become completely oblivious to everything else, are not at all implausible.[36]

Of course, al-Ghazālī himself was familiar with the halls of power in a quite literal sense. For less august members of his audience, sharp differences in social status – and thus experience with the pettier figurative "kings" of one's own local environment – were presumably so pervasive that most people might be expected to recognize the breathtaking awe of facing a superior with the power to patronize or harm. Certainly a general sense of the social logic of encounters with superiors was assumed by many authors. The Shāfiʿī thinker Ibn ʿAbd al-Salām al-Sulamī (d. 660/1262) argues that it is *ṣalāt*'s character as a personal audience that explains why one must face in one direction and refrain from turning about or engaging in extraneous speech or motion. Any physical or mental turning away from prayer would constitute discourtesy (*sūʾ adab*), as would be recognized by anyone who was invited to sit and converse intimately with a human grandee (*baʿḍ al-kubarāʾ*).[37]

Ibn Qayyim al-Jawzīya similarly uses the model of the royal audience to dramatize for his readers the inappropriate and shameful qualities of inattention during prayer. He assumes that his audience is at least generally aware of the etiquette and comportment that would be necessary to please a human dignitary from whom one wished to elicit favors, and that they can use this standard to evaluate their own performance at prayer (and presumably find it wanting). A person who prays with an inattentive heart

[35] al-Ghazālī, *Iḥyāʾ*, 1:192.
[36] Ibid., 1:193.
[37] al-Sulamī, *Qawāʿid al-aḥkām*, 1:156.

is like someone who goes to the gate of the king to apologize for his errors and mistakes and seeking rain from the clouds of his magnanimity, generosity, and compassion, and seeking food to nourish his heart so that he will have the strength to serve him, but when he arrives at his gate and all that remains is to converse with [the king] in private, he turns away from the king and his eyes roam away from him to the right and left, or he turns his back to him and is distracted from him by the thing that is most loathsome and trivial to the king and prefers it to him.[38]

Just as important as this model's ability to draw on people's sense of proper social performance is its role in dramatizing and exalting a ritual that, if only because of its constant incorporation into daily life, must have been in danger of becoming quotidian or mundane. Ibn al-Qayyim, who vividly evokes the spiritual grandeur of an activity woven into the most ordinary moments of everyday existence, uses the image of the royal court to affirm the elevated nature of an encounter with God whose true magnificence might easily be overlooked. Accordingly, somewhat like al-Muḥāsibī, he emphasizes not only the worshiper's role as a supplicant in the divine court, but the honor and acceptance that God lavishes on the individual by inviting him to this regular audience. For Ibn al-Qayyim, God not merely summons us to come to His gate, but invites us to a princely repast:

Since God Most High has tested His servant with desire and similar things . . . the perfection of His compassion and beneficence towards him dictated that He prepare for him a banquet that brings together all different kinds of dishes, boons (*al-tuḥaf*), ceremonial robes and presents, and invite him to it five times every day.[39]

A very elaborate rendition of the "royal audience" model of prayer is produced by al-Rāzī (d. 606/1209) in his commentary on verse 29:45 of the Qurʾān, which states that "prayer restrains from shameful and unjust deeds." Having established that only "true" prayer is efficacious against sin, al-Rāzī turns to analogies based on "custom" – that is, on ordinary human experience, in this case the experience of social relations in a monarchy. Just as someone who has achieved rank and preferment in the service of a great king will not turn aside to serve someone whom the king has irrevocably banished from his presence, someone who serves God in prayer will not turn aside to the service of Satan, whom God has banished from His presence. Similarly, it is customarily (*ʿurfan*) known that someone who is clothed in clean and luxurious garments will not willingly come into contact with refuse; the finer the clothing, the greater the wearer's distaste for handling garbage. As the "garments of piety" (*libās al-taqwā*, Qurʾān verse 7:26) that one dons for a personal audience with God are more resplendent than gold brocade and are associated with the heart more

[38] Ibn Qayyim al-Jawzīya, *Asrār al-ṣalāt*, pp. 67–8.
[39] Ibid., p. 57.

intimately than physical clothing with the body, a person who prays will naturally refuse to handle the "filth" of obscene or evil acts. Since the prayers succeed each other at such short intervals, in effect someone who prays regularly is always clothed in the "garments of piety."

Furthermore, someone who is his own master (*amīr*) may sit wherever he pleases, but when he enters the service of a king, the king assigns him a place; he may sit only there, so if he decides to sit in the back with the sandals, he will not be allowed to do so. Similarly, someone who enters into the service of God by praying is assigned a place to the right hand; someone who commits bad acts relegates himself to the left hand (cf. Qur'ān 56:8–10, 27–46) and God will not allow His servant to do so. Al-Rāzī notes that this interpretation is a reference to the impeccability (*'iṣma*) that God bestows on those who pray; just as someone with an assigned place at court is not only unwilling but unable to choose another, he suggests that God actually will not permit someone who (as a result of prayer) has been assigned a favorable place in His presence to choose an inferior one. In his next example he points out that a person who is of very low status and is very distant from the king will be unconcerned with how he acts; he may eat food from common vendors and consort with marginal people. If the person then attains some very modest position in the royal court (such as that of a stableman), he will be very little inhibited from his old behavior. However, if he attains greater intimacy and higher rank with the king, he will be sure not to eat in disreputable places or keep unsavory company. Similarly, someone who prays attains an intimacy with God that will inhibit him from doing or associating with bad things.[40]

A striking feature of al-Rāzī's series of analogies is the way in which they associate enhanced rank (which is identified with greater closeness to the human or divine king) with greater behavioral constraints. Low-ranking people can do as they please; they can sit where they like, eat what they fancy, and associate with whomever they choose. While some of the liberties enjoyed by the lowly are questionable privileges – the freedom to handle refuse is probably not widely desired – others appear to be simple pleasures; like a hotdog from a cart on a New York street, a ladleful of *harīsa* from a vendor in the market (one of al-Rāzī's two concrete examples of foods that must be eschewed by those who rise to high rank) may be tasty, even if it is déclassé. As every little girl who has coveted a party dress has discovered, even the demands of one's clean and fancy clothes can sometimes be burdensome. In al-Rāzī's model prestige is both generated and displayed by the exercise of self-control and the limiting of options. Prayer is a means of advancement and access at the divine court, whose protocols both exalt and

[40] al-Rāzī, *Tafsīr*, 25:72–3.

constrain those who frequent it. In his analogies sin is equated with the activities – themselves sometimes neutral – that one must leave behind as one pursues one's upward trajectory in the service of the divine court.

On one level, the metaphor of the royal audience presses into service the aspiring worshiper's familiarity with the affective states, physical postures, and supplicative strategies involved in encounters with powerful superiors. While theologians were divided on the question of whether analogies with this-worldly human relationships could properly be used to elucidate divine attributes such as justice, in this case Ashʿarīs such as al-Ghazālī and al-Rāzī resorted to human parallels without hesitation. The goal was not to generate true statements about the nature of God (which according to Ashʿarīs was impossible on the basis of parallels with human expectations and standards), but to evoke proper feelings and comportment. From this point of view ritual actions could make use of human conventions to express a proper relationship with an intellectually unknowable God. In his interpretation of verse 2:255 of the Qurʾān, which speaks of God's "footstool" or "throne," al-Rāzī invokes the opinion that

> when God addresses His creatures by making known His essence and attributes, He does so with that which they [humankind] recognize from their kings and notables. For example, He made the Kaʿba a house of His, around which people circumambulate, just as they circumambulate the houses of their kings, and He ordered people to visit it [His house] just as people visit the houses of their kings. He related of the Black Stone that it is the right hand of God on His earth, and then He appointed it a place to be kissed, just as people kiss the hand of their kings.[41]

Similarly, for thinkers who invoked the model of the royal audience the *ṣalāt* ritual utilized the familiarity of the institution of monarchy and the etiquette of social hierarchy to concretize the human relationship with God.

It might appear that, by sanctifying bodily gestures of submission and overtly relating them to the acts of obeisance offered to human potentates, classical Muslim thinkers' utilization of the "royal audience" model of prayer implicitly reinforced social hierarchies and served to legitimize monarchical power. A person who subscribed to this model, it might be assumed, would internalize postures and sentiments of deference that fit seamlessly into a steeply ranked social world where submission to those in power was not simply a prudential necessity but a deeply felt value. In fact, however, the works of scholars who evoked the royal audience model of prayer suggest that the opposite was true; imagining *ṣalāt* as an encounter with the divine King served as a subtle but

[41] Translated in Feras Hamza and Sajjad Rizvi, eds., *An Anthology of Qur'anic Commentaries*, vol. 1: *On the Nature of the Divine* (Oxford: Oxford University Press, in association with the Institute of Ismaili Studies, London, 2008), p. 197. This opinion is attributed to al-Qaffāl; it may be al-Rāzī's paraphrase of the opinions of al-Qaffāl al-Shāshī in his *Maḥāsin al-sharīʿa*.

devastating critique both of court ceremonial and of the attitudes of deference that it implied.

This is particularly clear from al-Ghazālī's great work *The Revival of the Religious Sciences*, which offers both his interpretation of *ṣalāt* and a lengthy discussion of the permissibility and etiquette of visiting the courts of worldly rulers. From the latter passages it quickly emerges that al-Ghazālī's views of contemporary monarchs are uncompromisingly dark. He assumes summarily that all contemporary rulers are unjust (*ẓalama*), and bases his legal reasoning on this supposition. However, he opposes political revolt on the grounds that as long as an ignorant and unjust ruler is capable of maintaining power, efforts to replace him would cause civil unrest and obedience to him is religiously obligatory.[42]

In al-Ghazālī's view it is thus obligatory both to obey rulers (for prudential reasons) and to deplore them (for religious and ethical ones). The two principles intersect in that religion demands fulfillment of the pragmatic needs of the Muslim community, which include both security and the existence of a governmental framework for legal transactions. Al-Ghazālī's principled quietism and loyalty are thus completely compatible with a stinging disdain for actual rulers.[43] Court etiquette – the model that he assumes as a basis for the *ṣalāt* ritual – is a primary arena for the expression of this disdain. While al-Ghazālī does not advocate the overthrow of an iniquitous ruler, he strongly opposes frequenting such a ruler's court. First of all he asserts that in most cases the site of the audience is itself a misappropriated building; to set foot in it is thus religiously forbidden.[44] Even supposing that the space is licit, however, all the pious visitor may do is enter and greet the ruler with a simple "Peace be upon you" (*al-salām ʿalayka*). If he prostrates, bows, or stands up to greet and serve him, then he is honoring the unjust ruler for the sake of his royal authority, by means of which he commits his injustice; it is religiously forbidden to humble oneself to an unjust person. Al-Ghazālī here uses the terminology of *ṣalāt*: standing, bowing, and prostration.[45] He then turns to the utterances appropriate to a royal audience, which (like those of *ṣalāt*) include supplication (*duʿāʾ*) and praise (*thanāʾ*). Neither of these is licit, although it is permissible (for instance) to pray for God to reform the ruler, help him to perform good deeds, or allow him a long life to perform acts of obedience. (It is, of course, questionable whether a monarch would be gratified to hear prayers for his ethical

[42] al-Ghazālī, *Iḥyāʾ*, 2:154.

[43] On al-Ghazālī's political thought see Patricia Crone, *God's Rule: Government and Islam* (New York: Columbia University Press, 2004), pp. 237–49. Crone notes that, while al-Ghazālī recognized the pragmatic necessity of temporal power exercised by those with the clout to govern, "his strongman is a brute enrolled in the service of Islam" (p. 245).

[44] al-Ghazālī, *Iḥyāʾ*, 2:157.

[45] Ibid., 2:157.

improvement.) Furthermore, it is to be feared that an audience with the sultan will lead to a secret appreciation for the favors he has bestowed, which detracts from the recognition of God's benefactions.[46]

It is striking how thoroughly the royal audience here appears as a negative mirror image of *ṣalāt*, with each of the elements of the prayer ritual appearing and being problematized. Even the category of the "misappropriated building" (*al-dār al-maghṣūba*) is one more often encountered in discussions of *ṣalāt*, where it is debated whether prayers performed in such spaces are invalid (or whether the act of entering such a space is a sin, but the prayer itself remains valid).[47] One might assume that the problem with acts of deference to human potentates is simply that certain acts of obeisance should be reserved exclusively for God – and this is presumably one rationale for al-Ghazālī's disapproval of prostration. However, his condemnation of other gestures of deference (including standing, bowing, and the kissing of hands) is related specifically to the injustice of the ruler; he allows them towards just rulers, scholars, or anyone else who merits such respect on religious grounds.[48] The royal audience is the evil double of prayer not simply because human beings are radically different from God (although this is certainly true), but because actual monarchs are radically different from what they should be; they do not merit gestures of deference or utterances of praise.

Related to the model of the royal audience is another image repeatedly evoked in the remarks of al-Muḥāsibī (and ubiquitous in almost all discussions of *ṣalāt*), that of *munājāt* or "intimate conversation." This term appears in several statements about prayer attributed to the Prophet. In a report transmitted in the *Ṣaḥīḥ* of al-Bukhārī the Prophet declares, "When one of you stands in prayer, he is in intimate conversation with his Lord" – or (in an alternative version) "his Lord is between him and the *qibla*" – "so one of you should not spit in the direction of the *qibla*, but to his left or beneath his feet."[49] A less well-authenticated *ḥadīth* warns, "Beware of turning about during prayer; as long as one of you is praying, he is in intimate conversation with his Lord."[50] A highly suspect transmission goes even farther, declaring: "When someone prays, blessings are scattered on his head from the clouds of the sky to the parting of his hair, and an angel calls out, 'If this servant [of God] knew with Whom he was in intimate conversation, he would never leave off [from prayer]!'"[51]

46 Ibid., 2:158.

47 See al-Zuḥaylī, *Fiqh*, 2:984–6. Al-Ghazālī himself states that prayer in a misappropriated building (including one built by an unjust ruler) is technically licit, but that a pious person should avoid it (*Iḥyā'*, 2:166).

48 al-Ghazālī, *Iḥyā'*, 2:157.

49 Bukhārī, *Ṣaḥīḥ*, *Kitāb al-Ṣalāt*, *Bāb ḥakk al-buzāq bi'l-yad min al-masjid*.

50 Badr al-Dīn al-ʿAynī, *ʿUmdat al-qāri sharḥ Ṣaḥīḥ al-Bukhārī* (Beirut: Muḥammad Amīn Damj, n.d.), 5:311 (citing al-Ṭabarānī).

51 Ibid., 5:311 (citing Ibn Ḥibbān's *Kitāb al-ḍuʿafā'*).

Although they range from the minimal affirmation that one should not spit in the direction of one's prayer to a vision of divine blessings raining down from heaven, these reports share the common theme that an awareness of engaging in a private personal encounter with God should evoke reverence and concentration.

The models of royal audience and of "intimate conversation" are not mutually exclusive (as we have seen, several of the authors discussed above use this term while depicting prayer as a visit to the divine King), but even when they overlap they are differently inflected. Much in the same vein as al-Muḥāsibī, al-Ghazālī writes that God "differs from sultans by opening the door, raising the curtain, and allowing the servants to engage in intimate conversation [with Him] by engaging in *ṣalāt* in whatever situation they may be, whether in groups or in solitude. . . . Other feeble [human] kings allow private meetings only after the presentation of presents and bribes."[52] Elaborating the model of the ritualized encounter with the divine King, Muslim thinkers emphasized gestures of humility and self-abasement. The concept of *munājāt*, in contrast, tended to evoke images of a more personal communing with a tender deity. It is notable that the term *munājāt* is usually accompanied by the designation of God by the title al-Rabb, rendered by the modern Qur'ān translator Abdullah Yusuf Ali as "Cherisher and Sustainer." This translation reflects the word's root, which according to some interpreters has overtones of nurture and care as well as of ownership and lordship.[53] While the model of the royal audience emphasizes the elements of deference and hierarchy, that of the intimate conversation implies privacy and mutuality. Etymologically, the root n-j-w refers to a private communication, a confidence, or something that is whispered (for instance, in the Qur'ānic verses 20:62, 21:3, 9:78 and 43:80, where it is paired with the root s-r-r, "secret").

The morphological form of the term *munājāt* also implies a two-sided dialogue. These overtones could be theologically problematic for some thinkers, who emphasized that the mutuality and privacy of the encounter were not literal truths but imaginative aids to focused worship. Badr al-Dīn al-ʿAynī (d. 855/1451) writes in his commentary on al-Bukhārī that "*Munājāt* and *najwā* mean a secret [that is shared] between two people. . . . *Munājāt* with the Lord is a figurative expression (*majāz*), because evidence indicates that it cannot be interpreted literally, as there is perceptible speech only from the side of the worshiper." For al-ʿAynī the metaphor of "intimate conversation" serves to ensure the worshiper's appropriate physical orientation and posture, "even

52 al-Ghazālī, *Iḥyā'*, 1:173.

53 Qurṭubī, *Tafsīr*, 1:96 (commentary on verse 1:2). Sometimes the title "Rabb" is also linked with the verb *rabbā* (to raise, nurture); Murtaḍā al-Zabīdī includes *al-murabbī* as one of the meanings of *rabb* (*Tāj al-ʿarūs*, 2:281 [s.v. r-b-b]).

though God is exalted above [all spatial] directions, because external and internal comportment are interconnected."[54]

Authors of a more mystical or pietistic bent, in contrast, sometimes embraced the implication of a genuinely two-sided exchange between the worshiper and God. This idea, as well, has a basis in *ḥadīth*; in a report transmitted by Muslim in his *Ṣaḥīḥ* the Prophet relays a statement directly in the divine voice (a *ḥadīth qudsī*) in which God declares:

> I have divided prayer (*ṣalāt*) in two halves between Myself and My servant; My servant shall receive what he asks for. When the servant says, "Praise be to God, the Cherisher and Sustainer of the Worlds" [i.e., the first line of the Fātiḥa], God Most High says, "My servant has praised Me." When he says, "Most Gracious, Most Merciful," God Most High says, "My servant has extolled Me." When he says, "Master of the Day of Judgment," God Most High says, "My servant has glorified Me." . . . When he says, "You do we worship, and Your aid we seek," God Most High says, "This is shared between Me and My servant, and My servant shall receive what he asks for." When he says, "The way of those on whom You have bestowed Your grace, those who are not the object of [Your] wrath, and who go not astray," God Most High says, "This is for My servant, and My servant shall receive what he asks for."[55]

The great Andalusian Sufi master Ibn ʿArabī (d. 638/1240) writes about the silences between the verses of the first chapter of the Qurʾān, which must be recited in every canonical prayer,

> [The word] *munājāt* ("intimate conversation") is [of the form] *mufāʿala*, and *mufāʿala* is the action of two actors. . . . So when the servant says "Praise be to God, the Cherisher and Sustainer of the Worlds," God is listening when the servant makes this utterance, and when the servant finishes the verse he ought to listen and observe and be silent so that he can see what the Truth [i.e., God] says to him about that, out of courtesy towards the Truth. He should not interrupt Him when He is speaking; that is part of the etiquette of dialogues, and the Truth is most worthy that one be courteous towards Him. God says, "My servant has praised Me." There are those among God's servants who hear that statement with their [faculty of] hearing. If you do not hear it by means of your hearing, hear it by means of your faith in it; [God] has informed [you] of it. Similarly He speaks to you at every verse according to what that verse demands; it is courteous to be attentive to what the speaker says to you, whomever you may speak to intimately. . . . Know that someone who has no courtesy is not taken as a companion, a confidant or an intimate by kings.[56]

For some thinkers the prayer rite evoked a specific instance of intimate dialogue with God, rather than merely a generalized model. The scenario most often invoked is that of the Prophet's ascension to heaven (the *miʿrāj*), when he prostrated himself in close propinquity to the divine Throne. As we have seen, the *miʿrāj* is also understood by most scholars to be the occasion on which the five

[54] al-ʿAynī, *ʿUmdat al-qāri*, 4:149.
[55] Muslim, *Ṣaḥīḥ*, *Kitāb al-ṣalāt*, *Bāb wujūb al-Fātiḥa fī kull rakʿa*.
[56] Muḥyī al-Dīn Ibn al-ʿArabī, *al-Futūḥāt al-makkīya* (Beirut: Dār Ṣādir, n.d.), 1:413.

daily prayers were imposed on the Muslim community by God; thus, there is a strong connection between this event and the *ṣalāt* ritual. The Prophet is even held by some to have stated, "*Ṣalāt* is the *miʿrāj* of the believer." However, this report was never supplied with a chain of transmission (*isnād*) or recognized as a valid *ḥadīth* by authorities in that field. The statement itself, albeit without an attribution to the Prophet, appears in al-Rāzī's Qurʾān commentary.[57] Although al-Rāzī does not present it as a *ḥadīth* of the Prophet, it is conceivable that he was indirectly responsible for putting it into circulation as a *ḥadīth*; it is the commentary of Niẓām al-Dīn al-Nīsābūrī (d. 727/1327), which draws heavily on al-Rāzī, that seems to have popularized the attribution of this statement to the Prophet.[58]

A central element in the equation of *ṣalāt* with *miʿrāj* is the dialogue that, in some accounts of the *miʿrāj*, occurred between the Prophet and God at the apex of his ascent. In one version of the narrative the Prophet relates that when he prostrates himself before the divine Throne, God invites him to lift up his head and glorify Him. The Prophet raises his head and pronounces the first line of what would come to be the *tashahhud* performed in every prayer, "Blessed greetings and pure prayers belong to God!" God replies with the second line of the *tashahhud*, "Peace be upon you, O prophet, and the mercy and blessings of God!" The Prophet rejoins (as in the third line of the *tashahhud*), "Peace be upon us, and upon [all of] God's righteous servants." Finally the angels, witnessing this exchange between God and the Prophet, exclaim, "I testify that there is no god but God, and I testify that Muḥammad is His servant and messenger!'"– that is, the fourth line of the *tashahhud*.[59] This dialogue does not form part of the earliest or best-authenticated narratives of the *miʿrāj*, and has been rejected by some modern scholars as a piece of baseless folklore.[60] However, it seems to have been widely circulated and accepted, even by some scholars, in the centuries following al-Rāzī.[61] Al-Rāzī writes of this exchange,

[57] Rāzī, *Tafsīr*, 1:275.

[58] Niẓām al-Dīn Muḥammad ibn al-Ḥusayn al-Qummī al-Nīsābūrī, *Gharāʾib al-qurʾān wa-raghāʾib al-furqān*, ed. Ibrāhīm ʿAṭwa ʿAwaḍ (Cairo: Sharikat Maktabat wa-Maṭbaʿat Muṣṭafā al-Bābī al-Ḥalabī wa-Awlādihi bi-Miṣr, 1981/1962), 1:115. For a description of this *tafsīr* (and its dependence on al-Rāzī) see Kristin Zahra Sands, *Ṣūfī Commentaries on the Qurʾān in Classical Islam* (London: Routledge, 2006), pp. 77–8.

[59] See, for instance, the translation by A. P. Courteille and A. Arnot in *Turkish Literature, Comprising Fables, Belles-Lettres, and Sacred Traditions*, rev. ed. (New York: Colonial Press, [1901]), pp. 208–9.

[60] Its authenticity is briskly dismissed in a fatwa by the Saudi Permanent Council for Scientific Research and Legal Opinions, available online at www.islamqa.com/ar/ref/117604 (accessed May 24, 2011). For a survey of the historical development of *miʿrāj* narratives see Frederick S. Colby, *Narrating Muḥammad's Night Journey: Tracing the Development of the Ibn ʿAbbās Ascension Discourse* (Albany: SUNY Press, 2008).

[61] For instance, the Ḥanafī jurist al-Bābartī notes that in the *tashahhud* one says "Peace upon you, O prophet" as a report (*ḥikāya*) of what God said to the Prophet on the night of the *miʿrāj*, and that because the Prophet praised God in three different ways, God responded to him with three different things (al-Bābartī, *ʿInāya*, 1:260).

When God blessed Muḥammad (peace be upon him!) by raising him to two bows' lengths [from the divine Presence, cf. Qur'ān 53:9], at that time he said, "Blessed greetings and pure prayers belong to God!" *Ṣalāt* is the *miʿrāj* of the believer, so when in his *miʿrāj* the believer reaches the utmost extent of being honored – which is that he sits before God [at the end of the prayer] – it is obligatory to recite the words that Muḥammad mentioned; he, too, recites the greetings, and this becomes like a reminder that this *miʿrāj* that has come to pass for him is a flame from the sun of the *miʿrāj* of Muḥammad and a drop from his sea.[62]

Prayer as communication

On an abstract level both the "royal audience" model of *ṣalāt* and the overlapping "intimate conversation" model are dependent on a very fundamental assumption about the nature of prayer: that it is in some sense a form of communication, combining verbal and nonverbal elements, and that it can thus be analyzed in terms of its effectiveness in expressing certain contents vis-à-vis the divine addressee. Although (as we have seen) not all ritual actions were seen as having inherent and universal meanings, there was a general consensus both that the actions of *ṣalāt* were signifiers and about what they signified. The standing, bowing, and prostration involved in *ṣalāt* were understood by most classical Islamic thinkers to express the self-abasement of the worshiper and the exaltation of God, which were inseparable correlatives of each other. In the words of Ibn ʿAbd al-Salām al-Sulamī (d. 660/1262), "Standing [in prayer] is one of the modes of glorification (*taʿẓīm*), as are bowing and prostration . . . because glory entails lowliness and submission, so when [the worshiper] enters the realm of self-abasement he acknowledges that the object of his worship possesses the glory that requires that submission."[63]

Implicit in the assumption that *ṣalāt* is inherently a form of *taʿẓīm* (exaltation) is that it is a form of symbolic speech, even if it is one that is not exclusively performed through verbal utterance. As al-Rāzī writes about prostration, "an action can become meaningful by convention, like a [verbal] statement" (*al-fiʿl qad yaṣīr biʾl-muwāḍaʿa mufīdan kaʾl-qawl*).[64] Al-Ghazālī explores this issue in greater depth, beginning with the invocations and recitations involved in *ṣalāt*. He argues that there are only two possible assumptions about these utterances. The first is that they are performed for their own sake, simply for the discipline they impose upon the believer. He deems this assumption untenable because the utterances are not in themselves onerous, and thus involve no significant discipline. The second, which al-Ghazālī believes to be true, is that they are

[62] al-Rāzī, *Tafsīr*, 1:275.
[63] al-Sulamī, *Maqāṣid al-ṣalāt*, p. 17.
[64] al-Rāzī, *Tafsīr*, 2:213 (commentary on verse 2:34).

acts of communication and must be performed in such a way as to fulfill this function.

As for remembrance, it is a form of proximity (*mujāwara*) and intimate conversation (*munājāt*) with God; its objective is either being a form of address (*khiṭāb*) and dialogue (*muḥāwara*), or [the pronunciation of] the consonants and vowels as a trial for the tongue by performing the action, as the stomach and the genitals are tried by abstinence during fasting, and as the body is tried by the hardships of the *ḥajj*. . . . There is no doubt that this [second] alternative is false. How easy it is for an inattentive person to move his lips with nonsense; it involves no trial in its capacity as an action, rather, the objective is the letters in their capacity as a [meaningful] utterance (*nuṭq*), and it is not a meaningful utterance unless it expresses what is in the mind, and it does not express [what is in the mind] without the presence of the heart. What request is there in "Lead us on the straight path" [Qur'ān 1:6] if the heart is inattentive? And if he does not intend it to be an entreaty and a supplication, what hardship is there in moving the lips with it while being inattentive, especially after becoming accustomed to it?[65]

Al-Ghazālī then likens prayer to a speech act directed at another human being:

I say: If a person were to take an oath and say, "I will surely thank so-and-so, praise him, and ask him for something," and then the words indicating these meanings passed over his tongue while he was asleep, he would not have fulfilled his oath. If they passed over the tongue in the dark and that person was present but he did not know that he was present and did not see him, he would not have fulfilled his oath because his speech would not be an address and a meaningful utterance directed toward [that person], as long as [the addressee] was not present in his heart. [Even] if these words passed over his tongue when [the person] was present in the broad light of day, but he was inattentive because he was completely preoccupied with some other thought and he did not have the intention to direct the address to him when he spoke, he [still] would not have fulfilled his oath. There is no doubt that the objective of the recitation and invocations [performed in prayer] is thanks, praise, entreaty, and supplication, and that the addressee is God Most High.

While it may be obvious that the verbal invocations involved in *ṣalāt* are acts of communication, al-Ghazālī argues that this is also true of the physical postures:

As for bowing and prostration, the objective of them both is definitely (*qaṭ'an*) glorification.[66] If it were possible for [the person performing the prayer] to glorify God with his action while he was oblivious to Him (*ghāfil 'anhu*), it would be possible for him to be glorifying an idol placed before him while he was oblivious or for him to be glorifying the wall that was in front of him while he was oblivious. If [the actions of bowing and prostration] cease to be glorification, nothing remains but the motions of the back and the head; and these do not involve sufficient hardship to constitute discipline [in themselves].[67]

65 al-Ghazālī, *Iḥyā'*, 1:189–90.
66 Reading *ta'ẓīm* for *'aẓīm* in the printed edition.
67 al-Ghazālī, *Iḥyā'*, 1:190.

Al-Ghazālī's insistence on the centrality of intentionality and awareness to the validity of prayer derives not merely from his perspective as a mystic preoccupied with the experiential qualities of worship, but also from his training as a legal theorist well versed in a sophisticated theory of communication. Summarizing the postulates of the legal theorists' theory of language and communication, Mohamed Mohamed Yunis Ali observes that "for an utterance to merit interpretation, it must meet at least three conditions:

i it must be uttered intentionally;
ii it must be intended to a particular hearer or hearers; and
iii the hearer must be rational and able to understand it."[68]

Al-Ghazālī's analysis both applies this general linguistic theory to the utterances involved in *ṣalāt* and extends it to the nonverbal elements, which are similarly treated as communicative acts. Just as medieval Islamic jurists conceptualized the meaning of an utterance as inhering in the intent of the speaker, so al-Ghazālī locates the meaning of prayer in the conscious intent of the worshiper.

The functional equivalence of verbal and nonverbal communication is also suggested by the eleventh-century Ḥanafī legal theorist al-Sarakhsī, in connection with the distinctively Ḥanafī position that the opening *takbīr* of *ṣalāt* (*Allāhu akbar*, "God is most great") need not be performed in precisely these words or in Arabic. He writes:

> What is obligatory is to glorify God with the tongue, because from one point of view the tongue is one of the external limbs, and *ṣalāt* is the glorification of God with all of the limbs. Thus, each limb is associated with the [mode of] glorification appropriate to it, and glorification with the tongue can occur by means of [any] praise and remembrance.[69]

Like words, physical gestures such as prostration might have widely recognized meanings, but these were understood by most medieval Muslim thinkers to have originated in an ultimately arbitrary act of designation (*waḍʿ*), and thus to be inherently variable. The exegete al-Rāzī argues with regard to the Qurʾānic narrative in which the angels prostrate themselves to Adam at God's command that prostration is not inherently and invariably a form of worship. Since gestures (like words) gain their meanings from convention (*muwāḍaʿa*), it is quite possible that at some time prostration expressed social deference, rather than worship.[70] Furthermore, the meaning of such a gesture is determined not only by preexisting "linguistic" conventions, but by the intent of the author of the "utterance" (i.e., the person performing the gesture). (The two are intimately linked by the fact that rational speakers use the established meanings of words to communicate their intentions.) Thus, some jurists argue that – while deeply

[68] Ali, *Medieval Islamic Pragmatics*, p. 42.
[69] Muḥammad ibn Aḥmad al-Sarakhsī, *Uṣūl al-Sarakhsī*, ed. Abū'l-Wafāʾ al-Sarakhsī (Hyderabad: Lajnat Iḥyāʾ al-Maʿārif al-Nuʿmānīya, n.d.), 2:169–70.
[70] al-Rāzī, *Tafsīr*, 2:213.

sinful – it does not constitute disbelief to prostrate oneself to a human king or dignitary as long as one intends it as a greeting, rather than an act of worship.[71]

As we have seen, the central significance attributed to the utterances and actions of *ṣalāt* by classical theorists is glorification or exaltation (*taʿẓīm*). On one level, *taʿẓīm* can be understood as a meaning, similar to the lexical meaning of a word. On another, medieval Islamic thinkers regarded it as (in modern terminology) a kind of speech act – that is, "exalting" may be seen as what one is *doing* by means of one's utterance. Thus, one might say number of different things by way of praise (*ʿalā wajh al-taʿẓīm*), just as one may say various things by way of welcoming, blaming, or ridiculing.

For medieval Islamic thinkers *taʿẓīm* was inextricably associated with a closely related kind of speech act, thanking (*shukr*). The intimate interconnection of the two concepts is suggested by al-Rāzī, who writes:

> Thanking consists of glorification (*taʿẓīm*). It has three components: one has to do with the heart, which is that he know that this benefaction is from Him and not from anyone else; the second [has to do] with the tongue, which is that he praise Him; and the third [has to do] with action, which is that he serve Him and humble himself to Him. *Ṣalāt* comprises all of these elements.[72]

We have seen that, for Muʿtazilīs, thanking a benefactor was one of the actions whose moral goodness was intellectually axiomatic. The concept of "thanking" played a particularly prominent role for those who sought a rational interpretation of the prayer ritual. Al-Qaffāl states succinctly, "As for prayer, its overall meaning is glorification of the Creator by means of various motions indicating self-abasement, in thanks to God for His favors."[73] He elaborates on this point by emphasizing the involvement of the entire body – the body itself being both a manifestation of divine beneficence and the instrument of human responses to it:

> The meaning of prayer refers to … humbling oneself (*tadhallul*) to God by performing motions of exaltation (*ḥarakāt al-taʿẓīm*) with the entire body, in thanks to God for the favors that He initiated with respect to the person praying, because He created him in a form that is appropriate for legal responsibility (*al-taklīf*), made him capable of performing actions (*tarkīb al-fiʿl fīhi*), and gave him a power by virtue of which he could be tested and by which he could perform the thanks of the benefactor that is incumbent upon him.[74]

Here, interestingly, *ṣalāt* is not simply a response to all of the various blessings that God has bestowed. Rather, it focuses specifically on the bestowal of the human body and its capacity for action. One prays with the whole body in

[71] *al-Mawsūʿa al-fiqhīya*, art. "*sujūd*," paragraph 11 (24:211; with reference to *al-Fatāwā al-hindīya*).
[72] Rāzī, *Tafsīr*, 32:129 (commentary on verses 108:1–2).
[73] Shāshī, *Maḥāsin*, p. 29.
[74] Ibid., p. 77.

acknowledgment that God has provided us with a body which is the means to moral agency and thus obedience to God.

The most extensive exposition of this understanding of prayer was produced by the great twelfth-century Ḥanafī jurist ʿAlāʾ al-Dīn al-Kāsānī, who offers it in his classic legal manual as one of the rational proofs for the obligatory nature of the five daily prayers. Al-Kāsānī, an outspoken opponent of the Muʿtazila, presumably regards the obligation to thank as being ultimately rooted in the arbitrary divine decree; however, based on that premise he offers a logical analysis of the relationship between gratitude to God and the actions of prayer:

One of [the rational proofs] is that these prayers are obligatory simply as thanks for benefactions (*niʿam*), including the benefaction of the way in which humans were created (*al-khilqa*), since [God] favored the human substance by forming it in the best form and stature, as God said, "He shaped you, and shaped you well" [Qurʾān 40:64] and "We indeed created humankind in the best stature" [Qurʾān 95:4]. ... [Also among the blessings for which one gives thanks through prayer] is the benefaction of the limbs' being sound and free of defects, because it is by means of them that one is capable of filling one's needs. God gave [the human being] all of that as a pure benefaction without his having previously done anything to merit any of that. Thus, he was commanded to use this blessing in the service of the benefactor in thanks for His benefaction, because giving thanks for a benefaction means using it in the service of the benefactor. Then, prayer combines the use of all the visible limbs, including standing, bowing, prostration, sitting, placing the hands in the right places, and restraining the eye, and also of the interior faculties,[75] including the occupation of the heart with the intent, and making it feel fear and hope, the focusing of the mind and the intellect on glorification and exaltation (*al-taʿẓīm waʾl-tabjīl*), in order that the work of each member will be thanks for what [God] bestowed on him with respect to that [member]. These [benefactions] include the blessing of flexible joints and obedient limbs by virtue of which he is able to use them in various situations, including standing, sitting, bowing and prostration; prayer encompasses [all] of those situations.[76]

Ṣalāt as an exercise in self-discipline

The "royal audience" model of prayer and its various modulations envision *ṣalāt* as an interpersonal encounter between the worshiper and God. An alternative model deemphasizes the bilateral nature of this encounter in order to focus on its inner dynamic as an act of self-mastery. The relevant hierarchy is no longer exclusively external (the lowly creature bowing before the supreme King), but also – and perhaps just as saliently – internal (the higher spiritual and intellectual faculties exercising authority over the individual's unruly impulses and desires). This model is associated both with the philosophical and with the mystical traditions, which intersect extensively despite their

[75] Lit., "interior limbs," *al-jawāriḥ al-bāṭina*.
[76] al-Kāsānī, *Badāʾiʿ al-ṣanāʾiʿ*, 1:280–1.

contrasting points of view on many individual issues; Muslim proponents of *falsafa* were sometimes deeply informed by mysticism, while Sufis often borrowed freely from *falsafa* even while some of them condemned it in principle.

Both Sufism and the Greek and Arabic philosophical thought by which the Sufi tradition was partially informed imagined the human person as complex and fragmented, rather than as an unproblematically unitary agent. Somewhat like modern psychoanalysis, both disciplines envision the psyche as having a dynamic inner life in which mutually conflicting (and hierarchically ordered) faculties compete for dominance. In this drama the *nafs* or "lower soul" functions as the locus of passions and desires and threatens to control and indulge the individual's senses and bodily members. The animalistic nature of the *nafs* is countered by the spiritual nature of the *qalb* (heart), whose dominance of the psyche and thus of the body will lead to the wise use of a person's faculties in the service of God. The physical body is lower still, and requires careful regulation and subordination by the intellect and spirit.

The prayer ritual was analyzed according to a version of this model by al-Ḥakīm al-Tirmidhī, a controversial mystic of the third–fourth/ninth–tenth century.[77] Al-Tirmidhī creatively mingled a number of trends in early Islamic piety and thought. He combined a commitment to the discipline of *ḥadīth* (and an affinity with Ḥanbalism) with a penchant for speculative interpretation of revealed texts; he borrowed discernibly from Shīʿī thought while rejecting Shīʿism, and "denounced philosophy, at least that of others, and accepted the cognomen of al-Ḥakīm ["the Sage"], evidently in the sense of monotheist and Muslim philosopher."[78] On one level al-Tirmidhī's interpretation of *ṣalāt* parallels the "royal audience" model by positing that canonical prayer is a periodic reaffirmation of the individual's covenantal commitment to the Lord, and an apology and expiation for the acts of disobedience and ingratitude that have occurred since the previous prayer.[79] Thus, for instance, the *takbīr* reaffirms the incomparable greatness of God after the servant's disobedience has expressed a misguided sense of his own grandeur.[80]

However, according to al-Tirmidhī the greater part of the drama of prayer transpires among the different components and faculties of the individual. He explains that the objective of Qurʾānic recitation in prayer is to exhort the lower soul (*nafs*). This contributes to the role of prayer in renewing the

77 For a general discussion of al-Tirmidhī and a description of his analysis of the "human organism and faculties" see *EI*^{2}, art. "al-Tirmidhī, Abū ʿAbd Allāh Muḥammad ibn ʿAlī al-Ḥakīm" (by Y. Marquet).

78 Ibid.

79 Muḥammad ibn ʿAlī al-Ḥakīm al-Tirmidhī, *Kitāb Ithbāt al-ʿilal*, ed. Khālid Zahrī (Rabat: Jāmiʿat Muḥammad al-Khāmis, Kullīyat al-Ādāb waʾl-ʿUlūm al-Insānīya, 1998), pp. 91–2.

80 Ibid., p. 97.

covenant between the worshiper and God, as it establishes God's proof (*ḥujja*) against the soul:

The Qurʾān is in the chest (*al-ṣadr*), and the chest is the domain of the heart, and the lower soul (*nafs*) is devoid of all of that. [God] commanded that [the worshiper] bring [the Qurʾān] forth from the heart and the chest to his tongue in recitation, so that his ear will hear and those exhortations will be transmitted to his "soul that commands evil" [cf. Qurʾān 12:53] . . . so that God's proof will be established against him. If it were not for that, the lower soul would be devoid of the knowledge of the next world that is in the heart and the chest.[81]

This process of instructing the *nafs* through Qurʾānic recitation in prayer is necessary because the *nafs* receives sensory data under the direction of the mind (*dhihn*), while the heart receives knowledge of the divine under the direction of the intellect (*ʿaql*), "So the mind is the director of the *nafs*, and the intellect is the director of the heart, and the heart seeks its Lord, and the *nafs* seeks its pleasure and desire. Whichever one of them prevails, the limbs are subordinate to it."[82] The "limbs" (*jawāriḥ*) to which al-Tirmidhī refers are both the extremities and organs of the physical body and the senses. The ritual of prayer serves to bring them back into their proper subordination to the higher faculties. He writes:

As for the rationale of *ṣalāt*, the "standing" (*qiyām*) is the surrendering of the lower self (*nafs*) to God Most High, because when [the worshiper] neglected his limbs they went forth to pursue their pleasures and desires in ways that they were not given permission to do, so he brought them to renew his surrender. . . . [*Ṣalāt*] is [God's] covenant with which He bound him, and with which He bound his seven limbs: the hearing, the sight, the tongue, the stomach, the genitals, the hand, and the foot.[83]

Al-Tirmidhī continues:

These seven limbs were commended to you as a trust (*amāna*), and you were commanded to guard them and made responsible to tend to them; if a shepherd neglects his sheep, he is taken to account, punished, and fined. When you get up in the morning, each of your limbs goes forth to graze in its own valley – the hearing in the valley of listening to sounds, the sight in the valley of looking at colors, the tongue in the valley of speech, and so on with each limb.[84]

It is through prayer and self-exhortation that one tends, nourishes, and heals the "flock" that constitutes one's physical and sensory self, an image that al-Tirmidhī develops at length.

In another metaphor al-Tirmidhī likens the *nafs* to a debtor for whom one has guaranteed a debt to a third party. Repayment is being demanded from you as

81 Ibid., pp. 100–1.
82 Ibid., p. 101.
83 Ibid., p. 91.
84 Ibid., p. 93.

guarantor, and you must attempt to extract the money from the *nafs* in order to pay it to the creditor, for "the heart is the partner (*sharīk*) of the *nafs* in good and evil, reward and punishment, praise and blame." Meanwhile, the intellect (*'aql*) plays the role of the debt collector.[85] Even in this less complex scenario the human being is not an unproblematic individual, but an unruly partnership whose members are constantly at odds due to their different proclivities and goals.

Al-Ḥakīm al-Tirmidhī was an eccentric and controversial figure in his own time, and few Muslims of later centuries claim him explicitly as a central religious authority. However, his direct and indirect influence was considerable. Al-Ghazālī reproduces the scenario of the debtor *nafs* and the guarantor heart so precisely that it clearly derives from al-Tirmidhī, although he does not identify a source.[86] The Sufi, *muḥaddith*, and jurist Quṭb al-Dīn al-Qasṭallānī (d. 686/1287) does name al-Tirmidhī as one of his major predecessors (along with al-Qaffāl al-Shāshī) in writing about the rationales of the sharia, and particularly of prayer.[87] He provides a highly elaborated version of al-Tirmidhī's model of seven refractory "limbs" pictured as animals under the pastoral care of the heart.[88]

The motif of the heart subduing the lower soul and the passions is one facet of a broader philosophico-mystical approach to *ṣalāt* as a form of discipline or training (*siyāsa*, *riyāḍa*). Another early and influential example of this approach appears in the "Epistles of the Brethren of Purity" (*Rasā'il Ikhwān al-Ṣafā*), an anonymous tenth-century compilation of treatises that encyclopedically surveys the intellectual and religious sciences. It is deeply informed by the amalgam of Aristotelian and Platonic thought that characterized early Islamic *falsafa*, but also reflects other influences. The Brethren identify with Sufism (*taṣawwuf*) and admiringly cite the stories of ascetics and mystics as exemplars of self-mastery and spiritual purification. They are also clearly Shī'ites who follow an imām possessing esoteric knowledge, and share many traits with the Ismā'īlīs who were so religiously and intellectually influential in their day.[89] In the neo-Platonic schema advanced by the Brethren, the cosmos issues forth from the First Cause in a descending chain of emanation beginning with the First Intellect and extending down to the planetary spheres, the sublunar world, the four elements, and the animal and mineral kingdoms. The goal of the human being, a microcosm of this entire schema, is to reascend to the spiritual realm

[85] Ibid., p. 109.
[86] al-Ghazālī, *Iḥyā'*, 1:100.
[87] Quṭb al-Dīn al-Qasṭallānī, *Marāṣid al-ṣalāt fī maqāṣid al-ṣalāt*, ed. Maḥmūd 'Abd al-Raḥmān 'Abd al-Mun'im (Cairo: Dār al-Faḍīla, n.d.), p. 31.
[88] Ibid., pp. 32–3.
[89] For a recent and accessible survey of the evidence about the identity and beliefs of the Ikhwān al-Ṣafā see Godefroid de Callataÿ, *Ikhwan al-Safa': A Brotherhood of Idealists on the Fringe of Orthodox Islam* (Oxford: Oneworld, 2005), particularly pp. 1–16.

through self-refinement and intellectual insight into the true nature of the One. Only an initiated elite is capable of this ascent; the larger mass of ordinary humans is governed by divinely revealed, concrete rules that order their individual and social lives.

The Brethren introduce the subject of ritual worship in the context of their dichotomy between ordinary humans ("the children of this world") and the spiritual–intellectual elite ("the children of the next world"):

> Know, my brother (may God support you and us with a spirit from Him! [cf. Qur'ān 58:22]) that the moral characteristics of the children of this world are those that nature embedded in their dispositions without acquisition, choice, thought, reflection, exertion or effort on their part; they pursue them and act according to them like beasts in seeking the benefits of their bodies and warding off harm from them, as God said: "They eat as cattle eat, and the Fire will be their abode" [Qur'ān 47:12]. As for the moral characteristics of the children of the next world, they are those that they have acquired by their [own] exertions, either on the basis of intellect, thought, and reflection, or by following the commandments of the Law (*al-nāmūs*) and its discipline (*ta'dīb*), as we shall explain; then [these characteristics] become habitual for them through their long persistence in them and the frequency of their practicing them; according to them they are recompensed and rewarded.[90]

The provisions of the divine/cosmic law serve to mold the human character by instilling desirable traits through constant repetition. The disciplinary function of the law lies in its pervasive demands for the control and frustration of impulses and desires. One who contemplates the Law (*nāmūs*) will observe that

> most of its commandments are in opposition to that which is in people's natures, and its prohibitions are against [the tendency] implanted in their dispositions to pursue pleasures and seek comfort, ease, and enjoyment. ... That is, that it commands fasting and refraining from eating and drinking when hunger and thirst are intense, ablutions when it is cold, getting up to pray and leaving off sleeping in a comfortable bed, sharing one's possessions when in scarcity and great need, remaining chaste when desire is aroused, clemency when assailed by anger, [etc.].[91]

However, it is difficult to discipline one's passions and desires. It is for this reason that God sent prophets who instituted revealed laws, including acts of worship:

> So they built temples, mosques, churches, places of prayer, and houses of worship for them, and commanded them to enter them after performing ablutions, cleansing themselves, and donning fine garments, with serenity, dignity, good comportment, piety, humility, proclamation of glory and seeking of forgiveness, and refraining from things that were [otherwise] permissible to them and acceptable for them to do in their homes, markets, gatherings, and paths – all of that in order to be an indication for every rational

[90] *Rasā'il Ikhwān al-ṣafā wa-khillān al-wafā'* (Beirut: Dār Ṣādir, 2006), 1:332–3.
[91] Ibid., 1:333.

> and discerning person that this is the way a person ought to behave who wishes to enter paradise and elevate his spirit into the kingdom of the heavens, as long as he lives and all the days of his life, so that it will become a habit, a disposition, and an established nature for him. . . . If any rational person ponders the sermons that he hears from the pulpits in all faiths and religious communities (*kull al-diyānāt waʾl-milal*) on holidays and sabbaths (*al-jumuʿāt*), the truth of what we have said and the correctness of what we have described will become clear to him.[92]

In this view, rites of prayer (as performed in designated places of worship) are limited and repetitive exercises in the kind of self-purification and self-restraint that the true philosopher would practice at all times on the basis of his abstract insight. They provide an arena in which strict behavioral norms – forbidding every activity not involved in the rites of worship themselves – can be practiced on a regular basis and on a manageably limited scale. They allow ordinary individuals to master by habituation the virtues necessary to embark on the upward spiritual journey.

In keeping with this view of prayer as an exercise in self-mastery, the Brethren also treat the issue of ritual worship within a discussion of different forms of discipline or training (*siyāsāt*). In this passage the Brethren distinguish between two kinds of worship (*ʿibāda*). Exterior acts of worship are relegated to a lower echelon among the means of spiritual refinement, below purely philosophical reflection. According to this epistle the first form of worship is "the form established by the divine Law [that is achieved] through following the bringer of the law (*al-sharʿīya al-nāmūsīya biʾttibāʿ ṣāḥib al-nāmūs*), obeying his commands and prohibitions." This category includes all of the formal acts of worship required by the sharia, which are identified by their conventional Islamic names, although it is not clear that these terms are intended to refer exclusively to their Islamic forms: "sacrifices, acts of worship, ablutions, prayers (*al-ṣalawāt*), fasting (*al-ṣawm*), almsgiving (*al-zakāt*), pilgrimage (*al-ḥajj*), struggle in the service of the faith (*jihād*), traveling to places of visitation and pure locations, affirming [the truthfulness] of God's books, messengers, angels, and revelation." The second category of worship is "divine philosophic worship" (*al-ʿibāda al-falsafīya al-ilāhīya),* which is defined simply as "affirmation of the oneness of God."[93]

While it might be supposed that pure philosophic worship would supersede the external acts of devotion known at second hand through God's messengers, the epistle is at pains to dispel this impression – whether straightforwardly or as a prudential concession to Islamic normativity, is difficult to determine. It proceeds:

92 Ibid., 1:335–6.
93 Ibid., 4:261–2.

Know, O brother, that if you fall short in the worship prescribed by the divine law (*al-ʿibāda al-sharʿīya*), you must not embark on any part of philosophic worship; otherwise you will be ruined and ruin others, go astray and lead others astray. That is because acting according to the divine Law (*al-sharīʿa al-nāmūsīya*), fulfilling the acts of worship required by it, and remaining obedient to its bringer (peace be upon him!) [is submission, *islām*[94]], and engaging in divine philosophical worship is faith (*īmān*), and a believer is not a [true] believer until he is a submitter [see Qurʾān 49:14].[95]

Here philosophy (much like the Sufi path, for mystical adepts) is the depth dimension that exceeds and completes obedience to the letter of the law without displacing it. The primary distinction between conventional Islamic acts of worship and their philosophic counterparts, according to this epistle, is that the latter are far more demanding. Philosophical worship demands "restraining the lower soul (*nafs*) from beloved things of all kinds, abandoning concessions (*al-rukhṣa*) to partake of any of them, and attaining to comprehension of the truths of all existent things."[96]

One might expect that "philosophic worship" would be strictly a matter of abstract contemplation. However, to the extent that the Brethren provide any specifics (albeit only with respect to the initial levels of philosophical training), it closely parallels the rites of worship prescribed by revealed texts. The major distinction, in addition to its enhanced rigor, would appear to be an explicit focus on the contemplation of the heavens.[97] Although the physical and external acts of worship imposed by the divine law are theoretically inferior to abstract contemplation, they are rendered necessary by the imperfection of the human constitution. In a debate between animals and humans at another place in the *Rasāʾil*, it is argued by a spokesman of the animals that *ṣalāt* is necessary only as a remedy for the moral failings with which human beings (unlike animals) are afflicted, likening its physical motions to the calisthenics prescribed by a doctor. Like the latter, external prayer is necessary only because people are morally "sick." Similarly, congregational worship would not be necessary if people (like animals) naturally lived in cooperation and harmony.[98]

Despite the small number and religious marginality of the Brethren of Purity themselves, their Epistles were widely circulated for centuries, even in Sunnī circles. Recent scholarship has demonstrated the degree to which they influenced later Islamic thinkers, even those who overtly decried their teachings (as was the case with al-Ghazālī).[99] In any case, their framing of Islamic rituals

94 This addition appears to be implied by the context.

95 Ibid., 4:262.

96 Ibid., 4:263.

97 Ibid., 4:263–5.

98 Ibid., 2:324, 326, 328; see Crone, *God's Rule*, p. 209.

99 See de Callataÿ, *Ikhwan al-Safa'*, pp. 107–11; cf. Martin Whittingham, *al-Ghazālī and the Qurʾān: One Book, Many Meanings* (London: Routledge, 2007), p. 69.

as concentrated exercises in self-control reflected a broader and preexisting trend that would prove attractive to many later Islamic thinkers. Al-Ghazālī himself accepted this model with respect to other Islamic rituals, although (as we have already seen) in the case of *ṣalāt* he did not consider the physical requirements of the rite sufficiently onerous to justify its interpretation as an exercise in discipline and self-denial.[100]

A more sophisticated mystico-philosophic account of prayer is attributed to a scholar who was influenced in his youth by the *Epistles of the Brethren of Purity*, Ibn Sīnā (d. 428/1037, the Avicenna of the Western tradition). Like the Brethren, Ibn Sīnā combined a neo-Platonic emanationist cosmology with a commitment to Islamic belief and the Qurʾānic revelation. Ibn Sīnā's views on prayer are set forth in a manuscript preserved in Cairo entitled *al-Ṣalāt wa-asrāruhā* (Prayer and its secrets).[101] Whether or not the epistle in question was actually authored by Ibn Sīnā, it uses authentically Avicennan categories and terminology and thus usefully reflects the application of his ideas to *ṣalāt*.

Ibn Sīnā (or the author of the work, if it is pseudonymous) begins his explanation of *ṣalāt* against the background of his cosmology and anthropology, which are interlinked because for him the human being is both the objective (*fāʾida*) of creation and its microcosm (*al-ʿālam al-aṣghar*). He recounts that God created animals (*al-ḥayawān*) after creating (in chronological sequence, and in descending order of rank): the intellects that are perfect in themselves (*al-ʿuqūl al-kāmila bi-dhātihā*), the abstract souls (*al-nufūs al-mujarrada*), the planets (*al-kawākib*), the celestial spheres (*al-aflāk*), the four elements (*al-arkān*), minerals, and plants. When He was completing His creation, he wanted to finish it with the most perfect species just as He had begun it with the most perfect genus, so He finished creation with the human being (*al-insān*) just as He had begun it with the Intellect.[102] Human beings are ranked, just as all extant beings are ranked in creation. Some human beings behave in an angelic way, and others in a satanic way. This is because the human being was not created out of one thing, so that its status would be uniform; rather, it was composed of disparate elements. Most basically, there are two aspects of the human being, the spirit and the body. The external or bodily aspect is adorned with the five senses; the inner, spiritual aspect is governed by the intellect.[103]

The dichotomy between body and spirit cross-cuts a three-tiered division of the human being into natural, animal, and human elements. God placed the

[100] Cf. al-Ghazālī, *Iḥyāʾ*, 1:189.

[101] al-Ḥusayn ibn ʿAbd Allāh ibn Sīnā, *al-Ṣalāt wa-asrāruhā*, MS Cairo, Dār al-Kutub, Ḥikma wa-Falsafa 389.

[102] For a chart enumerating the elements of Ibn Sīnā's cosmos in order of rank, based on several of his major works, see Peter Heath, *Allegory and Philosophy in Avicenna (Ibn Sînâ)* (Philadelphia: University of Pennsylvania Press, 1992), pp. 171–2.

[103] See ibid., p. 52.

natural (*ṭabīʿī*) soul in the liver; its function is to digest and expel, and to maintain the body through dissolution and nutrition. He linked the animal (*ḥayawānī*) soul with the (physical) heart; it is associated with the powers of anger and desire. It is the source of the five senses and the seat of imagination (*khiyāl*) and motion. Then God placed the rational human soul (*al-nafs al-insānīya al-nāṭiqa*) in the brain, the highest place in the human body, and put it in charge of reflection, retention, and recollection (*al-dhikr*).[104] By means of these three spirits the human being partakes of the different elements of the cosmos; it shares the animal spirit with animals, the natural spirit with plants, and the human spirit with angels. Each spirit has its own nature and action that is appropriate to it, and any one of them may predominate in a given individual. The benefit of the natural power is the growth and health of the body, and that of the animal power is the preservation of the body through self-defense and of the species through reproduction. Neither the natural nor the animal spirit is resurrected, experiences an afterlife, or receives divine reward (*thawāb*) for its actions; their benefits are exhausted in this life.[105] In contrast, the function of the rational human spirit (*al-nafs al-insānī al-nāṭiq*) is to meditate on the Creator (*al-taʾammul fīʾl-ṣāniʿ*), to ponder the wonders of creation (*al-tafakkur fī al-badāʾiʿ*), and to orient itself toward what is above (*al-tawajjuh ilā al-aʿlā*). It has no business with eating, drinking, or sexual intercourse. Its mission is to purify (or, perhaps, to abstract) physical things and to comprehend rational things (*taṣfiyat al-maḥsūsāt wa-idrāk al-maʿqūlāt*). The human spirit is distinguished by God with a unique power, that of rationality (*al-nuṭq*).

The objective of human existence is to progress upward through these levels, and rituals of worship are means toward this end. Through contemplation a person can recognize that the most perfect things in creation are the heavenly bodies, because they are the furthest from corruption, turbidities (*al-kudūrāt*), and composite things; he will find that in terms of its eternity (*baqāʾ*) and rationality (*nuṭq*), his rational soul (*al-nafs al-nāṭiqa*) resembles those bodies, and he will consider the Creator, which will lead him to ponder the stages of emanation (*fayḍ*) involved in creation. This will lead to a longing for the stations of the higher levels of emanation, which will lead the person to constant remembrance, prayer, and fasting. These actions have much (otherworldly) reward, since the human soul has intentions (*nawāyā*) that remain after the corruption of the body and do not wear out with the passage of time. After death it will be separated from the body and joined to those spiritual substances; its reward will be according to its actions. If its intellect was perfect and its human spirit predominated in this life, it will experience great reward after death;

[104] For an overview of Ibn Sīnā's model of the three souls (natural or vegetable, animal, and rational) see ibid., pp. 60–5.

[105] See ibid., p. 55.

otherwise, if its natural and animal spirits prevailed, it will experience sorrow and loss.

The author of the epistle concludes, "The meaning of prayer (*ṣalāt*) is for the rational soul to become similar to the heavenly bodies and constantly serve the absolute Truth for eternal reward. The Messenger of God (peace be upon him!) said, 'Prayer is the pillar (*'imād*) of religion'; religion (*al-dīn*) is the purification of the human soul from satanic turbidities and human (*basharīya*) notions, and turning away from lowly accidents." The resemblance between the rational soul and the heavenly bodies is understood here in terms of abstract contemplation and knowledge; he further defines prayer as knowledge (*ma'rifa*, *'ilm*) of the Necessary Existent with a pure heart and a soul that is preoccupied with nothing else, and offers the further explanation that "the true meaning of prayer is to know God Most High in His unicity, the necessity of His being, the exaltation of His essence [above all physical qualities] (*tanazzuh dhātihi*)."

What is the connection, if any, between this highly rarified definition of *ṣalāt* and the prayer rite mandated by Islamic law? The author devotes the second section of the work to an exploration of the relationship between the two. He states that prayer (*al-ṣalāt*) has an exterior/apparent (*ẓāhir*) part and an interior/hidden (*bāṭin*) part; it is the interior part that is the true (*ḥaqīqī*) essence of prayer. The exterior aspect is that which is commanded by the divine law and known by description; its numbers and times are known and stipulated. It is described as being a form of discipline or of physical training (*siyāsa*, *riyāḍa*); it is associated with bodies because it is composite, made up of positions and elements, just as the body is compound. It was imposed by God "so that the world would be ordered." In contrast, "the second part, which is the true, interior [prayer]," involves "witnessing the Truth with the pure heart and the soul whose vision is stripped of [selfish] hopes; this part does not go the way of bodily numbers and palpable elements, but the way of pure thoughts and eternal souls." The author takes this to be the true referent of the Prophet's statement that "the person engaged in prayer is in intimate converse with his Lord," because

> It is not hidden from a rational person that intimate converse with the Lord cannot be by means of the physical limbs, neither is it by means of palpable tongues. . . . A physical body can only sit and converse with a being that is located in space, palpable to the senses and visible to the eye. Thus, the Prophet's statement must be interpreted to refer to the abstract, intellectual contemplation of the divine that occurs outside of the boundaries of space and time. Thus, it has become clear that true prayer is divine contemplation and pure worship.

So far, the two aspects of prayer sound completely disparate. However, the two are related because God instituted physical, external prayer to correspond to spiritual, internal prayer.

> The law follows the order of the intellect; when the Lawmaker saw that the intellect made true, abstract prayer (*al-ṣalāt al-ḥaqīqīya al-mujarrada*) – which is the gnosis (*ʿirfān*) and knowledge (*ʿilm*) of God – obligatory on the rational soul, He made prayer obligatory on his body in imitation of that prayer and composed it of perfectly ordered numbers in the best form and most perfect shape, so that bodies would conform to souls in worship even if they do not correspond to them in rank. The Lawmaker knew that not all people would ascend the ladders of the intellect, so they needed an obligatory bodily discipline and training (*siyāsa wa-riyāḍa badanīya taklīfīya*) that would contradict their natural whims.

What the body seeks from the active intellect by means of this external prayer is its own physical preservation from harm for the time it remains in this world. In contrast, the true, interior prayer that has no (physical) forms and involves no change is the entreaty (*taḍarruʿ*) of the rational soul that knows the unicity of God for the contemplation of the divine.

The author concludes by relating the two aspects of prayer to the differing natures and ranks of human beings, based on his emanatory schema. The two kinds of prayer are incumbent on different varieties of people, based on which of the three different souls prevails in them. People who are dominated by the natural or animal soul are in love with their bodies and preoccupied with their needs, and at best can be disciplined by the external kind of prayer. People who are dominated by their spiritual and rational powers, in contrast, are obligated to engage in the true, interior prayer. This was the kind of prayer that was made obligatory on the Prophet Muḥammad on the night of the *miʿrāj*. On that occasion he was freed of his body and his worldly attachments, and no traces of animal desires or natural needs remained with him, so he engaged in intimate colloquy with his Lord with his soul and intellect.[106] He said, "O Lord, I have felt a strange delight this night; give it to me and facilitate a way for me to attain delight at all times." So God commanded him to perform *ṣalāt*.

Unlike the Ikhwān al-Ṣafā, who distinguished between the canonical prayer imposed by revelation and the "philosophical" devotion rooted in the Greek tradition and aimed at abstract contemplation of the universe, Ibn Sīnā located both sides of the dichotomy (at least potentially) within the Islamic prayer rite. "True, interior prayer" is simply the depth dimension of *ṣalāt*, not a separate activity. However, the physical actions of prayer and the concrete parameters set by Islamic law are merely subordinate means to a more rarified end. As Jon McGinnis observes:

[106] In his work on the Prophet's ascent to heaven, the *Miʿrājnāmeh*, Ibn Sīnā writes: "Rationalists know that [the Prophet's] intention in that was not that it was a sensible [i.e., physical] journey, but rather that it was intelligible perception that he related allegorically [*ramzī*] in sensible language" (Heath, *Allegory and Philosophy*, p. 123).

By Avicenna's lights the proper good of the human is to perform that function or operation that is the human's most complete or perfect activity, namely, to theorize and to contemplate, and particularly to contemplate the best and most noble thing, namely, the Necessary Existent.[107]

Because of the inaccessibility of this objective to most ordinary people, Ibn Sīnā's framework (like that of the Ikhwān) is an elitist one; in prayer, as with all other aspects of religion, the commonality possess only the husk or outer form of religion.[108] It is significant that, although the essay on prayer depicts the Prophet receiving *ṣalāt* from God on the occasion of the *miʿrāj*, Ibn Sīnā's account of the Prophet's ascent to heaven in his *Miʿrājnāmeh* depicts his encounter with God in terms of pure contemplation; unlike in other accounts, there is no mention of prostration or any other concrete element of the Islamic prayer ritual.[109]

In contrast with the approach of mainstream Islamic jurists, Ibn Sīnā's thought reflects a radical devaluation of the body and of the duties obligatory upon the body.[110] From this point of view, his approach is diametrically opposed to those of (for instance) al-Qaffāl al-Shāshī and al-Kāsānī, who emphasize the role of physical acts of obeisance as responses to God's bestowal of a body that is beautiful in form and capable of ethical action. Legal scholars who interpret the motions and utterances of prayer as constituting an act of obedience encompassing the whole person including body, tongue, and mind (and sometimes as an expression of thanks for all of the various components of the human person) imply a holistic sense of selfhood. All of the limbs and faculties together constitute a single whole, which is fully engaged in the activity of prayer. In contrast, Ibn Sīnā – and the philosophical tradition that he represents – distinguishes between the physical and the spiritual, the exterior and the interior. In this dichotomy the intellectual and spiritual are unambiguously valorized above the bodily and material. The true, universal core of worship is an act of contemplation performed in the mind. Bodily exercises are not without value, but their importance lies in the cultivation of self-mastery on the path to the recognition of philosophic truths; they do not constitute an end in themselves. Much as was the case with the Brethren of Purity, Ibn Sīnā also offers a vision of ideal prayer that lacks any dimension of interpersonal encounter. Just as external prayer is a form of bodily discipline lacking any dialogic element, interior prayer is the abstract contemplation of an impersonal ultimate

107 Jon McGinnis, *Avicenna* (Oxford and New York: Oxford University Press, 2010), p. 210.

108 See Heath, *Allegory and Philosophy*, p. 119 (trans. of Ibn Sīnā's *Miʿrājnāmeh*).

109 See ibid., pp. 135–7.

110 Ibn Sīnā writes: "The nobility of human beings . . . lies in two things: the rational soul and the intellect. Neither of these two are from the world of corporal bodies [*ajsâm*]; rather, they are from the higher world. They are the governors [*mutaṣarrif*] of the body, not its resident [*sâkin*]" (Heath, *Allegory and Philosophy*, p. 115 [trans. of Ibn Sīnā's *Miʿrājnāmeh*]).

Being. His vision is highly hierarchical, but his philosophical elitism is divorced both from the political hierarchies of society and the physical gestures by which they are expressed.

Ṣalāt as a reflection of the cosmos

When Ibn Sīnā (or pseudo-Ibn Sīnā) suggests that God "composed [external prayer] of perfectly ordered numbers in the best form and most perfect shape, so that bodies would conform to souls in worship even if they do not correspond to them in rank," his comments appear to imply some sort of homology between the forms and numbers of the canonical prayers and the structure of the cosmos as he understood it. Both the Brethren of Purity and Ibn Sīnā view the human person as a microcosm and posit complex interrelationships between different levels of being. However, neither of them offers a detailed interpretation of the *ṣalāt* ritual based on these principles. For this, we must look to other thinkers.

One group that interpreted *ṣalāt* in cosmic terms was the Ismāʿīlī Shīʿites, who posited dual dimensions (exoteric and esoteric, *ẓāhir* and *bāṭin*) of religious meaning in both in the text of the Qurʾān and in religious law and ritual. In keeping with their overall interest in temporal cycles and the successive dispensations of series of prophets and imāms, Ismāʿīlī interpretations of *ṣalāt* focus particular attention on the daily cycle of prayers and its correspondences with the phases of history as they envision it. The religious theorist of the early Fāṭimid state in the fourth/tenth century, al-Qāḍī al-Nuʿmān, equates *ṣalāt* with the *daʿwa*, the religious "call" or mission on behalf of the Ismāʿīlī imāms. The *ādhān* summons believers to prayer as the *daʿwa* summons them to follow the imāms.[111] A person who does not perform *ṣalāt*, like a person who fails to acknowledge the rightful imām, stands outside of the covenant of faith.[112] The five daily prayers correspond to the missions of the five "resolute" prophets (*ūlāʾl-ʿazm*), with the noon prayer corresponding to Noah, *ʿaṣr* to Abraham, *maghrib* to Moses, *ʿishāʾ* to Jesus, and *fajr* to Muḥammad.[113] (Ordinarily the "resolute" prophets, identified with the *nāṭiq* or "law-giving" prophets, number seven; here, presumably to yield the requisite total of five, both Adam and al-Qāʾim, the imām who is to come, are excluded from the list.)

Al-Nuʿmān's system of correspondences is multidimensional and complex; for instance, having associated the Prophet Muḥammad with the dawn prayer as the fifth and final daily prayer, he later returns to argue that Muḥammad is first in the series (having been the first to establish the five daily prayers in their Islamic

[111] Abū Ḥanīfa al-Nuʿmān ibn Muḥammad, *Taʾwīl al-daʿāʾim*, ed. ʿĀrif Tāmir (Beirut: Dār al-Aḍwāʾ, 1415/1995), 1:175.

[112] Ibid., 1:186.

[113] Ibid., 1:177–8.

form) and thus corresponds to the first (noon) prayer. In this context he observes that the noon prayer consists of four *rakʿa*s, which correspond to the four Arabic letters of Muḥammad's name. Furthermore, he states that the noon prayer is performed at the beginning of seven hours of the daytime (presumably on the basis of the period of daylight being divided into twelve equal hours); these seven correspond to the four letters of Muḥammad's name plus the three letters in the name of the first imām, ʿAlī, as well as to the seven law-giving prophets (*nāṭiqīn*) and the seven legatees (*awṣiyā*ʾ) who followed them.[114] He further states that there are seven different modes of prayer (including, for instance, *jumʿa* prayers, festival prayers, and a sick person's prayer without bowing or prostration), each of them corresponding to a different law-giving prophet (*nāṭiq*). Just as the legal dispensation of each law-giving prophet differs in its details from the others, so do the details of the modes of prayer performed in each of these different situations. The seventh, and culminating, mode of prayer is the invocation of blessings on the Prophet Muḥammad (*al-ṣalāt ʿalā al-nabī*), which involves no physical actions, just as the dispensation of the final imām – al-Qāʾim, who will bring on the end times – will abolish all external obligations.[115]

Another leading exponent of Ismāʿīlī thought in the fourth/tenth century who was not specifically affiliated with the Fāṭimid state, Abū Yaʿqūb al-Sijistānī (or al-Sijzī), focuses attention on the esoteric knowledge provided by the imāms as much as on the obligation to recognize them. He reasons that God has conferred no greater blessing upon His creation than the bestowal of the intellect upon them; thus, it is incumbent upon them to praise Him. Because the intellect was the first light that appeared from God's word, it is obligatory to follow and obey it. The prayer (*ṣalāt*) imposed upon the body corresponds to this truth; specifically, al-Sijistānī portrays the dawn prayer (which is performed from the first appearance of the light to the rising of the sun) as thanks for the dawning of the intellect by which we can distinguish truth from falsehood and good from evil, and by which is it possible to escape from the darkness of nature and achieve eternal reward.[116]

Correspondingly, al-Sijistānī interprets the sunset prayer as thanks for God's gift of the *nafs*, which mediates between the light of the intellect and the darkness of nature (*al-ṭabīʿa*).[117] The evening (*ʿishā*ʾ) prayer corresponds to (and is performed in thanks for) the imāms who sustain the Prophet's message in the darkness of ignorance that arises after his time.[118] As for the individual

[114] Ibid., 1:183.
[115] Ibid., 1:181.
[116] al-Sijistānī, *Kitāb al-Iftikhār*, pp. 117–18.
[117] Ibid., p. 118.
[118] Ibid., p. 120.

postures of prayer, al-Sijistānī states that bowing corresponds to the *asās* (the "foundation," i.e., the legatee or imām) and prostration corresponds to the *nāṭiq* (the "speaker," i.e., the prophet).[119] Once again, there are fundamental homologies among the components of the human person, the postures of prayer, and the temporal cycles of the day and of human history. Specific to the Ismāʿīlī worldview, of course, is the role of the imāms and their representatives.

The Andalusian mystic Muḥyī al-Dīn Ibn ʿArabī (d. 638/1240) was among both the most controversial and the most broadly and lastingly influential of premodern Islamic thinkers. His vision of reality posits that the cosmos is an expression of the many names of God (as derived from the Qurʾān and *ḥadīth*), which issue forth from the undifferentiated oneness of the divine and are refracted in a state of multiplicity and imperfection in the perceptible world. Based on this theory, Ibn ʿArabī posits that each act of worship (*ʿibāda*) legislated by God is connected with a specific divine name or reality (*ḥaqīqa*). Correlating acts of worship with divine names places them in a structurally mediatory role in his overall schema, where all things are manifestations of the divine attributes, and where the realization of divine attributes within the human microcosm is the objective of the journey back to and within God that closes the circle of emanation. As a result of this link, the performance of that act of worship yields distinctive stations and gnoses in the heart of the worshiper and distinctive signs and wonders in his life in this world; in the afterlife it yields special ranks and ways of beholding God in paradise.

Citing a *ḥadīth* in which the Prophet declares, "Prayer is light, almsgiving is a proof, patience is an illumination, and the Qurʾān is evidence for you or against you," Ibn al-ʿArabī focuses on the linkage between *ṣalāt* and the divine name "The Light" (*al-nūr*), which is Qurʾānically based in verse 24:35 ("God is the light of the heavens and the earth"). Combining this identification with the *ḥadīth* stating that one who is engages in *ṣalāt* partakes in intimate conversation with God (*yunājīhi*), he writes that

> God engages in intimate conversation with him from His name "The Light," not from any other name. Just as light dispels every gloom, *ṣalāt* cuts off every other preoccupation, in contrast to all other activities. . . . For that reason, [*ṣalāt*] is light. By means of that [statement] God gives [the worshiper] the good tidings that when He engages in intimate conversation with him from His name "The Light," He is alone with him and removes every created thing by means of beholding Him while engaging in intimate conversation with Him.[120]

The divine name "The Light" has a special place in Ibn ʿArabī's cosmology, in which the universe is an infinitely unfolding manifestation of the divine names.

119 Ibid., p. 120.
120 Ibn ʿArabī, *Futūḥāt*, 1:256.

Light is pure, undifferentiated being; it is associated with spirit, and opposed to the comparative darkness, density, and multiplicity of entities further down his emanatory hierarchy of being.[121] The linkage between the canonical prayers and the divine name "The Light" plays a prominent role in Ibn ʿArabī's interpretation of the distribution of the five prayers over the daily cycle of light and darkness. Reinforcing the association between prayer and light with a focus on the position and visibility of the sun as the arbiter of daily prayer times, he cites a *ḥadīth* in which the Prophet declares, "You will see your Lord as you see the sun." Ibn ʿArabī notes that the time for the noon prayer starts when the sun begins to decline from the zenith. It is at this moment that the worshiper regards the sun with an awareness of separation, as it moves toward setting and concealing itself from him. He thus worships in lowliness, need, and brokenness, seeking witnessing (*mushāhada*) of God. He continues in this mode as the glow of sunset passes away and the light of the sun begins to be reflected by the stars, and implores and begs God until the break of dawn. At this point he witnesses the signs of acceptance and worships God in a spirit of thankfulness; the worship of thankfulness and joy continues until the sun again reaches the point of decline and he returns to the worship of patience and neediness in the anticipation of separation. The cycle of prayers thus reflects an alternation between thanks and need, favor and affliction, difficulty and ease.[122]

Up to this point it would appear that the sun and its illumination straightforwardly function within the cycle of the daily prayers as physical correlatives of the divine presence. Indeed, on one level this appears to be the model Ibn ʿArabī is following. His esoteric interpretation of the fact that one does not pray when the sun is precisely at its zenith is that

> The sun is the Truth [i.e., God], and prayer is intimate conversation (*al-munājāt*). When the Truth is manifested (*tajallā*), bewilderment and annihilation occur, and neither speech nor intimate conversation is appropriate. . . . You know that the servant is absent at the time of witnessing because he is overpowered by the Witnessed, so there is no conversation. At the time of the sun's zenith (*al-istiwāʾ*), your shadow disappears from you within yourself; your shadow is your reality (*ẓilluka ḥaqīqatuka*); the light has surrounded you from all sides and submerged you, and there is nothing specific for you to prostrate yourself to but that it is behind you as well as in front of you, to your right and your left, and above you.[123]

In this passage it would appear that high noon, the moment of most direct and overpowering illumination and exposure to the sun, is the apex of the cycle of prayer.

[121] See William C. Chittick, *The Sufi Path of Knowledge: Ibn al-ʿArabi's Metaphysics of Imagination* (Albany: SUNY Press, 1989), pp. 23, 223–4.
[122] Ibn ʿArabī, *Futūḥāt*, 1:390.
[123] Ibid., 1:397.

However, on another level Ibn ʿArabī appears to invert the identification between divine manifestation and the light of the sun in order to suggest that the culmination of the daily round of canonical prayers occurs in the hours of darkness. He states that just as God divided the cosmos (*al-ʿālam*) into three levels, He divided the times of prayer into three levels. The world of witnessing (*ʿālam al-shahāda*) is the world of sense perception and manifestation; it corresponds to those prayers that are performed in the daytime. Thus, when performing those prayers one relates to God on the basis of the indications of Him that are provided by the world of witnessing and sense perception and of the divine names (i.e., attributes) that are physically perceptible. In contrast, the unseen world (*ʿālam al-ghayb*) is the world of the intellect (*al-ʿaql*); it corresponds to the *ʿishāʾ* prayer and other prayers performed from the disappearance of the afterglow of sunset to the break of dawn. At these times the worshiper communes with God on the basis of the evidences and proofs of God that are provided by the unseen world, the intellect, and cogitation. These are special evidences that lead to special gnosis, and thus these nighttime prayers belong to the lovers of God who possess secrets and obscure sciences.

The third division is the world of imagination and of the "isthmus" (*ʿālam al-takhayyul waʾl-barzakh*),[124] which is where abstract meanings are concretized in physically perceptible forms. It is not part of the unseen world because the concepts are clothed in physical forms, and it is not part of the perceptible world because they are fundamentally abstract concepts whose appearance in these forms is purely contingent. (This world is often exemplified by the phenomenon of dreams.) The prayer times that correspond to this world are the sunset and dawn prayers, which are neither of the day nor of the night; they are "isthmuses" or liminal zones (*barzakhān*) between the two.[125]

Ibn ʿArabī's multiple interpretations of the daily cycle of prayer appear to be different refractions of a complex and esoteric whole that is not subject to simple systematization. His schema is further complicated by the fact that, while *ṣalāt* as an overall category corresponds to the divine name "The Light," he also posits that there is a divine name specific to each prayer time, and that a worshiper who completely fulfills the act of worship corresponding to that time will manifest the effects of that divine name. In setting forth the esoteric interpretation (*iʿtibār al-bāṭin*) of the principle that the call to prayer may be sounded only when the given prayer time has commenced, he states that every "time has a ruler (*sulṭān*) other than whom none rules it; the one who is ruled must know the identity of the ruler of the time, which is the divine name specific to that time." He asks rhetorically, "Reflect: is it correct for you to give thanks

124 For the concept of the *barzakh*, and the translation of "isthmus," see Chittick, *Sufi Path of Knowledge*, p. 14.

125 Ibn ʿArabī, *Futūḥāt*, 1:395–6.

before the beginning of the rule of the name 'The Benefactor' (*al-munʿim*)?" (The connection here, of course, is that one gives thanks for benefactions.) He continues by remarking, "If your present time is [characterized by] benefit (*idhā kāna waqtuka al-niʿma)*, and its time begins by its existing for you, you are called to thank the benefactor."[126] Ibn ʿArabī does not seem to specify the divine names that correspond to specific prayers, and it appears that the relationship between individual prayers and divine names may be contingent on the spiritual state of the individual worshiper.

Central to this schema is the concept of the *maqām*, the spiritual "station" along the mystical path. Ibn ʿArabī likens the transition from one prayer time to another, and thus from one divine attribute to another, to the transition from one mystical station to another. Each station involves distinctive rules of conduct (*ādāb*) toward God that the aspirant must master before being established within that station; in each station special ethical qualities are acquired. Ibn al-ʿArabī likens the *maqām*s to the various acts that are commanded by the sharia, including *ṣalāt*, mandatory almsgiving (*zakāt*), fasting (*ṣawm*), pilgrimage (*ḥajj*), and struggle in service of the faith (*jihād*). Each station also has a knowledge (*ʿilm*) that is specific to it.[127] Ibn ʿArabī's suggestion that each act of worship corresponds to a specific *maqām* parallels his statement about their correspondences with divine names, and suggests that the *maqām*s themselves must be closely associated with individual divine names. Thus, there are complex interrelations among different prayers, different spiritual stations, and different attributes of God.

It is characteristic of Ibn ʿArabī's system that it posits a dense set of correspondences among various levels of being, from the divine attributes to the constitution of the individual person. Thus, Ibn ʿArabī places the entire system of Islamic canonical prayer within a complex set of homologies among various elements of the cosmos (prominently including its temporal cycles) and various levels and aspects of the human microcosm. In one passage he establishes a correlation between the various varieties of prayer (such as the Friday prayer, the daily prayers, and the festival prayers), which he states to be eight in number, and the substance and attributes of the human being, which he states to be eight as well: "substance (*al-dhāt*), life, knowledge, will, speech, power, hearing, and sight." Finally, "As for the obligation-bearing organs – I mean those with which the human being performs those actions that he is obligated to perform or to refrain from – they are [also] eight: the ear, the eye, the tongue, the hand, the stomach, the genitals, the foot, and the heart."[128] There is thus an overall homology between the prayers mandated by God and the component

[126] Ibid., 1:401.
[127] Ibid., 1:392.
[128] Ibid., 1:387.

elements of the human being, both on the physical level (which is here defined by its capacity for ethical action) and on that of substance and attributes.

Ibn ʿArabī also posits a homology between the temporal cycle of the day and night, over which the five daily prayers are distributed, and the four basic component elements (or "quarters") of the human being: the external person (*ẓāhir*); the *bāṭin*, which is the heart (*qalb*); the subtle essence (*laṭīfa*), which is the spirit (*rūḥ*) which is addressed (by the divine command); and the natural constitution (*ṭabīʿa*). He draws a parallel between this quadripartite division and the four six-hour quarters of the day. In particular, he suggests a correspondence between the quarter of the day from dawn to noon, which has no prescribed prayer and thus may be devoted to religiously neutral (*mubāḥ*) mundane activities, and the *ṭabīʿa*, which operates according to its own nature (*ṭabʿ*) in a way that is neutral with respect to the divine law (*mubāḥan lahu*).[129] In another work he states that the five daily prayers correspond to the five elements in the human constitution: "the noon prayer is associated with light (*ṣalāt al-ẓuhr nūrīya*), the afternoon prayer with fire, the sunset prayer with water, the evening prayer with earth, and the dawn prayer with air."[130] Here the classical four elements of Aristotelian natural science are supplemented with light, the supreme element in Ibn ʿArabī's cosmos, which stands above the dark density of the physical world but also pervades it.[131]

Much of Ibn ʿArabī's attention is absorbed by the temporal cycles of the daily prayers, whose alternations of light and darkness and modulations of spiritual mood mesh well with his teachings about divine attributes and spiritual states. He also reflects at great length on the utterances and recitations involved in the *ṣalāt* ritual.[132] He appears less interested in speculation about the bodily motions of prayer, perhaps due to his relative devaluation of the sensorially perceptible aspects of existence. However, he does offer some interpretations of the concrete components of *ṣalāt*. He observes that canonical prayer combines all of the basic motions (*ḥarakāt*): the upright, corresponding to humanity, which is the posture assumed while performing the recitation; the horizontal, corresponding to animals, which is the posture assumed in *rukūʿ* while reciting invocations; and the inverted (*al-mankūsa*), corresponding to plants, which is the posture assumed in prostration in order to seek proximity to God.[133]

129 Ibid., 1:391.

130 Muḥyī al-Dīn Ibn ʿArabī, *Tanazzul al-amlāk min ʿālam al-arwāḥ ilā ʿālam al-aflāk* (Beirut: Dār al-Kutub al-ʿIlmīya, n.d.), p. 31.

131 See Chittick, *Sufi Path of Knowledge*, p. 13.

132 See Michel Chodkiewicz, *An Ocean without Shore: Ibn ʿArabî, the Book, and the Law*, trans. from the French by David Streight (Albany: SUNY Press, 1993), pp. 109–12.

133 Ibn ʿArabī, *Tanazzul al-amlāk*, p. 30. For another interpretation of the bodily motions of prayer in terms of the four elements see Aḥmad ibn ʿImād al-Aqfahsī, *Kashf al-asrār ʿammā khafiya ʿan al-afkār*, ed. Muḥammad Khair Ramaḍān Yūsuf (Beirut: Dār Ibn Ḥazm, 1426/2005), pp. 187–8.

As usual with Ibn ʿArabī, the correspondences between physical postures and elements of the cosmos are multiple and complex. Thus, he also characterizes the bowing position (*rukūʿ*) as a liminal zone (*barzakh*), likening it to the acquired existence enjoyed by the creature, which mediates between the necessary existence of God (represented by *qiyām*) and the possible existence, which is nonbeing in itself, that is inherent to the creature (represented by *sujūd*).[134] Michel Chodkiewicz notes that

> Once more referring to prophetic traditions, Ibn ʿArabî establishes an analogy between the lowering of the body toward the earth and the descent of God toward the heavens of this lower world during the last third of the night. Lowering himself toward the place of his prosternation, the person who prays is in search of divine proximity. It is said: "Prostrate yourself and come closer" (Qur'ân 96:19).[135]

Ibn ʿArabī cites a *duʿāʾ* performed by the Prophet while prostrate in prayer:

> O Lord, place light in my heart, light in my hearing, light in my sight, light to my right, light to my left, light in front of me, light behind me, light above me, and light below me. Give me light! Make me light!

He concludes, "The second thing that the person says in prostrate prayer is 'Make me light,' that is, make me [Y]ou."[136] Like his analysis of the temporal cycles of prayer, Ibn ʿArabī's interpretation of its physical postures places them within a complex set of cosmic correspondences centering on, and suffused by, the divine Light.

Modern developments

Beginning in the later nineteenth century, reformist currents placed new emphasis on direct adherence to the example of the Prophet and his early followers, an approach that tended to prioritize formal correctness and obedience to the *sunna* over other frameworks for the interpretation of prayer. As John Bowen has observed, "Movements of Islamic reform and revival often have attempted to purify the historical links between the prophet's *ṣalāt* and current practice by opposing symbolic elaboration."[137] However, it is by no means the case that the models discussed above have passed into memory, even in modernist or Salafī circles. The anthropologist Bärbel Reuter, who worked with young Islamist women in Cairo in the 1990s, notes that with respect to *ṣalāt*, "like many others,

[134] Ibn ʿArabī, *Futūḥāt*, 1:428; see also Chodkiewicz, *Ocean*, p. 112.
[135] Chodkiewicz, *Ocean*, p. 112; see Ibn ʿArabī, *Tanazzul al-amlāk*, p. 71.
[136] Chodkiewicz, *Ocean*, p. 113; Ibn ʿArabī, *Futūḥāt*, 1:423–4.
[137] Bowen, "Salat in Indonesia," p. 615.

they emphasize dialogue with God, not obedience to a formal commandment";[138] the model of *munājāt* (firmly based in *ḥadīth*, as well as in devotional practice) continues to be vital for a wide range of Muslims. The idea that the underlying objective of *ṣalāt* is to cultivate bodily discipline and ethical virtue, which (as we have seen) was both widespread and suspect in earlier centuries, has been rearticulated in some circles with renewed force. The founder of the religiously and politically influential Muslim Brotherhood, Ḥasan al-Bannā (d. 1949), wrote that in Islam "rites were only laid down in so far as they conduced to the hallowing of moral character."[139]

As was the case in the premodern period, the virtues cultivated by prayer have often been conceived as social and political as well as personal in nature. While the religious appeal of the "royal audience" model seems to have waned in the contemporary period, Muslim thinkers have generated new interpretations of the human authority structures modeled or reflected by *ṣalāt*. Whereas medieval thinkers tended to regard the bilateral, hierarchical encounter between the individual worshiper and God as analogous to the awe-inspiring but flawed experience of confronting a human monarch, modern thinkers have often used prayer as a model of the Islamic individual or nation that they wished to reform and empower. Although they generally do not explicitly draw on the heritage of *falsafa* or Mu'tazilism, modern thinkers have revived the model of *ṣalāt* as a form of individual and social discipline that develops habits of organization and self-control. (Unlike premodern *falāsifa*, they do not subordinate this role to an ultimate goal of abstract contemplation of the Absolute that could supersede physical worship.)

Such reflections on prayer have been particularly prevalent among the Islamic activists of the twentieth century. Ḥasan al-Bannā argued that *ṣalāt* "reflects the social, political, and ethical values of the three major systems of government known to man – communism, dictatorship, and democracy."[140] He wrote, "Islamic prayer . . . is nothing but a daily training in practical and social organization, uniting the features of the Communist regime with those of the dictatorial and democratic regimes." The egalitarianism of the mosque, where all are equal before God, is equated with Communism; the solidarity of the community massed in a "compact block behind the imam" mimics "the principal merit of the dictatorial regime"; and the fact that the *imām* himself is subject to the laws of prayer, and can be corrected by any ordinary worshiper, is

[138] Bärbel Reuter, *Gelebte Religion: Religiöse Praxis junger Islamistinnen in Kairo* (Würzburg: ERGON Verlag, 1999), p. 199. Translation mine.

[139] From *The Theology of Unity*, trans. Ishaq Musa'ad and Kenneth Cragg, in John J. Donohue and John L. Esposito, eds., *Islam in Transition: Muslim Perspectives*, 2nd ed. (New York: Oxford University Press, 2007), p. 21.

[140] Cited in Ibrahim M. Abu-Rabi', *Intellectual Origins of Islamic Resurgence in the Modern Arab World* (Albany: SUNY Press, 1996), p. 77.

associated with democracy.[141] It is notable that al-Bannā, who himself nominally lived under a monarchy, did not invoke it as one of the basic forms of human rule. Rather, he saw *ṣalāt* as modeling the advantages of the regimes that were most politically and intellectually compelling in his own day – including dictatorship, a model that appeared successful in strengthening European nations in the 1930s but would be less likely to appeal to a Muslim thinker today.

Other thinkers focused on the internal transformation of the individual as much as on the external configuration and authority structure of congregational prayer. Muslim reformers in the Indonesian province of Aceh argued during the struggle for regional and national self-determination in the first half of the twentieth century that *ṣalāt* was central to the effort because of "the this-worldly discipline it imposed on the individual" as well as "the egalitarian and universal character of the congregation." Punctual performance of ritual duties such as *ṣalāt* allowed one to "increase one's power of reason (*ʿaql*) and the ability to control one's behaviour. ... Only when individuals had first improved themselves would the perfect society be realised. It would rise from the joint submission of all its members to God in a mechanical solidarity of universal *salāt* performance."[142]

For the Islamist activist Sayyid Quṭb (executed by the Egyptian government in 1966), prayer is a concentrated exercise in personal realization – through bodily action and mental focus – of the exclusive sovereignty of God, the central tenet of his political program. Prostrating oneself to God frees one of slavery to other human beings, and empowers one with the consciousness of a direct connection to the Necessary Existent so that one will no longer fear the power of other created beings. It is an important form of personal training (*tarbīya shakhṣīya*).[143]

A far more elaborate account of the role of acts of worship in the development of a socially and politically engaged individual was produced by the Iraqi Shīʿite *ʿālim* and activist Muḥammad Bāqir al-Ṣadr, who was executed in 1980 for his support of the Iranian revolution. He argues that, unlike other elements of the sharia, acts of worship (*ʿibādāt*) do not change with the development of society. Thus, these rituals must address a human need that is constant and unchanging. This might seem impossible, given the comprehensive transformations to which human societies are subject. For instance, while ablution and prayer may serve to impose hygiene and moral discipline on people, modern societies are capable

141 Ibid.

142 Bowen, "*Salat* in Indonesia," p. 602.

143 Sayyid Quṭb, *Fī ẓilāl al-qurʾān* (Beirut: Dār al-Shurūq, 1973–4), 1:40 (commentary on verse 2:3). The translation of Salahi and Shamis does not fully express this dimension of the passage (Sayyid Quṭb, *In the Shade of the Qurʾān*, ed. and trans. M. A. Salahi and A. A. Shamis [Leicester: Islamic Foundation, 1999/1420], 1:24).

of fulfilling these functions by other means. In contrast, al-Ṣadr argues that human beings have certain constant needs connected not to their relationship with nature – which changes as they master new technologies – but to their relationship with God and, thus, with each other. These include the need for a connection with the Absolute, the need for objectivity (*mawḍūʿīya*) and self-transcendence, and the need for an interior feeling of responsibility that motivates them to carry out their objectives.[144]

The need for a connection with the Absolute is threatened by two contrasting errors, one of which is nihilism and the other the transformation of relative things into false absolutes; in religious terms, the first of these is known as atheism (*ilḥād*), and the second as idolatry. Either of these errors can impede the progress of humankind. The objects of idolatry are not simply graven images, but objects of chauvinistic and excessive loyalty such as tribalism or even science. "Objectivity" is necessary because many of the goals that an individual must pursue do not benefit him directly; thus, a person must be trained to value and pursue objectives that transcend his selfish or material needs. Acts of worship, in order to be valid, must be performed for the sake of God and not for any personal gain or ulterior motive such as social esteem. Thus, they are a "necessary training" (*tarbīya ḍarūrīya*) in performing actions that are impartial, sincere, and based on feelings of responsibility; they allow the individual to experience "objective motivation" (*al-qaṣd al-mawḍūʿī*). Al-Ṣadr continues that "the path [i.e., the sake] of God" (*sabīl Allāh*) is the abstract term for "the path of serving humanity" (*sabīl khidmat al-insān*), because every act performed for God is in fact performed for the sake of God's creatures. God is without need of His creatures (and thus does not benefit from human worship); however, because God is above limitation, specification, or association with any group, in practical terms service of God is equivalent to service of all humanity.[145] Prayer, like other acts of worship, is thus a "spiritual and psychological drill" (*al-tadrīb al-rūḥī waʾl-nafsī*) for disinterested and altruistic action.[146] Furthermore, an inner feeling of responsibility is ensured by the awareness of scrutiny by an omniscient observer, which in turn is developed through acts of worship whose validity is based on internal factors that can be evaluated only by an all-knowing God.[147]

Finally, al-Ṣadr relates the ethical dispositions cultivated by acts of worship to proper behavior in society, writing that "it is by means of this feeling [of

144 Muḥammad Bāqir al-Ṣadr, *al-Fatāwā al-wāḍiḥa* (Beirut: Dār al-Kitāb al-Lubnānī, 1977), 1:584–5.
145 For a critique of this argument see Muḥammad Bāqir al-Ṣadr, *Falsafa wa-akhlāqīyat al-ṣalāt*, ed. and annotated by al-Sayyid Muḥsin al-Mūsawī (Beirut: Dār al-Ḥujja al-Bayḍāʾ, 1424/2003), p. 42.
146 Ṣadr, *Fatāwā*, 1:596.
147 Ibid., 1:598.

responsibility] that a good citizen is created," because it does not suffice that a person respect the rights of his fellow citizens simply "out of fear of the social reaction" to violations of those rights, which would allow people to evade their responsibilities whenever they could get away with it.[148] It may seem that he is returning to the argument of social utility already dismissed at the beginning of his discussion, by arguing that the value of prayer lies in the internalized awareness of an ominiscient and impartial observer monitoring one's actions far more effectively than any governmental agency. However, the heart of his argument is that social solidarity can be achieved only on the basis of the moral transformation effected by an awareness of the Absolute, not merely through the external discipline imposed by acts of worship (which could be effected by other means).

The approach to prayer advanced by thinkers such as al-Bannā, Quṭb, and Ṣadr produced objections from some more conservative religious scholars. With respect to the closely related school of thought of Quṭb's contemporary, the South Asian thinker Abū'l-Aʿlā al-Mawdūdī, some protested that "it is as though even the fundamental rituals of religion come to be conceived of by them not as practices Muslims must undertake because they are an irreducible part of being a believer, but rather because they are socially useful in inculcating the habits and the discipline that assist in the project of striving for an Islamic state."[149] Like their predecessors centuries before, they objected to functional and instrumental interpretations of *ṣalāt* – an objection that al-Ṣadr, at least, anticipates and attempts to defuse.

Not only activists devoted to the establishment of an Islamic state envisioned prayer as a form of training for political engagement, however. More politically moderate thinkers sometimes saw prayer as a form of training for civic values, rather than necessarily for revolutionary action. The politically centrist and immensely influential contemporary thinker Yūsuf al-Qaraḍāwī (known, among other things, for his television program on the al-Jazeera satellite channel) envisions ablution and *ṣalāt* as inculcating habits of cleanliness and hygiene, physical fitness, mental health, and ethical vigor. He emphasizes the good posture and muscular strength developed through the ritual, and compares it to the calisthenics practiced by athletes.[150] In his view, *ṣalāt* holistically develops physical, mental, and moral powers; however, it does so not merely in the service of individual well-being, but of the community and the polity. He characterizes congregational prayer as "military training," not in the sense that it encourages conflict with outsiders but in that it inculcates order and discipline. "How much

[148] Ibid., 1:599.

[149] Muhammad Qasim Zaman, *The Ulama in Contemporary Islam* (Princeton and Oxford: Princeton University Press, 2002), p. 104.

[150] Yūsuf al-Qaraḍāwī, *al-ʿIbāda fī'l-islām* (Beirut: Mu'assasat al-Risāla, 1397/1977), pp. 217–21.

developing nations – like the Arabs in the days of the Prophet – need to learn practically obedience to commands, adherence to order, submission to law, and respect of commanders – and this is what congregational prayer does."[151]

The idea that *ṣalāt* instills socially and politically vital habits of order and self-command is also reflected in the government textbooks that often introduce ideas about prayer to elementary-school children in modern Muslim-majority countries. In Egypt a second-grade religious studies textbook from the late 1980s taught that the five daily prayers "invigorate the body" and "accustom the Muslim to organization, and respect for appointed times."[152] Similarly, a privately published Egyptian manual teaches that "orderliness proceeds from faith." It illustrates this principle with the example of a bureaucrat presiding over a decorous and efficient office; he declares to the crowd in a disorderly neighboring office (where no one is getting served due to the chaos) that they must learn the lesson taught by prayer: "During collective prayer we must straighten the rows, just as in all our lives, we must have order, order."[153]

Thus, modern thinkers have interpreted *ṣalāt* as conditioning the habits and dispositions leading to both activism and docility, revolutionary engagement and orderly submission to bureaucratic control. These dichotomies do not exhaust the range of virtues that *ṣalāt* may be seen to produce, however. A liberal nationalist Egyptian journalist has emphasized "how rituals [*ṭūqūs*] and worship [*ʿibādāt*] prepare for the creation of a type of person who thinks freely, [and] is capable [*muʾahhal*] of enlightened criticism on important issues."[154] Drawing on a concept prominent in the thought of the Iranian revolution, the South African Muslim anti-apartheid activist Farid Esack has written that "prayer in Islam is truly an institution of *tawhid*, the oneness of Allah, reflecting it and directed towards it." For Esack, unlike many who promoted the ideal of the "tawḥīdī society" in the context of the Iranian revolution, this ideal is inherently pluralistic and inclusive. In prostration, he continues, "we become at one with the earth from which we come and to which we have to return. We are reminded of our being part of the ecosystem. . ."[155]

Other approaches emphasize the purely individual benefits of *ṣalāt*, such as the development of physical strength and health. As early as the fourteenth century, Ibn Qayyim al-Jawzīya had listed *ṣalāt* as a medical remedy and noted that it was "invigorating to the limbs" and had "an extraordinary effect in preserving the health of the body and heart," although he attributed this effect

151 Ibid., p. 224.
152 Cited in Gregory Starrett, *Putting Islam to Work: Education, Politics, and Religious Transformation in Egypt* (Berkeley: University of California Press, 1998), p. 150.
153 Cited in ibid., p. 150.
154 Cited in Mahmood, *Politics of Piety*, p. 132.
155 Farid Esack, *On Being a Muslim: Finding a Religious Path in the World Today* (Oxford: Oneworld, 1999), pp. 27–8.

primarily to the blessings of connection with God; some contemporary Muslims (including Ibn al-Qayyim's editor) go further, interpreting it as *riyāḍa* in the modern sense of "exercise" rather than the broader premodern sense of overall discipline and training.[156] If the modern period has seen a resurgence of the idea – first promoted by Muʿtazilīs and philosophers – that *ṣalāt* is an educational and disciplinary tool for the cultivation of certain virtues and capacities, there is great diversity of opinion on the nature of those virtues and their significance for society.

156 Ibn Qayyim al-Jawzīya, *Zād al-maʿād fī hady khayr al-ʿibād*, ed. Muḥammad al-Anwar Aḥmad al-Baltājī (Ṣaydā and Beirut: al-Maktaba al-ʿAṣrīya 1428/2007), 4:533. The editor observes in n. jīm on p. 532 that "salāt contains a medical component, which is exercise of the soul (*nafs*) and the body, because it includes standing, bowing, prostration, kneeling, and other postures in which most of the joints are moved and most of the organs are involved, particularly the stomach, the intestines, and all of the organs of respiration and digestion during prostration."

4 The community at prayer

Congregational prayer, prayer leadership (imāma), *and the boundaries of the religious community*

Muslim scholars of all schools agree on the religious value of congregational prayer. The Prophet is reported to have stated, "Prayer in congregation is superior to prayer by an individual by twenty-seven degrees" (or, in some versions, twenty-five), which was understood to mean that its merit and reward were multiplied this number of times.[1] In another well-authenticated report the Prophet declares:

> If you were to pray in your homes as this person who stays behind (*al-mutakhallif*) prays in his home, you would abandon the way of your Prophet, and if you abandon the way of your Prophet, you will go astray. Any man who purifies himself thoroughly and then sets out for one of these mosques, God will record a good deed for every step that he takes and raise him a degree because of it, and will take away one of his sins.[2]

The unique value of public prayer could even function as a rationale for favoring urban life; one *ḥadīth* text represents the Prophet as worrying that love of the milk of their flocks may lead recently sedentarized Muslims to "return to the desert, leaving the places where men pray together."[3]

Ḥanafīs and Mālikīs consider congregational *ṣalāt* to be a confirmed *sunna* (*sunna mu'akkada*) for all obligatory prayers, rather than a strict obligation; similarly, Imāmī Shīʿites regard it as desirable (*mustaḥabba*).[4] Ḥanbalīs are distinctive in regarding it as mandatory for individuals (or at least individual men). There was a difference of opinion within the school about whether failure to fulfill this obligation without a valid excuse (*ʿudhr*) voided one's prayers; most Ḥanbalīs held that a person who willfully prayed alone was sinful but that the prayer still counted. Shāfiʿīs consider congregational prayer to be obligatory upon the community as a whole (*farḍ kifāya*), rather than upon individuals;

[1] See Bukhārī, *Ṣaḥīḥ*, *Kitāb al-Ādhān*, *Bāb Faḍl ṣalāt al-jamāʿa*.

[2] See Muslim, *Ṣaḥīḥ*, *Kitāb al-Masājid wa-mawāḍiʿ al-ṣalāt*, *Bāb Ṣalāt al-jamāʿa min sunan al-hudā*.

[3] See Jonathan Berkey, *The Formation of Islam* (Cambridge: Cambridge University Press, 2003), p. 119.

[4] See al-Muḥaqqiq al-Ḥillī, *Sharāʾiʿ al-islām fī masāʾil al-ḥalāl waʾl-ḥarām* (Qumm: Dār al-Tafsīr, 1425 A.H.), 1:112.

enough adult males must participate in order for it to function as a visible emblem (*shiʿār*) of Islam.[5]

Technically, any prayer performed by two or more people, with one person serving as prayer leader (*imām*) to be followed by the rest, is a congregational prayer (*ṣalāt al-jamāʿa*). As Ibn Qayyim al-Jawzīya (d. 751/1350) observes, "Most people are able to pray in congregation in their homes, because a person usually has a wife, son, slave (*ghulām*), friend, or the like, so he can pray in congregation."[6] However, as reflected in the second *ḥadīth*, value is also placed on public prayer in the officially designated prayer space of mosques. Ḥanbalīs in particular hold that going to the mosque is obligatory (for adult men) in the absence of some specific excuse.[7] Furthermore, some prayers, such as the Friday and festival prayers, can only be performed in a public mosque or outdoor prayer ground (*muṣallā*).

Congregational prayer and the communal solidarity that it was believed to bring with it was a strong religious value that sometimes stood in tension with other ideals, including the impulse to hold oneself aloof from a materialistic or sinful environment. In general, withdrawal from the community was condoned only in cases of existential peril. Commenting on the Qur'ānic story of the "Men of the Cave" who took refuge in a cavern from a persecuting ruler, Ibn Kathīr (d. 774/1373) observes: "[A] person who fears for his religion should flee from his persecutors. . . . In such cases, it is allowed to seclude oneself from people, but this is not allowed in any other case, because by such seclusion one loses the benefits of congregational and Friday prayers."[8] Pious persons might not only withdraw from the strife of a turbulent society, but seek solitude for religious reasons; Ibn Taymīya (d. 728/1328) speaks bitterly of ascetics (presumably Sufis) who prefer to pray in seclusion.[9] Others were motivated by more mundane considerations; Ibn al-Ḥājj (d. 737/1336) complains that even a religious scholar may hear the call to prayer but remain at home to pray with a student or colleague (or even, as a last resort, with his wife), hoping to receive the reward for performing congregational prayer without the bother of going to the mosque and mixing with common folk (*al-ʿawāmm*).[10] In the view of Ibn al-Ḥājj, such a person not only forfeits the religious merit of going to the mosque, but proves himself to be elitist and lazy.

5 al-Zuḥaylī, *Fiqh*, 2:1167–9.
6 Ibn al-Qayyim, *Kitāb al-ṣalāt*, p. 140.
7 Ibid., p. 134. Ibn al-Qayyim states that "refraining from attending the mosque without an excuse is like refraining from praying in congregation altogether without an excuse" (p. 137).
8 Ibn Kathīr, *Tafsir Ibn Kathir (abridged)*, trans. and abridged under the supervision of Shaykh Safiur-Rahman al-Mubarakpuri (Riyadh: Darussalam Publishers & Distributors, 2000), 6:124. I have revised the translation to render both occurrences of the verb *tushraʿ* as "is allowed."
9 Ibn Taymīya, *Majmūʿ al-fatāwā*, 23:103–4.
10 Ibn al-Ḥājj, *Madkhal*, 2:300.

Ibn al-Ḥājj himself enumerates a staggering ninety-two different pious intents that one may frame when setting out to pray in the mosque, and many of them suggest the benefits he believed accrued to the community from congregational prayer and the social interactions accompanying it. Among other things, one should intend to acquire knowledge from those who possess it and impart it to the ignorant; visit with friends, scholars, and virtuous people (*al-ṣulaḥāʾ*) and acquire the blessing of gathering and praying with them; offer one's condolences to the afflicted; and inquire about the fortunes of the Muslim armies.[11] For Ibn al-Ḥājj, going out to pray in the mosque is not only a meritorious act in itself, but a context for engagement with the Muslim community that includes opportunities for teaching and learning, for practicing the etiquette of proper social intercourse, and for hearing and sympathizing with the fortunes of the Muslim polity.

Friday prayers

While cleaving to the community in shared prayer is always to be encouraged, in the case of Friday prayer it is integral to the validity of the ritual. The Friday (*jumʿa*) prayer takes the place of the ordinary noon prayer; instead of the usual four prostration cycles, it involves two short sermons separated by a short pause, followed by a two-*rakʿa* prayer. Scholars agree that it is obligatory only for free males above the age of puberty; one is exempted if traveling, ill, or suffering from other impediments (such as bad weather). However, Friday congregational prayer is not incumbent upon all individual males who fit these requirements. Shāfiʿīs traditionally held that *jumʿa* must be held only in villages or towns whose populations afforded a quorum of at least forty resident male worshipers, without which the prayer was invalid. Mālikīs and Ḥanbalīs did not set such a numerical standard, but limited Friday prayers to sedentary people; migratory tent-dwellers were not required to attend, even if they were currently located close to a town. Mālikīs added that the village in question must be built in a compact and contiguous fashion. At the other extreme, Ḥanafīs excluded villagers altogether; *jumʿa* was incumbent only on residents of a major town (*miṣr, al-miṣr al-jāmiʿ*), and invalid if held elsewhere.[12] Baber Johansen notes that while Ḥanafī jurists offer a number of different definitions of this term, most converge on the idea "that a town should be a comprehensive social and political entity embracing various groups, rallying different factions into one

[11] Ibid., 1:32, 35, 44.

[12] On this issue see Norman Calder, "Friday Prayer and the Juristic Theory of the Caliphate: Sarakhsī, Shīrāzī, Māwardī," *Bulletin of the School of Oriental and African Studies* 49 (1986), pp. 35–6.

community and uniting them under one leadership."[13] In the definition of ʿAlāʾ al-Dīn al-Kāsānī (d. 587/1191) a qualifying town "is a large locality in which there are streets and markets, to which rural districts (*rasātīq*) belong, in which there is a governor (*wālī*) who through his retinue and his knowledge, or the knowledge of other[s], can obtain justice for the oppressed from the oppressor . . . and to whom people turn in (all) calamities."[14]

The limitation of the performance of Friday prayers to communities fulfilling certain qualifications was taken very seriously, as emerges from the fatwa literature. A touching enquiry directed to Ibn Taymīya describes the situation of a group of people in Bahrain, who trace their tradition of holding Friday prayers back to the time of the Prophet but have been advised by some Iraqis to desist because their settlement is not sufficiently permanent in its construction. Ibn Taymīya reassures them that, although their homes are constructed from palm leaves, they qualify for Friday prayers because they are sedentary.[15]

In addition to the requirements relating to the individual worshiper and the town, Ḥanafīs established two further prerequisites: Friday congregational prayers must either be led by the ruler or his representative, or be performed with his permission; and the place where they are performed must be accessible to the public at large. Other schools disputed these requirements, in part based on the precedent that ʿAlī led Friday prayers while the caliph ʿUthmān was besieged and in duress.[16] The other school of law originating in Kufa, the Imāmī Shīʿites, similarly held that the permission of the ruler was necessary for Friday prayers to be legitimately convened; as we shall see, however, the permanent absence of the legitimate imām eventually made the implications of this requirement complex.

In some sense, the obligation to hold *jumʿa* prayers relates to the needs and qualifications of the local community, rather than of the individual worshiper. Women, slaves, villagers, and nomads are all regarded in Islamic law as fully responsible religious actors, but all of them are (at least according to some schools) permanently exempted from Friday prayers. According to the interpretations of classical Islamic scholars it would be possible to live one's entire life as an observant Muslim without ever participating in Friday prayers or being obligated to do so; on the other hand, Friday prayers are a constitutive feature of a well-regulated Islamic polity.

In practice, and over the course of many centuries, the most important political function of the Friday prayers was the public identification of the

[13] Baber Johansen, "The All-Embracing Town and Its Mosques," in Baber Johansen, *Contingency in a Sacred Law: Legal and Ethical Norms in the Muslim* Fiqh (Leiden: Brill, 1999), p. 82.
[14] Ibid., p. 85.
[15] Ibn Taymīya, *Majmūʿ al-fatāwā*, 24:75–8.
[16] Zuḥaylī, *Fiqh*, 2:1297–8.

ruler. To be mentioned in the sermon (*khuṭba*) was, next to having one's name stamped on coins by the mint, one of the primary insignia of rule. Because both Friday sermons and coins were accessible to a wide audience, they were central media for the communication of such information to the broader public. In cases of dynastic instability or transitions of power, the proclamation of the name of a specific claimant to the throne could be a potent political statement. Conversely, failure to invoke prayers upon the ruler in power could be taken as a subversive political commentary in itself (and thus might prove hazardous to the offending preacher).[17]

Given that prayers for the ruler were such a salient feature of Friday congregational worship, it might also be assumed that Friday prayers were an important religiously sanctioned form of legitimation for the powers that be. Despite the durability and political centrality of the practice, however, mentioning the ruling sovereign in the context of Friday prayers was recognized by scholars to lack any normative basis in Qurʾān and *ḥadīth*. It is arguable that this consensus itself reflected a significant political choice; because it was indeed *sunna* to invoke blessings upon the Prophet, and the Prophet was the political leader of the community in his lifetime, it would have been possible to argue that the *sunna* offered a relevant precedent. In fact, however, scholars did not choose to follow this approach. The closest thing adduced by scholars to a Prophetic warrant for praying for the ruler was a *ḥadīth*, transmitted by al-Ṭabarānī (d. 360/971) but not appearing in the best-authenticated collections, in which the Prophet declares, "Do not curse the rulers (*lā tasubbū 'l-aʾimma*); [rather], pray for their righteousness, for their righteousness is righteousness for you (*ṣalāḥuhum lakum ṣalāḥ*)."[18] Another, even less authoritative version states at greater length:

> Pray behind every pious or iniquitous prince; your prayer is to your own credit, and their sin is to their own detriment. Engage in jihad with every caliph; your jihad is to your own credit, and their sins are to their own detriment. Do not rebel against your rulers with the sword, even if they are oppressive; [rather,] pray for their righteousness and well-being (*waʾdʿū lahum bi 'l-ṣalāḥ wa 'l-muʿāfāt*).[19]

Neither of these reports, of course, reflects positive sentiments about the religious and ethical qualifications of actual leaders; both assume the likelihood or inevitability of tyranny, and encourage prayer for the reform of the ruler, rather than endorsement of his rule.

[17] *EI²*, art. "Ḵuṭba" (by A. J. Wensinck).

[18] Sulaymān ibn Aḥmad al-Ṭabarānī, *al-Muʿjam al-awṣaṭ* (Cairo: Dār al-Ḥaramayn, 1415/1995), 2:169.

[19] Shīrawayh ibn Shahradār al-Daylamī, *al-Firdaws bi-maʾthūr al-khiṭāb* (Beirut: Dār al-Kutub al-ʿIlmīya, 1406/1987), 2:384 (#3705).

Reports cited by classical jurists suggest that the custom of praying for the ruler was of very early date. One states that the Prophet's Companion Abū Mūsā al-Ashʿarī prayed for the current caliph, ʿUmar, and for his predecessor Abū Bakr when delivering the *khuṭba* in Kufa;[20] the Companion Ibn ʿAbbās is also said to have prayed for the caliph ʿAlī. However, neither of these precedents is well authenticated by the standards of the *ḥadīth* tradition, and neither was widely regarded as compelling evidence for the appropriateness of prayers for later and less exemplary rulers. Resistance to the custom of praying for the rulers seems to be almost as old as the practice itself. Al-Shāfiʿī cites the disapproval of the early Meccan scholar ʿAṭā' ibn Abī Rabāḥ (d. 114/732).[21] In the *Muṣannaf* of Ibn Abī Shayba (d. 235/849), the pious Umayyad caliph ʿUmar ibn ʿAbd al-ʿAzīz (r. 99–101/717–20) is cited as writing in a letter to a governor:

> Some people have begun to seek this world with the work of the next world [i.e., to seek worldly advancement through prayer]; some people among the preacher-storytellers (*quṣṣāṣ*) have innovated prayers for their caliphs and governors that are equal to their prayers upon the Prophet (peace be upon him!). When this letter of mine reaches you, command them that their prayers should be upon the prophets and their supplications should be for the Muslims in general; they should refrain from anything but that.[22]

Another concern was that rulers might be invoked with exalted titles that were theologically problematic or simply dishonest. The Ḥanafī theologian and jurist Aḥmad al-Ṣaffār (d. 336/947–8) is reported to have been consulted about "the titles of the sultan that are used by preachers who give the sermon from the pulpit on Friday," such as "the supreme and just sultan" or "the supreme king of kings." He replies that the use of such titles is not permissible, because some of them constitute disbelief, while others are acts of disobedience (i.e., to God) or lies. This view is reinforced with the opinion of the influential Ḥanafī theologian Abū Manṣūr al-Māturīdī (d. 333/944) that "whoever says about the ruler of our time that he is just is an unbeliever, because he is [known to be] a tyrant with certainty, and whoever calls tyranny justice has committed unbelief."[23]

The scholars who documented the classical doctrines of the schools of law from the fifth/eleventh century, in general, had little enthusiasm for prayers for the ruler in the context of the *khuṭba*. Abū Isḥāq al-Shīrāzī (d. 476/1083) states that "as for praying for the sultan, it is not recommended (*lā yustaḥabb*)."[24] The

20 Ibn Ḥajar al-Haytamī, *Tuḥfat al-muḥtāj bi-sharḥ al-Minhāj*, printed in margin of *Ḥawāshī al-Shirwānī wa-Aḥmad ibn Qāsim al-ʿAbbādī ʿalā Tuḥfat al-muḥtāj* ([Būlāq], n.d.), 2:449.

21 al-Shāfiʿī, *al-Umm*, 1:203; see also ʿAbd al-Razzāq Ibn Hammām al-Ṣanʿānī, *al-Muṣannaf*, ed. Ḥabīb Allāh al-Aʿẓamī (Beirut: al-Majlis al-ʿIlmī, n.d.), 3:216–17 (#5389).

22 Ibn Abī Shayba, *Muṣannaf*, 8:241.

23 ʿĀlim ibn ʿAlā' al-Anṣārī, *al-Fatāwā al-tātārkhānīya*, ed. Sajjād Ḥusayn (Karachi: Idārat al-Qur'ān wa'l-ʿUlūm al-Islāmīya, [1990–]), 5:523–4.

24 In al-Nawawī, *Majmūʿ*, 5:676.

eleventh-century Ḥanbalī authority Abū Yaʿlā ibn al-Farrāʾ is reported to have expressed the same opinion, as is the twelfth-century Mālikī Sind ibn ʿInān.[25] Norman Calder notes that the Ḥanafī al-Sarakhsī's failure to mention the practice must be intentional and pointed, as he was surely aware of it.[26]

A more explicitly critical position was asserted by the great Shāfiʿī jurist al-ʿIzz ibn ʿAbd al-Salām al-Sulamī (d. 660/1261). In a fatwa he declares uncompromisingly, "Mentioning the Companions [of the Prophet], the caliphs and the sultans [in the *khuṭba*] is an undesirable innovation (*bidʿa ghayr maḥbūba*); sermons should mention only things that are in harmony with their objectives, including praise [of God], supplication, the instilling of hope [of heaven] and fear [of hell], and the recitation of the Qurʾān."[27] Al-Sulamī's position in this area was characteristic of his outspokenly independent stance toward the political authorities, which led (among other things) to his exile from Syria to Egypt; a premodern biographer notes that "he avoided praising kings, rather, he lectured them."[28]

Other jurists were more pragmatic. In his encyclopedic compendium of *fiqh*, Ibn Qudāma (d. 620/1223) writes that if the *khaṭīb* "prays for the righteousness (*ṣalāḥ*) of the sultan of the Muslims, it is good (*ḥasan*)."[29] In the eighth/fourteenth century the great Tunisian Mālikī jurist Ibn ʿArafa stated that there was no legal basis for the practice of mentioning sultans in the *khuṭba*, even "with supplication and statements that are free of lying." However, "after its innovation and its continuous usage in sermons in all regions of the earth," failure to mention the sultan has become "likely grounds for the sultans to think things about the preacher (*khaṭīb*) from which calamitous results are to be feared and whose outcome is uncertain"; under these circumstances, "mentioning them in sermons is legally preferred or obligatory."[30]

[25] Abū Yaʿlā cited in Ibn Qudāma, *al-Mughnī*, 2:157; Sind ibn ʿInān cited in al-Ḥaṭṭāb al-Ruʿaynī, *Mawāhib al-jalīl li-sharḥ Mukhtaṣar Khalīl* (Beirut: Dār al-Kutub al-ʿIlmīya, 1416/1995), 2:529.

[26] Calder, "Friday Prayer," p. 36.

[27] ʿIzz al-Dīn ibn ʿAbd al-Salām al-Sulamī, *al-Fatāwā al-mawṣilīya*, ed. Iyād Khālid al-Ṭabbāʿ (Damascus: Dār al-Fikr, 1999), p. 36.

[28] *EI*², art. "al-Sulamī, ʿIzz al-Dīn" (by E. Chaumont).

[29] Ibn Qudāma, *al-Mughnī*, 2:157. In a later passage Ibn Qudāma remarks of the obligation to listen to supplications made in the context of the *khuṭba*, "it is also possible that if it is a mandated prayer, such as prayer for the male and female Muslims or for a just ruler, he must listen to it, and if it is some other [kind of prayer] it is not obligatory to listen to it" (Ibn Qudāma, *al-Mughnī*, 2:170) The specification that the ruler must be "just" seems significant. The eighteenth-century Shāfiʿī authority al-Bujayrimī states that it is *sunna* to pray for the leaders and rulers of the Muslims during the second *khuṭba*, but specifies that one should pray for their righteousness (*ṣalāḥ*) and that they be aided in doing what is right (*al-iʿāna ʿalā al-ḥaqq*) and upholding justice (*al-qiyām bi'l-ḥaqq*). All of this, again, seems to emphasize the rulers' need for guidance more than their entitlement to blessings (Sulaymān ibn Muḥammad al-Bujayrimī, *Ḥāshiyat al-Bujayrimī ʿalā Sharḥ Manhaj al-ṭullāb*, ed. ʿAbd Allāh Maḥmūd Muḥammad ʿUmar [Beirut: Dār al-Kutub al-ʿIlmīya, 1420/2000], 1:505).

[30] Ḥaṭṭāb, *Mawāhib al-jalīl*, 2:529.

The Syrian Ḥanafī Muḥammad al-Ḥaṣkafī (d. 1088/1677) writes in his influential manual of Ḥanafī law that it is not recommended to pray for the ruler, and that "it is reprehensible to the point of prohibition (*yukrah taḥrīman*) to describe him with attributes that he does not possess." However, political realities intruded here as well. The late Ottoman-period Syrian scholar Ibn ʿĀbidīn, commenting on al-Ḥaṣkafī's statement, notes that "prayer for the sultan from the pulpits has now become one of the insignia of sovereignty, and someone who omits it does so at his peril (*yukhshā ʿalayhi*). For this reason some scholars have held that if it were to be argued that it is obligatory to pray for him because of the disorder (*fitna*) usually involved in omitting it, it would not be implausible."[31]

Much like the Ḥanafī insistence that Friday prayers be held under the auspices of the rulers, tolerance of the invocation of blessings upon the ruler among Sunnī scholars reflected pragmatism and concern with the unity of the community, rather than a positive attitude toward the holders of political power.[32] Imāmī Shīʿite attitudes toward Friday prayer also reflected the close association between this institution and the role of the ruling authorities, but manifested less resignation toward the questionable legitimacy of the actual incumbents. Like the Ḥanafīs (whose early doctrines also crystallized in Kufa), Imāmīs recognized the authorization of Friday prayers as a prerogative of the ruler. However, unlike Ḥanafīs, they made this role contingent on the ruler's religious legitimacy. Since he enjoyed the exclusive and divinely bestowed entitlement to exercise the prerogatives of ruler, convening Friday prayers was therefore a privilege of the imām. However, since ʿAlī was the only imām to exercise temporal power (and then for only a few years), for most of Imāmī history the legitimacy of Friday prayers was subject to debate. A letter attributed to a partisan of al-Ḥusayn in the fateful year of 60 A.H. declares that the Umayyad governor occupies the palace, but "we do not congregate with him for Friday prayers."[33] Hamid Algar notes that "it is uncertain that any of the Imams after the first convened such prayers, even privately for his own followers."[34] More than one imām is reported to have counseled followers to attend congregational prayers with the non-Shīʿite majority, but such anecdotes often suggest the policy of prudent dissimulation (*taqīya*). (In one, a disciple approaches the Sixth Imām, Jaʿfar al-Ṣādiq, and says, "I am a man who lives

[31] Ibn ʿĀbidīn, *Ḥāshiyat Radd al-muḥtār*, 2:149.

[32] In fact, Norman Calder argues that at least as articulated in the *Mabsūṭ* of al-Sarakhsī, the Ḥanafī requirement of the permission of the ruler did not imply endorsement of his righteousness or even his legitimacy. "The primary aim . . . was to secure Islamic values; support for power was a means to that end" (Calder, "Friday Prayer," p. 38).

[33] Muḥammad ibn Jarīr al-Ṭabarī, *Ta'rīkh al-Ṭabarī*, ed. Muḥammad Abū'l-Faḍl Ibrāhīm (Beirut: Dār al-Turāth, n.d.), 5:352 (referenced in Crone, *God's Rule*, p. 290).

[34] *Encyclopaedia Iranica*, art. "Emām-e jomʿa" (by Hamid Algar).

near to the mosque of my clan (*qawmī*); if I don't pray with them they will attack me and say, 'He is such and such.'"[35])

However, this counsel of prudence did not imply that following non-Shīʿite and sinful leaders in prayer was legally valid. The imāms are reported to have counseled followers outwardly to follow the leader at Friday prayers, but to add two more *rakʿa*s (thus actually performing the noon prayer individually).[36] According to a twelfth-century anti-Shīʿite polemic, however, such surface participation was not necessarily carried out discreetly; it describes how they "would attend the congregational mosque at midday on Friday but perform the Friday prayer with obvious disdain, reserving their devotional sincerity for the regular noonday prayers they would perform immediately afterwards."[37] In Medina in the fourteenth century C.E. the stern Shāfiʿī scholar Ibn al-Amyūṭī led the Friday prayers:

> Once he came down from the pulpit to beat an Imāmī man who was performing supererogatory prayers in addition to the [two prostration cycles of] "greeting the mosque," and performing the four-cycle noon prayer in the course of those supererogatory prayers – because [the Imāmīs] believe in the performance of the Friday prayers only behind an infallible imām, and this was their custom with him [i.e., al-Amyūṭī] and other [Friday prayer leaders]. He forbade them to do that, and they desisted, except those whose Shīʿism and fanaticism were strong; he used to yell at them when he was on the pulpit, and order that they be dragged to him so that he could beat them.[38]

In other cases, of course, Shīʿites must have concealed their dissent more thoroughly and enjoyed the benefits of prudential dissimulation.

Al-Ṣādiq is also reported to have instructed Shīʿite communities that they could hold their own Friday prayers when this was possible; later Imāmī scholars debated whether this precedent demonstrated the necessity to seek permission from the imām, or whether it reflected the general permissibility of holding Friday prayers.[39] The issue of authorization by the imām became far more complex, of course, after the disappearance of the Twelfth Imām (believed to be in "occultation" on another plane of existence, to return at the end of history). Imāmī scholars debated the legitimacy of Shīʿites' holding their own Friday prayers in the period after the onset of the "Greater Occultation" in the fourth/tenth century, when all possibility of communication with the Hidden

[35] Muḥammad ibn al-Ḥasan al-Ḥurr al-ʿĀmilī, *Tafṣīl wasāʾil al-shīʿa ilā taḥṣīl masāʾil al-sharīʿa* (Beirut: Muʾassasat Āl al-Bayt li-Iḥyāʾ al-Turāth, 1413/1993), 8:300 (see also 8:301).

[36] Muḥammad ibn al-Ḥasan al-Ḥurr al-ʿĀmilī, *Wasāʾil al-shīʿa ilā taḥṣīl masāʾil al-sharīʿa* (Beirut: Dār Iḥyāʾ al-Turāth al-ʿArabī, 1403/1983), 5:44–5.

[37] Algar, "Emām-e jomʿa."

[38] Ibn Farḥūn, *Naṣīḥat al-mushāwir wa-tasliyat al-mujāwir*, ed. ʿAlī ʿUmar (Cairo: Maktabat al-Thaqāfa al-Dīnīya, 1427/2006), p. 263.

[39] See ʿAlī ibn ʿAbd al-ʿĀl al-Karakī, "Risāla fī ṣalāt al-jumʿa," in Rasūl Jaʿfariyān, ed., *Davāzdah risālah-i fiqhī dar bārah-i namaz-i jumʿah az rūzgār-i ṣafavī* (Qum: Intishārāt-i Anṣāriyān, 1423/2003), p. 114.

Imām (and thus of direct authorization of Friday prayers) was cut off. The great authorities of the fifth/eleventh century, al-Ṭūsī and al-Mufīd, considered Friday prayers permissible and recommended – but not actually obligatory – as long as they were led by a qualified person and caused no harm to the Shīʿite community. Other prominent scholars, such as their contemporary al-Sharīf al-Murtaḍā, held that Friday prayers were simply not permissible during the Greater Occultation.[40]

The argument that Friday prayers were actually incumbent upon Imāmī Shīʿites was encouraged both by the emergence of Shīʿite dynasties and by the development of the doctrine of "general deputyship" (*niyāba ʿāmma*), which held that Shīʿite legal scholars as a group served as representatives of the imām in exercising governmental functions. The first scholar to advance the position that Friday prayer was obligatory during the Occultation, if led by a jurist as a representative of the imām, was Muḥammad al-Makkī al-ʿĀmilī, known as al-Shahīd al-Awwal (d. 786/1384); he expressed this opinion in a manual of law produced for a Shīʿite ruler of the Sarbadarid dynasty in eastern Iran.[41] The debate over Friday prayers intensified enormously with the foundation of the Twelver Shīʿite Safavid dynasty in Iran at the beginning of the sixteenth century, when treatises representing all sides of the debate were produced in large numbers.[42] A particularly vigorous exposition of the view that religious scholars now exercised many prerogatives of the absent imām, and that the establishment of Friday prayers was thus obligatory (particularly now that Shīʿite rule had removed the fear of ill consequences) was presented by Nūr al-Dīn al-Karakī (d. 940/1530), who was officially designated as the Deputy of the Imām (*nāʾib al-imām*) by the Safavid Shah Ṭahmāsp, and arranged for the appointment of Shīʿite imāms to lead public prayers.[43] Some scholars emphasized that the duty to attend Friday prayers was contingent on the permission of a qualified legal scholar (a *mujtahid*), while others asserted an unqualified individual obligation to attend the prayer if it was convened by the ruler. Ideologically, the first of these positions advanced the prestige of the clerical establishment and of the individual scholar under whose auspices prayers were held, while the second stressed loyalty to the political leadership. However, there was ultimately little functional distinction between the two; the debate

40 Algar, "Emām-e jomʿa."

41 Ibid.

42 Devin Stewart estimates that approximately half of 200 extant works on this subject date from the Safavid period (Devin Stewart, "Polemics and Patronage in Safavid Iran: The Debate on Friday Prayer during the Reign of Shah Tahmasb," *Bulletin of the School of Oriental and African Studies* 72 [2009], p. 428). For the texts of twelve works of this kind see Jaʿfariyān, *Davāzdah risālah*.

43 al-Karakī, "Risāla fī ṣalāt al-jumʿa," pp. 103–30; *EI*^{2}, art. "al-Karakī, Nūr al-Dīn ʿAlī ibn al-Ḥusayn" (by W. Madelung); Algar, "Emām-e jomʿa."

reflects the rivalry of different scholarly claimants to Safavid patronage as much as substantive differences in religious interpretation.[44]

In any case, the establishment of Friday prayers in Safavid Iran was not an easy matter. In the mid-seventeenth century the official prayer leader of the capital (after long advocacy of the individual obligation of Friday prayer) ultimately "declared he now believed it was permissible to abandon the prayer in the event that performing it encouraged corruption, resistance, division, rebellion, contrariness, and mutual hatred."[45] The rite of Friday prayer was never as firmly established in Shīʿite Iran as in the Sunnī Ottoman domains. The traveler Jean Chardin (d. 1713) found the contrast striking, noting that most people did not believe that it was obligatory in the absence of the Imām. While it was an important ceremonial function of the Ottoman sultan to attend Friday prayers, the same was not true of Iranian dignitaries and monarchs. He described Friday prayers in particular, and mosque attendance in general, as being particularly popular among the lower classes.[46]

It was only in the twentieth century that the institution of Friday prayer was revived on a broad basis among Iranian Shīʿites. Efforts began on a modest scale; it is recounted of Sayyid ʿAli Muḥammad Vazīrī that when he initiated the performance of *jumʿa* in the city of Yazd in the 1920s, "[a] produce seller used to station himself at the gate [of the Congregational Mosque] and tell people, 'We are going to have Friday prayers, we need a quorum of five, please join us.'"[47] Ismāʿīl ibn Aḥmad al-Ḥusaynī al-Marʿashī (d. 1425/2004), who revived the practice of Friday prayers later in the century in his adopted city of Ahwaz, recounts that he became convinced of its obligatoriness through private study but continued to perform an individual four-*rakʿa* prayer afterwards in case it was actually invalid.[48] Individual scholars also initiated Friday prayers in other localities. It was the movement to overthrow the shah and the revolution of 1979, however, that led to the massive revival of *jumʿa* prayers. Friday prayers were instrumental in mobilizing people during the revolution, and Khomeini emphasized the centrality of *jumʿa* prayers as "a demonstration of the political and social power of Islam." After the revolution Friday sermons became a major venue for the dissemination of official political positions.[49]

[44] See Stewart, "Polemics and Patronage," p. 428 and *passim*; Andrew Newman, "Fayd al-Kashani and the Rejection of the Clergy/State Alliance," in Linda S. Wallbridge, ed., *The Most Learned of the Shiʾa* (Cary, N.C.: Oxford University Press, 2001), p. 34.

[45] Newman, "Fayd al-Kashani," p. 43.

[46] Chardin, *Voyages*, 7:14, 32; 9:196.

[47] Michael M. J. Fischer and Mehdi Abedi, *Debating Muslims: Cultural Dialogues in Postmodernity and Tradition* (Madison: University of Wisconsin Press, 1990), p. 57.

[48] Ismāʿīl ibn Aḥmad al-Ḥusaynī al-Marʿashī, *ʿUnwān al-ṭāʿa fī iqāmat al-jumʿa waʾl-jamāʿa* (Tehran: Manshūrāt Maktabat al-Ṣadr, 1367 H.Sh.), p. 8.

[49] Algar, "Emām-e jomʿa."

Leadership in prayer (*imāma*)

All congregational (*jamāʿa*) prayers require that an individual lead the other worshipers. A prayer leader (*imām*) leads and synchronizes the prayers of the congregation from a position in front of the rows, as well as performing the recitation of the Qurʾān on behalf of the group. In essence, the *imām* plays no fundamental mediatory or sacramental role.[50] Nevertheless, it is considered most appropriate and meritorious to pray behind someone who is both morally exemplary and knowledgeable about the prayer ritual. The role of prayer leader (*al-imāma al-ṣughrā*, or "lesser *imāma*," in contrast with the "greater *imāma*," the caliphate) is also a leadership role appropriately claimed by those in positions of social or political authority. The four classical Sunnī schools of law are in agreement that precedence in the leadership of prayer goes to a ruler (including the supreme ruler, his governors or commanders, and judges); if such a person is present the comprehensiveness of his authority (*wilāya*) supersedes all other claims. Similarly, they concur that if congregational prayer occurs in a private home, the master of the house is entitled to lead the prayer. It is only in the absence of individuals with such claims to authority that considerations of religious learning or piety (the only factors actually referenced in *ḥadīth*) come into play.[51]

For instance, al-Shāfiʿī holds that in the absence of either the ruler or the owner of the prayer space, the most deserving prayer leader is the member of the group with the greatest knowledge of Islamic law (*afqahuhum*), assuming that he has knowledge of Qurʾānic recitation adequate for prayer, because such a person will be in the best position to respond appropriately if an unexpected situation occurs in the ritual. Next in line is the person with the best mastery of Qurʾānic recitation (*aqraʾuhum*). If the candidates are equal in this respect – or if their accomplishments are unknown – the leadership should fall to the eldest. If all of these criteria are equal or indeterminate, the honor should go to the person with the most prestigious lineage, particularly if he belongs to the Prophet's tribe, Quraysh.[52] Other scholars give consideration to such factors as the person's scrupulosity in doubtful matters, his frequency of supererogatory worship, and even his physical attractiveness (which was considered likely to make him appealing to potential worshipers).[53]

[50] According to some scholars the validity of the *ṣalāt* of the followers is contingent on that of the *ṣalāt* of the *imām*. Thus, if the *imām* performs the prayer in a state of ritual impurity, according to the Ḥanafīs (but not the Shāfiʿīs) the prayers of the entire congregation would be canceled. Mālikīs distinguish between conscious and unintentional infractions (that is, if he *imām* did not know that he was in a state of pollution the prayers of the congregation would still be valid). See Ibn Rushd, *Bidāyat al-mujtahid*, 1:144.

[51] *al-Mawsūʿa al-fiqhīya*, art. "Imāmat al-ṣalāt," paragraphs 14–16 (6:207–8).

[52] See al-Shāfiʿī, *al-Umm*, 1:157–8.

[53] *al-Mawsūʿa al-fiqhīya*, art. "Imāmat al-ṣalāt," paragraphs 17–18 (6:208–9).

On the face of it, such broad acknowledgment of the prior claim of the ruler to leadership in prayer, combined with the textually based emphasis on the prayer leader's knowledge and probity, would seem to imply a high opinion of rulers. In fact (as perhaps already suggested by our discussion of prayers for the ruler in the context of the *khuṭba*), the opposite is the case; scholars generally assumed that the prayer leadership of rulers presented acute religious and ethical challenges to worshipers who aspired to technically correct prayer behind a virtuous leader. Deference to the ritual claims of rulers is based not on value judgments about their qualifications, but on the historical precedents set by the earliest Muslims (as well as, presumably, on pragmatic concerns about communal order). If the Prophet's Companion Ibn ʿUmar prayed behind the notoriously ruthless and bloodthirsty Umayyad governor al-Ḥajjāj, what doubt could remain that political authority trumped personal integrity? The Prophet's Companions even prayed behind ʿUthmān's governor of Kufa, al-Walīd ibn ʿUqba, who is famously reported to have drunkenly added two extra (and invalidating) *rakʿa*s to the dawn prayer and to have asked nonchalantly, "Want more?"[54] In addition to their personal faults, rulers might be usurpers or heretics; the third/ninth-century Iraqi scholar Ibn Abī Shayba found a precedent in the early Muslims who prayed behind the extremist Shīʿite rebel al-Mukhtār during his brief rule over Kufa in 66–7 A.H.[55] Personal prayer leadership by the caliph or his representative was an early practice that gradually gave way to the leadership of prayer (and the delivery of the sermon) by religious professionals; C. H. Becker notes that "in the case of Egypt we know the exact year – 242/856 – when the amīr [commander] led the Friday prayer for the last time."[56] Nevertheless, the problem of prayer leadership by iniquitous rulers (or their appointees) contributed to a broad and long-lasting religious discussion of the issue of prayer behind sinful *imām*s.

In the Mālikī school, the early and authoritative collection *al-Mudawwana* reports that Mālik affirmed that it was valid "for us to pray behind these rulers and [perform] Friday prayers behind them," a question that seems to imply a veiled critique of the powers that be. However, it also quotes him as saying, "If you know that the *imām* is a heretic (*min ahl al-ahwāʾ*), do not pray behind him."[57] He is further reported to have held that one must not pray behind a drunkard (*al-sakrān*), and that anyone who did so must repeat the prayer.[58] Taken together, these opinions could be interpreted to mean that one should

54 Cf. Ibn Qudāma, *al-Mughnī*, 2:24.
55 Ibn Abī Shayba, *Muṣannaf*, 2:272.
56 C. H. Becker, "On the History of Muslim Worship," in Gerald Hawting, ed., *The Development of Islamic Ritual* (Aldershot: Ashgate Publishing Limited, 2006), p. 73.
57 Mālik ibn Anas al-Aṣbaḥī [Saḥnūn ibn Saʿīd al-Tanūkhī], *al-Mudawwana al-kubrā* (Beirut: Dār al-Kutub al-ʿIlmīya, 1426/2005), 1:176.
58 Ibid., 1:177.

pray behind rulers unless one had positive knowledge of their heterodoxy or sinfulness. Alternatively, they could be taken to indicate that rulers enjoyed a special exception from Mālik's general conviction that one should not pray behind someone who was religiously deviant or morally degenerate. This view was advanced by the early Mālikī authority Ibn Ḥabīb (d. 238/853), who states that it is necessary to repeat a prayer performed behind someone who drinks an intoxicant "unless it is the caliph, his judge, or his chief of police, because to forbid prayer with him leads to rebellion against them (*al-khurūj ʿan ṭāʿatihim*) and is a cause of civil disturbances (*fitan*)."[59]

Mālikī ambivalence about public prayer under the auspices of questionable rulers, or under conditions of political dissension, is reflected in the tradition that for many years in his later life Mālik himself did not attend Friday or congregational prayers. Some anecdotes interpret his absence as an expression of pious aloofness from civil strife (*iʿtizāl*) in general, or of concern that he might encounter offenses that he would be obliged to denounce, or identify it as occurring specifically during the reign of a counter-caliph. Others have him explaining on his deathbed that he suffered from a ritual disability (urinary incontinence) so embarrassing that he chose to keep it secret.[60] It seems plausible that the latter explanation is intended to remove the implicit political valence of Mālik's nonattendance; in general, later scholars discouraged separation from the community as an expression of disapproval for its moral or political state, particularly where Friday prayers were concerned.

Regarding nonruling sinners, there was a range of interpretations among later Mālikīs. Some held that the *imām*'s sinfulness voided the prayer only if it was a matter subject to absolute consensus (*ijmāʿ*), such as adultery; if a person committed an offense based on an interpretation (*taʾwīl*) that was simply not accepted by Mālikīs (for instance, an Iraqi who drank potentially intoxicating beverages allowed by his school of law) the prayer was not inherently void – although it was still preferable for the Mālikī to repeat the prayer if there was enough time in left in the prayer period. Others held, on the contrary, that even serious and undisputed sins such as adultery or theft did not void the prayer as long as they had nothing to do with the performance of *ṣalāt*, unlike offenses relating to relevant matters such as ritual purity (which eroded the presumption that the *imām*'s prayer was technically valid).[61]

[59] Muḥammad ibn Yūsuf al-ʿAbdarī, known as al-Mawwāq, *al-Tāj wa'l-Iklīl li-Mukhtaṣar Khalīl*, printed in margins of Ḥaṭṭāb, *Mawāhib al-jalīl*, 2:413.

[60] See Michael Cook, *Commanding Right and Forbidding Wrong in Islamic Thought* (Cambridge: Cambridge University Press, 2000), p. 382; al-Qāḍī ʿIyāḍ, *Tartīb al-madārik wa-taqrīb al-masālik li-maʿrifat aʿlām madhhab Mālik*, ed. Aḥmad Bukayr Maḥmūd (Beirut: Dār Maktabat al-Ḥayāt, n.d.), 1:180–1.

[61] Ḥaṭṭāb, *Mawāhib al-jalīl*, 2:412–13.

The great Mālikī thinker and philosopher Abū'l-Walīd ibn Rushd (d. 595/1198) writes that the difference of opinion among jurists over the prayer leadership of the sinner (*al-fāsiq*) is a result of the fact that there is no textual basis for this specific ruling, so that they must base it upon analogy (*qiyās*). Some hold that the only criterion is the validity of the prayer of the *imām*, which is not affected by his state of sinfulness. Others, in contrast, draw an analogy with legal witnessing (*shahāda*). Since one must trust the prayer leader to perform the prayer correctly, just as one must trust a witness to give correct testimony, on the basis of that analogy the unreliability of the *imām* would vitiate the validity of the prayer.[62]

The standard of probity (*ʿadāla*) that applies to legal witnessing is both more exacting and more contextually specific than the criteria of major sin or heresy otherwise applied to the issue of prayer leadership. In order to maintain *ʿadāla* a person must not merely fulfill the basic requirements of the faith, but uphold a standard of propriety and dignity appropriate to his station and to the society in which he lives. For instance, many classical scholars held that it impaired *ʿadāla* to be seen eating in the marketplace, which was not forbidden by the sharia but was perceived as an act of vulgarity. Imāmī Shīʿites also consider *ʿadāla* a requirement for prayer leaders; as formulated by al-Shahīd al-Thānī (d. c. 965/1558), this means that "in addition to faith, he should have an ingrained disposition (*malaka rāsikha*) that impels him to piety and manliness (*murūwa*), such that he does not commit a major sin (*kabīra*) or persist in a minor one, and does not commit any [legally] neutral or undesirable act that indicates baseness or degradation based on what is customary for his peers according to his time and place." (The requirement of "faith" here specifically includes the stipulation that the individual be an Imāmī.)[63]

Mālikī fatwas suggest that the standard of *ʿadāla* for prayer leaders could be wielded as a form of religious leverage in cases where social or religious customs were under dispute. The fifteenth-century Moroccan compiler al-Wansharīsī presents, for instance, a set of legal opinions elicited by a question about an *imām* who does not veil his wife. Are his leadership of prayer and his testimony (*imāma* and *shahāda*) valid or not? The responses show that some scholars strove to assert the requirement of veiling by female relatives as a condition of prayer leadership, although they acknowledge that it is the custom of people in the countryside for a woman to go out and take care of her own affairs with her face and extremities exposed.[64] In the early modern period a

62 Ibn Rushd, *Bidāyat al-mujtahid*, 1:134.

63 al-ʿĀmilī, *al-Fawāʾid al-malīya*, 285–6.

64 Aḥmad ibn Yaḥyā al-Wansharīsī, *al-Miʿyār al-muʿrib waʾl-jāmiʿ al-mughrib ʿan fatāwā ahl ifrīqīya wa'l-andalus wa'l-maghrib* (Rabat: Wizārat al-Awqāf wa'l-Shu'ūn al-Islāmīya bi'l-Mamlaka al-Maghribīya, 1401/1981), 1:131. Also see related cases on 1:136, 159.

number of North African jurists discussed the validity of the testimony and prayer leadership of someone who smokes tobacco (a vice then newly imported from the New World); even those who considered smoking inherently licit often held that it impaired *ʿadāla* because it was incompatible with *murūʾa*, i.e., "manliness" or dignified comportment.[65]

Inquiries about the qualifications for prayer leadership collected by al-Wansharīsī reflect tensions not only over proper social norms, but over religious and political authority. Questioners sought to cast doubt on the qualifications of *imāms* who engaged in Sufi practices such as mystical audition (*samāʿ*) and ecstatic dancing, which were evidently prevalent and accepted by much of the population; jurists had varying responses to such concerns.[66] One enquirer probes the case of an *imām* who acts as a witness/notary for government business (*yashhadu fī'l-umūr al-makhzanīya*), an activity clearly assumed to be sufficiently compromising to warrant concerns about his religious probity.[67] In the eighteenth century the Moroccan Muḥammad ibn ʿAlī al-Sūsī complained about the popular reverence accorded to memorizers and reciters of the Qurʾān. He notes that while they are often preferred by ordinary people as prayer leaders (if only because they demand lower salaries than proper scholars), their lack of legal knowledge may lead them to err in matters of ritual purity and *ṣalāt*, invalidating their own prayers and those of those who pray behind them. Furthermore, they are disqualified by the permissive mores and distinctive religious customs characteristic of rural Morocco, including the fact that they shake hands with women and that their wives do not pray, and mix with men while insufficiently covered.[68]

Among Ḥanbalīs, debates over legitimate prayer leadership focused more centrally on issues of theological orthodoxy. This is perhaps unsurprising, since the origin narrative of the Ḥanbalī school centrally features its founder's conflict with the ruling powers, who persecuted him for resisting their imposition of a theological doctrine that he regarded as heretical.[69] In one report Ibn Ḥanbal's student al-Athram enquires about the case of someone who has prayed behind one of the Shīʿite "rejecters" (al-Rāfiḍa, i.e., those who repudiate Abū Bakr, ʿUmar, and ʿUthmān). He replies that such a person must repeat his prayer, implying that it was invalid. Another questioner enquires further, "Does that

[65] Laḥsan al-Yūbī, *al-Fatāwā al-fiqhīya fī ahamm al-qaḍāyā* (Rabat: al-Mamlaka al-Maghribīya, Wizārat al-Awqāf wa'l-Shuʾūn al-Islāmīya, 1419/1998), pp. 355–7.

[66] See Wansharīsī, *Miʿyār*, 1:133–4, 160.

[67] Ibid., 1:167.

[68] Muḥammad ibn ʿAlī ibn Ibrāhīm Akbīl al-Sūsī, *Tanbīh al-ikhwān ʿalā tark al-bidaʿ wa'l-ʿiṣyān*, ed. Muḥammad Sitītū (Wajdah: Kullīyat al-Ādāb wa'l-ʿUlūm al-Insānīya, Jāmiʿat Muḥammad al-Awwal, 2001), pp. 42–4.

[69] See Michael Cooperson, *Classical Arabic Biography: The Heirs of the Prophets in the Age of al-Maʾmūn* (Cambridge: Cambridge University Press, 2000), pp. 107–53.

apply to all heretics (*ahl al-bidaʿ*)?" Ibn Ḥanbal answers, "No; some of them remain silent, and some of them reserve judgment (*yaqif*) and do not speak." He is also supposed to have declared, "Do not pray behind any of the heretics if he is a propagandist (*dāʿiya*) for his heresy."[70]

This stipulation that one must avoid following prayer leaders who openly advocate for heretical doctrines (that is, doctrines deemed heretical from the point of view of Ibn Ḥanbal and his followers) was subject to more than one interpretation. The authoritative Ḥanbalī legal manual of ʿUmar al-Khiraqī (d. 334/946) states that someone who prays behind a leader who "openly proclaims his religious innovation" (*yuʿlin bi-bidʿatihi*) must repeat the prayer. Ibn Qudāma understands this statement to imply that a person who prays behind an individual who is secretly a heretic is excused (*maʿdhūr*), like someone whose prayer leader is in a state of ritual pollution unbeknownst to him; in both cases sincere ignorance of the true situation preserves the validity of the follower's prayer.[71] The Ḥanbalī scholar Abū Yaʿlā (d. 458/1066), in contrast, interprets al-Khiraqī's reference to someone who "proclaims" or "promulgates" his heresy (*al-muʿlin*) to mean someone who believes it on the basis of a proof (*dalīl*), in contrast to someone who is merely following a religious authority (*taqlīd*). While Ibn Qudāma rightly regards this as a somewhat strained interpretation of al-Khiraqī's wording, it serves to place the moral odium (and ritual exclusion) associated with religious deviance on the leaders who advocate for objectionable doctrines on their own authority, rather than on the rank and file who trustingly follow them.[72]

Despite a deep concern with the theological boundaries of the community, Ḥanbalī scholars did not encourage inquisitorial investigation or destabilizing doubt with respect to the faith of one's fellow believers who sought to lead the community in prayer. Ibn Taymīya likens the *imām* who conceals his religious deviancy to a sinner who conceals his misbehavior; such a person is not confronted but left to the judgment of God, because he harms only himself by sinning in secret (unlike an open sinner or heretic, who harms the wider public).[73]

Discussing the problem of prayer leadership by heretics and sinners, Ibn Taymīya offers a strikingly tolerant view of prayer even behind those whose beliefs are regarded as falling outside of the limits of Islam. While it may be

70 Ibn Qudāma, *al-Mughnī*, 2:21.

71 Ibid., 2:21, but see 2:26–7, where he argues that if the *imām* openly espouses his heresy one must repeat the prayer even if one was unaware of it at the time, since (unlike in the case of unwitting infractions of ritual purity) open heterodoxy is not ordinarily unknown to either the *imām* or the follower.

72 However, it is also reported that Ibn Ḥanbal declared, "One should not pray behind a heretic (*mubtadiʿ*) under any circumstances (*bi-ḥāl*)": ibid., 2:22.

73 Ibn Taymīya, *Majmūʿ al-fatāwā*, 23:150–1.

possible to state that a given religious tenet constitutes disbelief (*kufr*), he writes, it is not possible to determine that a given individual who espouses this tenet is a nonbeliever. For instance, the Qur'ān explicitly states that someone who wrongfully consumes the wealth of orphans will burn in hell (verse 4:10), but it is not possible to confirm that any specific person who commits this sin will go to hell, because some mitigating factor may be present (for instance, he may not have been aware of the prohibition, he may have repented, or his good deeds may suffice to counterbalance the offense). Similarly, someone who confesses a doctrine that itself constitutes *kufr* may not be aware of or understand the relevant texts; if the person is qualified to exercise independent legal reasoning (*ijtihād*), God will forgive him for being mistaken in his reasoning.[74] Given that Ibn Taymīya ordinarily has little tolerance for oppressors, heretics, and religious innovators, his theological generosity in this regard speaks volumes about his concern for the unity of the community gathered in prayer.

Aside from the question of doctrinal soundness, Ibn Ḥanbal's concerns also extended to general moral turpitude. He is reported to have declared that one should never pray behind someone who gets drunk; if one finds out about this habit after the fact, one should repeat the prayer. In response to a questioner who asked whether, in the case that the *imām* was a drunkard, he should rather pray by himself Ibn Ḥanbal is supposed to have retorted, "Where are you, in the desert? There are lots of mosques!"[75] Ḥanbalīs such as Ibn Qudāma took this attitude toward tippling prayer leaders as applicable to other cases of moral turpitude (*fisq*), up to an including the venial prayer leader who demands payment for his services during Ramaḍān.[76]

Significantly, however, Ḥanbalī scrupulosity with respect to prayer leaders was tempered by prudential deference to governmental power. Ibn Qudāma cites a *ḥadīth* in which the Prophet declares, "Let no woman lead a man in prayer, nor a sinner (*fājir*) a believer, unless the sultan overpowers [the believer] or he fears [the sultan's] whip or his sword."[77] This principle particularly applied to Friday and festival prayers, which were held under the auspices of the authorities and to which there was no private alternative. To eschew them was unacceptable; Ibn Qudāma cites a report from an early authority who, consulted about heretics who fail to attend Friday prayers, declares that they are directly defying God's commandment to hasten to prayer when called on Friday (Qur'ān 62:9) – an idea so overwhelming that he faints in awe. Ibn Qudāma observes that "Aḥmad [ibn Ḥanbal] used to attend them with the Muʿtazila [i.e., his opponents in the theological conflict of his time], and so

[74] Ibid., 23:151–3.
[75] Ibn Qudāma, *al-Mughnī*, 2:23.
[76] Ibid., 2:24.
[77] Ibid., 2:22–3.

did the [other like-minded] scholars who were in his time."[78] Varying reports suggest either that Ibn Ḥanbal advocated repeating such prayers later if the *imām* was a heretic or that he denounced such an action as itself being heretical; in any case, his support for participation in government-sponsored congregational prayer, even if led by a heterodox *imām*, seems to be undisputed. Similarly, while Ibn Qudāma cites Ibn Ḥanbal as directing, "Do not pray behind an immoral person (*fājir*)," he goes on to state, "As for Friday and festival prayers, they are performed behind every virtuous or immoral person (*kull barr wa-fājir*)."[79] Ibn Taymīya firmly declares that it is heresy to abstain from Friday and congregational prayers behind oppressive rulers, or to repeat the prayers on the assumption that they were invalid. Refraining from participation forfeits a religious benefit without preventing any corresponding harm, assuming that the ruler's injustice will not be stopped by these means.[80]

As summarized by his disciple al-Muzanī, al-Shāfiʿī's position was more lenient than that of Aḥmad ibn Ḥanbal. He writes that "Shāfiʿī said ... I disapprove of prayer being led by a sinner (*al-fāsiq*) or someone who openly displays religious innovations (*muẓhir al-bidaʿ*), [but] someone who follows them in prayer does not repeat [his prayer]."[81] While al-Shāfiʿī clearly finds prayer behind moral and religious deviants distasteful, the key point is that he holds it to be perfectly valid (and thus to require no repetition).[82] As we have seen, this was a concession that Ibn Ḥanbal appears to have made only with respect to Friday or festival prayers held under the auspices of the authorities. On the issue of prayers led by rulers, al-Shāfiʿī again takes a more tolerant position. About rulers who delay prayers after the ideal time, he cites a *ḥadīth* in which the Prophet states, "A group of people will come and lead you in prayer; if they do so perfectly, it is to their benefit and to yours, and if they do so inadequately, it is to their detriment and to your benefit." Only if the leader completely fails to perform the prayer until the allotted time expires is the follower counseled to pray individually instead.[83]

In the eleventh century the Shāfiʿī jurist al-Māwardī summarized the school's doctrine regarding the prayer leadership of heretics and sinners as follows. Firstly, he distinguished between those whose offenses excluded them from the Muslim faith community altogether and those who remained believers. The first category was exemplified by those who, for instance, drank wine and believed it to be licit, persisted in committing adultery or sodomy while denying that they were forbidden, or violated the property or shed the blood of others out

[78] Ibid., 2:25–6 (see also Ibn Taymīya, *Majmūʿ al-fatāwā*, 23:151).
[79] Ibid., 2:24, 25.
[80] Ibn Taymīya, *Majmūʿ al-fatāwā*, 23:151.
[81] *Mukhtaṣar al-Muzanī* (printed as final volume of al-Shāfiʿī, *al-Umm*), p. 22.
[82] al-Shāfiʿī, *al-Umm*, 1:158–9.
[83] Ibid., 1:159.

of impudence toward God. Such a person is a nonbeliever (presumably because he is denying the validity of revealed texts), and his prayer leadership is invalid. (Although it seems unlikely that many aspirants to the leadership of congregational prayer denied such basic Islamic tenets as the prohibition of wine or adultery, al-Māwardī's reference to arrogant confiscation of money or shedding of blood might well have been understood to apply to some rulers.) The second category, those who remained within the religious community despite their offenses, included both behavioral and doctrinal offenders. An example of the first would be someone who drank wine or committed other forbidden actions with regret and trepidation; an example of the second would be someone who believed in cursing the Companions of the Prophet (i.e., a hardline Shīʿite). The prayer leadership of such a person, al-Māwardī states, is repugnant but valid.[84]

In summarizing the Shāfiʿī position, Ibn Qudāma cites a precedent attributed to the Prophet's Companion Ibn ʿUmar. Observing that he was willing to pray with both parties in a time of civil war, someone asked him, "Do you pray with these and with these when they are killing each other?" Ibn ʿUmar replied, "Whoever says, 'Come to prayer,' I respond to him [positively] ...; whoever says, 'Come to kill your Muslim brother and take his property,' I say no."[85] In the final analysis, then, Shāfiʿī doctrine combines an idealistic emphasis on the qualifications of the ideal prayer leader (al-Māwardī cites a *ḥadīth* in which the Prophet exhorts believers to "test your prayer leaders as you test coins") with an inclusive affirmation that even the most sinful or doctrinally offensive leader will suffice if he does not actually forswear the basic tenets of the faith.

At the extreme lenient end of the spectrum is the position attributed to Abū Ḥanīfa by his school. Significantly, the most famous relevant statement occurs in two theological creeds that reflect Abū Ḥanīfa's strong denial that the commission of sins excludes a believer from the community of faith. This position represents a vigorous repudiation of the view that faith includes works and thus can be voided by serious infractions – one most notoriously associated with the Khārijites, who declared sinning or dissenting Muslims apostates and accordingly regarded their blood as licit. The *Fiqh al-absaṭ*, traditionally attributed to Abū Ḥanīfa, declares in response to the question of prayer behind a murderer (*qātil*), "Prayer behind every virtuous or sinning [believer] is valid, and you receive your reward." (A version of this statement was also attributed to the Prophet Muḥammad.)[86] Classical Ḥanafī legal manuals held that prayer behind a sinner or heretic was valid and yielded reward

[84] ʿAlī ibn Muḥammad al-Māwardī, *al-Ḥāwī al-kabīr fī fiqh madhhab al-imām al-Shāfiʿī raḍiya Allāhu ʿanhu*, ed. ʿAlī Muḥammad Muʿawwaḍ and ʿĀdil Aḥmad ʿAbd al-Mawjūd (Beirut: Dār al-Kutub al-ʿIlmīya, 1414/1994), 2:328–30.

[85] Ibn Qudāma, *al-Mughnī*, 2:22.

[86] A. J. Wensinck, *The Muslim Creed, Its Genesis and Historical Development* (New Delhi: Oriental Books Reprint Corporation, 1979), pp. 220–1.

(particularly in the case of Friday prayers, where choosing an alternate venue was not a possibility), although not as much reward as prayer behind a pious person.[87] Only opinions that excluded one from the faith community altogether actually disqualified one as a valid prayer leader, although scholars could differ on the precise tenets to which this principle applied. Opinions cited as excluding one from prayer leadership included denying the caliphate of ʿUmar (as did many Shīʿites), affirming that the Qurʾān was created (as did the Muʿtazilīs), attributing anthropomorphic characteristics to God, and denying the Prophet's power of intercession or the vision of God in the afterlife.[88]

Overall, among Sunnī scholars concern for the unity of the community and for the stability of its governance outweighed the desire for doctrinal purity or behavioral conformity. However, particularly for Mālikīs (who were more apt to apply the standard of *ʿadāla*), refusal to pray behind a sinning *imām* remained a potential avenue of social and political protest[89]. During a wave of civil unrest in Fez in the fifteenth century the Moroccan Sufi master Aḥmad Zarrūq expressed his disapproval of the religious excesses of the rebels by refusing to pray behind a scholar supporting the uprising, declaring, "I don't entrust my prayers to an arrogant and conceited show-off, since my prayers might become as hollow as he is."[90] Zarrūq's Moroccan Sufi contemporary ʿAlī ibn Maymūn al-Idrīsī, who traveled to Syria and was appalled by many of the religious practices he encountered there, declared the prayer leadership of the generality of *imāms* in the Islamic East to be invalid due to the ubiquitous practice of paying bribes to acquire the salaried state posts of prayer leader and preacher. He asked rhetorically, "How can the prayer leadership be valid of someone who wrongfully consumes the wealth of the people and wrongfully gives his own money in order to acquire many times the amount in return?"[91]

[87] Cf. Ibn Nujaym, *al-Baḥr*, 1:348; Ibn al-Humām al-Ḥanafī, *Sharḥ Fatḥ al-qadīr*, ed. ʿAbd al-Razzāq Ghālib al-Mahdī (Beirut: Dār al-Kutub al-ʿIlmīya, 1424/2003), 1:359–60.

[88] See, for instance, Ibn Nujaym, *al-Baḥr*, 1:611 (see also Ibn al-Humām, *Fatḥ al-qadīr*, 1:360). Here again, it is carefully specified that such persons are debarred because their opinions constitute *kufr* (disbelief), although one cannot declare them *kāfirs* as individuals.

[89] A related question was the issue of prayer in misappropriated spaces. Refusal to pray in a building erected by the ruler through the confiscation of property was an occasional form of religious protest against government abuses. The great Shāfiʿī jurist Abū Isḥāq al-Shīrāzī (d. 476/1083) refused for this reason to perform his prayers in the Niẓāmīya madrasa in Baghdad, constructed especially for him by the Saljuq vizier; several centuries later legal scholars declared prayer invalid in al-Māristān al-Manṣūrī in Cairo, which the sultan had seized from a dignitary whom he had then put to death. See George Makdisi, *The Rise of Colleges: Institutions of Learning in Islam and the West* (Edinburgh: Edinburgh University Press, 1981), pp. 42, 46.

[90] Scott Kugle, *Rebel between Spirit and Law: Ahmad Zarruq, Sainthood, and Authority in Islam* (Bloomington and Indianapolis: Indiana University Press, 2006), p. 94.

[91] ʿAlī ibn Maymūn al-Idrīsī, *Risālat Bayān ghurbat al-islām bi-wāsiṭat ṣinfay al-mutafaqqiha wa'l-mutafaqqira min ahl miṣr wa'l-shām wa-mā yalīyā min bilād al-aʿjām*, Princeton MS Garret 828H, 68b.

More discreet and personal protests were also possible; the seventeenth-century North African Mālikī Sufi ʿAbd al-Qādir al-Fāsī received an inquiry about the practice of the "early Muslims" (*al-salaf*) of performing one's prayers privately before attending congregational prayers behind iniquitous leaders. Al-Fāsī approvingly observes that this practice preserves the unity and comity of the community, and then proceeds to give detailed instructions for the application of this form of tacit dissent.[92] In a similar vein, the influential seventeenth-century Ḥanbalī scholar Manṣūr ibn Yūnūs al-Bahūtī suggests that, for the sake of safety from the authorities, one might either pray in congregation behind their sinful appointees and then repeat the prayer afterward, or pray in sync with the *imām* while inwardly intending to pray alone (or to follow someone else).[93]

The presumption of the invalidity of prayers led by official appointees, and the necessity of resorting to private ritual remedies, was an issue of lasting concern. As we have seen, Ibn al-Taymīya himself regarded such a position as extreme; however, it remained within the repertory of religious responses to governmental wrongdoing in subsequent centuries. In response to the question of whether it is obligatory (*wājib*) to perform a four-*rakʿa* prayer after Friday prayers to cover the eventuality that the *jumʿa* prayer was invalid, the eighteenth-century Ḥanafī ʿAbd al-Ghanī al-Nābulusī responds that it most likely is, particularly if one takes into account the fact that most of the prayer leaders of his time are appointed by government officials who obtain their positions through bribery, take bribes from others, or tolerate bribery on the part of their appointees or subordinates. Citing a precedent from the Ḥanafī school, he argues that all such officials are illegitimate and their legal actions void, including the appointment of prayer leaders.[94] It is significant that ʿAbd al-Ghanī is otherwise known to have been a loyal subject of the Ottoman state; this is not the opinion of a political agitator, but a standard expression of religious disillusionment with the corruption inherent in the exercise of power (from which he carefully exculpates the sultan himself).[95]

92 Muḥammad al-Mahdī al-ʿImrānī, *al-Nawāzil al-jadīda al-kubrā* ([Rabat]: al-Mamlaka al-Maghribīya, Wizārat al-Awqāf wa-al-Shuʾūn al-Islāmīya, 1996–), 1:375.

93 Manṣūr ibn Yūnus al-Bahūtī, *Kashshāf al-qināʿ ʿan matn al-Iqnāʿ*, ed. Hilāl Muṣayliḥī Muṣṭafā Hilāl (Riyadh: Maktabat al-Naṣr al-Ḥadītha, n.d.), 1:475 (for a less politically pointed discussion see Ibn Qudāma, *al-Mughnī*, 2:29).

94 ʿAbd al-Ghanī ibn Ismāʿīl al-Nābulusī, *Nihāyat al-murād fī sharḥ Hadīyat Ibn al-ʿImād*, ed. ʿAbd al-Razzāq al-Ḥalabī (Dubai: Qism al-Taḥqīq wa'l-Nashr, Markaz Jumʿa al-Mājid li'l-Thaqāfa wa'l-Turāth, 1414/1994), p. 682.

95 See Barbara von Schlegell, "Sufism in the Ottoman Arab World: Shaykh ʿAbd al-Ghanī al-Nābulusī (d. 1143/1731)," Ph.D. dissertation, University of California, Berkeley, 1997, pp. 96, 103–4.

Prayer behind a leader of another legal school

Because almost all premodern Sunnīs (like many modern-day believers) considered it obligatory to adhere to the teachings of one school of law, and because the details of the *ṣalāt* ritual varied slightly from school to school, the question arose whether it was desirable or even permissible to pray behind an *imām* of another school. Of course, even more acute questions were raised by congregational prayer across sectarian lines. Debates over this issue focused on the religious values of community solidarity and inclusiveness on the one hand, and of the pursuit of ideal ritual forms on the other.

Najam Haider has demonstrated that variant styles of performing *ṣalāt* were among the most visible and important signifiers of identity for the emerging religious groupings of the late first and second centuries of the Islamic calendar. For instance, the late first-century Baṣran traditionist Abū'l-ʿĀliya is quoted as declaring:

> We would follow the man from whom we wanted to transmit [traditions] to observe him when he prayed. If he knew how to perform [the prayer] expertly, we would sit down with him and say, "He must be correct in other matters." But if he performed [the prayer] incorrectly, we would move away from him and say, "He is wrong in other matters."[96]

A person's mode of prayer could be an indicator not only of religious proficiency but of the sectarian and school-based loyalties that were then crystallizing. Such distinctions influenced not merely personal preferences (such as the choice whether to transmit from an individual *muḥaddith*) but the formation of communities of worship. Haider notes a report in which the Kufan jurist Sharīk ibn ʿAbd Allāh (d. 177/793) counsels a questioner that if *qunūt* – a practice favored by early Kufan scholars, and carried on by Imāmī Shīʿites – is not performed in the mosque closest to one's home, one should go to another mosque where it is done.[97] The desire to worship with others who shared one's ritual preferences could be a powerful practical incentive to consolidate a like-minded community.

Over time prayer practices became not merely matters of personal discretion but insignia of identity, as Ibn Baṭṭūṭa and his traveling companions discovered in the fourteenth century when visiting the city of Sinop in Asia Minor. Being unfamiliar with Mālikī practice, the locals assumed that their posture in prayer (with the hands hanging down at the sides) indicated that they were Shīʿites. The travelers were able to clear themselves of this suspicion only when the sultan craftily presented them with a rabbit, an animal considered ritually impure by Shīʿites. "So we slaughtered it, cooked it and ate

[96] Haider, *Origins*, p. 219 (the translation is Haider's).
[97] Ibid., p. 234.

it; the servant went back to him and informed him of that, and then the accusation was removed from us."[98]

As time went by Shīʿites and Sunnīs generally preferred not to pray together, although in many cases Shīʿites acknowledged the need to pray with Sunnīs as a matter of practicality or dissimulation. Within the Sunnī community, in contrast, the situation was more complex. Particularly in the case of Friday prayer, but also on other occasions, Sunnīs often found it necessary or desirable to worship together. However, because the precise specifications of ideal (or even valid) prayer varied from school to school, there was also a tendency to prefer prayer leaders of one's own school of law (*madhhab*). The concerns raised by inter-*madhhab* worship included issues of ritual purity; because different schools disagreed on the precise actions (including touching a person of the opposite sex or one's own genitals) that canceled one's state of ritual purity and required *wuḍūʾ*, it was possible that the *imām* might be in a state of ritual purity by his own lights but not according to the school of a person following him in prayer. They also included differences of opinion about the required or desirable components of the prayer ritual – whether one should pronounce the *basmala* audibly as a verse of the Fatiḥa or not, whether one should perform *qunūt* in the dawn prayer, etc.

Discrepancies in such areas could either render one's prayer less meritorious or invalidate it altogether. Some of them would have been immediately apparent to the follower, demanding a decision about the desirability of following the *imām*; others, such as most issues of ritual purity, would have been undetectable but raised the possibility of invalidity. Whether one prayed alone or in congregation, inter-*madhhab* distinctions could give rise to disagreement and doubt. In the sixteenth century the Egyptian Sufi and jurist ʿAbd al-Wahhāb al-Shaʿrānī composed a book in response to the predicament of Sufi aspirants and ordinary craftspeople who complained (among other things) that "if we perform our ablutions according to one *madhhab* the [scholars] of the other *madhhab* tell us, 'Your ablutions are invalid!', and if we pray according to one *madhhab* the [scholars] of the other *madhhab* tell us, 'Your prayers are invalid!'"[99]

Although (as we shall see) most scholars accepted the validity of prayer behind an *imām* of another school of law under certain conditions, differences in the rules of prayer sometimes appear to have contributed to the formation of exclusivist group loyalties. Ibn Taymīya deplores the extent to which differences in the performance of *ṣalāt* have contributed to the development of

98 Ibn Baṭṭūṭa, *Riḥlat Ibn Baṭṭūṭa al-musammā Tuḥfat al-nuẓẓār fī gharāʾib al-amṣār* (Ṣaydā and Beirut: al-Maktaba al-ʿAṣrīya, 1425/2005), 1:288.

99 ʿAbd al-Wahhāb al-Shaʿrānī, *Kitāb Kashf al-ghamma ʿan jamīʿ al-umma* (Cairo: Muṣṭafā al-Bābī al-Ḥalabī, n.d.), p. 2.

unthinking and chauvinistic identification with those who adhere to the same rules and feelings of hostility and estrangement toward those who do not. Agreement in matters of ritual – and the consequent ability to worship together – leads to problematic group solidarities that may sway people in such matters as the distribution of patronage, regardless of the merits of the individuals involved.[100] The identity and solidarity of subgroups such as schools of law, which share rules and preferences on the details of *ṣalāt*, thus causes an internal fragmentation of the Muslim community. For Ibn Taymīya, in contrast, the internal solidarity of the believing community – which for him excludes such "heretics" as Muʿtazilīs and Shīʿites – is a primary religious value that is founded in the Qurʾān.

Ibn Taymīya argues that most differences of opinion relating to prayer do not involve the obligatory components of the ritual, but subsidiary matters that different schools of law consider desirable or undesirable (*al-mustaḥabbāt waʾl-makrūhāt*). Thus, most scholars regard alternative forms of *ṣalāt* (such as those preferred by schools of law other than their own) to be valid, if suboptimal. Regardless of whether one believes that the *basmala* should be recited out loud or under one's breath, for instance, the prayer will be valid in either case. It is universally accepted that some Companions of the Prophet pronounced it loudly and others whispered it, yet none of them invalidated each other's prayers.[101] Rather than adhering to a single mode out of either considered preference or habitual loyalty, Ibn Taymīya argues that it is superior to vary one's mode of worship, just as the Prophet is reported to have acted in one way on a given occasion and in a second way on another. This would eliminate rifts in the community based on preferences in the details of ritual practice.[102] Ibn Taymīya affirms that the unification of the hearts of the religious community (*iʾtilāf qulūb al-umma*) is of far greater importance than a nonbinding preference for some detail of ritual practice.[103] The best thing is for an *imām* to emulate the Prophet's prayer as faithfully as possible, even if it involves practices that are unfamiliar to most people in the congregation.[104]

In fact, however, abandonment of the forms of prayer sanctioned by the established schools in favor of practices documented in *ḥadīth* was no simple matter. Particularly when deep personal convictions and governmental power came into conflict, differences in the *ṣalāt* ritual could become existential. It is recounted of an Andalusian contemporary of Ibn Taymīya that as a Ẓāhirī who

100 Ibn Taymīya, *Majmūʿ al-fatāwā*, 22:179; Ibn Taymīya, *Risālat al-ulfa bayna al-muslimīn*, ed. ʿAbd al-Fattāḥ Abū Ghudda (Aleppo: Maktab al-Maṭbūʿāt al-Islāmīya, 1417/1996), p. 64.
101 Ibn Taymīya, *Majmūʿ al-fatāwā*, 22:184–5; Ibn Taymīya, *Risālat al-ulfa*, pp. 42–4.
102 Ibn Taymīya, *Risālat al-ulfa*, pp. 62–3; see also Ibn Taymīya, *Majmūʿ al-fatāwā*, 22:170.
103 Ibn Taymīya, *Risālat al-ulfa*, p. 47; see also Ibn Taymīya, *Majmūʿ al-fatāwā*, 22:202.
104 Ibn Taymīya, *Majmūʿ al-fatāwā*, 22:161–2.

believed in direct reference to *ḥadīth* texts rather than adherence to one of the established schools of law, he altered the position of his hands in prayer based on a report from the Prophet that he considered authentic. The sultan, learning of this, threatened to cut off the scholar's hands if he continued to position them based on his own textual interpretation. Lamenting the beleaguered status of the *sunna*, the scholar emigrated to Egypt.[105]

For those premodern Muslims who adhered to an established school of law, the validity and merit of prayer behind a leader of another *madhhab* was a legitimate area of concern. One view, most influentially expressed in a monograph by Raḥmatullāh al-Sindī (who lived in Medina and Mecca and died in 993/1585), is that the validity of a prayer performed behind an *imām* depends exclusively on the doctrines held by the person who is following. That is, both his or her own *ṣalāt* and that of the *imām* must conform to the standards established by the follower's school of law, regardless of the legal doctrines held by the *imām*. The somewhat paradoxical implication of this approach is that if the *imām* performs the prayer in a way that is invalid by the standards of his own school but valid by those of the follower, the follower's prayer is valid.[106] Al-Sindī's argument would presumably exclude many cases of inter-*madhhab* prayer leadership, since an *imām* is unlikely to perform prayer in ways that diverge from his own school but fairly likely to do so in ways that diverge from the standards held by a follower of another school. However, al-Sindī affirms that it is permissible to follow an *imām* of another *madhhab* if he performs the prayer in such a way as to avoid disputed actions that would invalidate the prayer for members of other schools.[107] Al-Sindī's Ḥijāzī contemporary Mullā ʿAlī al-Qāriʾ similarly held that one could pray behind an *imām* of another school if the *imām* observed the principle of *iḥtiyāṭ*, which requires that one piously choose the stricter of the two options in any case of juristic disagreement.[108] This guaranteed that the *imām* would not invalidate his prayer in the eyes of the follower by, for instance, taking advantage of the more lenient tenets of his school with respect to ritual purity. (In cases such as the loud or silent pronunciation of the *basmala*, where neither option was obviously more demanding than the other, he allowed discretion to the individual worshiper.)

[105] Ignaz Goldziher, *The Ẓāhirīs: Their Doctrine and Their History*, trans. Wolfgang Behn (Leiden: E. J. Brill, 1971), p. 177.

[106] Raḥmat Allāh al-Sindī al-Ḥanafī, *Risāla fī bayān al-iqtidāʾ biʾl-shāfiʿīya wa ʾl-khilāf fī dhālika*, MS Cairo 347 Majāmīʿ, p. 3.

[107] Ibid., p. 2.

[108] ʿAlī al-Qāriʾ argues that what is at stake is not the technical validity of the follower's prayer, but whether it is legally repugnant. However, most worshipers presumably would choose not to pray behind a member of another *madhhab* if it involved repugnance (*karāha*). Mullā ʿAlī al-Qāriʾ, Risālat al-Ihtidāʾ fīʾl-iqtidāʾ, MS Cairo, Uṣūl Taymūr 172, p. 9.

However, al-Qāri' observed that in his own time *imāms* observing *iḥtiyāṭ* were "as rare as a gryphon."[109]

The opposite view, expressed by the Ḥanbalī authority al-Bahūtī in an influential manual, is that even if the *imām* performs the prayer in a way that is invalid from the point of view of the follower, the prayer is valid for both of them as long as the *imām*'s action is based on legitimate interpretation or on emulation (*taqlīd*) of an authority. This is because the *imām*'s prayer is valid by virtue of fulfilling the conditions to which he himself adheres; since the *imām*'s prayer is valid, so is that of the follower.[110] Addressing another possible source of recrimination among schools, al-Bahūtī specifies that an *imām* is also not disqualified by the performance of actions that are sinful according to the follower's school of law but permitted according to the *imām*'s; legitimately disputed actions are not a source of moral opprobium. (However, he does entertain the possibility that such a person would be disqualified by chronic commission of such an action.)[111]

Both al-Sindī's and al-Bahūtī's positions reflect a concern for conciliation and solidarity within the Sunnī community, although al-Sindī establishes a more exacting standard for cross-*madhhab* participation. In practice, however, people often preferred to pray behind an *imām* who performed the ritual in the manner to which they were accustomed. In a place with a religiously mixed population such as medieval Damascus, Friday prayers were generally led by an *imām* representing the school favored by the ruler in a cathedral mosque (*jāmiʿ*) that accommodated adherents of all *madhhab*s. Smaller mosques (*masjid*), in contrast, might be devoted to a single *madhhab* by the stipulation of their founder (although this practice was disapproved by some scholars). On occasions other than Friday prayers, great mosques such as the Umayyad Mosque of Damascus hosted multiple congregational prayers led by *imāms* of different *madhhabs* presiding at designated prayer niches.[112]

A particularly important and controversial case was the Sacred Mosque of Mecca, where separate *imāms* for the different schools of law were appointed at the beginning of the sixth/twelfth century by the command of the ʿAbbāsid caliph. This development raised the legal question whether it was permissible for them to lead prayers one at a time, as was the custom for a number of

[109] Patrick Franke, "Ritual prayer and *madhhab* identity in Mecca at the turn of the seventeenth century: some texts by the Hanafi scholar Ali al-Qari," unpublished conference paper delivered at the conference Performing Religion: Actors, Contexts, and Text, Orient-Institut Beirut, November 18, 2011.

[110] al-Bahūtī, *Kashshāf al-qināʿ*, 1:478.

[111] Ibid., 1:478–9.

[112] Makdisi, *Rise of Colleges*, p. 17; Daniella Talmon-Heller, *Islamic Piety in Medieval Syria: Mosques, Cemeteries and Sermons under the Zangids and Ayyubids (1146–1260)* (Leiden and Boston: Brill, 2007), p. 46.

centuries thereafter. Was the first prayer to be performed most meritorious, thus making it inadvisable to wait for the *imām* of one's own *madhhab*? And was the Sacred Mosque to be considered one mosque, in which case it might be repugnant to have multiple congregational prayers performed one after another? Scholars produced fatwas and epistles on both sides of these questions.[113] Because the Sacred Mosque was of unique symbolic importance for all Muslims, it was the arrangements within its precincts that gave rise to much of the reflection about inter-*madhhab* prayer.

Knowledge of prayer and its distribution in the community

The *ṣalāt* ritual creates and expresses community identity and solidarity not only through the performance of congregational prayer, but through the sheer fact that each individual Muslim is obligated to pray. Even when the rite is performed individually in the privacy of the home or the solitude of a remote place, it ties Muslims together in a community of knowledge and practice. This fact is reflected in the famous travel narratives of al-Muqaddasī in the fourth/tenth century and of Ibn Baṭṭūṭa in the eighth/fourteenth; no matter how distant or unfamiliar the areas to which they traveled, they could not only participate in prayer, but evaluate local prayer practices based on their knowledge of relevant legal debates and their shared sense of ideal Islamic piety.

Responsibility for organizing and encouraging regular prayer, both on the individual and the communal level, was incumbent upon the ruler at the top of the hierarchy, the market inspector or censor of morals (*muḥtasib*) in the middle, and the ordinary believer at the bottom. For rulers it was a central attribute and obligation of legitimate power. For *muḥtasib*s as a professional duty and individual believers as a moral one it was an important facet of "commanding the good and forbidding the evil," a central Qurʾānic duty of the community (cf. Qurʾān 3:104, 3:110, 3:114, 7:157, 9:71, 9:112).

The Cordoban jurist and Friday prayer leader Ibn al-Munāṣif (d. 620/1223) regards the enforcement of regular prayer on the part of ordinary Muslims as an obligation of the ruler, but one that must accommodate the limitations of simple Muslims. He writes that in the case of a rough and uncivilized person believed not to perform his prayers, the ruler should question him gently and courteously to determine whether he knows the requirements of proper *ṣalāt* – not according to the technical terminology and categories of the jurists, but in a way that the (suspected) culprit can understand. If the individual in question can tell him how many prostration cycles are included in each prayer, what recitations and actions are required for each cycle, and the like, then he should be released, because this constitutes evidence that he actually prays. If it emerges that he does not possess

[113] See Ibn ʿĀbidīn, *Ḥāshiyat Radd al-muḥtār*, 1:377; Wansharīsī, *Miʿyār*, 1:200–1.

this basic knowledge, then there may be mitigating circumstances, for instance if he is newly converted or a "rough commoner." In this case he should be instructed until he can pray properly. If, on the other hand, his ignorance is a result of lack of practice in praying and a contempt for it, then he should be roundly and thoroughly punished – after which arrangements should be made for his instruction.[114]

The fourteenth-century Egyptian manual of Ibn al-Ukhuwwa exhorts the *muḥtasib* to patrol the markets on Friday, ensuring that merchants attend prayers and chastising them without fear or favor for failure to do so.[115] However, authorities also emphasized the religious autonomy of communities and individuals, generally accepting that rulers and *muḥtasib*s could not intervene if they prayed in any way authorized by legitimate religious authority. For instance, if the *muḥtasib* and the community disagreed about the quorum required to hold Friday prayers, the school followed by the community prevailed even if this led to the *muḥtasib*'s tolerating the nonperformance of congregational prayers he considered obligatory. This deference to legal pluralism was not absolute, however; some scholars held that the *muḥtasib* could impose his own religious doctrine, and others emphasized that public policy required (for instance) that Friday prayers be held when appropriate even over the objections of the community.[116] Public enforcement of attendance at congregational prayers was also not intended to be intrusive; the Ḥanbalī authority Abū Yaʿlā ibn al-Farrāʾ notes that although someone who fails to pray should be told to do so, "if he says, 'I perform the prayers in my home,' they are left to his responsibility and he is not compelled to perform them where people can see him."[117] According al-Māwardī's manual of government a *muḥtasib* is not entitled to intervene if an individual fails to attend Friday prayers, because the person may have a valid excuse of which he is unaware; however, if it is feared that a person's habitual nonattendance will influence others, the *muḥtasib* should compel him to participate for the sake of the public welfare.[118]

In practice, governmental enforcement of mosque attendance seems to have been sporadic at best. Boaz Shoshan notes that in Egypt "in 1509 Sultan Qānṣawh al-Ghawrī called on Muslims to perform the five daily prayers in congregational mosques. Commenting on the people's response, a

114 Muḥammad ibn ʿĪsā Ibn al-Munāṣif, *Tanbīh al-ḥukkām ʿalā maʾākhidh al-aḥkām*, ed. ʿAbd al-Ḥafīẓ Manṣūr (Tunis: Dār al-Turkī li'l-Nashr, 1988), p. 331.

115 Muḥammad ibn Muḥammad Ibn al-Ukhūwa, *The Maʿālim al-qurba fī aḥkām al-ḥisba of Ḍiyāʾ al-Dīn Muḥammad ibn Muḥammad al-Qurashī al-Shāfiʿī, known as Ibn al-Ukhuwwa*, trans. Reuben Levy (London: E. J. W. Gibb Memorial, 1938), pp. 61–2.

116 See ʿAlī ibn Muḥammad al-Māwardī, *al-Aḥkām al-sulṭānīya wa'l-wilāyāt al-dīnīya*, ed. Samīr Muṣṭafā Rabāb (Ṣaydā and Beirut: al-Maktaba al-ʿAṣrīya, 1424/2003), pp. 263–4.

117 Abū Yaʿlā Muḥammad ibn al-Ḥusayn al-Farrāʾ, *al-Aḥkām al-sulṭānīya* (Cairo: Sharikat Maktabat wa-Maṭbaʿat Muṣṭafā al-Bābī al-Ḥalabī wa-Awlādihi bi-Miṣr, 1386/1966), p. 261. (See also al-Māwardī, *Aḥkām*, pp. 264–5.)

118 al-Māwardī, *Aḥkām*, p. 264.

contemporary chronicler stated that the sultan's appeal 'entered one ear and left through the other.'"[119] Ibn Baṭṭūṭa describes several communities and rulers who strictly enforced attendance at congregational prayers, albeit with an admiration that suggests the rarity of the phenomenon. Describing Sultan Muḥammad ibn Tughluq of Delhi, he writes approvingly that he was unusually strict in the imposition of regular congregational prayer and severe in punishing nonattendance. Men were sent to the markets to punish people found lingering at prayer time; Ibn Baṭṭūṭa even claims (exceptionally, as we shall see) that some people were executed for their refusal to pray. The sultan's minions also quizzed commoners about the rules of ablution and prayer, and chastised them if they proved ill informed – an effort that motivated people to study together even in the markets.[120] Ibn Baṭṭūṭa also describes with appreciation the practice in the Central Asian city of Khwārizm, where he reports that the *mu'adhdhin*s would circulate through the neighborhood summoning people to pray, and that the *imām* would beat anyone who failed to attend with a whip that was kept hanging in each mosque for this purpose.[121] Legal and bureaucratic enforcement of congregational prayer seems to have become more institutionalized under the Ottomans, where failure to pray regularly or to attend Friday prayers was subject to legal regulation. Ottoman dynastic law stipulated monetary fines for these offenses, a practice that stimulated legal controversy among scholars who debated whether it was a misappropriation of property.[122]

Most instruction and exhortation for the performance of *ṣalāt*, however, was carried out by private individuals. These might be trained scholars or ordinary believers; since everyone was obligated to master the rules of ablution and prayer by puberty, everyone was potentially in a position to inform or correct someone else. The obligation to do so was pressing because lack of the requisite knowledge might lead even sincerely devoted individuals to perform prayers that were technically faulty, and thus did not discharge their obligation for *ṣalāt*. Aḥmad ibn Ḥanbal composed a passionate epistle admonishing the members of a congregation with which he had prayed on several occasions that they were invalidating their prayers by getting ahead of the *imām* as they moved from one stage of *ṣalāt* to another, which could render all of their efforts – including rising early and facing darkness, rain, or scorpions on the way to the mosque – completely vain.[123]

[119] Boaz Shoshan, *Popular Culture in Medieval Cairo* (Cambridge: Cambridge University Press, 1993), pp. 9–10.

[120] Ibn Baṭṭūṭa, *Riḥla*, 2:80.

[121] Ibid., 1:332. He states that offenders also paid a fine that was spent on the maintenance of the mosque and the feeding of the poor.

[122] See Uriel Heyd, *Studies in Old Ottoman Criminal Law*, ed. V. L. Ménage (Oxford: Clarendon Press, 1973), pp. 30–1, 122, 211, 232, 242, 281.

[123] Abū'l-Ḥusayn Muḥammad Ibn Abī Ya'lā, *Ṭabaqāt al-fuqahā' al-ḥanābila*, ed. 'Alī Muḥammad 'Umar (Būr Sa'īd: Maktabat al-Thaqāfa al-Dīnīya, 1419/1998), 1:478.

Because of the vital importance of correct performance of the prayer ritual, it is incumbent upon the possessors of knowledge to disseminate it to the ignorant and help them to rectify their prayers. Ibn Ḥanbal writes:

Know that if a man performs his prayer well, completely and correctly, then sees someone perform his prayer poorly and ruin it, preceding the *imām*, and he remains silent and does not instruct him that he has performed his prayer poorly and preceded the *imām* or forbid him to do so, and does not give him counsel, then he shares in the onus and shame of [the other person's faulty prayer]. . . . It is reported from the Prophet that he said, "Woe to the learned person from the ignorant one, if he does not instruct him."[124]

Ideally, the obligation to instruct and correct one's fellow Muslims leads to a community of mutual instruction and support. Ibn Ḥanbal exhorts his readers to

perform your prayers correctly, and be mindful of God in performing them; support each other in performing them, and give each other sincere counsel by learning from one another and reminding each other in case of inadvertence or forgetfulness. God has commanded you to support one another in good works and piety [Qurʾān 5:2], and prayer is the best of good works.[125]

Ibn Ḥanbal's vision is of an egalitarian community where any individual who acquires some degree of religious knowledge has the obligation to edify and exhort his fellow Muslims. However, he acknowledges that even well-meaning intervention may be met with indifference or hostility. In another work Ibn Ḥanbal is reported to have been asked about the situation of a person who observes that many or most of the people in the mosque are praying improperly. He insists that such a person must set them straight even if he is sorely outnumbered, but acknowledges that he will have discharged his obligation if he repeats his exhortation two or three times, even if it remains without effect.[126] Because the dissemination of information about the proper performance of prayer was a duty that could devolve upon anyone, there was no guarantee that the individual in question would enjoy any authority in the eyes of the intended objects of his instruction. Indeed, because almost anyone was in a position to learn about the requirements of prayer, this was a notable instance in which any given believer might find him- or herself in a position to instruct and encourage others. The twelfth-century exegete al-Zamakhsharī notes in his commentary on verse 3:104 of the Qurʾān, which proclaims the Islamic community as one "enjoining what is right, and forbidding what is wrong," that since everyone knows that it is wrong not to pray, every believer can undertake

[124] Ibid., 1:477.
[125] Ibid., 1:479.
[126] Abū Dāwūd Sulaymān ibn al-Ashʿath al-Sijistānī, *Kitāb Masāʾil al-imām Aḥmad*, with an introduction by Muḥammad Rashīd Riḍā (Cairo: Maṭbaʿat al-Manār, [0]1353/1942), p. 278.

the duty of "enjoining the right and forbidding the wrong" in this particular instance.[127]

The obligation to instruct those ignorant of the basic requirements of ablution and prayer extended outward from a person's own household to the wider society, where such knowledge was far from evenly distributed. Al-Ghazālī (d. 505/1111) writes that

> It is the duty of every Muslim to start with himself and reform himself by consistently performing his religious duties and refraining from forbidden actions. Then he must teach the members of his household, and after finishing with them he must go on to [instruct] his neighbors, then the people dwelling in his quarter [of the town], then the people dwelling in his town [as a whole], then the people dwelling in the hinterland surrounding his town, then the people dwelling in the hinterlands (*bawādī*)[128] such as Kurds, Bedouin, etc.; and so on to the farthest reaches of the earth.[129]

Furthermore:

> Every ordinary person (*ʿāmmī*) who knows the requirements of prayer is obligated to inform others; otherwise, he participates in the sin [of their failure to pray properly]. . . . Anyone who learns about a single legal point is a scholar with respect to that issue. . . . A person is not entitled to remain in his home and not go out to the mosque because he sees that people do not know how to pray correctly; rather, if he knows that he is obligated to go out to teach and admonish [them].[130]

Given the centrality of prayer, it might be assumed that their superior mastery of the knowledge constitutive of legally valid prayer must have ensured the authority of religious scholars in the lives of ordinary Muslims. To a certain extent this is certainly true. Insofar as legal scholars commanded the expertise to define and communicate the requirements of *ṣalāt*, all Muslim adults were in need of them, and certainly many ordinary Muslims sought out scholars to clarify their concerns about various aspects of prayer. Thousands of fatwas elicited by questions posed to scholars over the centuries attest to this fact. The virtues and requirements of prayer were also among the subjects most widely recommended by scholars for preaching and teaching.

However, it is also true that non-scholars did not always assume the technical knowledge of jurists to be the ultimate standard of valid prayer, or automatically turn to them as the natural authorities in this area. Other standards of piety and religious distinction competed with the jurists' criteria of technical proficiency. In one anecdote from a Sufi source the early Islamic thinker and ascetic al-Ḥasan al-Baṣrī is rebuked by God for his unwillingness to pray behind a devout

127 See Cook, *Commanding Right*, p. 19, n. 21.
128 *Bādiya* can literally mean "desert," but is used as the opposite of *ḥaḍar*, "settled area."
129 al-Ghazālī, *Iḥyāʾ*, 2:371.
130 Ibid., 2:370; see also Cook, *Commanding Right*, p. 445.

worshiper whose bad Arabic mars his recitation in *ṣalāt*.[131] In another anecdote recounted by a premodern jurist, but reflecting Sufi ideals of unmediated devotion to the divine, the passengers of a ship visit a remote (but apparently Muslim) island. There,

> the passengers saw a black woman performing the ritual prayer (*ṣalāt*) incorrectly. They told her this was not the right way to pray, and she asked them to show her the correct procedure. They taught her the Fātiḥa, the first Sūra of the Qurʾān, and also demonstrated the correct way to perform the prayers. As the ship sailed away, however, the passengers were startled to see the woman racing after them across the surface of the water. She implored them to teach her again how to pray because she had already forgotten.

The passengers assure her that her prayers are clearly quite satisfactory to God just as they are.[132] Regardless of its historicity, this story illustrates the conviction that the value of prayer was not fully defined by standards of formal correctness.

Most people probably learned to pray at home, in the context of the family, and prayer practices reflected the priorities and needs of ordinary people. Ultimately, scholars were often unable fully to control popular perceptions of the legitimacy and value of prayer practices, particularly the new customs that arose over time. The medieval period saw the introduction of a number of special prayers performed in congregation at particularly holy times in the Islamic calendar. Ordinary people eagerly embraced these practices, which combined opportunities to reap extraordinary quantities of religious merit with festive and sometimes carnivalistic nocturnal gatherings in mosques. One particularly popular innovation was the *raghāʾib* ("wishes") prayer, so called because it was believed that God was particularly receptive to petitions made on that occasion. It is said to have arisen spontaneously in Jerusalem in the middle of the fifth/eleventh century, and to have swiftly become widespread in that city and beyond. The prayer, held on the eve of the first Friday in the Islamic month of Rajab, was an elaborate one involving a preparatory fast, a prayer of twelve prostration cycles with recitation of specific passages of the Qurʾān, and two additional prostrations. With the notable exception of al-Ghazālī, most scholars rejected the *raghāʾib* prayer as an impermissible innovation (*bidʿa*), particularly because it came to be institutionalized as a public practice (often with the support of the ruler) in ways that conflated it with the congregational prayers established by the *sunna*.[133]

131 Padwick, *Muslim Devotions*, pp. 51–2 (citing al-Hujwīrī's *Kashf al-maḥjūb*).

132 Christopher Schurman Taylor, *In the Vicinity of the Righteous: Ziyāra and the Veneration of Saints in Late Medieval Egypt* (Leiden and Boston: Brill, 1999), p. 135.

133 See Raquel Margalit Ukeles, "Innovation or Deviation: Exploring the Boundaries of Islamic Devotional Law," Ph.D. dissertation, Harvard University, 2006, pp. 239–59; Talmon-Heller, *Islamic Piety*, pp. 62–6.

Significantly, one of the main issues raised for scholars by this practice was precisely the way in which it challenged the authority of *ʿulamāʾ* by catering to the religious agendas and longings of ordinary people. The most prominent scholar after al-Ghazālī to endorse the practice, Ibn al-Ṣalāḥ al-Shahrazūrī (d. 643/1245), argues that the objective "is for the people to remain engaged in worship (*ʿibāda*) during this time as they are accustomed to."[134] Ibn al-Ṣalāḥ in turn was accused of capitulating "to suit the whim of the Sulṭān and the masses of the time."[135] His primary antagonist in this controversy, ʿIzz al-Dīn Ibn ʿAbd al-Salām, charged that his position was a usurpation of the exclusive authority of religious scholars in favor of the custom (*iʿtiyād*) of the masses and of "those who do not have a foot planted in the science of the law."[136] Nevertheless, scholarly efforts to assert the top-down dissemination of religious knowledge were ineffective. The contemporary historian Abū Shāma (d. 665/1268) observes:

> I have seen one of the common people castigate the *imām* of a mosque and rebuke him because he did not know how to pray it right. I asked [the *imām*] about that, and he said that he led them in praying the *raghā'ib* prayer and did not know how to perform the two cycles of prostration after it. I saw the commoner teach it to him, expressing wonderment that he was the *imām* of a mosque and not well informed about it – the *imām* being like a prisoner in his hands, unable to say that it was an objectionable innovation or that it was not a *sunna*. How many an *imām* has said to me that he prays it only to keep the hearts of the common people by it and in order to keep hold of his mosque, fearing that it might be seized from him.[137]

Daniella Talmon-Heller remarks of this and several other non-canonical festival prayers: "Commoners, who to the dismay of scholars regarded special prayers as more meritorious than regular daily ones, made *Niṣf Shaʿbān*, *ṣalāt al-raghāʾib* and *al-taʿrīf* part of the liturgical calendar in the very bastion of official religion – the congregational mosque."[138] Scholarly opposition could have unintended consequences. The seventeenth-century Ottoman scholar Ḥajjī Khalīfa observed pragmatically of the *raghā'ib* prayers and other similar practices, "It is better not to forbid any custom that takes the shape of worshipping God, for that would give rise to zeal and persistence"; ordinary people only became more devoted to such rites in the face of official condemnation.[139]

134 Cited in Ukeles, "Innovation," p. 279.
135 Cited in ibid., p. 251.
136 Cited in ibid., p. 280.
137 ʿAbd al-Raḥmān ibn Ismāʿīl Abū Shāma, *al-Bāʿith ʿalā inkār al-bidaʿ wa'l-ḥawādith*, ed. ʿUthmān Aḥmad ʿAnbar (n.p.: Dār al-Hudā, 1398/1978), p. 67.
138 Talmon-Heller, *Islamic Piety*, p. 245.
139 Kātib Chelebi, *The Balance of Truth*, trans. G. L. Lewis (London: George Allen & Unwin Ltd., 1957), p. 99.

(Nevertheless, the *raghā'ib* prayer has largely fallen into disuse in modern times, with the exception of some Sufi and Turkish circles.[140])

Although jurists strongly emphasized the importance of inculcating information about the technical requirements of prayer, preachers and teachers were subject to the pressures and incentives of their actual audiences. It appears that lectures on topics such as the distinction between *shurūṭ* (conditions) and *arkān* (components) may not have been the stuff of popular preaching – "popular" not in the sense of a folk piety diverging from the scholarly norm, but in the sense of attracting large audiences of engaged listeners. A sixteenth-century Syrian scholar and preacher, ʿAlī ibn ʿAṭīya al-Hītī (known as Shaykh ʿAlwān), complains that preachers prefer to indulge in popular storytelling, immoderate lamentation, or vain displays of erudition rather than communicating basic doctrines and practices in a straightforward and approachable manner. As a result, if you were to ask members of the audience how to perform the basic kinds of ablution they would know nothing about them. Consequently, a man or woman among them may perform invalid prayers all of his or her life, simply because he or she does not know how to perform *wuḍūʾ* or the *arkān* of prayer.[141] Shaykh ʿAlwān complains bitterly that many able-bodied men and women neglect to pray altogether. Furthermore, those of them who do perform *ṣalāt* disdain to humble themselves to the religious scholars by seeking instruction from them (presumably because of the elementary nature of the knowledge involved, or because they assume they already have mastery of the ritual).[142] Thus, the religious scholars' prerogative and duty to define and disseminate the correct performance of prayer was more an ideal to be pursued (sometimes in the face of opposition or indifference) than a consistent de facto reality.

Failure to pray

Scholars agree that someone who overtly denies that *ṣalāt* is obligatory places him- or herself outside of the community of faith. In this respect prayer is no different from any other religious obligation, prohibition, or tenet that is unambiguously established by a revealed text of undeniable authenticity (in this case, the Qurʾān). To deny the truth of any verse of the Qurʾān is to be guilty of unbelief (*kufr*). The more difficult issue relates to the person who acknowledges in principle the obligation to pray, but fails to do so in practice. In general, behavioral infractions do not impair one's status as a believing member of the

[140] Ukeles, "Innovation," p. 240, n. 3.

[141] ʿAlī ibn ʿAṭīya al-Hītī, known as al-Shaykh ʿAlwān, *Nasamāt al-asḥār fī manāqib wa-karāmāt al-awliyāʾ al-akhyār*, ed. Aḥmad Farīd al-Mazīdī (Beirut: Dār al-Kutub al-ʿIlmīya, 1421/2001), pp. 339–41.

[142] Ibid., p. 343.

Muslim *umma*; while some scholars hold that belief can increase and decrease (or that faith and disbelief can coexist in varying proportions within a single soul), as a matter of legal status bad conduct does not render one a nonbeliever. To argue otherwise smacked of the doctrines of the Khārijites. However, both texts and authoritative precedents suggested that prayer was a special case in this respect. A *ḥadīth* of the Prophet states, "Between a person and unbelief is refraining from prayer (*tark al-ṣalāt*)."[143] In another *ḥadīth* the Prophet declares that "I was commanded to do battle against people until they bear witness that there is no god but God and that Muḥammad is the messenger of God, establish regular prayer, and pay alms tax; if they do that, their blood and property are immune from me." Similarly, verse 9:5 of the Qurʾān states that one should cease hostilities against polytheists "if they repent, and perform the prayer, and pay the alms."[144] Furthermore, the first caliph Abū Bakr had done battle (without demur from the other Companions of the Prophet) against "apostates" whose offense was to withhold *zakāt*, although they did not necessarily deny the obligation. On this analogy, it seemed logical that prayer as well could be a behavioral prerequisite for membership in the faith community.[145]

Based on this evidence, three of the four classical Sunnī schools of law regarded failure to pray as grounds for execution if the person failed to repent – although, as we shall see, they limited it to certain scenarios that exempted the ordinary imperfect Muslim. (Imāmī Shīʿites held that a person who failed to pray without denying the obligation in principle should be subject to discretionary punishment for the first and second offenses, and executed after the third – or possibly the fourth.[146]) Aḥmad ibn Ḥanbal argued that a person who did not pray was thus rendered a nonbeliever, based on the *ḥadīth* to this effect. Other scholars argued that faith was constituted by belief in God, the angels, and the prophets; it was thus an action of the heart, and could not be negated by actions of the limbs (including failure to pray).[147] They thus regarded execution of someone who refrained from prayer as a textually stipulated punishment (*ḥadd*) like that for adultery, rather than for apostasy. (The difference might appear technical, but in fact it would affect whether the offender could be buried as a Muslim and whether his or her Muslim relatives would inherit the estate.) The Ḥanafī school, distinctively, argued that someone who refused to pray

[143] Muslim, *Ṣaḥīḥ*, *Kitāb al-Īmān*, *Bāb Iṭlāq ism al-kufr ʿalā man taraka al-ṣalāt*; Abū Dāwūd, *Sunan*, *Kitāb al-Sunna*, *Bāb Fī radd al-irjāʾ*.

[144] See Muḥammad ibn ʿAbd Allāh al-Zarkashī, *Sharḥ al-Zarkashī ʿalā Mukhtaṣar al-Khiraqī*, ed. ʿAbd Allāh ibn ʿAbd al-Raḥmān al-Jabrīn (Riyadh: Maktabat al-ʿUbaykān, 1993), 2:269–70, 274.

[145] Muḥammad ibn ʿAlī al-Tamīmī al-Māzirī, *Sharḥ al-Talqīn*, ed. Muḥammad al-Mukhtār al-Salāmī (Beirut: Dār al-Gharb al-Islāmī, 1997), 1:372.

[146] See al-Ḥillī, *Sharāʾiʿ al-islām*, 1:112.

[147] Ibid., 1:370.

should be imprisoned and chastised, but not killed. They invoked a *ḥadīth* stating, "The blood of a Muslim is rendered licit only by one of three things: disbelief after faith, adultery after being married, and the wrongful killing of a human being." They also argued that execution frustrated the purpose of punishing someone for failure to pray, as the individual would be permanently incapable of praying after being killed.[148] (Their opponents, of course, argued for the deterrent value of execution.)

Despite the universal consensus that failure to pray was a dire crime, it also appears to have been a common one in medieval Islamic societies. This is not to deny that vast numbers of Muslims prayed regularly and conscientiously; however, even the most pious and idealistic scholars often acknowledged the prevalence of inconsistency in prayer, or even abstention from it. Ibn Taymīya remarks frankly in passing, "Most people pray sometimes, and fail to do so at others."[149] ʿIzz al-Dīn ibn ʿAbd al-Salām observes that people's distaste for a sin diminishes in proportion to its prevalence: "Don't you see that most people fail to perform the obligatory prayers and [the repugnance of that] is not as severe as the repugnance of breaking one's fast in Ramaḍān without an excuse, because that is not usual?"[150] As we have seen, the belief that many ordinary people failed to pray regularly was reiterated by Shaykh ʿAlwān in the sixteenth century.

Recognition of widespread (if often intermittent) failure to pray raised a number of legal questions. For instance, the sinfulness (*fisq*) of failure to pray would theoretically disqualify a guardian from validly marrying off his female ward. It also impaired the probity (*ʿadāla*) required of legal witnesses, two of whom were required to authenticate the marriage contract. As one questioner enquired of Ibn Ḥajar al-Haytamī, if failure to pray was prevalent, could one assume that any two given witnesses were qualified? Al-Haytamī responds with resignation that a marriage is not validly witnessed by someone who does not pray, "but the upshot of the matter is that because of the frequency of its occurrence and the difficulty of finding people with both interior and exterior [i.e., actual and apparent] probity to witness it, it suffices to use people about whom one does not know [any disqualifier, *al-mastūrīn*]."[151] However, the possibility that the bride's guardian failed to pray could be strategically exploited when useful – as sometimes occurred when, for instance, the couple desired to remarry after a hasty threefold (and thus irrevocable) divorce. Yossef Rapoport writes of the Mamlūk period:

148 Sibt ibn al-Jawzī, *Wasāʾil al-aslāf ilā masāʾil al-khilāf*, ed. Sayyid Mahnī (Beirut: Dār al-Kutub al-ʿIlmīya, 1419/1998), pp. 44–5.

149 Ibn Taymīya, *Majmūʿ al-fatāwā*, 22:30.

150 ʿIzz al-Dīn ibn ʿAbd al-Salām al-Sulamī, *Fatāwā Shaykh al-Islām ʿIzz al-Dīn ibn ʿAbd al-Salām*, ed. Muḥammad Jumʿa Kurdī (Beirut: Muʾassasat al-Risāla, 1416/1996), p. 339.

151 al-Haytamī, *al-Fatāwā al-kubrā*, 4:10.

When a couple that had been separated by triple divorce could prove that their marriage was voidable due to a major defect in the original contract, it meant that the husband did not have the legal capacity to issue a divorce. For this reason, we find spouses retroactively claiming that, at the time of the marriage contract, the bride's father was in the habit of drinking of wine or of not attending prayers.[152]

For Ḥanbalīs, the issue of failure to pray raised the even more acute problem of apostasy. After discussing the procedure for exhorting someone to pray and giving him or her three days to repent before proceeding with execution, a Ḥanbalī commentator observes that a person is not declared a nonbeliever before being exhorted officially in this way, "and from this it is known that marriages of the women of our time are valid, even according to [the doctrine of] Aḥmad [Ibn Ḥanbal]."[153] In other words, the key element in a person's condemnation to punishment and his or her exclusion from the faith community was not simply de facto failure to pray, but willful persistence in the refusal to pray after being formally summoned to do so and placed under duress by the authorities. This was a rare scenario indeed, and it seems unlikely that many people who omitted prayers out of laziness, preoccupation, or indifference would have resisted under such conditions. In support of the contention (denied by other schools of law) that failure to pray indicates unbelief (*kufr*), Ibn Qayyim al-Jawzīya writes:

It is remarkable that anyone could doubt the unbelief of someone who persists in refraining from [prayer] when he has been exhorted to perform it in front of the assembly, he sees the glint of the sword over his head, he is tied up to be killed, his eyes are blindfolded, and he is told, "Pray, or we will kill you" – and he says, "Kill me – I will never pray!"[154]

This dramatic vignette reflects Ibn al-Qayyim's assumptions about the situation in which a nonpraying person is subject to execution; under ordinary circumstances negligent believers were not subjected to this test, and their intermittent or chronic failure to pray did not result in legal exclusion from the community (let alone death).

In arguing that people who fail to pray are not, in fact, apostates (although he believes that they should be executed), Ibn Qudāma points to the continuous practice of the community:

We do not know of anyone who failed to pray in any age who was not washed, prayed over, and buried in the cemetery of the Muslims, or whose heirs were prevented from

152 Yossef Rapoport, *Marriage, Money and Divorce in Medieval Islamic Society* (Cambridge: Cambridge University Press, 2005), p. 95.

153 ʿAbd al-Ḥamīd al-Shirwānī and Aḥmad ibn Qāsim al-ʿAbbādī, *Ḥawāshī al-Shirwānī wa'l-ʿAbbādī ʿalā Tuḥfat al-muḥtāj bi-sharḥ al-Minhāj* (Beirut: Dār Ṣādir, 1972), 7:188.

154 Ibn Qayyim al-Jawzīya, *Kitāb al-Ṣalāt wa-ḥukm tārikihā*, ed. Muḥammad ʿAbd al-Razzāq al-Raʿūd (Amman: Dār al-Furqān, 1423/2003), pp. 61–2.

inheriting from him, or who was prevented from inheriting from a kinsman, or that spouses were ever separated because of failure to pray on the part of one of them, because so many people fail to pray.[155]

Ibn al-Munāṣif observes that "today sometimes there are venerable old men who have never prayed at all."[156] Despite theoretical recognition that failure to pray may be a capital offense, he clearly believes that nonpraying men routinely survive to advanced ages.

Indifference toward regular prayer seems to have been particularly common in certain sectors of the population; unsurprisingly, medieval authors describe failure to pray as being particularly widespread among people whose work was pressing, or whose time was not at their own disposal. Ibn al-Munāṣif makes clear that he considers even attendance at Friday prayers – the most visible form of *ṣalāt*, and probably one of the most appealing – to be rare in some sectors of the population. He complains of

> the neglect by many people, including merchants, artisans, and hired laborers (*al-ujarāʾ*), of attendance at Friday prayers – which is an individual obligation on every legally responsible man who is not sick or traveling. . . . These days many artisans join with the hired laborers and others in refraining from it and discarding attendance at it, and they are abetted in that by many of the elite and the prominent people who employ them, being too stingy to relinquish their labor during the time necessary to attend prayers. Some people of this sort do not perform Friday prayers or any others as long as they are at work.[157]

Although Ibn al-Munāṣif urges that the authorities take decisive action in this regard, it seems likely that workmen continued to labor through Friday prayers. A century later Ibn Taymīya was consulted about people who delay their prayers "because of work that they have, such as planting or tilling, or [being affected by] ritual pollution (*janāba*), or the service of a master (*ustādh*) [i.e., as an apprentice]." Ibn Taymīya responds sternly that it is never permissible to do this, regardless of one's tasks as a cultivator or a craftsman; however, the question implies the difficulty of combining timely prayer (and ritual purity) with certain forms of livelihood.[158]

Demanding labor or lack of facilities for ablution were not the only obstacles to regular prayer by people not of the urban elite, however. Scholars also repeatedly refer to the prevalence of ignorance of such religious matters as the rules of ritual ablution and prayer among people outside of the urban elites. People dwelling in remote areas or tribal societies were perceived as particularly lacking in religious knowledge. Al-Ghazālī writes that "most people in the

155 Ibn Qudāma, *al-Mughnī*, 2:301.
156 Ibn al-Munāṣif, *Tanbīh*, p. 331.
157 Ibid., pp. 332–3.
158 Ibn Taymīya, *Majmūʿ al-fatāwā*, 22:17.

towns are ignorant of the law relating to the requirements of prayer, so what of the [people in the] villages and the hinterlands, including the Bedouin, Kurds, Turcoman, and the rest of the peoples?" His solution was that in the mosque of every city quarter and village there should be a religious scholar to instruct people in their ritual duties. Religious scholars had an obligation to go out and teach tribal peoples dwelling in the vicinity of their towns – although without accepting food from them, because most of it (presumably rustled livestock) was stolen.[159]

Al-Ghazālī's view was that ill-informed rustics could not be blamed for their ignorance; seeing such a person perform his prayers incorrectly, one should tactfully instruct him without humiliating him for his ignorance.[160] Ibn Qudāma argued that if a person actually denied the obligation of prayer, the claim could be accepted as an expression of innocent ignorance if the person grew up in the hinterland (*al-bādiya*). If the offender came from a city or village, however, a claim of ignorance could not be accepted.[161] The perception that rural dwellers might be deficient in their knowledge and performance of basic ritual duties such as prayer was widespread. In a work lampooning rural Egyptian life and mores in the seventeenth century, Yūsuf al-Shirbīnī uses the peasants' deficient knowledge and proficiency in the area of canonical prayer as a recurring trope. Their buffoonish inability to grasp and apply the basic rules of worship, combined with their oblivious mangling of the Qur'ānic text that must be recited for valid prayer, is emblematic of their location outside of the boundaries of respectable Muslim society. Unlike Ibn Qudāma's hypothetical desert dweller, al-Shirbīnī's peasants appear to live in a world where mosques and prayer are ubiquitous (if often honored mainly in the breach).[162] Nevertheless, their inability to get prayer right – and their flagrant lack of interest in doing so, at least according to the standards of a provincial sophisticate such as al-Shirbīnī – marks them as irreducibly inferior. One passage of the book consists of a series of humorous anecdotes about the absurd errors rustics make in prayer. In one of them, after reciting the Fātiḥa a peasant clutches his head and cries, "Oh, my head!" Told by a better-informed onlooker that he has voided his prayer, he

159 al-Ghazālī, *Iḥyā'*, 2:370; see also Cook, *Commanding Right*, p. 445.

160 al-Ghazālī, *Iḥyā'*, 2:357; Cook, *Commanding Right*, p. 439.

161 Ibn Qudāma, *al-Mughnī*, 2:298–9.

162 Al-Shirbīnī does introduce some anecdotes featuring peasants who are altogether unfamiliar with prayer, including one about a bewildered rustic who wanders into a village mosque during Friday prayers because he thinks the people are going to a party, and flees in confusion at the first *takbīr* because he thinks they are starting a riot (Yūsuf al-Shirbīnī, *Yūsuf al-Shirbīnī's* Brains Confounded by the Ode of Abū Shādūf Expounded *(*Kitāb Hazz al-Quḥūf bi-Sharḥ Qaṣīd Abī Shādūf*)*, translation, introduction, and notes by Humphrey Davies [Leuven: Uitgeverij Peeters en Departement Oosterse Studies, 2007], 2:49–52). The contrast here seems to be between life in a substantial village and that in a remote hamlet; the point, of course, is that a man who has lived to adulthood without participating in Friday prayers is truly outside of civilization.

retorts, "I wasn't complaining to you, I was complaining to my Lord, of the pain in my head." He then proceeds to complete his (legally invalid) prayer.[163] In another, a peasant interrupts his prayer to tell his son to milk the cow.[164] In yet other cases, peasants make blasphemous nonsense out of the Qurʾānic verses they recite.[165]

Rural bumpkins were not the only people suspected of failure to pray properly. Elite urban sophisticates could also excite doubts, particularly if they followed schools of thought that relegated the formal ritual of prayer to a subordinate "external" level that might be superseded by more rarified forms of worship. Daniella Talmon-Heller recounts that

> the students of the renowned Shāfiʿī jurist, theologian and physician Sayf al-Dīn al-Āmidī (d. 631/1223) ... suspected that he did not pray, most likely because of his works in logic, *kalām* and philosophy, and claimed to have proven their assertion with the following trick. They marked one of his feet with ink while he was sleeping, and observed the place for two consecutive days. The persistence of the mark convinced them that al-Āmidī did not perform the ritual ablutions.[166]

(However, *falsafa* did not always entail neglect of prayer; Ibn Sīnā recounts of himself that he performed *ṣalāt* regularly through his long nights of philosophical study and writing, although he also fueled them with draughts of wine.[167]) Ismāʿīlī Shīʿism, which was attractive to members of the intellectual elite, also raised questions about the value of formal, bodily prayer. Patricia Crone notes that "external observance and inner understanding alike were required for salvation remained the standard Fatimid doctrine," and thus the practice of the greatest Ismāʿīlī state. However, when more extreme Ismāʿīlīs took over Bahrain in the eleventh century C.E., the Ismāʿīlī visitor Nāṣir-i Khusraw observed that "the locals did not pray, but there was a mosque for visitors."[168]

Although the majority of Sufis adhered to regular prayer, some also believed that it was possible to achieve a spiritual level transcending physical worship. Abū'l-Qāsim al-Qushayrī, who wrote a manual in the fifth/eleventh century systematizing Sufism and demonstrating its orthodoxy, alluded to contemporary Sufis' laxity in the performance of duties such as prayer and fasting as one of motivations behind his composition.[169] Ibn Taymīya disdainfully catalogues a number of relevant beliefs, including the ideas "that God has an elite for whom *ṣalāt* is not obligatory, having been exempted from it because they have arrived

163 Ibid., p. 68.
164 Ibid., p. 69.
165 Ibid., p. 70.
166 Talmon-Heller, *Islamic Piety*, p. 61.
167 See William E. Gohlman, *The Life of Ibn Sina: A Critical Edition and Annotated Translation* (Albany: SUNY Press, 1974), pp. 29, 79.
168 Crone, *God's Rule*, p. 208.
169 al-Qushayrī, *Risāla*, p. 37.

in the divine Presence or because they have replaced it with something that is more important and appropriate, or that the objective is the presence of the heart with the Lord, or that *ṣalāt* involves separation [between the worshiper and God], so if the worshiper is united with God he does not require *ṣalāt*." He also rejects the belief "that *ṣalāt* is accepted [by God] without ablutions, or that those who are distracted (or pretend to be distracted) by the love of God or the madmen who dwell in graveyards" are "God's intimates."[170] All of these attitudes certainly existed in some circles. Sufis who did not pray (or who might be suspected of failure to do so) ranged from respected mystical masters to those whose religious ecstasy or mental illness relegated them to the margins of society. In somewhat later times Sufis who adopted the deliberately transgressive *qalandar* style of mysticism sometimes lived in a state of ritual pollution and undress that precluded regular, conventional prayer. When one such antinomian group in Ottoman Syria transitioned to more orthodox Sufism, their transformation included securing a regular water supply and beginning to perform regular ablutions and *ṣalāt*.[171]

Not only mystical or philosophical beliefs that relativized the importance of formal prayer, but simple laziness or indifference affected people at all levels of the social hierarchy. Particular issues could arise when rulers were observed or suspected to be negligent in this regard. The fiercely independent Ibn ʿAbd al-Salām al-Sulamī, who was well known to admonish rulers when necessary, was asked in a legal inquiry about "someone who is appointed to a post of authority by someone who does not pray consistently, how can his commands, prohibitions, and rulings be upheld?" Al-Sulamī replies pragmatically that in such a case, "if they judge according to what is just . . . or rule in any part of their area of authority according to what is right and correct, we execute it in order to secure the welfare (*maṣāliḥ*) of the Muslims."[172]

Other scholars were sometimes more idealistic or less accommodating. Despite the fact that (as we have seen) individual delinquents were not generally excluded from the faith community for their indifference toward prayer, in certain political and cultural situations knowledge and performance of *ṣalāt* could be used as an indicator of the boundaries of the *umma*. In the case of culturally alien or newly converted dynasties, concerns about the arrogant irreligiosity of rulers could converge with cultural disdain toward uncouth outsiders. Questioned about the religious status of the newly converted Mongol overlords of the Islamic Near East, Ibn Taymīya replied that they were non-Muslims. For Ibn Taymīya, failure to pray was one of the fundamental

170 Ibn Taymīya, *Majmūʿ al-fatāwā*, 10:222.
171 Heghnar Zeitlian Watenpaugh, "Deviant Dervishes: Space, Gender, and the Construction of Antinomian Piety in Ottoman Aleppo," *IJMES* 37 (2005), p. 554.
172 al-Sulamī, *al-Fatāwā al-mawṣilīya*, p. 49.

criteria according to which the majority of Mongols – despite their overt Islamic religious identity – failed to qualify as members of the community and thus rendered themselves legitimate objects of jihad: "They pronounce the confession of faith if they are asked to do so, and venerate the Prophet [Muḥammad]; [yet] among them there are only a very few who pray."[173]

Similar issues sometimes arose when the rulers were indigenous but relatively recently converted. Askia Muḥammad I, who led a coup against the dynasty of Sunnī ʿAlī in 1493 to seize control of the Songhay Empire of western Africa, sent a legal enquiry to the Moroccan mufti Muḥammad ibn ʿAbd al-Karīm al-Maghīlī seeking legitimation for the deposition of his predecessor. As one important element of his argument, Askia Muḥammad asserted that Sunnī ʿAlī never attended the Friday prayers and that no one in his court ever prayed or fasted. He also alleged that rather than performing the five obligatory prayers properly at their assigned times, Sunnī ʿAlī did them all together once a day and simply gestured from a sitting position, rather than prostrating himself, even though he had no physical illness that would justify this. Furthermore, he did not know the first chapter of the Qurʾān by heart and did not do any recitations in the context of his daily prayers.[174]

Such accusations could be leveled not only at ruling elites new to Islam, but at non-urban populations within the Islamic heartland. The early nineteenth-century Yemeni scholar al-Shawkānī viewed the failure of tribal dwellers in the hinterlands to perform their basic ritual duties as a deliberate act of disbelief, a judgment that had severe legal consequences. Asked whether rural Bedouin who do not perform any of their religious duties but the pronouncing of the confession of faith were unbelievers (*kuffār*), and whether it was the duty of Muslims to engage in military campaigns against them on this basis, he replied:

> The protection of [a person's] property is only by virtue of his performance of the Pillars of Islam. What is incumbent upon any Muslim who dwells in the neighborhood of this nonbeliever ... is to exhort him to perform the Pillars of Islam ... to strive to educate him, speak to him gently, make things easy for him, and instill desire for the reward [for performing his religious duties] and fear of the punishment [for omitting them]. ... If that nonbeliever persists in his unbelief, it is obligatory for the Muslims who hear about this to fight him until he completely fulfils the requirements of Islam.[175]

Ordinarily, however, knowledge of prayer and regularity of practice varied across social milieus without giving rise to accusations of disbelief. Members of

[173] Ibn Taymīya, *Majmūʿ al-fatāwā*, 28:224.

[174] Muḥammad ibn ʿAbd al-Karīm al-Maghīlī, *Asʾilat al-asqiya wa-ajwibat al-Maghīlī* (Algiers: al-Sharika al-Waṭanīya li'l-Nashr wa'l-Tawzīʿ, 1974), p. 36.

[175] Muḥammad ibn ʿAlī al-Shawkānī, *al-Rasāʾil al-salafīya fī iḥyāʾ sunnat khayr al-barīya* (Beirut: Dār al-Kutub al-ʿIlmīya, 1348/1930), pp. 43–4. See Brinkley Messick, "Kissing Hands and Knees: Hegemony and Hierarchy in Shari'a Discourse," *Law & Society Review*, 22, 4, Special Issue: Law and Ideology (1988), p. 647.

the scholarly elite even sometimes acknowledged that simple fervency of prayer could compensate for technical imperfection, particularly for people without access to the religious and ritual training available to urban folk. The twelfth-century Andalusian traveler Ibn Jubayr describes the wildly unorthodox *ṣalāt* of Yemeni tribesmen in Mecca with a mixture of derision and awe. "They are noble, eloquent, rough, robust Bedouin," he declares, and "all you find with them of the acts of worship is sincerity of intent."

> As for their *ṣalāt*, nothing more amusing has been recounted among the funny anecdotes of the Bedouin. That is that they face the Noble House [i.e., the Kaʿba], prostrate themselves without bowing, and bob their heads to the ground.[176] Some of them perform one prostration, others two, three, or four. Then they lift their heads from the earth a bit with their arms resting upon it and turn to the right and left as if they were alarmed. Then they make the *taslīm* or arise without it; there is no sitting to perform the *tashahhud*. Sometimes they talk in the process of doing this, and sometimes one of them raises his head from his prostration, looks at his companion, yells at him and instructs him with whatever he likes, then returns to his prostration. . . . Despite what we have described of their behavior, they are people of true belief in the faith; it is said that the Prophet mentioned them and praised them, saying, "Teach them prayer (*ṣalāt*), and they will teach you invocation (*duʿāʾ*)."[177]

Indeed, Ibn Jubayr's description of the fervor of their devotions at the Kaʿba – and of the other pilgrims' heartfelt response to their invocations – suggests a genuine respect for their religiosity, even if it is combined with an arch incredulity at their lack of mastery of the basic rules of prayer.

The differential distribution of proficiency in the performance of *ṣalāt* (and in opportunities to perform it regularly) among different sectors of society persisted in many places over the centuries. The perception that nomads did not pray was not limited to Arabia.[178] The ability (if not, in some cases, the desire) to pray could also vary with wealth and class. When the anthropologist Reinhold Loeffler did fieldwork in a village in southern Persia in the 1970s, he found prayer practices to be unevenly distributed (and differently interpreted) across social strata. At the top of the hierarchy, a former landlord proudly declares that he prays regularly and promptly. He boasts that, while some will fail to pray for months at a time, "with me it's a habit, like my opium smoking."[179] (It goes without saying, of course, that smoking opium is

176 The verb *naqara* (here translated as "bob") refers to the action made by a bird pecking for grain, and is explicitly forbidden in *ḥadīth* as a motion during *sujūd*.

177 Muḥammad ibn Aḥmad Ibn Jubayr al-Kinānī al-Andalusī, *Riḥlat Ibn Jubayr, wa-hiya al-risāla al-maʿrūfa taḥta ism Iʿtibār al-nāsik fī dhikr al-āthār al-karīma wa'l-manāsik* (Beirut: Dār al-Kutub al-ʿIlmīya, 1424/2003), p. 107. For a parallel from the late nineteenth century see Charles M. Doughty, *Travels in Arabia Deserta* (New York: Boni & Liveright, [1920]), 1:238, 244.

178 See, for instance, Pococke, *A Description of the East*, 1:181, 184.

179 Reinhold Loeffler, *Islam in Practice: Religious Beliefs in a Persian Village* (Albany: SUNY Press, 1988), p. 34.

forbidden by the sharia.) A poor peasant, in contrast, replies when asked if he prays regularly, "No, one day we say them, the other day we don't. That's worse that not saying them at all."[180] Another poor peasant elaborates, "I . . . do not steal nor do I bother anyone, but I don't say the prayers. How this will be judged – that again only God Himself knows." He points out that it is easier to pray in fall and winter than during the main seasons of agricultural work.[181] At the bottom of the hierarchy, a destitute informant says that he prays when possible, but that the requirement of ritual ablution is difficult to fulfill.[182] While the peasants' views do seem to reflect some critique of economic privilege (it is questionable whether they would affirm that the landlord neither steals nor bothers anyone) they also express a sense of religious disadvantage based on their inability or failure to pray regularly.

This is certainly not to say that peasants, the poor, or even nomadic groups are never devoted to regular *ṣalāt*. For instance, in a study of the Azawagh Arabs of Niger, a group of newly sedentarizing nomadic pastoralists, Rebecca Popenoe observes that "both men and women drop whatever they are doing to pray."[183] It is generally true, though, that prayer is often differentially distributed across different strata and subcultures within a given society, and that commitment or indifference toward *ṣalāt* can form part of the self-identity and pride of a given group. Particularly in the twentieth century, the constraints of the modern workplace and of the secular state affected the ability of certain sectors of some Muslim societies (particularly the adult, urban, and middle-to-upper-strata men who might have had the most expertise and leisure for prayer in the past) to perform the five daily prayers on a regular basis (as well as the class and political valence of being observed to perform them). Tone Bringa notes of villagers in Bosnia in the 1980s that regular attendance at prayers in mosque was "impossible for [men] as long as they were participants in the secular (and "Yugoslav") public workplace. As men retired they became more like women, walking around the village, visiting neighbors, and observing the fast and the daily prayers."[184]

Modern developments

The modern period has seen profound challenges to many of the structures of authority and interpretation that informed the debates discussed in this chapter.

180 Ibid., p. 207.
181 Ibid., p. 210.
182 Ibid., p. 223.
183 Rebecca Popenoe, *Feeding Desire: Fatness, Beauty, and Sexuality among a Saharan People* (London and New York: Routledge, 2004), pp. 57, 60.
184 Tone Bringa, *Being Muslim the Bosnian Way: Identity and Community in a Central Bosnian Village* (Princeton: Princeton University Press, 1995), p. 165.

Among many modern Sunnī Muslims, questions have been raised about the necessity of adhering to one or another of the established schools of law (although *madhhab* loyalties remain strong in many places). The impact of divisive school loyalties on congregational prayer was one of the factors that elicited critiques of *madhhab*-based fragmentation of the community. However, newer religious trends also led to new forms of ideological – and ritual – differentiation among groups of Muslims. In some cases they also questioned the political attitudes that had led premodern scholars to endorse participation in Friday and festival prayers under the auspices of oppressive or religiously suspect rulers.

An influential critique of adherence to *madhhab*s was produced by Muḥammad Sulṭān al-Maʿṣūmī al-Khujandī (b. 1880), whose Central Asian environment was characterized by a fierce devotion to the Ḥanafī school. His account suggests that the issue of group solidarity in congregational prayer was a key stimulus for his rejection of the authority of the legal schools. When al-Maʿṣūmī performed the *ḥajj* in 1906 he was profoundly disturbed by the sight of believers refraining from congregational prayer in order to pray behind the *imām* of their own *madhhab*. He regarded legal opinions forbidding Ḥanafīs to pray behind Shāfiʿīs as the culmination of the community fragmentation caused by *madhhab* chauvinism.[185] Unlike in the premodern period, in the twentieth century such critiques had a deep impact. The Saudis, following the teachings of Muḥammad ibn ʿAbd al-Wahhāb (who in turn was deeply influenced by Ibn Taymīya), identified as Ḥanbalīs but deemphasized exclusive *madhhab* loyalties in favor of direct reference to the Prophet's *sunna*. In 1925, after the Saudi dynasty assumed control of Mecca, the separate locations for *imām*s of the four schools of law were eliminated in favor of a single, unified congregation.

Over the course of the twentieth century the Salafī movement (named after the "pious predecessors" of the Islamic community, the *salaf al-ṣāliḥ*) challenged the established interpretations and authority structures of premodern Islam to advocate renewed and direct adherence to the primary texts of Qurʾān and *sunna*. In the 1940s the Egyptian al-Sayyid Sābiq (d. 2000), who was a disciple of Ḥasan al-Bannā, the founder of the Muslim Brotherhood, began to write *Fiqh al-sunna*, a simplified manual of Islamic law prominently featuring relevant *ḥadīth* texts. Giving particularly extensive coverage to ritual law, it made *fiqh* rulings available to ordinary believers in a form that circumvented the authority of the four schools. In a somewhat similar vein, a highly influential Albanian student of *ḥadīth*, Nāṣir al-Dīn al-Albānī (d. 1999) produced a manual entitled "Description of the Prayer of the Prophet (peace be upon him!) from the

[185] Muḥammad Sulṭān al-Maʿṣūmī al-Khujandī, *Hal al-muslim mulzam biʾttibāʿ madhhab muʿayyan min al-madhāhib al-arbaʿa*ʾ, ed. Sulaym al-Hilālī (Cairo: Maktabat al-Tawʿīya al-Islāmīya/Amman: al-Maktaba al-Islāmīya, 1405), pp. 47–8. I thank Erol Sinan for drawing my attention to this work.

[opening] *Takbīr* to the [closing] *Taslīm*, As If You Were Seeing It."[186] It argues that the merit and reward of prayer depend on the degree of its correspondence to the Prophet's example, but that each of the existing *madhhab*s follows only selected elements of the *sunna*, while also adhering to *ḥadīth* of questionable authenticity.[187] The intent of his concise and simplified survey of the relevant *ḥadīth* is not only to enable more perfect prayer through closer adherence to the *sunna*, but to unify the *umma* by eliminating divisive commitments to the detailed ritual prescriptions of the individual schools. In contrast to the intentional pluralism of the *madhhab* tradition, he argues that differences of interpretation (*khilāf*) are a purely negative phenomenon – particularly when they prevent the solidarity of the community in prayer.[188] In this sense he revives the message of Ibn Taymīya, who raised similar arguments six centuries earlier.

Works such as those of Sābiq and al-Albānī have been highly influential, as have the broader religious currents that they reflect. Their impact is observable, for instance, when one sees large numbers of worshipers in a Moroccan congregation – which would historically have been monolithically Mālikī – folding their hands in front of their stomachs during the *qiyām* rather than letting them hang at their sides, as is the traditional Mālikī practice. However, on a wider scale Salafī influence has not always unified Sunnīs by eliminating distinctions in prayer style, but in many cases added yet another distinctive style of prayer to those already available. The contemporary British scholar Abdal-Hakim Murad, who asserts the continued obligation to adhere to one of the four established schools of law, laments that the new tendency for laypeople to refer directly to collections of *ḥadīth* has "provoked sharp arguments over issues settled by the great Imams over a thousand years ago. It is common now to see young activists prowling the mosques, criticising other worshippers for what they believe to be defects in their worship, even when their victims are following the verdicts of some of the great Imams of Islam."[189]

Because styles of prayer can be highly visible indicators of group identity and ideological commitment (much as they were in the early centuries of Islam), diverging modern interpretations can lead to reconfiguration or even division of communities. As early as the 1930s (before the works of Sābiq and al-Albānī) Muslim reformers in Indonesia used textual arguments to dispute traditional

186 Muḥammad Nāṣir al-Dīn al-Albānī, *Ṣifat ṣalāt al-nabī [sws] min al-takbīr ilā al-taslīm ka'annaka tarāhā*, 12th printing (Beirut: al-Maktab al-Islāmī, 1405/1985).

187 Ibid., pp. 14–16. He implies that the *ḥadīth* stating that a person may perform *ṣalāt* and be credited with only a fraction of it refers to the proportion of the prayer that correctly reflects the Prophet's example (p. 14).

188 Ibid., pp. 43–4.

189 Abdal-Hakim Murad, "Understanding the Four Madhhabs," www.al-fikr.name.my/understanding_the_four_madhabs.htm (accessed August 11, 2011). I thank Erol Sinan for drawing my attention to this passage.

prayer practices such as the audible recitation of the *nīya* (intent to pray). The resulting differences in practice led to schisms in mosques and even the foundation of new villages.[190] Not only did people take prayer profoundly seriously, but the rules of prayer could be a universally relevant and highly visible microcosm of larger issues about religious interpretation, authority, and the society's relationship to its own past.

More militant modern Islamic groups have sometimes insisted on praying only with the like-minded, drawing sharp lines of exclusion toward other Muslims. In an impassioned fatwa, Yūsuf al-Qaraḍāwī responds to an inquiry from a group of students at the historic al-Azhar University of Cairo (by some measures the most influential Sunnī institution of higher learning). They note that some "extremists" (*mutaṭarrifūn*) are refusing to pray in the public mosques, insisting upon performing *ṣalāt* at home. For authority they cite Sayyid Quṭb's interpretation of verse 10:87 of the Qur'ān, in which Moses and Aaron instruct the Israelites in Egypt to "make your dwellings into places of worship and establish regular prayers." Quṭb argues that this counsel applies to all believers who are pursued by godless governments and corrupt societies. By his criteria Egyptian society is *jāhilī* (non-Islamic) – a term that was traditionally used to designate the pre-Islamic pagan period in Arabia, but which he used to designate all social orders not ruled by God's law. Thus, some followers concluded that they were obligated to shun "*jāhilī*" society and all of its institutions, including the mosques. Al-Qaraḍāwī responds fervently and at length, citing Qur'ānic and *ḥadīth* texts emphasizing the sacredness of mosques and the merit of worshiping in congregation in them. He dismisses Quṭb's interpretation of verse 10:87 as a mere personal opinion unsupported by textual evidence. In closing, he forcefully rejects the underlying view that the majority of Muslims are in effect unbelievers living in a state of *jāhilīya*, and emphasizes that the orthodox Sunnī approach is to pray in mosques "behind every virtuous or sinful person" (*khalfa kull barr wa-fājir*).[191]

Due to the theological and political implications of refusal to pray with other Muslims, the boundaries of permissible congregational prayer can be a sensitive issue. In Nigeria starting in 1978, the reformist group Izala (the Society for the Eradication of Innovations and the Establishment of the Sunna) militantly opposed the forms of piety and worship traditionally espoused by the influential Tijānīya Sufi order. "Whoever adopted the prayer posture and the recitations of this group made himself an unbeliever. . . . Further, Izala reformers resisted the idea that 'heretics' were allowed to lead righteous Muslims in public prayers."[192]

[190] Bowen, "Salat in Indonesia," pp. 602–3.
[191] Yūsuf al-Qaraḍāwī, *Hudā al-islām: fatāwā mu'āṣira* (Cairo: Dār Āfāq al-Ghadd, 1981), 1:229–37.
[192] Johannes Harnischfeger, *Democratization and Islamic Law* (Frankfurt and New York: Campus Verlag, 2008), p. 75.

Even when carried out more discreetly, the invalidation of public prayers could be taken as a sign of theological and political radicalism. In an interview about three brothers accused by the Egyptian government of the bombing of the Hilton in Taba in 2004, a local resident reported that "at first, there was no problem with them. They came to the mosque and prayed with us. . . . Then I learned that, after praying with us in the mosque, they would go out to the desert with other men and pray again. From that time, I wanted to have nothing to do with them." His assumption, based on their prayer behavior, was that they were practicing *takfīr* (that is, declaring the rest of the community to be unbelievers).[193]

At the other, more secular, end of the political spectrum, congregational prayers can be a potent symbol of the solidarity and will of the community for people who may have no interest in promoting an overtly religious public sphere, let alone an Islamic state. The prevalence of mass protests following Friday prayers (and of mass prayers during protests) during the "Arab Spring" in 2011 have demonstrated the role of *ṣalāt* in mobilizing vast numbers of people around an activity with deep historical and cultural, as well as religious, resonance.

[193] Scott Anderson, "Under Egypt's Volcano," *Vanity Fair*, October 2006, p. 339, columns 1–2.

5 Women and prayer

The fundamental obligation to pray, and the components of prayer, are neutral with respect to gender. As Ibn Qudāma (d. 620/1223) puts it, "The basic principle is for the same rules of prayer to apply to women as to men, because the [divine] address includes them."[1] That is, the scriptural commandments mandating and describing prayer apply to believers of both sexes. However, because menstruation precludes valid *ṣalāt*, ritual purity law affects women of reproductive age differently from men. Furthermore, classical Islamic law stipulated a number of distinctions between the ideal prayer practices of the two sexes. These distinctions were extremely minor in the case of individual prayer and far-reaching in the case of congregational prayer. As we shall see, a number of the gender-based distinctions in the performance of public and communal prayer have been subject to some debate in the contemporary world, although they remain authoritative for many believers.

Menstruation cancels the state of ritual purity required for valid *ṣalāt*, so a woman cannot perform her canonical prayers until her flow ceases and she performs full ablutions (*ghusl*). The same applies to any person in a state of major pollution (*janāba*), for instance if one has had sexual intercourse. However, unlike the other bodily functions entailing *janāba*, a menstrual period is of relatively long duration and cannot be omitted at will. Unlike days of Ramaḍān fasting, which must be made up at another time, prayers omitted due to menstruation need not be performed later; a menstruating woman simply is not obligated to perform the prayers for the duration of her period, so she does not "owe" them later. The fact that women of reproductive age are cyclically excluded from prayer could be taken to imply their religious imperfection. In one widely cited but controversial *ḥadīth* recorded in the *Ṣaḥīḥ* of al-Bukhārī, the Prophet is cited as stating that women are "deficient in intellect and religion" (*nāqiṣāt ʿaql wa-dīn*). Immediately questioned about the nature of these deficiencies by the women present, the Prophet is reported to have replied that the deficiency of their intellect was indicated by the fact that "a woman's testimony is equivalent to half of a man's" (cf. Qurʾān 2:282) and the deficiency of their

[1] Ibn Qudāma, *al-Mughnī*, 1:599.

religion by the fact that "when [a woman] menstruates, she does not pray or fast."[2] Nevertheless, classical scholars logically observed that according to the principles of Islamic law, menstruating women could not be religiously culpable for failing to engage in a ritual that they were incapable of validly performing. Unlike a traveler, who is allowed to curtail his prayers but has it in his power to perform them in their complete form (if only by staying at home), a woman is compelled by her circumstances and bears no blame at all.[3]

In general, the issue of menstrual pollution is not one that entails severe consequences or evokes intensive concern on the part of scholars. Reports attributed to the Prophet's wife ʿĀʾisha state that in the poverty of the early days of the Islamic community, the women of his household used to have only one garment apiece; if they found that some menstrual blood had soiled it, they would moisten it with a bit of saliva and scrape it off with a fingernail. (In another *ḥadīth* the Prophet states that a woman should scrape the blood off her garment and then wash it before praying.) Scholars regarded this precedent as demonstrating that it was valid to pray in a garment on which traces of menstrual blood remained.[4]

There was general agreement that a menstruating woman – like any person in a state of major impurity (*janāba*) – should not linger in a mosque, based on *ḥadīth* reports (although a small minority of scholars contested the texts' validity).[5] However, this limitation is not based on the idea that menstrual pollution is in any way contagious or inherently threatening to the sanctity of the mosque. (In a *ḥadīth* recorded in the *Ṣaḥīḥ* of Muslim (d. 261/875), the Prophet tells ʿĀʾisha, "Hand me the mat from the mosque"; when she objects that she is menstruating, he declares, "Your menstruation is not in your hand!"[6]) Some scholars considered it permissible for menstruating women to pass through the mosque, although others found this problematic as well. In any case, the underlying concern was not that menstruating women were inherently polluting, but that blood might actually drip on the floor of the mosque. The eleventh-century Shāfiʿī jurist al-Māwardī frankly states that a woman ought not to pass through the mosque if her flow is heavy and she has taken inadequate precautions to bind it, but that she may do so if the opposite is true.[7] In the

[2] Bukhārī, *Ṣaḥīḥ, Kitāb al-Ḥayḍ, Bāb Tark al-ḥāʾiḍ al-ṣawm.* The influential contemporary Egyptian scholar Yūsuf al-Qaraḍāwī has argued that this report must be interpreted in context as a respectful and even playful exhortation to the women the Prophet was addressing, rather than as a general statement about the attributes and status of women; see, for instance, www.qaradawi.net/library/78/3941.html (accessed June 4, 2012).

[3] See Marion Holmes Katz, *Body of Text: The Emergence of the Sunnī Law of Ritual Purity* (Albany: SUNY Press, 2002), pp. 199–200.

[4] ʿAbd al-Karīm Zaydān, al-*Mufaṣṣal fī aḥkām al-marʾa wa bayt al-muslim fī al-sharīʿa al-islāmīya* (Beirut: Muʾassasat al-Risāla, 1420/2000), 1:181.

[5] Ibid., 1:168–9.

[6] Muslim, *Kitāb al-Ḥayḍ, Bāb Jawāz ghasl al-ḥāʾiḍ raʾs zawjihā.*

[7] al-Māwardī, *al-Ḥāwī al-kabīr*, 2:267.

modern period, a few otherwise extremely conservative scholars have argued that the prohibition on menstruating women frequenting mosques is textually and legally unfounded.[8]

People of both sexes are required to cover those parts of the body that they are not permitted to display to strangers (*ʿawra*) to perform valid prayers. However, a woman's *ʿawra* is more extensive than a man's. She must cover all of her body and hair except for her face and hands; schools of law differ on whether she must cover her feet, and if so whether both the top and the bottom of the foot must be covered. Interestingly, in premodern Islamic law slave women's private parts were defined like those of men, rather than like those of free women; thus, in theory a slave woman could pray with not only her hair but her breasts exposed.[9] Of course, this rule tells us more about classical jurists' symbolic construction of gender and status that about actual social practice. Although many religiously observant women routinely wear clothing that fulfills the requirements of coverage for *ṣalāt*, some women keep special prayer garments that cover their ordinary clothing with a clean and enveloping outer layer.

Most classical and modern scholars do not consider a woman's face to be *ʿawra*; however, particularly among premodern scholars, many advocated that women conceal their faces from unrelated men as a measure against *fitna* (sexual temptation). The wearing of face veils was thus customary, particularly for high-status urban women, in many premodern Islamic societies; it continues to be widespread in some localities (such as Saudi Arabia and Yemen) and favored by individual women, depending on their ideological convictions and modes of personal piety, in various parts of the world. However, scholars agree that in prayer a woman should not cover her face, just as she should remove her face veil (even if she wears one in public in everyday life) while performing the pilgrimage to Mecca. Ibn Qudāma explains the prohibition on wearing a face veil during *ṣalāt* pragmatically, in terms of the need for the woman's forehead and nose to touch the floor directly during prostration;[10] however, the analogy with *iḥrām* (the special ritual state assumed during pilgrimage, which is not structurally focused on the needs of prostration) suggests a deeper significance, possibly reflecting the intimacy of the encounter with God or the liminality that minimizes social and gender distinctions at particularly sacred times.

With respect to the physical positions of prayer, the differences between women and men are extremely minor. The most pervasive distinction relates to the general posture of the body during *ṣalāt*. Scholars recommended that men

[8] See, for instance, Muḥammad Nāṣir al-Dīn al-Albānī, *al-Thamar al-mustaṭāb fī fiqh al-sunna wa'l-kitāb* (Kuwait: Ghirās, 1422), 2:738–55.

[9] For the rules of *satr* (covering) during prayer, including those relating to free and slave women, see al-Zuḥaylī, *Fiqh*, 1:743–54.

[10] Ibn Qudāma, *al-Mughnī*, 1:638–9.

maintain some separation between the limbs and the trunk (*al-tajāfā*), based on *ḥadīth* texts stating that during prostration the Prophet was observed to hold his arms somewhat apart from his body, so that his underarms were visible. For women, in contrast, a more compact posture was considered to preserve modesty. Al-Shāfiʿī (d. 204/820) writes that it is preferable for a man to "keep himself open" by, for instance, holding his wrists and arms clear of his sides and keeping his feet and legs somewhat separated. In contrast,

> God Most High taught women to conceal themselves (*addaba Allāh taʿālā al-nisāʾ biʾl-istitār*), and the Messenger of God (peace be upon him!) taught them that [as well]; I prefer for a woman performing prostration to hold her body together, pressing her stomach to her thighs and prostrating in the way that best conceals her. I similarly prefer for her to perform bowing, sitting, and all of *ṣalāt* in the way that best conceals her.[11]

Interestingly, al-Shāfiʿī – the leading proponent of the legal authority of *ḥadīth* in his time – presents no textual evidence supporting the specific prayer postures he recommends for women; rather, he is applying what he argues to be a textually established systemic principle that modesty and self-concealment are divinely prescribed for women. Some scholars also held that a woman should not raise her hands while pronouncing the opening *takbīr*, or that she should raise them to a lower level than a man. Others followed a report attributed to Abū Ḥanīfa indicating that a woman should hold her hands at the same level as a man, as the palms of the hands are not a body part that a woman is obligated to conceal.[12]

Women's prayer leadership (*imāma*) and placement within the congregation

If the differences between the rules of individual *ṣalāt* for men and women are extremely minor, those relating to congregational prayer are far more extensive. Firstly, scholars debated whether *ḥadīth* emphasizing the enhanced merit of congregational prayer applied to both sexes without distinction, or whether it might be less imperative for a woman to pray in congregation or even preferable for her to worship in the privacy of her home. In this area, as we shall see, the issue of communal prayer intersected with (although it was not identical to) the question of public, mixed worship in the context of the mosque. Secondly, in congregational prayer the placement and conduct of women differ from those of men. A well-attested *ḥadīth*, transmitted in the *Ṣaḥīḥ* of Muslim as well as many other collections, states that "the best [prayer] row for men is the first and the

[11] al-Shāfiʿī, *al-Umm*, 1:115.
[12] Zaydān, *Mufaṣṣal*, 1:217–18.

worst is the last; the best row for women is the last and the worst is the first."[13] While men are urged to seek out the foremost available position in the congregation, women are urged to fill in the rows from the rear. Although most scholars agreed that a woman's ordinary speaking voice is not technically *ʿawra* (the female Companions of the Prophet were known to have conversed with unrelated men), they also made distinctions between men and women in terms of vocal participation in prayer. A woman praying in the presence of unrelated men is instructed to lower her voice so that her recitation is not audible to them. While a man who needs to draw attention to something during prayer (such as an omission by the *imām*) is instructed to cry out, "Glory be to God!" (*subḥān Allāh*), a woman should clap her hands.[14]

Most scholars (including the eponymous founders of the four Sunnī schools and the authorities of the Imāmī Shīʿite tradition) considered it impermissible for a woman to lead a male or mixed congregation in prayer.[15] However, a few early scholars affirmed that a woman could do so – including the Iraqi jurist Abū Thawr (d. 240/854) and the Egyptian al-Muzanī (d. 264/878), both disciplines of al-Shāfiʿī (and thus proponents of the authority of *ḥadīth*) but independent legal thinkers in their own right, and Ibn Jarīr al-Ṭabarī (d. 310/923), the historian and Qurʾān commentator and the founder of a short-lived independent school of law.[16]

Among the classical schools the Ḥanbalīs alone affirmed that a woman could lead men in congregational prayer, specifically in the context of the special nighttime *tarāwīḥ* prayers in Ramaḍān. (According to some sources al-Ṭabarī similarly held that a woman could lead the *tarāwīḥ* if no man was available who could perform the requisite Qurʾānic recitations, rather than endorsing women's prayer leadership unconditionally.[17]) Some Ḥanbalī authorities added the proviso that she could do so only if she was the sole member of the group capable of reciting the Qurʾān, or if she was at least a better reciter of the Qurʾān than any of the men, or if she was a family relation, or if she was old (*ʿajūz*), but in general the permission was considered to be unqualified. Even in this limited context, Ḥanbalī scholars manifested some ambivalence; the authoritative compiler al-Mardāwī (d. 885/1480) insists, citing a number of scholars within the school, that if a woman leads men in the *tarāwīḥ* prayers she must stand behind them, because "it conceals her better" (*liʾannahu astar*). In this case she would "lead" by performing the recitation, while a man at the front of the congregation would

[13] Muslim, *Ṣaḥīḥ, Kitāb al-ṣalāt, Bāb taswiyat al-ṣufūf wa-iqāmatihā wa-faḍl al-awwal faʾl-awwal* . . . .
[14] See Zuḥaylī, *Fiqh*, 2:935.
[15] See Zaydān, *Mufaṣṣal*, 1:251; al-Shahīd al-Thānī, *Rawḍa*, 1:317.
[16] See Ibn Rushd, *Bidāyat al-mujtahid*, 1:135; Ibn Qudāma, *al-Mughnī*, 2:33.
[17] See Muḥammad ibn Ismāʿīl al-Ṣanʿānī, known as al-Amīr, *Subul al-salām*, ed. Khālid ʿAbd al-Raḥmān al-ʿAkk (Beirut: Dār Ṣādir, 1998), 2:63.

frame the intention of serving as *imām* and lead the physical motions of prayer.[18]

The *ḥadīth* evidence for women's leadership of mixed prayers is ambiguous. A report transmitted by Abū Dāwūd (d. 275/889), Ibn Saʿd (d. 230/845), and Ibn Ḥanbal (d. 241/855) states that the Prophet gave his Companion Umm Waraqa bint Nawfal al-Anṣārīya (a distinguished early convert who had memorized the Qurʾān) permission to lead the people of her household in prayer.[19] Her household is said to have included an elderly man who performed the call to prayer as well as a male and a female slave. Some scholars concluded from this that it was permissible for a woman to lead her own household in prayer even if it included adult males.[20] However, other versions of the report specify that the Prophet only gave her permission to lead the women of her household.[21] Ibn Māja (d. 273/887) transmits a *ḥadīth* stating, "Let no woman lead a man in prayer, nor any Bedouin a *muhājir* [i.e., someone who has migrated to Medina and become sedentary], nor any sinner (*fājir*) a believer." However, the chain of transmission of this report was recognized by *ḥadīth* specialists to be weak. Furthermore, many Sunnī jurists (including the Shāfiʿīs and Ḥanafīs) did not hold that it was actually invalid for a sinner to lead believers in prayer, which suggested that even if authentic the statement might indicate undesirability rather than absolute prohibition.[22]

The textual precedents for women leading other women in prayer are less ambiguous. One report states that ʿĀʾisha led women in obligatory prayers, and another more specifically that she led them in performing *maghrib*, standing in the center of the row and reciting the requisite Qurʾānic passages audibly. Her co-wife Umm Salama is reported to have led women in congregational prayer during Ramaḍān, and the Companion Ibn ʿUmar is said to have appointed a woman to lead the female congregation during that month.[23] Nevertheless, neither early scholars nor the classical Sunnī schools of law were unanimous that a woman could or should lead other women in communal prayer. Some early authorities held that it was desirable for her to do so, some that it was undesirable but valid, others that she could do so for a supererogatory but not an obligatory prayer, and yet others that it was impermissible for any kind of prayer.[24] Mālikīs hold that it is impermissible for a woman to serve as prayer

[18] ʿAlī ibn Sulaymān al-Mardāwī, *al-Inṣāf fī maʿrifat al-rājiḥ min al-khilāf ʿalā madhhab al-imām al-mubajjal Aḥmad ibn Ḥanbal*, ed. Muḥammad Ḥāmid al-Faqqī (Beirut: Dār Iḥyāʾ al-Turāth al-ʿArabī, 1406/1986), 2:264–5.

[19] See Simonetta Calderini, "Contextualizing Arguments about Female Ritual Leadership (Women Imāms) in Classical Islamic Sources," *Comparative Islamic Studies* 5, 1 (2009), p. 12.

[20] al-Amīr al-Ṣanʿānī, *Subul al-salām*, 2:75.

[21] See Calderini, "Contextualizing Arguments," pp. 12–13; Ibn Qudāma, *al-Mughnī*, 2:33.

[22] See al-Amīr al-Ṣanʿānī, *Subul al-salām*, 2:62–3.

[23] See ʿAlī ibn Aḥmad Ibn Ḥazm al-Andalusī, *al-Muḥallā bi'l-āthār* (Beirut: Dār al-Kutub al-ʿIlmīya, 1425/2003), 3:136–7.

[24] For a list of scholars see Ibn Qudāma, *al-Mughnī*, 2:35.

leader for other women, on analogy with the ruling that it is legally undesirable for a woman to perform the call to prayer. The Ḥanafīs hold that it is valid but undesirable for a woman to lead other women in prayer, arguing that the apparent desirability of this practice at the rise of Islam was abrogated. Shāfiʿīs consider it desirable for women to pray in an all-female congregation and permissible for a woman to act as an *imām* in that context; despite a conflicting report from Ibn Ḥanbal, some Ḥanbalīs also hold that it is desirable for a woman to do so.[25] Imāmī Shīʿites also consider it permissible for a woman to lead a group of other women.[26]

The fact that the textual evidence against women's prayer leadership was slender did not escape some premodern scholars. The influential and controversial Ibn al-ʿArabī (d. 638/1240) was simultaneously a visionary mystic and a textual literalist (*ẓāhirī*) in matters of Islamic law. After declaring his own conviction that a woman may serve as prayer leader for men and women alike, he writes, "The default assumption (*al-aṣl*) is that [a woman's] leadership of prayer is permissible; whoever claims that it is forbidden without evidence should not be listened to, and the person who forbids this has no text."[27] In fact, at first glance it would appear that the textual evidence that women can lead mixed congregational prayers is stronger than the evidence that they are forbidden to do so (that is, the Umm Waraqa report is better regarded by scholars than the report stating that a woman may not lead a man). However, given that none of the reports involved were irreproachably authenticated by the standards of the *ḥadīth* discipline, for some scholars (particularly Mālikīs) the lack of evidence for continuing practice of women's prayer leadership of mixed groups in the early community was decisive.[28]

Classical scholars also drew on broader ideas about gender relations to argue that women's leadership of mixed groups was in fact unacceptable. One argument was that since women were instructed to pray in the back of the congregation, and female Companions reported to have led groups of other women in prayer during the Prophet's time did so from the center of the row (rather than standing in front of the rows where they would be more visible), women's prescribed placement conflicted with the ideal location and role of an *imām*.[29]

Some scholars argued that a man's prayer would actually be rendered invalid if a woman prayed next to or in front of him, an idea completely incompatible with a woman's leading from the front or even the first row of a mixed group.

[25] See Zaydān, *Mufaṣṣal*, 1:253.

[26] al-Shahīd al-Thānī, *Rawḍa*, 1:317.

[27] Ibn ʿArabī, *Futūḥāt*, 1:447.

[28] See Ahmed Elewa and Laury Silvers, "'I *Am* One of the People': A Survey and Analysis of Legal Arguments on Woman-Led Prayer in Islam," *Journal of Law and Religion* 26 (2010), pp. 155–7; Calderini, "Contextualizing Arguments," pp. 14–15.

[29] See, for instance, Ibn Ḥazm, *al-Muḥallā*, 3:136–7.

This idea was distinctively promoted by Ḥanafīs, who developed complex schemas to determine precisely whose prayers would be invalidated in different configurations of men and women. Regardless of the details, the clear implication was that women (if present at all at public prayers) should be rigorously limited to the back of the assembly.[30] This rule is presumably historically related to the idea (based on a *ḥadīth* transmitted in the *Ṣaḥīḥ* of Muslim) that a man's prayer could be invalidated by a woman (or a donkey or a dog) passing before him, unless a symbolic barrier such as the back of a saddle was interposed between them.[31] It is possible that the idea that women could rupture men's prayers was historically rooted in early Islamic concerns about the contagiousness of ritual pollution, although in classical Islamic law, no believer – including a menstruating woman – is considered to be contagiously impure.[32]

Whatever the historical origins of the idea that an adjacent woman could invalidate a man's prayer, classical Ḥanafī thinkers did not justify it in terms of ritual purity. Instead, they supported it with a supposed *ḥadīth* commanding, "Keep them [feminine plural] behind in what God has kept them behind" (*akhkhirūhunna min ḥaythu akhkharahunna Allāh*). It is a sign of the original independence of the disciplines of *fiqh* (Islamic law) and *ḥadīth* that it took centuries for Ḥanafī scholars to acknowledge that this statement lacked a credible chain of transmission (*isnād*), and was more reliably attributed to the Companion Ibn Masʿūd than to the Prophet.[33] However, the Ḥanafī discovery of this problem did not lead to substantive revision of the school's doctrine; instead, it was provided with an alternative proof-text in the Qurʾānic verse 2:228, which states that "men have a degree [of precedence] over [women]."[34] Behnam Sadeghi argues on the basis of examples such as this one that jurists were far more certain of their desired legal outcomes than of the precise textual

30 On this issue see Behnam Sadeghi, *The Logic of Law-Making in Islam: Women and Prayer in the Legal Tradition* (Cambridge: Cambridge University Press, 2012), pp. 50–75. I thank Professor Sadeghi for access to the page proofs.

31 Muslim, *Ṣaḥīḥ*, *Kitāb al-Ṣalāt*, *Bāb Qadr mā yastur al-muṣallī*. The implications of this report seem to have been disturbing to the sensibilities of some Muslims at a very early date; in the *Ṣaḥīḥ* of al-Bukhārī the Prophet's wife ʿĀʾisha is reported to have heard this report and to have retorted, "You have made us [equivalent to] dogs! I have seen the Prophet (peace be upon him!) pray when I was between him and the direction of prayer, lying on the bed" (Bukhārī, *Ṣaḥīḥ*, *Kitāb al-ṣalāt*, *Bāb Istiqbāl al-rajul ṣāḥibahu aw-ghayrahu fī ṣalātihi wa-huwa huwa yuṣallī*). For a vigorous modern critique of the report see Fatima Mernissi, *The Veil and the Male Elite: A Feminist Interpretation of Women's Rights in Islam*, trans. Mary Jo Lakeland (Reading, Mass.: Addison-Wesley Publishing Company, Inc., 1991), pp. 62–81.

32 Sadeghi, *Logic of Law-Making*, pp. 51–2.

33 Ibid., pp. 57–8, 66–9. This maxim is attributed in several sources to Ibn Masʿūd (see Ibn Khuzayma, *Ṣaḥīḥ Ibn Khuzayma*, 3:99; al-Ṭabarānī, *al-Muʿjam*, 9:296 [#9485]; al-Ṣanʿānī, *al-Muṣannaf*, 3:139 [#5115]).

34 Sadeghi, *Logic of Law-Making*, p. 69.

evidence from which they were ostensibly derived; Ḥanafī scholars were sure that women must not pray next to or in front of men, even if they were not always sure what text justified the rule. Even some non-Ḥanafīs cited the same highly dubious report in support of the rule that a woman cannot lead a man in prayer.[35]

The principle that women should be located at the back of the congregation also supported the inference that the overall ideal for women was concealment (*satr*), which was corroborated by other evidence (such as the *ḥadīth*s demonstrating a general concern for female modesty). Closely related to the preference for concealment of women from the male gaze was a concern with women's sexual allure; as the Shāfiʿī authority al-Māwardī (d. 450/1058) puts it, "A woman is *ʿawra* [that is, all of her must be concealed from sight], and her acting as *imām* would be seductive (*fī imāmatihā iftitān bihā*)."[36] It was also argued by some that the peril of sexual temptation underlay the Ḥanafī rule invalidating men's prayers performed next to or behind a woman. The eleventh-century authority al-Sarakhsī argues that since *ṣalāt* is an intimate dialogue with God (*munājāt*), it is not appropriate that it be sullied with any element of sexual desire, which (so he states) ordinarily accompanies adjacency to a woman.[37] Other scholars, however, disputed this inference. ʿAlāʾ al-Dīn al-Kāsānī (d. 587/1189) rejects the possibility that adjacency to a woman voids a man's prayer due to the probability of sexual desire, in part "because the woman is the same as the man in this respect" – that is, she may feel sexual desire if praying in proximity to a man – "so her prayer should be invalidated as well, but there is a consensus that it is not invalidated."[38] Interestingly, in later centuries scholars also sometimes questioned the relevance of sexual attraction to the spatial positioning of men and women at prayer because they did not perceive erotic desire to be exclusively heterosexual. In particular, most assumed that adolescent boys were alluring to adult men, but not that the adjacency or prayer leadership of a handsome youth (*al-amrad*, the young man whose beard had just begun to sprout) actually invalidated a man's prayers.[39]

Another issue raised by the question of women's prayer leadership was that of precedence and authority. Al-Shāfiʿī writes, "If a woman leads men, women, and male youths in prayer, the prayers of the women is valid and that of the men and the male youths is invalid, because God made men the caretakers of women (*jaʿala al-rijāl qawwāmīn ʿalā al-nisāʾ*) and made [women] unqualified to be in

[35] See Ibn Rushd, *Bidāyat al-mujtahid*, 1:135; Māwardī, *al-Ḥāwī al-kabīr*, 2:326.
[36] Māwardī, *Ḥāwī*, 2:326.
[37] al-Sarakhsī, *al-Mabsūṭ*, 1:340; see Sadeghi, *Logic of Law-Making*, p. 113.
[38] al-Kāsānī, *Badāʾiʿ al-ṣanāʾiʿ*, 2:617–18; see also Sadeghi, *Logic of Law-Making*, p. 114.
[39] See Ibn al-Humām, *Sharḥ Fatḥ al-qadīr*, 1:372–3; Ibn ʿĀbidīn, *Ḥāshiyat Radd al-muḥtār*, 1:562. Cf. Sadeghi, *Logic of Law-Making*, p. 115.

authority [over men]."[40] Here al-Shāfiʿī is invoking verse 4:34 of the Qurʾān, which states that "men are *qawwāmūn* over/towards women." The somewhat unusual word *qawwāmūn* is derived from a root whose semantic range includes the concepts "to be in charge of, to take responsibility for, to protect." It need not be taken in a rigidly hierarchical sense, and has been interpreted diversely by modern Muslim translators.[41] However, premodern interpreters generally took it to indicate – as implied by al-Shāfiʿī – that men properly exercised authority over women, and that women were thus unqualified to stand in positions of superiority or authority (*wilāya*) over men.[42] In a similar vein, some scholars supported the invalidity of women's prayer leadership of men by citing a *ḥadīth* in which the Prophet reportedly declared, "No people has flourished who commended their affairs to a woman."[43]

The diversity of opinion among classical scholars about the inherent merit and comparative status of women is suggested by the reasoning attributed to Abū Thawr, who (as we have seen) supported the unconditional validity of a woman's prayer leadership of men. He argued, firstly, that the Prophet had directed that a group of people be led in prayer by whomever among them was most knowledgeable in the recitation of the Qurʾān. Implicitly, he affirms that since either a man or a woman may prove to be the most accomplished in this respect, a person of either sex may be most entitled to the role of *imām*. Secondly, he is reported to have argued that since a man's prayers could validly be performed behind a (male) slave, *a fortiori* it must be permissible to pray behind a woman; after all, "the deficiency (*naqṣ*) of slavery is greater than the deficiency of femaleness."[44] At the other end of the spectrum, "the Mālikī al-Māzarī (d. 453/1061) . . . goes as far as to state that women's deficiency involves *ʿaql* (reason) and *dīn* making women essentially and hopelessly deficient: minors with no legal capacity can grow up, slaves can be manumitted, infidels can convert, but women are essentially and permanently deficient, hence they cannot lead in prayer."[45]

The degree to which the question of prayer leadership was symbolically intertwined with deeper issues of merit and rank is suggested by the discussion

[40] al-Shāfiʿī, *al-Umm*, 1:164.

[41] Abdullah Yusuf Ali has influentially translated *qawwāmūn* as "protectors and maintainers," a formulation which emphasizes nurture and support rather than discipline or superiority. This rendition has been adopted even by the conservative Saudi-sponsored translators Muhammad Taqi-ud-Din al-Hilali and Muhammad Muhsin Khan.

[42] For a survey of premodern commentaries on this verse see Karen Bauer, "'Traditional' Exegeses of Q 4:34," *Comparative Islamic Studies* 2 (2006), pp. 129–42.

[43] Māwardī, *Ḥāwī*, 2:326; Bukhārī, *Ṣaḥīḥ*, *Kitāb al-Maghāzī*, *Bāb Kitāb al-nabī (ṣ) ilā kisrā wa-qayṣar*; the authenticity of this *ḥadīth* is interrogated in Mernissi, *The Veil and the Male Elite*, pp. 49–61.

[44] Māwardī, *Ḥāwī*, 2:326.

[45] Calderini, "Contextualizing Arguments," p. 10.

of Ibn ʿArabī, which boldly addresses underlying questions about the religious status of women. In addressing the "deeper significance" (*iʿtibār*) of the rule regarding women's prayer leadership, he first observes that "the Messenger of God attested to the perfection of some women just as he attested to the perfection of some men, even if [the men] were more numerous than the women." He then identifies perfection (*kamāl*) with prophecy (*nubuwwa*). While most classical scholars denied the existence of female prophets, as textual literalists Ibn ʿArabī and his Ẓāhirī predecessor Ibn Ḥazm affirmed on the basis of several Qur'ānic passages that God had indeed made revelations to women.[46] Prophecy is leadership (*imāma*), Ibn ʿArabī further reasons; thus, the *imāma* of a woman is valid. Ibn ʿArabī's gender egalitarianism is not unqualified; based on his overall cosmology, he goes on to analyze the relationship between men and women at prayer in terms of parallelism with the human microcosm, identifying the man with the intellect (*ʿaql*) and the woman with the lower or appetitive soul (*nafs*). The leadership of the woman thus appears somewhat suboptimal, since the ideal hierarchy within the human psyche is headed by the intellect; however, the only impermissible configuration is the leadership of the passions (*al-hawā*), which significantly is not identified with women.[47] While Ibn ʿArabī's views are eccentric in their details, he does usefully suggest the deeper religious resonance of rules relating to ritual behavior – as well as suggesting the diversity of attitudes toward gender among medieval Muslim thinkers.

Women's prayer leadership is an area that has recently evoked lively debate among Muslim scholars and laypeople alike. A particularly intense controversy was aroused when the American Muslim scholar Amina Wadud led a mixed-sex Friday prayer at the Cathedral of St. John the Divine in New York City in 2005. Wadud argues that "exclusive male leadership in the role of religious ritual is not a requirement. Although it has served as a convenience which later became legally inscribed, it was merely customary and should not be prescribed as a religious mandate."[48] In her view, the foundational principle of God's unicity (*tawḥīd*) implies that God's position as supreme Creator holds men and women "on a horizontal line of constant equality. . . . Neither can be above the other because the divine function establishes their reciprocal relationship."[49] In contrast to the egalitarianism and solidarity of a common humanity united in submission to God, "hierarchy is what is exemplified when women pray in the rear or in a place invisible to the leader of the prayer."[50]

[46] See Maribel Fierro, "Women as Prophets in Islam," in Manuela Marín and Randi Deguilhem, eds., *Writing the Feminine: Women in Arab Sources* (London: I. B. Tauris, 2002), pp. 185–6.
[47] Ibn ʿArabī, *Futūḥāt*, 1:447.
[48] Amina Wadud, *Inside the Gender Jihad: Women's Reform in Islam* (Oxford: Oneworld, 2006), p. 169.
[49] Ibid., p. 168.
[50] Ibid., p. 175.

Wadud's position is based both on her overall understanding of the social and ethical implications of Islamic theological postulates and on her argument that much traditional Islamic interpretation reflects the cultural values and practical needs of specific past Islamic societies, rather than any explicit divine mandate that gender relations be structured in one specific fashion.[51] Both because of the novel nature of her ritual leadership (which was heavily covered in the international media) and because she declined to engage in more traditional forms of textual argumentation on the specifics of the legal questions involved, her actions and their justifications were criticized by a large number of Muslim scholars.[52] A particularly interesting response was produced by Yūsuf al-Qaraḍāwī, an al-Azhar-trained *ʿālim* closely associated with the Muslim Brotherhood who gained global fame as the on-air mufti for the al-Jazeera satellite network. Al-Qaraḍāwī's relatively moderate attitudes on issues of gender often lead him to propose significant modifications of traditional interpretations, while simultaneously rejecting Western-style assumptions about the negotiability of gender roles in favor of an affirmation of divinely mandated complementary roles.

Al-Qaraḍāwī bases his rejection of women's leadership of mixed-sex prayer on the observation that Islamic prayer is not composed merely of supplications and invocations, but of bodily movements such as bowing and prostration; these, he states, are inappropriate for a woman to perform in front of men – particularly in the context of an act of worship that requires a reverent and serene frame of mind. God in His wisdom created the female body in such a way as to arouse the desires of men, so that people will enter into marriage and perpetuate the species.[53] Thus, as a way of "blocking the means" to sin (*sadd al-dharīʿa*), the divine law mandated that women be separated from and behind men. This is because Islam is a pragmatic religion; it does not treat human beings as if they were angels, but takes into account their instincts and drives and protects them from temptation, particularly in the context of intimate communion with God.[54]

Interestingly, al-Qaraḍāwī straightforwardly observes that "if we look at the texts, we do not find a direct, authentic text forbidding a woman to . . . lead [men and women] in prayer."[55] He dismisses the *ḥadīth* stating "Let no woman lead a man in prayer, nor any Bedouin a *muhājir*" as "very weak" and unfit to form the basis for legal argumentation. Thus, al-Qaraḍāwī's argument is fundamentally

[51] See Amina Wadud, *Qur'an and Woman* (New York and Oxford: Oxford University Press, 1999), especially pp. 62–91.

[52] For a thoughtful discussion of reactions on both sides of the debate see Elewa and Silvers, "'I *Am* One of the People,'" pp. 144–53.

[53] Jamāl al-Bannā, *Jawāz imāmat al-marʾa al-rajul* (n.p., n.d.), p. 30.

[54] Ibid., p. 31.

[55] Ibid.

structured around his assumptions about the conditions necessary for focused prayer and their practical implications for the roles of the two sexes within ritual. Conversely, he does seem to acknowledge some textual foundation for women's prayer leadership (if only in very limited contexts). He observes that the chain of transmission of the Umm Waraqa *ḥadīth* is also subject to criticism, but then treats it as a valid precedent – with the qualification that it is specific to a woman who is proficient in the recitation of the Qurʾān leading the members of her own household, who are not subject to the hazard of sexual temptation in her presence.[56] Here he offers more latitude than classical scholars, who do not envision women leading mixed-sex congregational prayers even at home within the family circle.

Ultimately, however, al-Qaraḍāwī advocates primarily that women pray in congregation with other women, particularly in the context of the *tarāwīḥ* prayers. He muses, "If only our sisters who are zealous for women's rights would revive the *sunna* that has died out – of a woman's leading [other] women in prayer – instead of introducing this objectionable innovation of a woman's leading men in prayer."[57] He finishes his fatwa with a discussion of the special place of acts of worship (*ʿibādāt*) in Islamic law, arguing that "the Islamic principle is adherence to precedent (*al-ittibāʿ*, that is, following the *sunna*) in matters of religion, and innovations in matters of worldly life (*shuʾūn al-dunyā*)." In contrast, other religions were falsified when their followers introduced innovations into their sacred rites. He asks plaintively, "Is this what the Muslim woman lacks – to lead men in Friday prayers?!" Instead of fomenting discord among the ranks of Muslims, he urges, Muslim women should focus on the more serious crises that face the Islamic community.[58]

A more categorical rejection of Wadud's intervention was expressed by the Muftī of Egypt, ʿAlī Jumʿa. Much like al-Qaraḍāwī, he based his argument for the illegitimacy of women's leadership of mixed congregations on the principle that Islam commands chastity and modesty and forbids fornication; for this reason, believers of both sexes are obligated to avert their eyes from each others' charms to avoid temptation:

> Another of Islam's commands for this objective is that God Most High commanded women, as an honor to them (*takrīman lahunna*), to stand behind the rows of men, because the Muslims' prayer includes prostration. That was in the spirit of the Arab proverb, "He kept you back only to advance you." Keeping women back in the rows for prayer is not a form of dishonor to them, but a way of exalting them.[59]

[56] Ibid., p. 32.
[57] Ibid., p. 34.
[58] Ibid., p. 35.
[59] Ibid., p. 24.

Both al-Qaraḍāwī and Jumʿa make the threat of sexual temptation unambiguously central to their reasoning about women's prayer leadership. This is also true of other modern commentators. Suʿād Ṣāliḥ, a female Egyptian scholar, declares that "the origin [of the prohibition] is that the woman's body, even if veiled, stirs desire."[60] These contemporary scholars' confidence that the underlying rationale of the relevant rules is the issue of erotic allure far exceeds that of their premodern counterparts. However, perhaps mindful both of Muslim women's sensibilities and of critical external observers of Islam, they are careful to frame this focus in terms of concern for the dignity of women and the welfare of society rather than stigmatizing women as sexual temptresses. The blunt assertions of male authority and hierarchical superiority found in many medieval texts are largely replaced by concerns for public propriety and for the religious and cultural authenticity of Islamic ritual norms.[61]

Women's mosque access

A large number of *ḥadīth* reports suggest that women took part in communal prayers in Medina during the Prophet's lifetime, a practice that could only have taken place with his knowledge and approval and thus in principle forms part of the *sunna*. The historical reliability of this information is supported by the fact that the presence of women is often simply assumed or casually alluded to, rather than asserted as the central point of the reports in question. Thus, the participation of women appears as a widely shared early assumption, rather than as a polemical (and thus perhaps tendentious) contribution to a controversy over women's public prayer.[62] For instance, one report recounts that when the revelation of the change in the *qibla* from Jerusalem to Mecca was announced to the congregation in Medina (thus requiring everyone to turn from north to south), "the women changed to the men's place and the men to the women's, and we prayed the remaining two prostrations toward the Sacred House."[63]

The Prophet is also reported to have declared, "Do not prevent the maidservants of God from [going to] the mosques of God" (*lā tamnaʿū imāʾ Allāh masājid Allāh*). This is the best-authenticated *ḥadīth* explicitly addressing women's right to frequent public places of worship; among Sunnī collections it is transmitted in the *Ṣaḥīḥ*s of Bukhārī (d. 256/870) and Muslim and the

[60] Elewa and Silvers, "I *Am* One of the People," p. 148.

[61] On the concern that secular egalitarian values may threaten the authority of textually, theologically, and culturally authentic norms see ibid., pp. 147–8.

[62] A wide selection of relevant *ḥadīth*, mainly drawn from the *Ṣaḥīḥ*s of Bukhārī and Muslim, is presented by ʿAbd al-Ḥalīm Muḥammad Abū Shuqqa in his *Taḥrīr al-marʾa fī ʿaṣr al-risāla* (Kuwait: Dār al-Qalam, 1430/2009), 2:178–93.

[63] Ibid., 2:179 (report from Ibn Abī Ḥātim al-Rāzī).

Sunan of Abū Dāwūd, among other early compilations.[64] In addition to fulfilling the exacting requirements of the most prominent *ḥadīth* specialists of the mid-third century of the Islamic calendar, this report seems to have been circulated and accepted beyond the possibility of refutation – even among those who wished to circumvent its legal implications – even before that time. Both Mālik (d. 179/795) and al-Shāfiʿī (d. 204/820) were aware of it. It is notable that this report, while affirming women's right to go to the mosque, clearly addresses resistance to it – which must have arisen early, conceivably even during the lifetime of the Prophet.

Another, related, report dramatizes the tensions that may have surrounded the command not to prevent women from visiting the mosque. As reported in the *Muwaṭṭaʾ* of Mālik, it recounts that ʿĀtika bint Zayd, the wife of ʿUmar ibn al-Khaṭṭāb, used to ask the latter's permission to go to the mosque. He would remain silent, upon which she would declare, "By God, I will go out, unless you forbid me" – and he would not forbid her.[65] This anecdote implicitly acknowledges the prohibition on detaining women from going to the mosque; it is unclear whether it reflects admiration for ʿUmar's (apparently reluctant) adherence to an authoritative rule or disapproval of ʿĀtika's somewhat defiant exploitation of it. Various versions of this anecdote about ʿĀtika are reported in different sources, and seem to reflect evolving attitudes toward the issue. In variations presented in the *Ṭabaqāt* of Ibn Saʿd (d. 230/845) and Ibn Ḥanbal (d. 241/855), ʿUmar's resistance seems to be based in his unusual jealousy or in his personal preference to have her stay at home. Ibn Saʿd's anecdote indicates that she persists in going; she is in the mosque when her husband is assassinated there.[66] A version presented by a compiler a generation younger than Ibn Ḥanbal, Ibn Qutayba al-Dīnawarī (d. 276/889), states that ʿĀtika married her next husband, al-Zubayr, when she was already advanced in age. She used to go out to the mosque at night, although al-Zubayr objected. As in the version in the *Muwaṭṭaʾ*, she retorts that she will continue to go until he forbids her. However, al-Zubayr finds a way around this problem; he lurks in the darkness and pinches her ample rear end as she is on her way to the mosque, after which she declares that "the people have become corrupt" and keeps to her house.[67] Interestingly,

[64] Bukhārī, *Ṣaḥīḥ*, *Kitāb al-Jumʿa*, Bāb 13; Muslim, *Ṣaḥīḥ*, *Kitāb al-Ṣalāt*, *Bāb Khurūj al-nisāʾ ilā al-masājid idhā lam yatarattab ʿalayhi fitna*; Abū Dāwūd, *Sunan*, *Kitāb al-Ṣalāt*, *Bāb Mā jāʾa fī khurūj al-nisāʾ ilā al-masjid* (#565, 566); see additional references in Muḥammad al-Saʿīd ibn Basyūnī Zaghlūl, *Mawsūʿat aṭrāf al-ḥadīth al-nabawī al-sharīf* (Beirut: Dār al-Kutub al-ʿIlmīya, n.d.), 7:218–19.

[65] Mālik, *Muwaṭṭaʾ*, *Kitāb al-Qibla*, *Bāb Mā jāʾa fī khurūj al-nisāʾ ilā al-masājid*.

[66] Ibn Saʿd, *Kitāb al-Ṭabaqāt al-kubrā*, ed. Iḥsān ʿAbbās (Beirut: Dār Ṣādir/Dār Bayrūt, 1377/1958), 8:267; Ibn Ḥanbal, *Musnad*, 1:381.

[67] Ibn Qutayba al-Dīnawarī, *ʿUyūn al-akhbār* (Cairo: Maṭbaʿat Dār al-Kutub al-Miṣrīya, 1349/1930), 4:115.

in yet later sources she is stated to have stipulated in her marriage contracts to both ʿUmar and al-Zubayr that they not prevent her from going to the mosque.[68]

Although it would require more evidence to construct a firm chronology for the development of this anecdote (it is quite possible that later sources present versions that originated earlier than they were recorded in preserved books), there appears to be a progression in the assumptions of the sources. In the versions presented by Mālik, Ibn Saʿd, and Ibn Ḥanbal it seems perfectly reasonable that a high-status woman would frequent the mosque; it is only her husband's personal preferences and character traits that may stand in her way. In Ibn Qutayba it is clear that she is going to the mosque only to pray, that she does so only at night, and that she is privileged to do so as a woman of advanced years. In the later sources her frequenting of the mosque is implied to be a special privilege explained by her ability (as a woman of beauty and prestige) to negotiate exceptionally favorable conditions in her marriage contracts.

Other reports place disapproval of women's public prayer in the mouth of the Prophet himself. In a report not canonized by al-Bukhārī or Muslim – although variations of it appear in the *Musnad* of Ibn Ḥanbal and the *Ṣaḥīḥ*s of Ibn Khuzayma (d. 311/923) and Ibn Ḥibbān (d. 354/965) as well as being attributed by Shīʿites to the sixth Imām, al-Ṣādiq (d. 148/765) – a female Companion named Umm Ḥumayd approaches the Prophet and says, "I like [or want] to pray with you!" (*uḥibb al-ṣalāt maʿaka*). The Prophet replies, "I know that you like to pray with me, but it is better for you to pray in your closet than in your chamber, better for you to pray in your chamber than in your outer room [or courtyard], better for you to pray in your outer room than in the mosque of your clan, and better for you to pray in the mosque of your clan than in my mosque." The report concludes, "So she ordered that a prayer room (*masjid*) be built in the most remote and gloomy part of her house (*aqṣā shayʾ min baytihā wa-aẓlamihi*), and prayed there until she died."[69] In addition to being less widely circulated and (by the standards of classical *ḥadīth* scholars) less reliably authenticated than the *ḥadīth* affirming women's right to attend mosques, this report seems to bear some hints of Iraqi provenance. The existence of separate mosques associated with specific clans, alluded to in Ibn Ḥanbal's version of the

68 Ibn al-Athīr, *Usd al-ghāba fī maʿrifat al-ṣaḥāba*, ed. Khalīl Maʾmūn Shīḥā (Beirut: Dār al-Maʿrifa, 1418/1997), 5:338; Ibn Ḥajar al-ʿAsqalānī, *al-Iṣāba fī tamyīz al-ṣaḥāba* (Cairo: Maktabat al-Kullīyāt al-Azharīya, 1397/1977), 13:34; Ibn ʿAbd al-Barr, *al-Istīʿāb fī maʿrifat al-aṣḥāb*, in margin of Ibn Ḥajar, *Iṣāba*, 13:80.

69 Ibn Ḥanbal, *Musnad*, 45:37; Zaghlūl, *Mawsūʿa*, 5:675; Muḥammad ibn ʿAlī Ibn Bābawayh al-Qummī, known as al-Ṣadūq, *Man lā yaḥḍuruhu al-faqīh* (Beirut: Dār Ṣaʿb/Dār al-Taʿāruf li'l-Maṭbūʿāt, 1414/1994), 1:306. It is not completely clear what is intended by each of the terms in the series referring to different parts of the house, and the precise wording varies among versions of the report; here I am following an understanding of the report prevalent among later commentators.

ḥadīth, was typical of the garrison cities of early Islamic Iraq[70] rather than of Medina during the Prophet's lifetime. Furthermore, more than one scholar has argued that in the eighth century opposition to women's public ritual participation was a distinctively Kufan phenomenon.[71] However, it is difficult and speculative to associate the report with one specific location.

The Umm Ḥumayd report suggests that, while congregational prayer in general and prayer in the Prophet's mosque in particular yield vastly enhanced merit for male worshipers, women's prayer is more meritorious when performed privately within the home. Thus, the scale of values is implicitly inverted for women; while a man (at least with regard to obligatory prayers) earns greater religious reward for venturing forth to join in prayer with the community, and even more if he walks or travels further to visit a particularly holy mosque, a woman's prayer is depicted as becoming more religiously valuable the more she remains secluded within concentric circles of privacy. If taken as authoritative, the *ḥadīth* thus has significant implications for women's ideal prayer behavior. Nevertheless, it does not prohibit women's participation in public congregational prayer.

The idea that women's frequentation of mosques actually was (or at least should be) forbidden was not attributed to the Prophet himself, but (perhaps pointedly) to his influential widow, ʿĀʾisha. She is said to have declared, "If the Messenger of God had lived to see what women have innovated, he would have forbidden them from visiting the mosque, as the women of the Israelites were forbidden."[72] The report appears in the *Ṣaḥīḥ*s of Bukhārī and Muslim, the *Muwaṭṭaʾ* of Mālik, the *Sunan* of Abū Dāwūd, the *Musnad* of Aḥmad ibn Ḥanbal, and the *Ṣaḥīḥ* of Ibn Khuzayma; like the *ḥadīth* forbidding women from being barred from mosques, it thus appears to have been in broad circulation by the first half of the third century A.H. and is well authenticated by the criteria of the classical discipline of *ḥadīth*. However, of course, it is not technically a *ḥadīth*; it reports not a statement by the Prophet, but an opinion hypothetically attributed to him after his death. Nevertheless, over the centuries it was widely cited in the legal debates over the permissibility or desirability of women's presence at mosques.

[70] For a discussion of the transition "from tribal mosque to sectarian space" in Kufa see Haider, *Origins*, pp. 231–4. He notes that "at the turn of the 1st/7th century, most Muslims frequented their local clan mosques except on special occasions (e.g., the Friday prayer) when they would venture to the cathedral mosque in the geographic center of the city" (p. 232).

[71] See Leor Halevi, *Muhammad's Grave: Death Rites and the Making of Islamic Society* (New York: Columbia University Press, 2007), pp. 127–33 (on funeral processions); Sadeghi, *Logic of Law-Making*, p. 77.

[72] Bukhārī, *Ṣaḥīḥ*, *Kitāb al-Adhān*, *Bāb Intiẓār al-nās qiyām al-imām al-ʿālim*; Muslim, *Ṣaḥīḥ*, *Kitāb al-Ṣalāt*, *Bāb Khurūj al-nisāʾ ilā al-masājid idhā lam yatarattab ʿalayhi fitna*; Abū Dāwūd, *Sunan*, *Kitāb al-Ṣalāt*, *Bāb al-Tashdīd fī dhālika* [*khurūj al-nisāʾ ilā al-masājid*]; Mālik, *Muwaṭṭaʾ*, *Kitāb al-Qibla*, *Bāb Mā jāʾa fī khurūj al-nisāʾ ilā al-masājid.*

The complexity of the attitudes attributed to the Prophet is reflected in the opinions attributed to the scholars retrospectively regarded as the founders of the classical schools of law.[73] The early compilation *al-Mudawwana*, which records Mālik's legal opinions as collected by Saḥnūn ibn Saʿīd al-Tanūkhī (d. 240/ 854),[74] records the question, "Did Mālik disapprove of women going out to the mosque . . .?" The informant replies that "he used to say, 'They should not be forbidden (*lā yumnaʿna*) to go out to mosques.'"[75] This statement, which (like the anecdote about ʿUmar and ʿĀtika) uses the same verb as the Prophetic *ḥadīth* forbidding the exclusion of women from mosques, implies that Mālik believed this maxim to be legally binding. However, another report transmitted by Saḥnūn's somewhat younger contemporary Muḥammad al-ʿUtbī al-Qurṭubī (d. 255/869) suggests that Mālik qualified his application of this rule somewhat.

He was asked about women's going to attend prayers at mosques; he said, "That varies with respect to the mature woman (*al-mutajālla*) and the young woman (*al-shābba*). The *mutajālla* goes out to the mosque but does not frequent it often, and the young woman goes out to the mosque once in a while.[76]

The word *mutajālla* is an odd and distinctive one, occurring very rarely outside of Mālikī legal discourse; there are several other words that would ordinarily be used to refer to a woman of advanced years.[77] Outside of Mālikī *fiqh*, the locus classicus (cited, for instance, by the lexicographer Ibn Manẓūr[78]) is a report in the *Kitāb al-ṭabaqāt al-kubrā* of Ibn Saʿd. In it, the Companion of the Prophet Umm Ṣubayya Khawla bint Qays recounts:

In the time of the Prophet, Abu Bakr, and the beginning of the caliphate of ʿUmar, we used to be in the mosque, women who had grown old (*niswa qad tajālalna*). Sometimes we would spin, and sometimes some of us would work braiding palm leaves in it [i.e., the mosque]. ʿUmar said, "I will surely make you into free/noble women again!"

[73] For a general survey of classical legal opinions on women's mosque attendance see Christopher Melchert, "Whether to Keep Women Out of the Mosque: A Survey of Medieval Islamic Law," in B. Michalak-Pikulska and A. Pikulski, eds., *Authority, Privacy and Public Order in Islam: Proceedings of the 22nd Congress of L'Union Européenne des Arabisants et Islamisants, Cracow, Poland 2004* (Leuven: Peeters, 2006), pp. 59–69.

[74] On the authenticity and dating of the *Mudawwana* see Norman Calder, *Studies in Early Muslim Jurisprudence* (Oxford: Clarendon Press, 1993), pp. 1–38, and the critique of his arguments in Jonathan Brockopp, *Early Mālikī Law: Ibn ʿAbd al-Ḥakam and His Major Compendium of Jurisprudence* (Leiden: Brill, 2000), esp. pp. 66–114.

[75] Mālik, *al-Mudawwana*, 1:195.

[76] Abū'l-Walīd Ibn Rushd, *al-Bayān wa'l-taḥṣīl wa'l-sharḥ wa'l-tawjīh wa'l-taʿlīl fī masāʾil al-Mustakhraja*, ed. Muḥammad Ḥajjī (Beirut: Dār al-Gharb al-Islāmī, 1404/1984), 1:420; cf. Ibn Abī Zayd al-Qayrawānī, *al-Nawādir wa'l-ziyādāt ʿalā mā fī'l-Mudawwana min ghayrihā min al-ummahāt*, ed. ʿAbd al-Fattāḥ Muḥammad Ḥilw (Beirut: Dār al-Gharb al-Islāmī, 1999), 1:536.

[77] The *Mudawwana* also reports that Mālik allowed the *mutajālla* to go to prayers for the two festivals, for rain (*al-istisqāʾ*), and on the occasion of eclipses (*al-khusūf*). (Mālik/Saḥnūn, *Mudawwana*, 1:195, 242).

[78] Ibn Manẓūr, *Lisān al-ʿarab*, art. j-l-l.

(*la-arudannakunna ḥara'ir*), and he expelled us from it, except that we used to attend the [obligatory] prayers at the [set] time.[79]

This report itself has interesting implications. The women in the anecdote appear to be enjoying a privilege of their seniority, engaging in productive labor in the public space of the mosque. It is unclear whether they have chosen this space for its commercial potential (conceivably they hope to sell the resulting thread or mats) or for its social pleasures. ʿUmar, in a recognizable trope,[80] asserts a different form of social differentiation among women: as free women they should not linger in the mosque, although they may frequent it on a limited basis for obligatory prayers.

Even outside of the context of women's mosque attendance, the *mutajālla* is an important category in the gender discourse of early Mālikī legal texts. Mālik is reported to have held that a mature women could bargain publicly with craftsmen and travel to Mecca without a male guardian.[81] For Mālik (or at least for his early disciples) it appears that the public activities and roles of women vary with age and social status; there is no single set of behavioral constraints that applies to all women.

It is more difficult to reconstruct the opinions of Abū Ḥanīfa from available reports. However, statements transmitted by his disciple Muḥammad ibn al-Ḥasan al-Shaybānī (d. 189/805) suggest that a distinction between women of different age cohorts was prevalent among early Ḥanafīs as well. Al-Shaybānī writes:

I said: Do you consider it objectionable for [women] to attend Friday and obligatory [i.e., the five daily] prayers in congregation? He said: Yes. I said: Do you give them a dispensation to go to any [prayers at all]? He said: I give a dispensation for a very old woman (*al-ʿajūz al-kabīra*) to attend the nighttime and dawn prayers and the two festival prayers; as for anything else, no.[82]

It is notable that the Kufan Abū Ḥanīfa is represented as taking a significantly more restrictive approach to women's mosque attendance than the Medinian

79 Ibn Saʿd, *Kitāb al-Ṭabaqāt al-kubrā*, 8:296. Both of these editions have "*takhālalnā*" rather than "*tajālalnā*"; however, this does not make sense. Furthermore, the lexicographer Ibn Manẓūr (who discusses the report under the root j-l-l) clearly understood the word to be "*tajālalnā*," meaning "to become mature/elderly."

80 ʿUmar is said to have belabored any slave woman whom he saw veiled with his whip, crying, "Cast off your veil, bondswoman! Are you trying to look like a free woman?!" (See Ibn Abī Shayba, *Muṣannaf*, 2:134–5; Sarakhsī, *al-Mabsūṭ*, 1:212.)

81 Abū Muḥammad ʿAbd Allāh Ibn Abī Zayd al-Qayrawānī, *Kitāb al-Jāmiʿ fī'l-sunan wa 'l-ādāb wa 'l-ḥikam wa 'l-maghāzī wa 'l-tārīkh wa-ghayr dhālika*, ed. ʿAbd al-Majīd Turkī (Beirut: Dār al-Gharb al-Islāmī, 1995), pp. 243, 283; Abū'l-ʿAbbās Aḥmad al-Qabbāb al-Fāsī, *Mukhtaṣar kitāb al-Naẓar fī aḥkām al-naẓar bi-ḥāssat al-baṣar li-Ibn al-Qaṭṭān* (Riyadh: Maktabat al-Tawba, 1418/1997), p. 229; Ibn Qayyim al-Jawzīya, *al-Ṭuruq al-ḥukmīya fī'l-siyāsa al-sharʿīya aw al-firāsa al-murḍiya fī aḥkām al-siyāsa al-sharʿīya* (Cairo: Dār al-Ḥadīth, 1423/2002), p. 239.

82 al-Shaybānī, *Kitāb al-Aṣl*, 1:343–4.

Mālik. Not only does he categorically disapprove of mosque attendance by younger women, but the privileges of seniority are deferred to the end of life – the advanced age of the "very old woman" is redundantly emphasized – and limited in scope to daily prayers held in the twilight of dawn or the darkness of night. However, Abū Ḥanīfa's disciples Abū Yūsuf and Muḥammad al-Shaybānī reportedly permitted old women to attend all prayers without distinction.[83]

Early Shīʿite sources express restrictive opinions on women's mosque attendance similar to those that were typical of Kūfa (where the early Shīʿite community flourished). Muḥammad al-Kulaynī (d. 328–9/939–41) transmits in his canonical Imāmī *ḥadīth* compilation *al-Kāfī* that Imām al-Ṣādiq was asked about women going out to attend Friday and festival prayers and replied, "No, unless the woman is aged (*lā illā imraʾa musinna*)."[84] He is also reported to have stated that "the best places of worship (*masājid*) for women are their houses" and that the most meritorious location was an interior chamber.[85] Al-Shaykh al-Mufīd (d. 413/1032) wrote that there was no harm in elderly women (*al-qawāʿid min al-nisāʾ*, whom he defines as "old women who are no longer fit for marriage") attending Friday and festival prayers.[86]

The most substantial discussion of the issue of women's mosque access attributed to al-Shāfiʿī occurs in a short work entitled "Book on discrepancies among *ḥadīth*" (*Kitāb ikhtilāf al-ḥadīth*).[87] As suggested by its title, this piece deals most centrally with an issue of legal theory (the proper approach to apparent contradictions among statements transmitted from the Prophet), rather than with the substantive question whether women should frequent mosques. The discussion opens with a challenge by al-Shāfiʿī's hypothetical interlocutors, who confront him with the legal implications of the *ḥadīth* "Do not forbid the maidservants of God from going to the mosques of God." They point out that "according to you, a negative command from the Prophet indicates that [the action] is forbidden (*taḥrīm*) unless there is an indication from the Messenger of God that he did not intend to signify that it is forbidden." Furthermore, the

83 See Sadeghi, *Logic of Law-Making*, p. 84.

84 Muḥammad ibn Yaʿqūb al-Kulaynī, *Furūʿ al-Kāfī*, ed. Muḥammad Jaʿfar Shams al-Dīn (Beirut: Dār al-Taʿāruf li'l-Maṭbūʿāt, 1413/1993), 4:542.

85 Ibn Bābawayh al-Qummī (al-Ṣadūq), *Man lā yaḥḍuruhu al-faqīh*, 1:223; Muḥammad ibn al-Ḥasan al-Ṭūsī, *Tahdhīb al-aḥkām* (Beirut: Dār al-Aḍwāʾ, 1406/1985), 3:252–3. However, there is some ambiguity about the imāms' teachings; al-Ṣādiq's son Mūsā is reported to have stated that women bore the same obligation to attend Friday and festival prayers as men, while another report declares that a woman's Friday noontime prayer would be deficient if performed in congregation in the mosque (ʿAbd Allāh ibn Jaʿfar al-Ḥimyarī, *Qurb al-isnād* [Beirut: Muʾassasat Āl al-Bayt li-Iḥyāʾ al-Turāth, 1413/1993], p. 223; al-Ḥurr al-ʿĀmilī, *Tafṣīl*, 7:338; al-Ṭūsī, *Tahdīb*, 3:241).

86 al-Shaykh al-Mufīd, *Aḥkām al-nisāʾ*, vol. 9 of *Muṣannafāt al-Shaykh al-Mufīd* (n.p.: al-Muʾtamar al-ʿĀlamī li-Alfiyat al-Shaykh al-Mufīd, 1413), p. 58.

87 al-Shāfiʿī, *al-Umm*, final (unnumbered) volume with *Mukhtaṣar al-Muzanī*, pp. 513–15.

statement refers generally to the "mosques of God."[88] In short, the opponents claim that if al-Shāfiʿī applies his methodology consistently to this text, he is compelled to concede that a woman may never be denied the opportunity to go to the mosque.

Al-Shāfiʿī unhesitatingly replies that the *ḥadīth* is, in fact, specific (*khāṣṣ*) – that is, it applies only to some (as yet unspecified) instances of women's mosque-going. To demonstrate that it cannot possibly forbid all instances of forbidding women to visit mosques, al-Shāfiʿī invokes the case of the pilgrimage to Mecca, here construed as simply one instance of going to the mosque (in this case, the Sacred Mosque of Mecca). Since the male guardian can under some circumstances prevent a woman from making the long and costly journey to Mecca, al-Shāfiʿī argues, the *ḥadīth* cannot be general; there is at least one exception. He also invokes the overall consensus of the community by asking, "Do you know of anyone who disputes that a man is entitled to forbid his wife from going to the mosque of her clan (*ʿashīra*), even if it is next to her house, and to Friday prayers, which are the most obligatory prayers in a city?" The hypothetical opponent concedes, "I am not aware of any."

Now that al-Shāfiʿī has demonstrated that the *ḥadīth* in question does not mean that men are categorically forbidden to prevent the women of their households from frequenting mosques, his opponents demand to know precisely what it does mean. Having just demonstrated the specific nature of the *ḥadīth* by arguing that men may sometimes forbid women to visit the Sacred Mosque of Mecca, al-Shāfiʿī executes a startling about-face to argue that the Sacred Mosque of Mecca is precisely the one mosque to which the *ḥadīth* specifically refers. The *ḥadīth* does not mean that men must allow their womenfolk to visit all mosques at all times; rather, it means that they must allow them to visit one mosque (the mosque of Mecca) one time (for the obligatory pilgrimage).

Although it has been accurately observed that al-Shāfiʿī takes a relatively negative attitude toward women's mosque access in this passage,[89] we must be attentive to the precise points that he is making. To the extent that his interests address behavioral norms rather than legal theory, his overriding concern here is with the authority of the husband or male guardian, and thus with the power structure of the Muslim family. Al-Shāfiʿī's interpretive energies are expended to preserve male authority at home (and his hermeutic principles vis-à-vis other scholars), not to empty mosques of women. Indeed, in his survey of positive

[88] The distinction between general (*ʿāmm*) and specific or particular (*khāṣṣ*) statements is an important feature of al-Shāfiʿī's jurisprudence; see al-Shāfiʿī, *Risāla*, pp. 53–62, 226–8.

[89] Asma Sayeed notes that al-Shāfiʿī's position "is perhaps the most elaborate rationalization of the view that women can indeed be prevented from attending mosques" (Asma Sayeed, "Early Sunni Discourse on Women's Mosque Attendance," *ISIM Newsletter* 7 [2001], p. 10).

law, *al-Umm*, al-Shāfiʿī remarks, "I prefer that (*uḥibb*) aged women and those who do not have [attractive] appearances attend [congregational] prayers and festivals; I prefer more strongly that they attend the festival [prayers] than that they attend other obligatory prayers (*al-ṣalawāt al-maktūbāt*)."[90] Here al-Shāfiʿī indicates not only the permissibility but the positive desirability of mosque attendance by old women (*al-ʿajāʾiz*). In another passage, discussing the Friday congregational prayers, al-Shāfiʿī notes that it is not incumbent upon women to attend, but that "I prefer (*uḥibb*) . . . for old women [to do so] if they are given permission" (i.e., presumably by their husbands).[91]

Ḥanbalī legal sources generally do not attribute their doctrines on women's mosque attendance directly to the eponym of their school, Aḥmad ibn Ḥanbal, although they make passing references to his opinions. The Ḥanbalī authority Ibn Hubayra (d. 560/1165) states that the scholars of all four schools "are in agreement that it is objectionable for young women to attend the congregational prayers of men (*jamāʿāt al-rijāl*)"; however, "they differ with respect to attendance by old women." On this point, he states, Mālik and Ibn Ḥanbal agree that there is no objection whatsoever to their attendance, while Abū Ḥanīfa and al-Shāfiʿī have some reservations even with respect to older women.[92] Reports claim that Ibn Ḥanbal responded, when asked about women's attendance at the prayers for the two festivals, that "people will be tempted, unless she is a woman far advanced in age,"[93] or "as for in this time of ours, no, because they are a temptation."[94] If authentic, Ibn Ḥanbal's comments reflect a distinctively early and explicit concern with *fitna* (sexual temptation or disorder) and a sharp awareness of the decadence of his times.

It is worth observing that overall, *fitna* was not theorized as a structurally central component of legal reasoning in the discussion of women's mosque access until the fifth/eleventh century. Although it is a plausible inference (one drawn by many later scholars of various schools) that early authorities' pervasive distinction between older and younger women was based on concerns about younger women's sexual allure, this is not made explicit by the earliest sources. It is equally plausible that they envisioned varying social roles for women at different stages of the life cycle, with ideals of modesty and seclusion

90 al-Shāfiʿī, *al-Umm*, 1:24.

91 Ibid., 1:189.

92 Yaḥyā ibn Muḥammad ibn Hubayra, *al-Ifṣāḥ ʿan maʿānī al-ṣiḥāḥ* (Beirut: Dār al-Kutub al-ʿIlmīya, 1417/1996), 1:103–4.

93 Muḥammad ibn Mufliḥ, *Kitāb al-Furūʿ* (Beirut: ʿĀlam al-Kutub, 1404/1984), 1:578.

94 Aḥmad ibn Ḥanbal (attrib.), *Aḥkām al-nisāʾ*, ed. ʿAbd al-Qādir Aḥmad ʿAṭāʾ (Beirut: Dār al-Kutub al-ʿIlmīya, 1406/1986), p. 46. This work, whose attribution to Aḥmad is dubious but which may be the work of al-Khallāl, provides two versions of this report and another in which Aḥmad states, "Women used to sit with men at teaching sessions (*al-majālis*); as for now, a single finger of a woman is a temptation." For the work in question see Fuat Sezgin, *Geschichte des arabischen Schrifttums* (Leiden: E. J. Brill, 1967), 1:508.

emphasized for nubile virgins (whose value on the marriage market they would enhance) more than for mature matrons. The greater freedoms accorded senior women in early *fiqh* may quite possibly reflect assumptions about their enhanced autonomy and status in their post-reproductive years, rather than about their putative lack of sex appeal.

At least by the fifth/eleventh century, however, *fitna* was explicitly established as the central rationale for limitations on women's mosque attendance. The Mālikī jurist Abu'l-Walīd Ibn Rushd (grandfather of the philosopher of the same name, d. 520/1126) harmonizes the statements attributed to Mālik (who, as we have seen, both discouraged men from forbidding women to go to the mosque and discouraged women from going there often) with reference to the concept of *fitna*:

> The rationale (*wajh*) for Mālik's statement that young women should not be forbidden to go out to mosques is the general meaning of the Prophet's statement, "Do not forbid the maidservants of God from going to the mosques of God." The rational for his deeming it repugnant (*karāhīyatihi*) for them to go out frequently is the temptation (*fitna*) that it is feared they will cause for men. [The Prophet], may God bless him and grant him peace, said, "I have left no temptation after me that is more harmful to men than women."[95]

The fifth/eleventh-century Ḥanafī al-Sarakhsī explains the difference of opinion attributed to Abū Ḥanīfa and his two disciples in terms of the criterion of *fitna*:

> Abū Yūsuf and Muḥammad (may God Most High have mercy upon them!) said: "It is permitted for old women to attend all prayers . . . because old women's going out involves no *fitna* and people rarely desire them . . ." Abū Ḥanīfa (may God be satisfied with him!) said: "At the nighttime prayers, the old woman goes out covered up and the darkness of night protects her from men's glances, unlike the daytime prayers, and [unlike] Friday prayers, which are held in the city – because of the great crowds, she may be buffeted and jostled, and that would cause *fitna*. Even if a young man would not desire an old woman, an old man like her would desire her; extreme lechery might drive even a young man to desire her and jostle her on purpose."[96]

Neither Abu Ḥanīfa nor Abū Yūsuf and Muḥammad are credited with these precise words; rather, al-Sarakhsī is interpreting and justifying their views in terms of the potential for sexual attraction, which he assumes to be the basis of their arguments.

By the sixth/twelfth century some Ḥanafīs held that no women should attend any public prayers. Ṭāhir ibn Aḥmad al-Bukhārī (d. 542/1147) writes after outlining the difference of opinion between Abū Ḥanīfa and his two disciples on mosque attendance by elderly women: "We have mentioned the preferred

95 Ibn Rushd, *al-Bayān*, 1:420.
96 al-Sarakhsī, *al-Mabsūṭ*, 2:63.

opinion in our time, [which is] that they should not go out [for congregational prayers]; [similarly], an old woman should not travel without a close male relative (*maḥram*), and should not be alone with a man, whether young or old."[97] Al-Bukhārī's repudiation of mosque attendance even by elderly women, which is related to the conditions of "our time" without further specification, is placed within the context of a more general rejection of the social prerogatives of old women. ʿAbd Allāh al-Mawṣilī (d. 683/1284) states that "the preferred opinion in our time is that none of that is permissible [i.e., women are never permitted to go to mosques], because of the corruption of the times and the open commission of obscene acts."[98] In the Ḥanafī literature no individual authority is credited with establishing this view; rather, in the sixth century A.H. and later it appears as an anonymous and yet pervasive view that gradually established itself as the new doctrine of the school. Only Zayn al-Dīn Ibn Nujaym (d. 970/1563) acknowledges the objection that this trend is in violation of established school doctrine, a reservation that found little favor with later Ḥanafīs.[99]

The opinion that the corruption of latter-day Muslims rendered it inadvisable for women of any age to attend public prayers was also expressed in other schools of law. The sentiment that women ideally should not go to mosques at all is expressed by the Shāfiʿī al-Ghazālī in his *Iḥyāʾ* a generation before Ṭāhir al-Bukhārī.[100] Nevertheless, al-Ghazālī's pious exhortations for women to remain at home coexisted with his acceptance of classical Shāfiʿī legal doctrine, which did not categorically preclude women's mosque attendance. Among Shāfiʿī scholars it is not until Taqī al-Dīn al-Ḥiṣnī (d. 829/1426) that it is proposed that the currently valid legal judgment (*al-fatwā*) should be to prevent women from going to mosques altogether,[101] and more restrictive new attitudes never fully displaced the classical doctrine of the school. The influential Mālikī scholar Ibn Isḥāq al-Jundī (d. 767/1366) stated in one of his works that "what is appropriate in our time is that [women] should be prevented [from going to mosques]; this is indicated by ʿĀʾisha's famous statement, 'If the Messenger of God had seen what women have innovated . . .'."[102] However, in his authoritative legal manual he reiterates the classical doctrine of his school.[103] Only in

97 Ṭāhir ibn ʿAbd al-Rashīd al-Bukhārī, *Khulāṣat al-fatāwā* (Lahore: Amjad Akīdīmī, 1397/[1977]), 1:214.

98 ʿAbd Allāh ibn Mahmūd al-Mawṣilī, *al-Ikhtiyār li-taʿlīl al-mukhtār* (Amman: Dār al-Fikr, 1420/1999), 1:122–3; Sadeghi, *Logic of Law-Making*, p. 89. As the title of al-Mawṣilī's book suggests, his objective was to establish the most accepted doctrines of the Ḥanafī school.

99 Ibn Nujaym, *al-Baḥr*, 1:628.

100 al-Ghazālī, *Iḥyāʾ*, 2:365 (but see also 2:53, where he excepts elderly women).

101 Taqī al-Dīn al-Ḥiṣnī, *Kifāyat al-akhyār fī ḥall Ghāyat al-ikhtiṣār* (n.p.: Dār al-Bashāʾir, 1418/1998), p. 185.

102 Cited in Shihāb al-Dīn Aḥmad ibn ʿAbd al-Ghaffār al-Mālikī, *Izālat al-ghishāʾ ʿan ḥukm ṭawāf al-nisāʾ baʿd al-ʿishāʾ*, MS Cairo, Dār al-Kutub, 109 Fiqh Mālik, microfilm 1965, 103b.

103 Khalīl, *Mukhtaṣar*, published with al-Haṭṭāb, *Mawāhib al-jalīl*, 2:449, 547, 549.

the Ḥanafī school is the apparent shift in scholarly sentiment reflected in a genuine shift in legal doctrine.

Another approach was to establish behavioral guidelines and conditions for women who ventured forth to mosques. The Mālikī authority ʿIyāḍ ibn Mūsā al-Yaḥṣubī (al-Qāḍī ʿIyāḍ, d. 544/1103), who lived in North Africa and Spain, transmits a set of criteria for the permissibility of a woman's venturing out to the mosque:

> The scholars (*al-ʿulamāʾ*) have set as conditions for [women's] going out that it be during the night, that [they] not be adorned or wearing perfume, that they not crowd close to men, and that [the individual in question] not be a young woman from whom *fitna* is to be feared. Equivalent to perfume is displaying adornments and pretty jewelry. If any of these occurs, it is obligatory to prohibit them [from going out] for fear of *fitna*.

He adds, "If they are prohibited from going to mosques" (i.e., if they violate one or more of these conditions), "then *a fortiori* [they should be prohibited] from [going to] other places."[104] Here, interestingly, he implies that the mosque is the best place for a woman to go if she leaves her home at all.

Al-Qāḍī ʿIyāḍ's list of conditions is based not on the school tradition rooted in the statements of Mālik, but directly on *ḥadīth* reports. Over time, similar lists of *ḥadīth*-based requirements appeared among scholars of other legal schools who cultivated a particular concern for *ḥadīth*, particularly Shāfiʿīs. A very similar (and highly influential) list of conditions is presented by the Damascene Shāfiʿī Abū Zakarīyā al-Nawawī (d. 677/1278) – significantly, not in one of his legal compendia, but in his commentary on the *Ṣaḥīḥ* of Muslim. Discussing the *ḥadīth* "Do not prevent the maidservants of God from [going to] the mosques of God," he writes that "the clear meaning of this and the other similar *ḥadīth* texts on the subject is that [a woman] should not be prevented from [going to] the mosque, but [this is subject to] conditions mentioned by the scholars that have been drawn from [other] *ḥadīth*s."[105] In some ways, such lists of conditions for women's mosque attendance could be regarded as more restrictive than the mainstream doctrine of the Malikī or Shāfiʿī school. If each item on the list is regarded as a necessary condition for allowing a woman's attendance at a mosque, then it represents a more comprehensive and exacting standard for women's presentation and behavior than a simple endorsement of attendance by older and less alluring women. However, by shifting the focus away from the woman's age and personal appearance to standards of dress and comportment,

[104] Cited in Muḥammad ibn Khalīfa al-Washtānī al-Ubbī, *Ikmāl Ikmāl al-muʿallim*, printed with Muslim ibn Ḥajjāj al-Qushayrī al-Naysābūrī, *Ṣaḥīḥ Muslim* (Beirut: Dār al-Kutub al-ʿIlmīya, 1415/1994), 2:332–3.

[105] Muḥyī al-Dīn al-Nawawī, *Ṣaḥīḥ Muslim bi-sharḥ al-imām Muḥyī al-Dīn al-Nawawī al-musammā al-Minhāj sharḥ Ṣaḥīḥ Muslim ibn al-Ḥajjāj* (Beirut: Dār al-Maʿrifa, 1414/1994), 4:382–3.

such requirements also suggests a new focus on women's good behavior and pious agency rather than their physical characteristics.

Thus, beginning roughly in the twelfth century C.E., scholars challenged the earlier consensus making a sharp distinction among women of different age cohorts. They did so for two, diametrically opposed, reasons: while some (particularly, but not exclusively, Ḥanafīs) began to argue that women should not frequent mosques at any age, others (particularly, but not exclusively, Mālikī and Shāfiʿī *ḥadīth* specialists) began to emphasize issues of dress and propriety more prominently than the factor of age. In the sixteenth century the Mālikī scholar Ibn ʿAbd al-Ghaffār observed that there were two basic positions on the legal status of women's mosque attendance among latter-day scholars: one holding that it was forbidden for all women, and the other holding that it was permissible subject to conditions relating either to the woman's inherent qualities (i.e., her age and attractiveness) or to factors such as her self-presentation and the timing of the prayer.[106]

Of course, the normative opinions of legal scholars tell us very little about the actual behavior of women. Ibn ʿAbd al-Ghaffār observes about the opinion that women as a class should be barred from mosques: "This is an opinion that has not been accompanied by practice, because women in the Islamic domains in all eras have always attended mosques" (*idh al-nisāʾ fī al-mamālik al-islāmīya lam yazilna fī jamīʿ al-aʿṣār yaḥḍurna al-masājid*). If people objected, it was not to the mere fact of women's going to mosques, but because of incidental circumstances accompanying their presence (presumably here he is referring to allegations of religious innovation and general bad behavior).[107] A century earlier, Ibn Ḥajar al-ʿAsqalānī (d. 852/1449) had similarly referred to "the continuous practice based on the permissibility of women's going out to mosques, markets, and journeys when they are veiled so that men cannot see them" (*istimrār al-ʿamal ʿalā jawāz khurūj al-nisāʾ ilā al-masājid wa'l-aswāq wa'l-asfār mutanaqqibāt li-allā yarāhunna al-rijāl*).[108]

Nevertheless, it should not be assumed that women's mosque attendance has historically been equal in magnitude or similar in kind to men's. While patterns have varied widely over time and place, it seems that focusing attention on Friday congregational prayers (mandatory for men, and thus often a good diagnostic for the frequency of their attendance) fails to account for the forms of mosque usage that have been preferentially cultivated by many women. Of course, in some places women did attend Friday prayers; the Aqṣā Mosque of Jerusalem seems to have been notable in this regard. In a polemic of the first half

[106] Ibn ʿAbd al-Ghaffār, Izāla, 95a–b.
[107] Ibid., 95b.
[108] al-ʿAsqalānī, *Fatḥ al-bārī*, 19:401.

of the seventeenth century against objectionable practices current in the Aqṣā Mosque, one of the abuses listed is

> the mixing of women with men on Friday without a barrier between them; indeed, some of [the women] remove the horsehair veils[109] from their faces, despite their beauty, adornment, and perfume – and what temptation (*fitna*) could be greater than that?! By God, [the women] sit in various [study] circles among the men, as if the men were close relatives (*maḥārim*) of theirs, or they were in their homes.[110]

However, as suggested even by this passage, in many cases women seem to have been particularly attracted to mosque sessions of preaching and teaching, which were often held at other times of the day and week. In his monitory handbook for preachers, the Baghdādī Ibn al-Jawzī (d. 597/1201) observes that "these [preaching] assemblies are never lacking in attractive women."[111] Ibn Baṭṭūṭa, who traveled through Iran around 726/1326, observes in wonder of the women of Shiraz that "an astonishing circumstance about them (*min gharīb ḥālihinna*) is that they gather to hear the preacher (*al-wāʿiẓ*) every Monday, Thursday, and Friday in the Great Mosque; sometimes one or two thousand of them gather, holding fans that they use to fan themselves because of the intense heat."[112] Based on the polemical complaints of disgruntled scholars, droves of women also seem to have attended the great nocturnal festivals that illuminated mosques on occasions such as the middle night of the month of Shaʿbān (Niṣf Shaʿbān), the Prophet's birthday and the night of his ascent to heaven (*miʿrāj*).[113]

Doctrinal disapproval of women's mosque attendance does seem to have had an impact over time. For instance, accounts of nineteenth-century Ottoman mosques suggest that in that context (presumably strongly influenced by restrictive Ḥanafī norms), women rarely attended congregational or Friday prayers. Nevertheless, women flocked to the major mosques during Ramaḍān.[114] Describing a childhood visit to the Suleimaniye Mosque in Istanbul in the 1890s, the Turkish female author Halide Edib describes how on the first day of Ramaḍān "there were more groups of women than men

109 Moshe Perlmann provides Dozy's definition of *al-shaʿārī*, a word which refers to small, black horsehair veils that cover only the eyes and are worn with the *niqāb*, a larger veil that covers the face and leaves an opening for the eyes (Moshe Perlmann, "A Seventeenth Century Exhortation Concerning al-Aqṣā," *Israel Oriental Studies* 3 [1973], p. 286, n. 16).

110 Quoted in Perlmann, "Seventeenth Century Exhortation," p. 286.

111 ʿAbd al-Raḥmān Ibn al-Jawzī, *Ibn al-Jawzī's* Kitāb al-Quṣṣāṣ wa'l-Mudhakkirīn, trans. Merlin L. Swartz (Beirut: Dār al-Mashriq, 1971), p. 200.

112 Ibn Baṭṭūṭa, *Riḥla*, 1:183.

113 Cf. Ibn al-Ḥājj, *Madkhal*, 1:211, 214, 221; Aḥmad ibn Ibrāhīm al-Dimashqī, known as Ibn al-Naḥḥās, *Tanbīh al-ghāfilīn ʿan aʿmāl al-jāhilīn wa-taḥdhīr al-sālikīn min aʿmāl al-hālikīn* (Ṣaydā and Beirut: al-Maktaba al-ʿAṣrīya, 1424/2003), p. 330.

114 Fanny Janet Blunt, *The People of Turkey*, ed. Stanley Lane Poole (London: Elibron Classics, 2005; facsimile of edition of London: John Murray, 1878), 2:280.

around the preachers" holding forth on the main floor of the mosque.[115] Mosques (or at least major urban mosques) were also used by women for private devotion and even for moments of rest and socializing outside of the home; Julia Pardoe, who made an extended residence in Istanbul in the 1830s, observed that "the presence of females in the different mosques was of constant and hourly occurrence,"[116] and the traveler Edmondo de Amicis described how a typical Turkish woman "enters the nearest mosque to say a prayer, and then stays for a quarter of an hour under the portico chatting with a friend."[117]

In the twentieth century, while older patterns persisted in many places, modernist and Islamist scholars reframed the issue of women's mosque attendance to reflect newer concerns. On the one hand, they often emphasized the educational role of mosques in informing women of normative Islamic teachings and combating traditional forms of piety that these thinkers increasingly regarded as deviant. Reformers such as the Syrian Jamāl al-Dīn al-Qāsimī (d. 1914) emphasized that women should be given access to mosques because "closing the door [of the mosque] against them completely means opening it to endless ignorance." He advocated that women should be given formal religious instruction at designated mosques (at which times men should be excluded from the buildings), "since innovations, objectionable practices, deviant beliefs, disobedience of husbands, and uncountable forbidden things have become prevalent among them."[118] Muslim thinkers who had come to think of mothers as the educators and guides of the next generation of Muslims – a view generally alien to medieval scholars, who had assumed fathers to be responsible for the moral and religious training of children[119] – were newly concerned that women's religious instruction be brought out of the shadows of informal and autonomous female networks and into the purview of formal, public, implicitly male-led Islam.

Furthermore, both in the context of national anticolonial struggles and of the objectives of groups that sought the Islamization of society later in the century, the mobilization of women was an additional source of strength that could be furthered by their inclusion in the religious and political space of the mosque. However, a countervailing trend was the increasing emphasis on female domesticity. While premodern scholars' concerns about the mobility and visibility of

115 Halidé Edib, *Memoirs of Halidé Edib* (New York: The Century Co., n.d.), pp. 68–9.

116 Pardoe, *The City of the Sultan*, 2:53.

117 Edmondo de Amicis, *Constantinople*, trans. Stephen Parkin, foreword by Umberto Eco (London: Hesperis Classics, 2005), p. 129.

118 Jamāl al-Dīn al-Qāsimī, *Iṣlāḥ al-masājid*, cited in Khayr al-Dīn Wānilī, *al-Masjid fī'l-islām: risālatuhu, niẓām binā'ihi, aḥkāmuhu, ādābuhu, bida'uhu* (n.p., n.d.), p. 300. On al-Qāsimī's views regarding women see David Dean Commins, *Islamic Reform: Politics and Social Change in Late Ottoman Syria* (New York: Oxford University Press, 1990), pp. 82–4.

119 Cf. Afsaneh Najmabadi, "Crafting an Educated Housewife in Iran," in Lila Abu-Lughod, ed., *Remaking Women: Feminism and Modernity in the Middle East* (Princeton: Princeton University Press, 1998), pp. 91–2.

women had revolved around issues of sexual temptation and public propriety, in the late nineteenth and twentieth century greater emphasis was laid on their duties within the family and the home.[120] Modernist and Islamist scholars increasingly framed their reservations about women's public activities less in terms of *fitna* than of the domestic obligations of a wife and mother. Classical scholars, in contrast, had very rarely invoked a wife's duties toward her husband as a rationale for limiting her frequentation of mosques and almost never referred to her need to attend to her children.[121]

An influential fatwa on women's mosque attendance was produced by Yūsuf al-Qaraḍāwī.[122] Referring specifically to the special nighttime prayers (*tarāwīḥ*) held during the month of Ramaḍān (which historically have been particularly attractive to women), he notes their meritorious (although not obligatory) character and continues:

> This includes both men and women, except that it is better for a woman to pray in her home than in the mosque, as long as there is no other benefit resulting from her going to the mosque other than prayer alone, such as hearing a religious exhortation or a lesson in [religious] knowledge, or hearing the Qur'ān from a reverent and excellent reciter. Going to the mosque for this purpose is more meritorious and more appropriate, particularly since most men in our time do not instruct their women in the religion.

Furthermore, many women would not "find the desire or resolve that helps them to perform the *tarawīḥ* prayers alone, unlike in the mosque and in congregation." Al-Qaraḍāwī affirms that a wife must seek her husband's permission to go out of the house, "even to the mosque," because of his general authority over the affairs of the house. Nevertheless, he may not forbid her without a valid reason, such as "if the husband is sick and needs her to remain by his side to serve him and take care of his needs, or if she has small children who will be harmed by being left alone in the house for the time required for prayer and there is no one to watch them."[123]

[120] On the new focus on domesticity and home economics in the Egyptian women's press see Beth Baron, *The Women's Awakening in Egypt: Culture, Society, and the Press* (New Haven: Yale University Press, 1994), pp. 155–67.

[121] See Sayeed, "Early Sunni Discourse," p. 10 ("The various jurists referred to for this research focus resolutely on the disorder that may result from women's attendance at mosques and pay little or no attention to domestic duties that may prevent a woman from joining congregational prayers"). Among the rare exceptions is the twelfth-century Ḥanafī authority al-Kāsānī, who writes that a woman is exempted from Friday prayers because "she is busy serving her husband" as well as because she is "forbidden to go out to gatherings of men" (*Badā'i' al-ṣanā'i'*, 2:659–60).

[122] For the role of al-Qaraḍāwī see Bettina Gräf and Jakob Skovgaard-Petersen, eds., *Global Mufti: The Phenomenon of Yusuf al-Qaradawi* (New York: Columbia University Press, 2009), particularly the contribution "Yūsuf al-Qaraḍāwī and the Muslim Brothers: The Nature of a Special Relationship," by Husam Tammam (pp. 55–83).

[123] www.qaradawi.net/site/topics/article.asp?cu_no=2&item_no=5442&version=1&template_id=130&parent_id=17 (accessed May 5, 2010).

In al-Qaraḍāwī's fatwa the importance of women's mosque attendance lies in the mosque's centrality as a site for the acquisition of religious knowledge, as well as in its capacity to evoke religious feeling and motivate acts of worship. Here he displays a notable sensitivity to the woman's own spiritual needs as compared to premodern scholars, who tended to neglect the subjective benefits of women's participation in public worship. However, he subordinates these considerations to a woman's fulfillment of her familial role, subject to the lawfully exercised authority of her husband. The problem is no longer perceived as being women's potentially disruptive presence in the public sphere, but their potentially neglectful absence from the home. Given al-Qaraḍāwī's overall views, it is reasonable to assume that he understands women's exposure to religious knowledge and practice to have broader social and political implications; however, he does not make these connections explicit.

A much younger Egyptian female scholar, Hiba Raʾūf (b. 1965), has put women's mosque access into a more explicitly politicized context. A political scientist by training, she has independent political views and has sometimes been critical of the Muslim Brotherhood; yet her views have clear elements in common with the trend established by thinkers of the Ikhwān. She writes:

> The study of the rules of the sharia makes clear that the intent of the Lawgiver was to raise the consciousness of the Muslim community through the acts of worship. The objective of connecting political and social activity with the mosque as an arena of worship was to ensure the continuation of political participation and the development of political consciousness for the Muslim individual by linking it to the rites without which the Muslim's faith is not complete.[124]

Raʾūf notes that a woman may suffer a deficit in knowledge of public affairs when she is near-confined to the home by pregnancy or breastfeeding. In addition to the role of modern mass media, she emphasizes that in this case the religious duties of a Muslim woman – including public worship – will provide her with at least the minimum degree of awareness of public events requisite for political participation.[125] While the very minimum is for a woman to attend the two yearly festival prayers, she continues: "As for women who enjoy special competency (*ahlīya*) and a higher degree of consciousness, and whose circumstances permit them to attend Friday and congregational prayers, the Prophetic guidance has guaranteed that to them and commanded the man not to prevent them from going."[126]

The value of women's attendance at public prayers in the mosque for political mobilization (as well as, of course, for the religious development of the women

[124] Hiba Raʾūf ʿIzzat, *al-Marʾa wa'l-ʿamal al-siyāsī: ruʾya islāmīya* (Herndon, Va.: al-Maʿhad al-ʿĀlamī li'l-Fikr al-Islāmī, 1416/1995), p. 112.
[125] Ibid., p. 102.
[126] Ibid., p. 108.

themselves) has also been recognized in Shīʿite Iran before and after the revolution. While acknowledging the received doctrine that it was more meritorious for a woman to pray in an interior chamber of her home, for instance, Khomeini opined that if she was able to conceal herself from the gaze of unrelated men, it was superior for her to pray in a mosque.[127] Friday prayers were a source of religious and political information for female as well as male revolutionary activists.[128]

A newly affirmative attitude toward women's mosque attendance has not been exclusive to those who sought social and political change, however. Probably the most influential Saudi scholar of the late twentieth century was ʿAbd al-ʿAzīz Bin Bāz (1909–99), whose positions on social questions were profoundly conservative. In a fatwa that is widely available in print, as a text on the internet, and as an audio recording, he is asked by a female questioner: "Is it permissible for a woman to pray in the mosque if she is [fully] covered and modest, has not applied perfume, and does not engage in vain display, and she does so only out of devotion to God, except that her husband is not pleased with her [doing so]?" Bin Bāz replies:

> A woman is entitled to pray in the mosque if she is [fully] covered and does not wear perfume; her husband is not entitled to prevent her from doing so if she adheres to proper comportment as defined by the sharia, because the Prophet (peace be upon him!) said, "Do not prevent the maidservants of God from going to the mosques of God," and he also said, "If the wife of one of you asks his permission to go to the mosque, he should not prevent her" – [al-Bukhārī and Muslim] agree on the soundness of [this report]. If she goes out modestly and without perfume there is no harm in it, even if her husband is not happy, because of the two aforementioned *ḥadīth*s. [However], if she prays in her home and does not go out in order to please her husband and avoid causes of *fitna*, it is better, because the Prophet (peace be upon him!) said, "Do not prevent the maidservants of God from going to the mosques of God, and their homes are better for them."[129]

Although Bin Bāz prefers that a woman voluntarily defer to the wishes of her husband and limit her mobility in the interests of preventing *fitna*, he also acknowledges the ability of a pious woman to realize ideals of modesty and piety as an autonomous religious agent. He also, unlike most of his premodern predecessors, treats the Prophet's prohibition on barring women from mosques as a binding legal norm rather than a moral exhortation. In this respect, he inverts the traditional

[127] Ayatollah Sayyed Ruhollah Mousavi Khomeini, *A Clarification of Questions: An Unabridged Translation of* Rasaleh Towzih al-Masael, trans. J. Borujerdi (Boulder and London: Westview Press, 1984), p. 123.

[128] See Abdolrahmane Mahdjoube, "The Inner Revolution of a Khomeyni Activist," in Monique Gadant, ed., *Women of the Mediterranean* (London: Zed, 1986), p. 65.

[129] ʿAbd al-ʿAzīz ibn ʿAbd Allāh Ibn Bāz, *Majmūʿ fatāwā wa-maqālāt mutanawwiʿa taʾlīf al-faqīr ilā ʿafw rabbihi ʿAbd al-ʿAzīz ibn ʿAbd Allāh ibn ʿAbd al-Raḥmān ibn Bāz*, collected and arranged by Muḥammad ibn Saʿd Shuwayʿir (Riyadh: Dār Aṣdāʾ al-Mujtamaʿ, 1421), 12:79–80.

juristic understanding that a man is encouraged rather than commanded to allow his wife to go to the mosque, while a woman is commanded rather than encouraged to remain modestly at home. However, regardless of the mufti's official status and high prestige, it is worth observing that Bin Bāz's opinion does not necessarily reflect actual contemporary practice in Saudi Arabia.[130]

The greater encouragement of women's mosque attendance in various modern contexts has not always been perceived as unambiguously positive for women. It can sometimes be seen as limiting women's autonomy and displacing other forms of religious practice centered in spaces more thoroughly controlled by women.[131] In some places mosques are also regarded as spaces where religious and political messages are subject to manipulation by the government. In terms of the division of space within mosques, as well, greater accommodation has sometimes come hand in hand with enhanced control. While premodern mosques did not routinely feature separate balconies (and balconies, when they existed, were often reserved for purposes other than women's worship), designated women's space – often on another level from the main prayer space – became a routine feature of modern mosques. Renata Holod and Hasan-Uddin Khan note of this development that it "has had a paradoxical impact on the place of women in the mosque" since the 1950s:

> Insistence on a clearly defined physical separation for them, unlike the more flexible arrangements adopted in the past, has in practice limited the actual and potential use of the space by women. On the other hand, by making the provision of some space for them nearly obligatory in a new mosque, the programming has ensured the inclusion of facilities for women in instances where they had previously been denied access.[132]

The introduction of artificial amplification and even, in some cases, closed-circuit TV has allowed some mosques to create women's prayer spaces that are sharply divided from the usually much larger space reserved for men. It has been noted by several authors that in the US and Canada, for instance, there has been a broad trend in the last several decades toward the separation of women's prayer space, with the same double-edged effects described by Holod and Khan. For instance Mohja Kahf observed in 2005 that "my local mosque until recently

[130] For descriptions of limitations on the accommodation of women in Saudi mosques by Muslims from other regions see Jeffrey Lang, *Even Angels Ask: A Journey to Islam in America* (Beltsville, Md.: Amana Publications, 1418/1997), p. 111; Mohja Kahf, *The Girl in the Tangerine Scarf* (New York: Carroll & Graf Publishers, 2006), pp. 166–7.

[131] See, for instance, Diane D'Souza, "Women's Presence in the Mosque: A Viewpoints" [*sic*], in Asghar Ali Engineer, ed., *Islam, Women and Gender Justice* (New Delhi: Gyan Publishing House, 2001), pp. 193–217. Azam Torab describes how one Iranian woman preacher advises her audience to pray at home, rather than in mosques that are dominated by men and deliver the politicized messages of the state (Azam Torab, *Performing Islam: Gender and Ritual in Iran* [Leiden, Boston: Brill, 2007], pp. 57, 96).

[132] Renata Holod and Hasan-Uddin Khan, *The Contemporary Mosque: Architects, Clients and Designs since the 1950s* (New York: Rizzoli, 1997), p. 20.

had little space or welcome for women at *juma*, and now that the new mosque is built women can pray *juma* only on a mezzanine with opaque fiberglass cutting off all visual contact with the main hall."[133] A 2001 survey by the Council of American Islamic Relations (CAIR) found that "in 1994, 52% of mosques reported that women make prayers behind a partition or in another room, but that practice was adopted by 66% of mosques in 2000."[134] This development has led to resistance and activism on the part of some North American Muslim women, such as Asra Nomani, who protested the "isolated balcony" that was allotted to women in her community's new mosque in West Virginia.[135] Although more rigidly separated women's prayer space has become prevalent in modern mosques in many other parts of the world as well, globally the overall trend is toward greater accommodation of women for purposes of both prayer and religious teaching.

Knowledge and mastery of prayer

Classical scholars envisioned the basic task of inculcating the knowledge and habit of prayer as occurring within the authority structure of the family. They held that it was the duty of the male head of household to acquire religious learning and then to instruct everyone under his authority in the knowledge necessary for the performance of their basic religious duties. This applied not only to his minor children, but to his wife or wives. The standard Qur'ānic proof-texts for this rule were verses 20:132 ("Order your family to pray, and be constant in it") and verse 66:6 ("O you who believe! Save yourselves and your families from a fire whose fuel is men and stones"); in each case the word family (*ahl*) can also mean "wife." The male head of household's responsibility for the religious training of his dependents was also widely argued to be demonstrated by a *ḥadīth* stating, "Each of you is a shepherd, and each of you is responsible for his flock. The *imām* who is in authority over the people is a shepherd, and he is responsible for them; a man is a shepherd over the members of his family, and he is responsible for them."[136] The twelfth-century Andalusian scholar Ibn al-Munāṣif derived from this "a man's particular [duty] to make sure that the people of his household, his servants, and his minor children of seven years and

[133] Mohja Kahf, "The Muslim in the Mirror," in Saleemah Abdul-Ghafur, ed., *Living Islam Out Loud: American Muslim Women Speak* (Boston: Beacon Press, 2005), p. 131.

[134] See the booklet "Women Friendly Mosques and Community Centers: Working Together to Reclaim Our Heritage," available at www.isna.net/assets/ildc/documents/womenandmosques booklet.pdf (accessed September 21, 2011), p. 9.

[135] Asra Q. Nomani, *Standing Alone in Mecca: An American Woman's Struggle for the Soul of Islam* (New York: HarperSanFrancisco, 2005), p. 197. Another engaging work on this subject is Zarqa Nawaz's film *Me and the Masjid* (2005), produced by the National Film Board of Canada.

[136] See, for instance, Ibn al-Munāṣif, *Tanbīh*, p. 332; al-Qurṭubī, *Tafsīr*, 18:127–8; Ibn al-Ḥājj, *Madkhal*, 1:152.

up keep up their prayers and perform them regularly at their [proper] times" as well as that he instruct them in the requirements of prayer and ablution.[137] A man's obligation to instruct and encourage his wife in the proper performance of prayer was acknowledged beyond the confines of technical legal works. A twelfth-century Persian work of advice for rulers, which reduces Islamic legal doctrines to a simple and palatable form, lists as the seventh duty of men toward their wives that "the religious knowledge that applies to women, such as (the rules of) prayer, purification, and menstruation, should be taught them. . . . If he falls short of his duty in this he is impious, for God says, 'Save your souls, and those of your families, from the fire' (66:6), that is, save yourself and your family from Hell."[138]

Nevertheless, the recognition that all Muslims required knowledge in order to fulfill the fundamental duty of prayer affirmed, at least in principle, the basic right and duty of all believers to acquire religious learning for themselves. Even as an ideal, the duty to instruct and exhort one's family for the performance of prayer was potentially a reciprocal and egalitarian one. Al-Qurṭubī cites a *ḥadīth* stating, "May God have mercy on a man who gets up during the night to pray and wakes his wife, and if she does not wake up, he sprinkles her face with water; God have mercy on a woman who gets up during the night to pray and wakes her husband, and if he does not wake up, she sprinkles his face with water."[139] Furthermore, the duty to acquire knowledge about the requirements of ritual purity and prayer, because it is an irreducible requirement for every legally responsible Muslim, also entails a corresponding right to seek knowledge if it is not immediately available. The anonymous author of the Persian "mirror for princes" cited above succinctly states that "if the man does not teach her, the woman is required to go out without permission and enquire (about these things)."[140] Ibn al-Ḥājj, who is otherwise passionately committed to the principle that women should leave the home rarely and only with their husbands' permission (a principle that was clearly little observed in the actual society of his time) held that a woman could go out without her husband's consent if he were incapable or unwilling to instruct her on basic religious duties such as purity and prayer.[141]

It is notable that in this schema instruction in ritual purity and prayer is an entitlement of the wife, rather than a disciplinary privilege of the husband. Although premodern jurists generally held that a husband was entitled to

137 Ibn al-Munāṣif, *Tanbīh*, p. 332.
138 Julie Scott Meisami, trans., *The Sea of Precious Virtues* (Salt Lake City: University of Utah Press, 1991), p. 163. Being instructed about prayer, fasting, and menstrual purity is also listed as one of the eight rights enjoyed by wives (p. 119).
139 al-Qurṭubī, *Tafsīr*, 18:128.
140 Meisami, *Sea*, p. 163.
141 Ibn al-Ḥājj, *Madkhal*, 2:199.

physically discipline his wife (although within strict limits, and without causing physical injury), they debated whether he could punish her if she refused to pray. This was because prayer was not a right (*ḥaqq*) of the husband, but of God; a woman's failure to pray was an infraction of her rightful relationship with God, not of her marital duties, and as long as she was legally competent she bore the onus as an individual.[142] Even Muslim slaves were, from the point of view of their ritual duties, regarded as morally autonomous. Ultimately, prayer took place within a relationship between the individual and God, an arena where moral personhood was not limited by the hierarchies and social roles recognized in many other areas of the sharia.

In reality, women were probably just as likely as men to play the role of instructor in prayer – and did not always recognize the authority of male "heads of household" when men attempted to exercise it. Aḥmad ibn Ḥanbal was reportedly consulted about a man who observed that his mother was (at least in his opinion) performing her ablutions and praying improperly. Instructed to "order and teach" her, his questioner revealingly enquired what to do if she dismissed him with the sarcastic retort, "I'm older than you; are you going to teach me?" Ibn Ḥanbal told him that, rather than proceeding to disciplinary measures, he should continue to inform and exhort her gently.[143] The autobiography of the great fifteenth-century Sufi Zarrūq recounts how his grandmother, who raised him after the death of his parents, induced him to pray by rewarding him with a coin tucked under his pillow. Another North African Sufi, the eighteenth-century authority Ibn ʿAjība, "used to get himself and his clothing so wet doing his ablutions before prayer that his mother tricked him into believing that it was permissible to do ablutions with a stone," a dispensation that is actually valid only when traveling or when circumstances prevent the use of water; he did not discover the deception for years.[144]

The instruction of a mother or grandmother could carry the authority of formal religious training; the women of Zarrūq's family had scholarly accomplishments.[145] However, as suggested by the pragmatic ruse of Ibn ʿAjība's mother, instruction within the family did not always faithfully reproduce the dictates of legal scholarship. In a humorous anecdote presented by the seventeenth-century Egyptian author al-Shirbīnī, a village woman comes to the Qurʾānic school (*kuttāb*) to complain to the teacher that her young son bothers her and even urinates on her when she is trying to do her prayers. When the boy confirms this,

142 See *al-Mawsūʿa al-fiqhīya*, art. "Taʾdīb," paragraph 4, 10:21–2; Ibn Qudāma, *al-Mughnī*, 8:164; Zaydān, *Mufaṣṣal*, 7:309; Cook, *Commanding Right*, p. 355, n. 132.

143 Abū Dāwūd, *Masāʾil*, p. 278 (see Cook, *Commanding Right*, p. 93).

144 "The Literary Portrayal of the Self," in Dwight F. Reynolds, ed., *Interpreting the Self: Autobiography in the Arabic Literary Tradition* (Berkeley: University of California Press, 2001), pp. 84, 85.

145 Kugle, *Rebel between Spirit and Law*, pp. 47, 48.

the teacher asks him why he would do such a thing. The son replies, "I do it because her worship is invalid and worthless. Ask her yourself what she says and how she recites her prayers." So the teacher asks her, "Do you know the prayer well?" "How should I not," she replies, "when I learnt it from my mother and my grandmother and my grandmother's grandmother?" The teacher tells her, "Recite the Fātiḥa!" and she promptly recites, "In the name of God the Merciful, the Compassionate! Praise be to God, Lord of the Worlds! If al-Ḥajj Naṣr al-Dīn comes to you, open the door to him. Lo! He was once a maker of bricks." The teacher is compelled to admit that the son is in the right.[146] Shirbīnī's story is obviously intended to poke fun at peasants as well as women, but it is likely that in fact ordinary people were often perfectly content with what they learned "from my mother and my grandmother and my grandmother's grandmother" and unimpressed with those who tried to convince them otherwise. The polemic of Ibn al-Ḥājj suggests that this was particularly true with respect to the purity practices of women, which threatened the validity of their prayers as well as the permissibility of marital intercourse. Women clearly had customs in this regard that may, in their own eyes, have enjoyed an authority that was not dependent on the imprimatur of religious scholars.[147]

Classical scholars' concern for the religious education of women, and in particular for their instruction in the obligatory components of prayer, was sometimes frustrated by very ideals of gender segregation that they themselves promoted. As Ibn al-Jawzī writes, "A girl (*ṣabīya*) ordinarily grows up in her chamber (*makhdaʿ*); she is not taught the Qurʾān, and does not know how to purify herself from menstruation; she is also not taught the obligatory components (*arkān*) of *ṣalāt*." Of course, the inner chamber (*makhdaʿ*) was precisely where, based on a *ḥadīth*, many scholars advocated that a woman do her prayers. Due to this relative isolation from the venues where religious knowledge was disseminated by male authorities, women sometimes followed autonomous practices that did not fulfill officially recognized requirements; as Ibn al-Jawzī notes, "Perhaps she sees her mother delay her ablutions (*ghusl*) after menstruation until she washes the clothes," or performs her prayers sitting down when she is capable of standing up.[148] As we have seen, scholars such as Ibn al-Ḥājj did regard the acquisition of necessary religious knowledge, such as the rules of obligatory prayers, to be an obligation that entitled a woman to leave her home without her husband's permission if he was unwilling or incapable of instructing her himself. However, Ibn al-Ḥājj clearly sees this as a last resort,

146 Ibid., p. 71. The woman's nonsense verses bear some phonetic resemblance to verses from the Qurʾān.
147 Ibn al-Ḥājj, *Madkhal*, 1:154–5.
148 ʿAbd al-Raḥmān ibn ʿAlī Ibn al-Jawzī, *Kitāb Aḥkām al-nisāʾ* (Ṣaydā and Beirut: al-Maktaba al-ʿAṣrīya, 1424/2003), p. 95.

rather than as a open-ended rationale for women's frequentation of places of public religious instruction; he expresses discomfort both with women's presence at mosque teaching sessions (which potentially entails mixing with men) and female teachers' instruction of groups of women (which potentially entails the perpetuation of deviant female beliefs and practices).[149]

The ambivalence of some medieval scholars toward the practicalities of women's religious instruction (even though they supported it in the abstract) is reflected in a fatwa by the Andalusian mufti Abū Isḥāq al-Shāṭibī (d. 790/1388). The question regards the legitimacy of the activities of a woman in the rural hinterland (*al-bādiya*) who is teaching the Qur'ān to women and girls. Al-Shāṭibī replies that "if this woman teaches girls and women what they need to know for the validity of their prayers, then it is good." However, he raises the concern that her knowledge of the Qur'ān may be inaccurate, in which case the the prayers of those she trains will be invalid. He concludes that the people of the village should take steps to train and examine this female teacher, since "the most likely thing is that this woman is ignorant of all of that."[150]

Nevertheless, women with greater access to normative religious instruction could earn admiration for the proficiency as well as the fervency of their prayers. In a biographical notice written by her father, whom she predeceased, Fāṭima bint al-Qāsim (d. 707/1308) is described as follows:

> She was a blessed woman who performed all of her obligatory and supererogatory prayers. . . . On the day when she went to the public bath, she would take pains not to delay her obligatory prayer; she would not go in until she had performed the noon prayer, and she would take pains to leave in time to make the afternoon prayer. . . . When I saw her pray, I used to rejoice and say [to myself], "I hope that God will benefit me by means of her." She used to perform her prayers perfectly and do her invocations earnestly. . . . I benefited from her in this world, and I hope that God will benefit me by means of her in the next.[151]

The Syrian nobleman Usama ibn Munqidh (d. 584/1188) writes admiringly of his grandmother's performance of *ṣalāt*, and recounts an anecdote in which she refuses to perform her prayers from a sitting position on the sacred night of Niṣf Shaʿbān despite her advanced age of almost one hundred.[152] The traveler John Lewis Burckhardt, who traveled to the Arabian Peninsula in 1814, backhandedly acknowledges the regard that could accrue to a woman through her mastery of prayer when he claims that Arab women's husbands "care little about

[149] Ibn al-Ḥājj, *Madkhal*, 1:198–200, 2:388.

[150] Abū Isḥāq Ibrāhīm ibn Mūsā al-Shāṭibī al-Andalusī, *Fatāwā al-imām al-Shāṭibī*, ed. Muḥammad Abū'l-Ajfān, 2nd ed. (Tunis: n.p., 1406/1985), p. 122; Manuela Marín, *Mujeres en al-Ándalus* (Madrid: Consejo Superior de Investigaciones Científicas, 2000), p. 281.

[151] Khalīl ibn Aybak al-Ṣafadī, *Aʿyān al-ʿaṣr wa-aʿwān al-naṣr*, ed. ʿAlī Abū Zayd et al. (Damascus: Dār al-Fikr/Beirut: Dār al-Fikr al-Muʿāṣir, 1418/1998), 4:31.

[152] Usama ibn Munqidh, *The Book of Contemplation*, trans. Paul M. Cobb (London: Penguin Books, 2008), p. 139.

their strict observance of religious rites, and many of them even dislike it, because it raises them to a nearer level with themselves; and it is remarked, that the woman makes a bad wife, who can once claim the respect to which she is entitled by the regular reading [i.e., performance] of prayers."[153]

In more recent times increased female access to mosques and other media of religious instruction has increased the possibility that a woman may possess knowledge of (and commitment to) *ṣalāt* equal or greater than that of her male kin.[154] This is reflected, for instance, in the fact that modern muftis consider much more frequently and extensively than their premodern predecessors the scenario of a religiously knowledgeable and observant wife whose husband fails to pray. The influential Saudi mufti Ibn ʿUthaymīn states flatly that a man who does not pray is not a Muslim, and that thus his marriage to a practicing woman is de facto dissolved; she must separate from him and refuse to have marital relations, and he has no right to custody of their children. Of course, it is questionable how practical this counsel would be in real life; his closing advice is that men should not marry their daughters and wards to nonpraying men in the first place.[155] Female Islamic teachers appear to take varying approaches to this problem, some venturing that in intractable cases a woman might have to deny sex to her nonpraying husband or even leave him; others argue that because a woman does not exercise *sharʿī* authority (*wilāya*) over her husband, she bears no responsibility for such religious shortcomings on his part.[156] What seems clear is that, even if marital rebellion and divorce remain rare and extreme solutions, increasing numbers of women can display a mastery of prayer and other pious achievements that lends them moral authority within their marriages and their communities.[157] The proliferation of sources of religious instruction that require no potentially inappropriate mixing with men, including mosque classes for women and technologically mediated forms of instruction such as religious TV programming and DVDs, have contributed to resolving some of the ambivalence about women's religious instruction that can be detected among earlier scholars.

[153] John Lewis Burckhardt, *Travels in Arabia* (London: Frank Cass & Co. Ltd., 1968; reprint of London: Henry Colburn, 1829), p. 347.

[154] This is, of course, not universally the case. Judy Brink, writing of an Egyptian village in the 1990s, recounts how when one mother "tried to teach her daughter the words to the prayer, which she has performed five times a day since she was a girl, it quickly became apparent that she did not know the words well enough to teach them to her daughter. Because she is illiterate and unfamiliar with written Arabic, the words of the prayer had become over the years a jumble of meaningless sounds." Judy Brink, "Lost Rituals: Sunni Muslim Women in Rural Egypt," in Judy Brink and Joan Mencher, eds., *Mixed Blessings: Gender and Religious Fundamentalism Cross Culturally* (New York: Routledge, 1997), pp. 204–5.

[155] Muḥammad ibn Ṣāliḥ ʿUthaymīn, *Fatāwā arkān al-islām* (Riyadh: Dār al-Thurayyā li-l-Nashr, 1421/2000–1), p. 280.

[156] Torab, *Performing Islam*, p. 35; Mahmood, *Politics of Piety*, pp. 184–6.

[157] Cf. Mahmood, *Politics of Piety*, p. 177.

Conclusion

In his religio-political memoir *The Islamist*, the British Muslim Ed Husain recounts his youthful journey from the Sufi piety of his South Asian family, through his deepening involvement in Islamic political activism as a university student, and finally back to Sufism as an adult. At each turning point in Husain's account of his religious trajectory, it is the practice of prayer – the specific style of its performance, the nature of the knowledge that is mobilized to authenticate it, and its affective and spiritual qualities – that most centrally characterizes his evolving identity as a Muslim. His "first act of rebellion" is to pray with his head uncovered, emulating slightly older activists whom he assumes to be "well versed in their religion." This act of religious self-assertion marks a break with the authority of his family; "I prayed that evening with confidence, with a feeling of difference, of greater ease."[1] Later he becomes involved with an Islamist group that "prayed in a way I had not seen in any of Britain's mosques, standing in perfectly straight rows, touching ankles, constantly checking to see that their feet were touching one another, and holding their arms in a martial position on their chests." For Husain, their posture in congregational prayer is simultaneously a potent marker of difference, a performative indicator of the militance of their political stance, and a claim to religious knowledge and authority. (He writes that "they flooded the college with books explaining how they prayed and giving 'evidence' and 'references' in support."[2]) Husain attributes his ultimate disillusionment with his Islamist comrades in part to their deficient knowledge of (and devotion to) prayer, writing that even as they called others to Islam, many did not know how to pray properly or neglected prayer in favor of political activism.[3] His culminating return to Sufism is also authenticated by the depth and authenticity of his *ṣalāt*: "Now, to bow and prostrate myself in prayer had meaning for me: abject humility, total lack of vanity in following the Prophet Mohammed's motions of prayer before the unseen but

[1] Ed Husain, *The Islamist* (London: Penguin Books, 2007), p. 29.
[2] Ibid., pp. 71, 72.
[3] Ibid., pp. 146–8.

all-seeing God. . . . Suddenly there was sweetness to prayers, nourishment for the soul, where previously they had been a dull chore."[4]

It seems likely that many of the activists Husain condemns would confirm his view that they deemphasize purely ritual duties in favor of more active forms of mobilization, although presumably they would dispute his claim that their mode of *ṣalāt* inadequately reflects the Prophetic *sunna* or Muslim ideals of connection to God. Husain's representation functions on more than one level, tacitly addressing non-Muslim readers' assumptions about appropriate "spirituality" as well as his own conviction that *ṣalāt* (its regularity, fidelity to the example of the Prophet, and emotional depth) is the ultimate diagnostic of Islamic legitimacy. What is unmistakable, however, is that *ṣalāt* functions for him in a number of ways that are not ultimately separable, but inextricably intertwined. As much as he emphasizes the interiority and affective depth of sincere prayer, modes of performing *ṣalāt* also centrally determine (and are determined by) group identification and religious authority. Prayer makes him the person that he is at the end of the book (both affectively and politically), but his trajectory is also shaped by his ability to evaluate and select better forms of prayer.

Ultimately, the contrasting concerns raised in the introduction of this book – of politics and gender versus spirituality and contemplation – prove to be interdependent. To strive for ideal – or even minimally valid – *ṣalāt* is to raise questions of religious knowledge and authority; to pray in congregation (or to forsake the congregation in favor of pious solitude) is to address the issues of communal solidarity and human leadership in an imperfect world. However, the sincerity, commitment, and authenticity of prayer – even the prayer of rough tribesmen or secluded women – have a recognized value that can compel acknowledgment and respect even in a world of inequality and domination. If the analysis of prayer has been an occasion for Muslim thinkers and practitioners to confront issues of legitimacy and hierarchy, it has never been completely reduced to them.

[4] Ibid., p. 191.

Bibliography

I. PRIMARY SOURCES

Abū Dāwūd Sulaymān ibn al-Ash'ath al-Sijistānī. *Kitāb Masā'il al-imām Aḥmad*. With an introduction by Muḥammad Rashīd Riḍā. Cairo: Maṭba'at al-Manār, 1353/[1942].

Abū Shāma, 'Abd al-Raḥmān ibn Ismā'īl. *al-Bā'ith 'alā inkār al-bida' wa'l-ḥawādith*. Ed. 'Uthmān Aḥmad 'Anbar. N.p.: Dār al-Hudā, 1398/1978.

Abū Shuqqa, 'Abd al-Ḥalīm Muḥammad. *Taḥrīr al-mar'a fī 'aṣr al-risāla*. 6 vols. Kuwait: Dār al-Qalam, 1430/2009.

Abū Ya'lā Muḥammad ibn al-Ḥusayn al-Farrā'. *al-Aḥkām al-sulṭānīya*. Cairo: Sharikat Maktabat wa-Maṭba'at Muṣṭafā al-Bābī al-Ḥalabī wa-Awlādihi bi-Miṣr, 1386/1966.

al-Albānī, Muḥammad Nāṣir al-Dīn. *Ṣifat ṣalāt al-nabī [sws] min al-takbīr ilā al-taslīm ka'annaka tarāhā*. 12th printing. Beirut: al-Maktab al-Islāmī, 1405/1985.

al-Thamar al-mustaṭāb fī fiqh al-sunna wa'l-kitāb. 2 vols. Kuwait: Ghirās, 1422.

'Alī ibn Maymūn al-Idrīsī. *Risālat Bayān ghurbat al-islām bi-wāsiṭat ṣinfay al-mutafaqqiha wa'l-mutafaqqira min ahl miṣr wa'l-shām wa-mā yalīyā min bilād al-a'jām*. Princeton MS Garret 828H.

al-'Āmilī, Zayn al-Dīn (al-Shahīd al-Thānī). *Asrār al-ṣalāt*. Ed. Muḥsin 'Aqīl. Beirut: Dār al-Balāgha, 1410/1990.

al-Fawā'id al-malīya li-sharḥ al-Risāla al-naflīya. Qum: Markaz Intishārāt-i Dafar-i Tablīghāt-i Islāmī, 1420/2000.

al-Rawḍa al-bahīya fī sharḥ al-Lum'a al-dimashqīya. 4 vols. Qum: Majma' al-Fikr al-Islāmī, 1429.

al-Amīr al-Ṣan'ānī, Muḥammad ibn Ismā'īl. *Subul al-salām*. Ed. Khālid 'Abd al-Raḥmān al-'Akk. 4 vols. Beirut: Dār Ṣādir, 1998.

al-'Āmirī, Abū'l-Ḥasan. *al-I'lām bi-manāqib al-islām*. Ed. Aḥmad Sharī'atī and Ḥusayn Manūchehrī. Tehran: Markaz-i Nashr-i Dāneshgāhī, 1347 H.Sh.

Anon. *Rasā'il Ikhwān al-ṣafā wa-khillān al-wafā'*. 4 vols. Beirut: Dār Ṣādir, 2006.

al-Anṣārī, 'Ālim ibn 'Alā'. *al-Fatāwā al-tātārkhānīya*. Ed. Sajjād Ḥusayn. 5 vols. Karachi: Idārat al-Qur'ān wa'l-'Ulūm al-Islāmīya, [1990–].

al-Aqfahsī, Aḥmad ibn 'Imād. *Kashf al-asrār 'ammā khafiya 'an al-afkār*. Ed. Muḥammad Khair Ramaḍān Yūsuf. Beirut: Dār Ibn Ḥazm, 1426/2005.

al-'Asqalānī, Ibn Ḥajar. *Badhl al-mā'ūn fī faḍl al-ṭā'ūn*. Ed. Aḥmad 'Iṣām 'Abd al-Qādir al-Kātib. Riyadh: Dār al-'Āṣima, 1411.

Fatḥ al-bārī bi-sharḥ Ṣaḥīḥ al-Bukhārī. Ed. Ṭāhā 'Abd al-Ra'ūf Sa'd and Muṣṭafā Muḥammad al-Hawārī. 28 vols. in 14. Cairo: Maktabat al-Kullīyāt al-Azharīya, 1398/1978.

al-Iṣāba fī tamyīz al-ṣaḥāba. 13 vols. Cairo: Maktabat al-Kullīyāt al-Azharīya, 1397/1977.

al-ʿAynī, Badr al-Dīn. *ʿUmdat al-qāri sharḥ Ṣaḥīḥ al-Bukhārī*. 25 vols. in 12. Beirut: Muḥammad Amīn Damj, n.d.

al-Bābartī, Muḥammad ibn Muḥammad al-Ḥanafī. *al-ʿInāya sharḥ al-Hidāya*. Ed. Abū Maḥrūs ʿAmr ibn Maḥrūs. 6 vols. Beirut: Dār al-Kutub al-ʿIlmīya, 1427/2007.

al-Bahūtī, Manṣūr ibn Yūnus. *Kashshāf al-qināʿ ʿan matn al-Iqnāʿ* Ed. Hilāl Muṣayliḥī Muṣṭafā Hilāl. 6 vols. Riyadh: Maktabat al-Naṣr al-Ḥadītha, n.d.

al-Bannā, Jamāl. *Jawāz imāmat al-marʾa al-rajul*. N.p., n.d.

Bird, Mary R. S. *Persian Women and Their Creed*. London: Church Missionary Society, 1899.

Blunt, Fanny Janet. *The People of Turkey*. Ed. Stanley Lane Poole. 2 vols. London: Elibron Classics, 2005; facsimile of edition of London: John Murray, 1878.

al-Bujayrimī, Sulaymān ibn Muḥammad. *Ḥāshiyat al-Bujayrimī ʿalā Sharḥ Manhaj al-ṭullāb*. Ed. ʿAbd Allāh Maḥmūd Muḥammad ʿUmar. 4 vols. Beirut: Dār al-Kutub al-ʿIlmīya, 1420/2000.

al-Bukhārī, Ṭāhir ibn ʿAbd al-Rashīd. *Khulāṣat al-fatāwā*. 4 vols. in 2. Lahore: Amjad Akīdīmī, 1397/[1977].

Burckhardt, John Lewis. *Travels in Arabia*. London: Frank Cass & Co. Ltd., 1968; reprint of London: Henry Colburn, 1829.

Chardin, Jean. *Voyages du chevalier Chardin en Perse, et autres lieux de l'orient, enrichis d'un grand nombre de belles figures en taille-douce, représentant les antiquités et les choses remarquables du pays*. New edn, rev. L. Langlès. 10 vols. Paris: Le Normant, Imprimeur-Libraire, 1811.

al-Daylamī, Shīrawayh ibn Shahradār. *al-Firdaws bi-maʾthūr al-khiṭāb*. 6 vols. Beirut: Dār al-Kutub al-ʿIlmīya, 1406/1987.

de Amicis, Edmondo. *Constantinople*. Trans. Stephen Parkin, foreword by Umberto Eco. London: Hesperis Classics, 2005.

al-Dimashqī, Aḥmad ibn Ibrāhīm, known as Ibn al-Naḥḥās. *Tanbīh al-ghāfilīn ʿan aʿmāl al-jāhilīn wa-taḥdhīr al-sālikīn min aʿmāl al-hālikīn*. Ṣaydā and Beirut: al-Maktaba al-ʿAṣrīya, 1424/2003.

d'Ohsson [Mouradgea d'Ohsson, Ignatius]. *Tableau Général de l'Empire Othoman*. 7 vols. Paris, 1788.

Doughty, Charles M. *Travels in Arabia Deserta*. 2 vols. New York: Boni & Liveright, [1920].

Edib, Halidé. *Memoirs of Halidé Edib*. New York: The Century Co., n.d.

Esack, Farid. *On Being a Muslim: Finding a Religious Path in the World Today*. Oxford: Oneworld, 1999.

Fabri, Felix. *The Wanderings of Felix Fabri*. The library of the Palestine Pilgrims' Text Society, vol. VII. New York: AMS Press, 1971 (reprinted from London edition of 1887–97).

al-Fāsī, Abū'l-ʿAbbās Aḥmad al-Qabbāb. *Mukhtaṣar kitāb al-Naẓar fī aḥkām al-naẓar bi-ḥāssat al-baṣar li-Ibn al-Qaṭṭān*. Riyadh: Maktabat al-Tawba, 1418/1997.

al-Fāsī, Muḥammad ibn ʿAbd al-Qādir. *Tuḥfat al-mukhliṣīn bi-sharḥ ʿUddat al-ḥiṣn al-ḥaṣīn min kalām sayyid al-mursalīn*. 4 vols. in 2. Ed. Muḥammad ibn ʿAzzūz. Casablanca: Markaz al-Turāth al-Thaqāfī al- Maghribī, 1428/2007.

al-Fayrūzābādī, Majd al-Dīn Muḥammad ibn Yaʿqūb. *al-Qāmūs al-muḥīṭ*. Cairo: Muṣṭafā al-Bābī al-Ḥalabī, 1371/1952.

Geyer, Rudolf, ed. *Gedichte von ʾAbû Baṣîr Maimûn ibn Qais al-ʾAʿšâ*. London: E. J. W. Gibb Memorial, 1928.

al-Ghazālī, Abū Ḥāmid. *Faḍāʾiḥ al-bāṭinīya*. Ed. ʿAbd al-Raḥmān Badawī. Cairo: al-Dār al-Qawmīya li'l-Ṭibāʿa wa'l-Nashr, 1383/1964.

Iḥyāʾ ʿulūm al-dīn. 4 vols. Beirut: Dār al-Fikr, 1414/1994.

Gohlman, William E. *The Life of Ibn Sina: A Critical Edition and Annotated Translation*. Albany: SUNY Press, 1974.

Gonzales, Antonius. *Le Voyage en Egypte du Père Antonius Gonzales, 1665–1666*. Ed., trans. from the Dutch, and annotated by Charles Libois, S.J. 2 vols. Cairo: Institut Français d'Archéologie Orientale du Caire, 1977.

Guillaume, A. *The Life of Muhammad: A Translation of Ibn Ishaq's Sirat Rasul Allah*. Karachi: Oxford University Press, 1967.

al-Ḥaddād, Abū Bakr ibn ʿAlī al-Zabīdī. *al-Jawhara al-nayyira sharḥ Mukhtaṣar al-Qudūrī*. Ed. Ilyās Qablān. 2 vols. Beirut: Dār al-Kutub al-ʿIlmīya, 1427/2006.

al-Ḥamawī, Aḥmad ibn Muḥammad. *Ghamz ʿuyūn al-baṣāʾir fī sharḥ al-Ashbāh wa'l-naẓāʾir*. Ed. Nuʿaym Ashraf Nūr Aḥmad. 3 vols. Karachi: Idārat al-Qurʾān wa'l-ʿUlūm al-Islāmīya, 1424/2004.

al-Ḥaṭṭāb al-Ruʿaynī, Muḥammad ibn Muḥammad. *Mawāhib al-jalīl li-sharḥ Mukhtaṣar Khalīl*. 8 vols. Beirut: Dār al-Kutub al-ʿIlmīya, 1416/1995.

al-Haytamī, Ibn Ḥajar. *al-Fatāwā al-kubrā al-fiqhīya*. 4 vols. Beirut: Dār al-Kutub al-ʿIlmīya, 1417/1997.

Tuḥfat al-muḥtāj bi-sharḥ al-Minhāj, printed in margin of *Ḥawāshī al-Shirwānī wa-Aḥmad ibn Qāsim al-ʿAbbādī ʿalā Tuḥfat al-muḥtāj*. 10 vols. [Būlāq], n.d.

al-Ḥillī, al-Muḥaqqiq Abū'l-Qāsim Jaʿfar ibn al-Ḥasan. *Sharāʾiʿ al-islām fī masāʾil al-ḥalāl wa'l-ḥarām*. 2 vols. Qumm: Dār al-Tafsīr, 1425 A.H.

al-Ḥimyarī, ʿAbd Allāh ibn Jaʿfar. *Qurb al-isnād*. Beirut: Muʾassasat Āl al-Bayt li-Iḥyāʾ al-Turāth, 1413/1993.

al-Ḥiṣnī, Taqī al-Dīn. *Kifāyat al-akhyār fī ḥall Ghāyat al-ikhtiṣār*. N.p.: Dār al-Bashāʾir, 1418/1998.

al-Ḥurr al-ʿĀmilī, Muḥammad ibn al-Ḥasan. *Tafṣīl wasāʾil al-shīʿa ilā taḥṣīl masāʾil al-sharīʿa*. 30 vols. Beirut: Muʾassasat Āl al-Bayt li-Iḥyāʾ al-Turāth, 1413/1993.

Wasāʾil al-shīʿa ilā taḥṣīl masāʾil al-sharīʿa. 9 vols. Beirut: Dār Iḥyāʾ al-Turāth al-ʿArabī, 1403/1983.

Husain, Ed. *The Islamist*. London: Penguin Books, 2007.

Ḥusayn, Ṭāhā. *al-Ayyām*. 3 vols. [Cairo]: Dār al-Maʿārif bi-Miṣr, n.d. Trans. as Taha Hussein, *The Days*. Trans. E. H. Paxton, Hilary Wayment, and Kenneth Cragg. Cairo: American University in Cairo Press, 1997.

Ibn ʿAbd al-Ghaffār, Shihāb al-Dīn Aḥmad al-Mālikī. *Izālat al-ghishāʾ ʿan ḥukm ṭawāf al-nisāʾ baʿd al-ʿishāʾ*. MS Cairo, Dār al-Kutub, 109 Fiqh Mālik.

Ibn Abī Shayba. *Muṣannaf Ibn Abī Shayba fī al-aḥādīth wa'l-āthār*. Ed. Saʿīd al-Laḥḥām. 9 vols. Beirut: Dār al-Fikr, 1428–9/2008.

Ibn Abī Yaʿlā, Abū'l-Ḥusayn Muḥammad. *Ṭabaqāt al-fuqahāʾ al-ḥanābila*. Ed. ʿAlī Muḥammad ʿUmar. 2 vols. Būr Saʿīd: Maktabat al-Thaqāfa al-Dīnīya, 1419/1998.

Ibn Abī Zayd al-Qayrawānī, Abū Muḥammad ʿAbd Allāh. *Kitāb al-Jāmiʿ fī'l-sunan wa'l-ādāb wa'l-ḥikam wa'l-maghāzī wa'l-tārīkh wa-ghayr dhālika*. Ed. ʿAbd al-Majīd Turkī. Beirut: Dār al-Gharb al-Islāmī, 1995.

al-Nawādir wa'l-ziyādāt ʿalā mā fī'l-Mudawwana min ghayrihā min al-ummahāt. Ed. ʿAbd al-Fattāḥ Muḥammad Ḥilw. 15 vols. Beirut: Dār al-Gharb al-Islāmī, 1999.

Ibn ʿĀbidīn, Muḥammad Amīn. *Ḥāshiyat Radd al-muḥtār ʿalā al-Durr al-mukhtār: sharḥ Tanwīr al-abṣār*. 8 vols. Cairo: Muḥammad Maḥmūd al-Ḥalabī wa-Shurakāʾhu, 1386/1966.

Ibn ʿĀbidīn, Muḥammad ibn Muḥammad Amīn. *Majmūʿat rasāʾil Ibn ʿĀbidīn*. 2 vols. n.p., n.d.

Ibn al-ʿArabī, Muḥyī al-Dīn. *al-Futūḥāt al-makkīya*. 4 vols. Beirut: Dār Ṣādir, n.d.

Tanazzul al-amlāk min ʿālam al-arwāḥ ilā ʿālam al-aflāk. Beirut: Dār al-Kutub al-ʿIlmīya, n.d.

Ibn al-Athīr. *Usd al-ghāba fī maʿrifat al-ṣaḥāba*. Ed. Khalīl Maʾmūn Shīḥā. 5 vols. Beirut: Dār al-Maʿrifa, 1418/1997.

Ibn ʿAṭīya, ʿAbd al-Ḥaqq al-Gharnāṭī. *al-Muḥarrar al-wajīz fī tafsīr al-kitāb al-ʿazīz*. Ed. Aḥmad Ṣādiq al-Mallāḥ. 2 vols. Cairo: al-Majlis al-Aʿlā li'l-Shuʾūn al-Islāmīya, 1394/1974.

Ibn Bābawayh al-Qummī, Muḥammad ibn ʿAlī, known as al-Ṣadūq. *Man lā yaḥḍuruhu al-faqīh*. 4 vols in 2. Beirut: Dār Ṣaʿb/Dār al-Taʿāruf li'l-Maṭbūʾāt, 1414/1994.

Ibn Baṭṭūṭa. *Riḥlat Ibn Baṭṭūṭa al-musammā Tuḥfat al-nuẓẓār fī gharāʾib al-amṣār*. 2 vols. in 1. Ṣaydā and Beirut: al-Maktaba al-ʿAṣrīya, 1425/2005.

Ibn Bāz, ʿAbd al-ʿAzīz ibn ʿAbd Allāh. *Majmūʿ fatāwā wa-maqālāt mutanawwiʿa taʾlīf al-faqīr ilā ʿafw rabbihi ʿAbd al-ʿAzīz ibn ʿAbd Allāh ibn ʿAbd al-Raḥmān ibn Bāz*. Collected and arranged by Muḥammad ibn Saʿd Shuwayʿir. 17 vols. Riyadh: Dār Aṣdāʾ al-Mujtamaʿ, 1421.

Ibn Farḥūn. *Naṣīḥat al-mushāwir wa-tasliyat al-mujāwir*. Ed. ʿAlī ʿUmar. Cairo: Maktabat al-Thaqāfa al-Dīnīya, 1427/2006.

Ibn Fāris, Abū al-Ḥusayn Aḥmad. *Mujmal al-lugha*. Ed. Hādī Ḥasan al-Ḥammūdī. 5 vols. Kuwait: al-Munaẓẓama al-ʿArabīya li'l-Tarbīya wa'l-Thaqāfa wa'l-ʿUlūm, 1405/1985.

Ibn al-Ḥājj, ʿAbd Allāh ibn Muḥammad. *al-Madkhal ilā tanmiyat al-aʿmāl bi-taḥsīn al-nīyāt wa'l-tanbīh ʿalā baʿḍ al-bidaʿ wa'l-ʿawāʾid al-latī untuḥilat wa-bayān shanāʿatihā*. Ed. Tawfīq Ḥamdān. 4 vols. Beirut: Dār al-Kutub al-ʿIlmīya, 1415/1995.

Ibn Ḥanbal, Aḥmad. *Aḥkām al-nisāʾ*. Ed. ʿAbd al-Qādir Aḥmad ʿAṭāʾ. Beirut: Dār al-Kutub al-ʿIlmīya, 1406/1986.

Musnad al-imām Aḥmad ibn Ḥanbal. Supervised by ʿAbd Allāh ibn ʿAbd al-Muḥsin al-Turkī, ed. Shuʿayb Arnaʾūṭ et al. 52 vols. Beirut: Muʾassasat al-Risāla, 1421/2001.

Ibn Ḥazm, ʿAlī ibn Aḥmad al-Andalusī. *al-Muḥallā bi'l-āthār*. 12 vols. Beirut: Dār al-Kutub al-ʿIlmīya, 1425/2003.

Ibn Hubayra, Yaḥyā ibn Muḥammad. *al-Ifṣāḥ ʿan maʿānī al-ṣiḥāḥ*. Beirut: Dār al-Kutub al-ʿIlmīya, 1417/1996.

Ibn al-Humām al-Ḥanafī. *Sharḥ Fatḥ al-qadīr*. Ed. ʿAbd al-Razzāq Ghālib al-Mahdī. 10 vols. Beirut: Dār al-Kutub al-ʿIlmīya, 1424/2003.

Ibn al-Jawzī, ʿAbd al-Raḥmān ibn ʿAlī. *Kitāb Aḥkām al-nisāʾ*. Ṣaydā and Beirut: al-Maktaba al-ʿAṣrīya, 1424/2003.

Ibn al-Jawzī's Kitāb al-Quṣṣāṣ wa'l-Mudhakkirīn. Trans. Merlin L. Swartz. Beirut: Dār al-Mashriq, 1971.

Ibn Jubayr al-Kinānī al-Andalusī, Muḥammad ibn Aḥmad. *Riḥlat Ibn Jubayr, wa-hiya al-risāla al-maʿrūfa taḥta ism Iʿtibār al-nāsik fī dhikr al-āthār al-karīma wa'l-manāsik*. Beirut: Dār al-Kutub al-ʿIlmīya, 1424/2003.

Ibn Kathīr. *Tafsir Ibn Kathir (abridged)*. Trans. and abridged under the supervision of Shaykh Safiur-Rahman al-Mubarakpuri. 10 vols. Riyadh: Darussalam Publishers & Distributors, 2000.

Ibn Khuzayma, Muḥammad ibn Isḥāq. *Ṣaḥīḥ Ibn Khuzayma*. Ed. Muḥammad Muṣṭafā al-Aʿẓamī. 4 vols. Beirut: al-Maktab al-Islāmī, 1391/1971.

Ibn Manẓūr. *Lisān al-ʿarab*. Beirut: Dār Ṣādir, 1410/1990.

Ibn Mufliḥ, Muḥammad. *Kitāb al-Furūʿ*. 6 vols. Beirut: ʿĀlam al-Kutub, 1404/1984.

Ibn al-Munāṣif, Muḥammad ibn ʿĪsā. *Tanbīh al-ḥukkām ʿalā maʾākhidh al-aḥkām*. Ed. ʿAbd al-Ḥafīẓ Manṣūr. Tunis: Dār al-Turkī li'l-Nashr, 1988.

Ibn Nujaym, Zayn al-Dīn. *al-Baḥr al-rāʾiq sharḥ Kanz al-daqāʾiq*. 9 vols. Beirut: Dār al-Kutub al-ʿIlmīya, 1418/1997.

Ibn Qayyim al-Jawzīya. *Asrār al-ṣalāt wa'l-farq wa'l-muwāzana bayna dhawq al-ṣalāt wa-'l-samāʿ*. Ed. Iyād ibn ʿAbd al-Laṭīf ibn Ibrāhīm al-Qaysī. Beirut: Dār Ibn Ḥazm, 1424/2003.

al-Jawāb al-kāfī li-man saʾala ʿan al-dawāʾ al-shāfī. Ed. Ḥusayn ʿAbd al-Ḥamīd. al-Manṣūra: Dār al-Yaqīm, 1420/2000.

Kitāb al-ṣalāt wa-ḥukm tārikihā. Ed. Muḥammad ʿAbd al-Razzāq al-Raʿūd. Amman: Dār al-Furqān, 1423/2003.

al-Ṭuruq al-ḥukmīya fī'l-siyāsa al-sharʿīya aw al-firāsa al-murḍiya fī aḥkām al-siyāsa al-sharʿīya. Cairo: Dār al-Ḥadīth, 1423/2002.

Zād al-maʿād fī hady khayr al-ʿibād. Ed. Muḥammad al-Anwar Aḥmad al-Baltājī. 9 vols. Ṣaydā and Beirut: al-Maktaba al-ʿAṣrīya, 1428/2007.

Ibn Qudāma al-Maqdisī, Muwaffaq al-Dīn ʿAbd Allāh ibn Aḥmad. *Dhamm al-waswās*. Damascus: Maktabat al-Fārūq, 1411/1990.

al-Mughnī. 14 vols. Beirut: Dār al-Kutub al-ʿIlmīya, n.d.

Ibn Qutayba al-Dīnawarī. *ʿUyūn al-akhbār*. 4 vols. Cairo: Maṭbaʿat Dār al-Kutub al-Miṣrīya, 1349/1930.

Ibn Rushd, Abū'l-Walīd. *al-Bayān wa'l-taḥṣīl wa'l-sharḥ wa'l-tawjīh wa'l-taʿlīl fī masāʾil al-Mustakhraja*. Ed. Muḥammad Ḥajjī. 20 vols. Beirut: Dār al-Gharb al-Islāmī, 1404/1984.

Ibn Rushd, Muḥammad ibn Aḥmad al-Qurṭubī. *Bidāyat al-mujtahid wa-nihāyat al-muqtaṣid*. 2 vols. Beirut: Dār Ibn Ḥazm, 1424/2003.

Ibn Saʿd. *Kitāb al-Ṭabaqāt al-kubrā*. Ed. Iḥsān ʿAbbās. 9 vols. Beirut: Dār Ṣādir/Dār Bayrūt, 1377/1958.

Ibn al-Ṣalāḥ. *Fatāwā wa-masāʾil Ibn al-Ṣalāḥ fī'l-ḥadīth wa'l-uṣūl wa'l-fiqh*. Ed. ʿAbd al-Muʿṭī Amīn Qalʿajī. Beirut: Dār al-Maʿrifa, 1406/1986.

Ibn Sīnā, al-Ḥusayn ibn ʿAbd Allāh. *al-Ṣalāt wa-asrāruhā*. MS Cairo, Dār al-Kutub, Ḥikma wa-Falsafa 389.

Ibn Taymīya, Taqī al-Dīn Aḥmad ibn ʿAbd al-Ḥalīm. *Kitāb al-Īmān*. Beirut: Dār al-Kutub al-ʿIlmīya, 1403/1983.

Majmū' al-fatāwā. Ed. Muṣṭafā 'Abd al-Qādir 'Aṭā. 37 vols. Beirut: Dār al-Kutub al-'Ilmīya, 1421/2000.

Risālat al-ulfa bayna al-muslimīn. Ed. 'Abd al-Fattāḥ Abū Ghudda. Aleppo: Maktab al-Maṭbū'āt al-Islāmīya, 1417/1996.

Ibn Ṭufayl. *Qiṣṣat Ḥayy ibn Yaqẓān*. Ed. 'Iṣām Fāris al-Ḥarastānī. Amman: Dār 'Ammār, 1416/1995. Trans. Lenn Evan Goodman as *Ibn Tufayl's Hayy Ibn Yaqzān: A Philosophical Tale*. Chicago: University of Chicago Press, 2009.

Ibn al-Ukhūwa, Muḥammad ibn Muḥammad. *The Ma'ālim al-qurba fī aḥkām al-ḥisba of Ḍiyā' al-Dīn Muḥammad ibn Muḥammad al-Qurashī al-Shāfi'ī, known as Ibn al-Ukhuwwa*. Trans. Reuben Levy. London: E. J. W. Gibb Memorial, 1938.

al-Iṣfahānī, Abū'l-Faraj. *Kitāb al-Aghānī*. 24 vols. Cairo: al-Mu'assasa al-Miṣrīya al-'Āmma li'l-Ta'līf wa'l-Tarjama wa'l-Ṭabā'a wa'l-Nashr, n.d.

'Iyāḍ, al-Qāḍī. *Tartīb al-madārik wa-taqrīb al-masālik li-ma'rifat a'lām madhhab Mālik*. Ed. Aḥmad Bukayr Maḥmūd. 3 vols. Beirut: Dār Maktabat al-Ḥayāt, n.d.

'Izzat, Hiba Ra'ūf. *al-Mar'a wa'l-'amal al-siyāsī: ru'ya islāmīya*. Herndon, Va.: al-Ma'had al-'Ālamī li'l-Fikr al-Islāmī, 1416/1995.

Ja'fariyān, Rasūl, ed. *Davāzdah risālah-i fiqhī dar bārah-i namaz-i jum'ah az rūzgār-i ṣafavī*. Qum: Intishārāt-i Anṣāriyān, 1423/2003.

al-Jawharī, Ismā'īl ibn Ḥammād. *al-Ṣiḥāḥ*. Ed. Aḥmad 'Abd al-Ghafūr 'Aṭṭār. 6 vols. Beirut: Dār al-'Ilm li'l-Malāyīn, 1399/1979.

Johnson, Sarah Barclay. *Hadji in Syria, or Three Years in Jerusalem*. Philadelphia: James Challen & Sons, 1858; repr. New York: Arno Press, 1977.

al-Juwaynī, 'Abd al-Malik ibn 'Abd Allāh. *Nihāyat al-maṭlab fī dirāyat al-madhhab*. Ed. 'Abd al-'Aẓīm Mahmūd al-Dīb. 21 vols. Jeddah: Dār al-Minhāj, 1428/2007.

al-Kafawī, Abū'l-Baqā'. *al-Kullīyāt*. Ed. 'Adnān Darwīsh and Muḥammad al-Miṣrī Beirut: Mu'assasat al-Risāla, 1412/1992.

Kahf, Mohja. *The Girl in the Tangerine Scarf*. New York: Carroll & Graf Publishers, 2006.

"The Muslim in the Mirror." In Saleemah Abdul-Ghafur, ed., *Living Islam Out Loud: American Muslim Women Speak*. Boston: Beacon Press, 2005, pp. 130–8.

al-Kāsānī, 'Alā' al-Dīn Abū Bakr Ibn Mas'ūd. *Badā'i' al-ṣanā'i' fī tartīb al-sharā'i'*. 7 vols. Cairo: Zakarīyā 'Alī Yūsuf, n.d.

Kātib Chelebi. *The Balance of Truth*. Trans. G. L. Lewis. London: George Allen & Unwin Ltd., 1957.

Khomeini, Ayatollah Sayyed Ruhollah Mousavi. *A Clarification of Questions: An Unabridged Translation of Rasaleh Towzih al-Masael*. Trans. J. Borujerdi. Boulder and London: Westview Press, 1984.

[Rūḥ Allāh Khumaynī] *Islam and Revolution: Writings and Declarations of Imam Khomeini*. Trans. Hamid Algar. Berkeley: Mizan Press, 1981.

al-Khujandī, Muḥammad Sulṭān al-Ma'ṣūmī. *Hal al-muslim mulzam bi'ttibā' madhhab mu'ayyan min al-madhāhib al-arba'a*. Ed. Sulaym al-Hilālī. Cairo: Maktabat al-Taw'īya al-Islāmīya/Amman: al-Maktaba al-Islāmīya, 1405.

al-Kulaynī, Muḥammad ibn Ya'qūb. *Furū' al-Kāfī*. Ed. Muḥammad Ja'far Shams al-Dīn. 5 vols. Beirut: Dār al-Ta'āruf li'l-Maṭbū'āt, 1413/1993.

Labīd ibn Rabī'a. *Sharḥ Dīwān Labīd ibn Rabī'a al-'Āmirī*. Ed. Iḥsān 'Abbās. Kuwait: Wizārat al-Irshād wa'l-Inbā', 1962.

Lane, Edward William. *An Account of the Manners and Customs of the Modern Egyptians*. Introduced by Jason Thompson. Cairo: American University in Cairo Press, 2003.

Arabic–English Lexicon. 8 vols. Beirut: Librairie du Liban, 1980; reprint of London, 1872.

Lang, Jeffrey. *Even Angels Ask: A Journey to Islam in America*. Beltsville, Md.: Amana Publications, 1418/1997.

Lucas, Paul. *Troisieme voyage du Sieur Paul Lucas, fait en MDCCXIV, &c. par ordre de Louis XIV dans la Turquie*... 3 vols. Rouen: Robert Machuel le jeune, 1719.

al-Maghīlī, Muḥammad ibn ʿAbd al-Karīm. *Asʾilat al-asqiya wa-ajwibat al-Maghīlī*. Algiers: al-Sharika al-Waṭanīya li'l-Nashr wa'l-Tawzīʿ, 1974.

al-Mahdī al-ʿImrānī, Muḥammad. *al-Nawāzil al-jadīda al-kubrā*. 12 vols. [Rabat]: al-Mamlaka al-Maghribīya, Wizārat al-Awqāf wa-al-Shu'ūn al-Islāmīya, 1996–.

Maimonides, Moses. *The Guide of the Perplexed*. Trans. Shlomo Pines. Chicago: University of Chicago Press, 1963.

Mālik ibn Anas al-Aṣbaḥī [Saḥnūn ibn Saʿīd al-Tanūkhī]. *al-Mudawwana al-kubrā*. 5 vols. Beirut: Dār al-Kutub al-ʿIlmīya, 1426/2005.

al-Maqdisī, Muṭahhar ibn Ṭāhir. *Kitāb al-badʾ wa'l-tārīkh*. Ed. Clément Huart. 5 vols. Paris: Ernest Leroux, 1916.

al-Marʿashī, Ismāʿīl ibn Aḥmad al-Ḥusaynī. *ʿUnwān al-ṭāʿa fī iqāmat al-jumʿa wa'l-jamāʿa*. Tehran: Manshūrāt Maktabat al-Ṣadr, 1368 H.Sh.

al-Mardāwī, ʿAlī ibn Sulaymān. *al-Inṣāf fī maʿrifat al-rājiḥ min al-khilāf ʿalā madhhab al-imām al-mubajjal Aḥmad ibn Ḥanbal*. Ed. Muḥammad Ḥāmid al-Faqqī. 12 vols. Beirut: Dār Iḥyāʾ al-Turāth al-ʿArabī, 1406/1986.

Martineau, Harriet. *Eastern Life, Past and Present*. 3 vols. London: Edward Moxon, 1848.

al-Māwardī, ʿAlī ibn Muḥammad. *al-Aḥkām al-sulṭānīya wa'l-wilāyāt al-dīnīya*. Ed. Samīr Muṣṭafā Rabāb. Ṣaydā and Beirut: al-Maktaba al-ʿAṣrīya, 1424/2003.

al-Ḥāwī al-kabīr fī fiqh madhhab al-imām al-Shāfiʿī raḍiya Allāhu ʿanhu. Ed. ʿAlī Muḥammad Muʿawwaḍ and ʿĀdil Aḥmad ʿAbd al-Mawjūd. 18 vols. Beirut: Dār al-Kutub al-ʿIlmīya, 1414/1994.

al-Mawṣilī, ʿAbd Allāh ibn Mahmūd. *al-Ikhtiyār li-taʿlīl al-mukhtār*. 3 vols. Amman: Dār al-Fikr, 1420/1999.

al-Mawwāq, Muḥammad ibn Yūsuf al-ʿAbdarī. *al-Tāj wa'l-Iklīl li-Mukhtaṣar Khalīl*, printed in margins of al-Ḥaṭṭāb, *Mawāhib al-jalīl*. Beirut: Dār al-Kutub al-ʿIlmīya, 1416/1995.

al-Māzirī, Muḥammad ibn ʿAlī al-Tamīmī. *Sharḥ al-Talqīn*. Ed. Muḥammad al-Mukhtār al-Salāmī. 3 vols. Beirut: Dār al-Gharb al-Islāmī, 1997.

Meisami, Julie Scott trans. *The Sea of Precious Virtues*. Salt Lake City: University of Utah Press, 1991.

Memon, Muhammad Umar, trans. *Ibn Taimīya's Struggle against Popular Religion: With an Annotated Translation of His Kitāb iqtiḍāʾ aṣ-ṣirāṭ al-mustaqūm [*sic*] mukhālafat aṣḥāb al-jaḥīm*. The Hague: Mouton, 1976.

al-Muḥāsibī, al-Ḥārith ibn Asad. *Fahm al-ṣalāt*. Ed. Muḥammad ʿUthmān al-Khisht. Cairo: Maktabat al-Qurʾān, 1984.

Mullā Khusraw Muḥammad ibn Farāmūz. *Durar al-ḥukkām fī sharḥ Ghurar al-aḥkām*. 2 vols. Istanbul: n.p., 1329.

al-Nābulusī, ʿAbd al-Ghanī ibn Ismāʿīl. *Nihāyat al-murād fī sharḥ Hadīyat Ibn al-ʿImād.* Ed. ʿAbd al-Razzāq al-Ḥalabī. Dubai: Qism al-Taḥqīq wa'l-Nashr, Markaz Jumʿa al-Mājid li'l-Thaqāfa wa'l-Turāth, 1414/1994.

al-Nafrāwī, Aḥmad ibn Ghunaym. *al-Fawākih al-dawānī ʿalā Risālat Ibn Abī Zayd al-Qayrawānī.* 2 vols. Beirut: Dār al-Kutub al-ʿIlmīya, 1418/1997.

al-Nawawī, Yaḥyā ibn Sharaf. *Kitāb al-Adhkār al-muntakhab min kalām sayyid al-abrār.* Cairo: al-Dār al-Miṣrīya al-Lubnānīya, 1408/1988.

al-Majmūʿ sharḥ al-Muhadhdhab. 27 vols. Ed. ʿĀdil Aḥmad ʿAbd al-Mawjūd et al. Beirut: Dār al-Kutub al-ʿIlmīya, 1423/2002.

Ṣaḥīḥ Muslim bi-sharḥ al-imām Muḥyī al-Dīn al-Nawawī al-musammā al-Minhāj sharḥ Ṣaḥīḥ Muslim ibn al-Ḥajjāj. 18 vols. in 9. Beirut: Dār al-Maʿrifa, 1414/1994.

Nomani, Asra Q. *Standing Alone in Mecca: An American Woman's Struggle for the Soul of Islam.* New York: HarperSanFrancisco, 2005.

al-Nuʿmān ibn Muḥammad, Abū Ḥanīfa. *Daʿāʾim al-islām.* Ed. Āṣif ibn ʿAlī Aṣghar Fayẓi. 2 vols. Cairo: Dār al-Maʿārif bi-Miṣr, 1389/1969.

Taʾwīl al-daʿāʾim. Ed. ʿĀrif Tāmir. 2 vols. Beirut: Dār al-Aḍwā', 1415/1995.

Pardoe, [Julia]. *The City of The Sultan; and Domestic Manners of the Turks, in 1836.* 2nd ed. 3 vols. London: Henry Colburn, Publisher, 1838.

Pitts, Joseph. *A True and Faithful Account of the Religion and Manners of the Mohammetans, with an Account of the Author's Being Taken Captive.* Exon, 1704.

Pococke, Richard. *A Description of the East, and Some Other Countries.* 3 vols. London: W. Bowyer, 1743.

Postel, Guillaume. *Des Histoires Orientales, text modernisé, introduction et notes par Jacques Rollet.* Istanbul: Les Editions Isis, 1999.

Prynne, William. *A moderate, seasonable apology for indulging just Christian liberty to truly tender consciences, conforming to the publike liturgy...* London: Printed for the author by T.C. and L.P., 1662 [electronic resource].

al-Qaffāl al-Shāshī, Abū Bakr Muḥammad ibn ʿAlī. *Maḥāsin al-sharīʿa fī furūʿ al-shāfiʿīya.* Beirut: Dār al-Kutub al-ʿIlmīya, 1428/2007.

al-Qaraḍāwī, Yūsuf. *Hudā al-islām: fatāwā muʿāṣira.* 3 vols. Cairo: Dār Āfāq al-Ghadd, 1981.

al-ʿIbāda fī'l-islām. Beirut: Mu'assasat al-Risāla, 1397/1977.

al-Qarāfī, Shihāb al-Dīn Aḥmad ibn Idrīs. *al-Dhakhīra.* 14 vols. Beirut: Dār al-Gharb al-Islāmī, 1994.

al-Furūq wa-Anwār al-burūq fī anwāʾ al-furūq. 4 vols. Beirut: Dār al-Kutub al-ʿIlmīya, 1418/1998.

al-Qāriʾ, Mullā ʿAlī. *Risālat al-Ihtidāʾ fī'l-iqtidāʾ.* MS Cairo, Uṣūl Taymūr 172.

al-Qasṭallānī, Quṭb al-Dīn. *Marāṣid al-ṣalāt fī maqāṣid al-ṣalāt.* Ed. Maḥmūd ʿAbd al-Raḥmān ʿAbd al-Munʿim. Cairo: Dār al-Faḍīla, n.d.

al-Qummī, Niẓām al-Dīn Muḥammad ibn al-Ḥusayn al-Nīsābūrī. *Gharāʾib al-qurʾān wa-raghāʾib al-furqān.* Ed. Ibrāhīm ʿAṭwa ʿAwaḍ. 30 vols. in 10. Cairo: Sharikat Maktabat wa-Maṭbaʿat Muṣṭafā al-Bābī al-Ḥalabī wa-Awlādihi bi-Miṣr, 1981/1962.

al-Qurṭubī, Muḥammad ibn Aḥmad. *Tafsīr al-Qurṭubī (al-Jāmiʿ li-aḥkām al-qurʾān).* Ed. Sālim Muṣṭafā al-Badrī. 21 vols. in 11. Beirut: Dār al-Kutub al-ʿIlmīya, 1424/2004.

al-Qushayrī, ʿAbd al-Karīm ibn Hawāzin. *al-Risāla al-qushayrīya fī ʿilm al-taṣawwuf.* Ed. Maʿrūf Zurayq and ʿAlī ʿAbd al-Ḥamīd al-Balṭajī. Beirut: Dār al-Jīl, n.d.

Quṭb, Sayyid. *Fī ẓilāl al-qurʾān.* 6 vols. Beirut: Dār al-Shurūq, 1973–4.

In the Shade of the Qur'ān. Ed. and trans. M. A. Salahi and A. A. Shamis. 18 vols. Leicester: Islamic Foundation, 1999/1420.

al-Rāzī, al-Fakhr. *al-Tafsīr al-kabīr*. 32 vols. in 16. Beirut: Dār Iḥyā' al-Turāth al-ʿArabī, n.d.

Riccold de Monte Croce. *Pérégrination en Terre Sainte et au Proche Orient, Texte latin et traduction*. Ed. and trans. René Kappler. Paris: Honoré Champion Éditeur, 1997.

al-Ṣadr, Muḥammad Bāqir. *Falsafa wa-akhlāqīyat al-ṣalāt*. Ed. and annotated by al-Sayyid Muḥsin al-Mūsawī. Beirut: Dār al-Ḥujja al-Bayḍā', 1424/2003.

al-Fatāwā al-wāḍiḥa. Beirut: Dār al-Kitāb al-Lubnānī, 1977.

al-Ṣafadī, Khalīl ibn Aybak. *Aʿyān al-ʿaṣr wa-aʿwān al-naṣr*. Ed. ʿAlī Abū Zayd et al. 6 vols. Damascus: Dār al-Fikr/Beirut: Dār al-Fikr al-Muʿāṣir, 1418/1998.

al-Ṣanʿānī, ʿAbd al-Razzāq Ibn Hammām. *al-Muṣannaf*. Ed. Ḥabīb Allāh al-Aʿẓamī. 11 vols. Beirut: al-Majlis al-ʿIlmī, n.d.

al-Sarakhsī, Muḥammad ibn Aḥmad. *al-Mabsūṭ*. Ed. Muḥammad Ḥasan Muḥammad Ḥasan al-Shāfiʿī. 30 vols. in 15. Beirut: Dār al-Kutub al-ʿIlmīya, 1421/2001.

Uṣūl al-Sarakhsī. Ed. Abū'l-Wafā' al-Sarakhsī. 2 vols. Hyderabad: Lajnat Iḥyā' al-Maʿārif al-Nuʿmānīya, n.d.

al-Shāfiʿī, Muḥammad ibn Idrīs. *al-Risāla*. Ed. Aḥmad Muḥammad Shākir. Beirut: Dār al-Kutub al-ʿIlmīya, n.d.

al-Umm. 8 vols. in 4. Beirut: Dār al-Maʿrifa, n.d.

al-Shaʿrānī, ʿAbd al-Wahhāb. *Kitāb Kashf al-ghamma ʿan jamīʿ al-umma*. Cairo: Muṣṭafā al-Bābī al-Ḥalabī, n.d.

al-Shāṭibī, Abū Isḥāq Ibrāhīm ibn Mūsā. *Fatāwā al-imām al-Shāṭibī*. Ed. Muḥammad Abū'l-Ajfān. 2nd ed.Tunis: n.p., 1406/1985.

al-Iʿtiṣām. 2 vols. Beirut: Dār al-Maʿrifa, n.d.

al-Muwāfaqāt fī uṣūl al-sharīʿa. Ed. Muḥammad al-Iskandarānī and ʿAdnān Darwīsh. Beirut: Dār al-Kitāb al-ʿArabī, 1423/2002.

al-Shawkānī, Muḥammad ibn ʿAlī. *al-Rasā'il al-salafīya fī iḥyā' sunnat khayr al-barīya*. Beirut: Dār al-Kutub al-ʿIlmīya, 1348/1930.

al-Shaybānī, Muḥammad. *Kitāb al-Aṣl al-maʿrūf bi'l-Mabsūṭ*. Ed. Abū'l-Wafā' al-Afghānī. 5 vols. Beirut: ʿĀlam al-Kutub, 1410/1990.

al-Shaykh ʿAlwān, ʿAlī ibn ʿAṭīya al-Hītī. *Nasamāt al-asḥār fī manāqib wa-karāmāt al-awliyā' al-akhyār*. Ed. Aḥmad Farīd al-Mazīdī. Beirut: Dār al-Kutub al-ʿIlmīya, 1421/2001.

al-Shaykh al-Mufīd. *Muṣannafāt al-Shaykh al-Mufīd*. 50 vols. [Qum]: al-Mu'tamar al-ʿĀlamī li-Alfīyat al-Shaykh al-Mufīd, 1413.

al-Shirbīnī, Yūsuf. *Yūsuf al-Shirbīnī's Brains Confounded by the Ode of Abū Shādūf Expounded (Kitāb Hazz al-Quḥūf bi-Sharḥ Qaṣīd Abī Shādūf)*. Trans. and introduction by Humphrey Davies. 2 vols. Leuven: Uitgeverij Peeters en Departement Oosterse Studies, 2007.

al-Shirwānī, ʿAbd al-Ḥamīd, and al-ʿAbbādī, Aḥmad ibn Qāsim. *Ḥawāshī al-Shirwānī wa'l-ʿAbbādī ʿalā Tuḥfat al-muḥtāj bi-sharḥ al-Minhāj*. 10 vols. Beirut: Dār Ṣādir, 1972.

Sibt ibn al-Jawzī. *Wasā'il al-aslāf ilā masā'il al-khilāf*. Ed. Sayyid Mahnī. Beirut: Dār al-Kutub al-ʿIlmīya, 1419/1998.

al-Sijistānī, Abū Yaʿqūb. *Kitāb al-Iftikhār*. Ed. Muṣṭafā Ghālib. Beirut: Dār al-Andalus, 1980.

Kitāb Ithbāt al-nubū'āt. Ed. ʿĀrif Tāmir. Beirut: al-Maṭbaʿa al-Kāthūlīkīya, 1966.
al-Sindī, Raḥmat Allāh. *Risāla fī bayān al-iqtidāʾ bi'l-shāfiʿīya wa'l-khilāf fi dhālika*. MS Cairo, 347 Majāmīʿ.
Spencer, Rev. J. A. *The East: Sketches of Travel in Egypt and the Holy Land*. New York: George G. Putnam, 1850.
al-Subkī, ʿAlī ibn ʿAbd al-Kāfī Taqī al-Dīn. *Fatāwā al-Subkī*. 2 vols. Beirut: Dār al-Maʿrifa, n.d.
al-Sulamī, ʿIzz al-Dīn ibn ʿAbd al-Salām. *al-Fatāwā al-mawṣilīya*. Ed. Iyād Khālid al-Ṭabbāʿ. Damascus: Dār al-Fikr, 1999.
al-Fatāwā al-miṣrīya. Ed. Iyād Khālid al-Ṭabbāʿ. Damascus: Dār al-Fikr, 1428/2007.
Fatāwā Shaykh al-Islām ʿIzz al-Dīn ibn ʿAbd al-Salām. Ed. Muḥammad Jumʿa Kurdī. Beirut: Muʾassasat al-Risāla, 1416/1996.
Maqāṣid al-ṣalāt. Ed. Iyād Khālid al-Ṭabbāʿ. Beirut: Dār al-Fikr al-Muʿāṣir/Damascus: Dār al-Fikr, 1413/1992.
Qawāʿid al-aḥkām fī maṣāliḥ al-anām. 2 vols. in 1. Beirut: Muʾassasat al-Rayyān, 1410/1990).
al-Sūsī, Muḥammad ibn ʿAlī ibn Ibrāhīm Akbīl. *Tanbīh al-ikhwān ʿalā tark al-bidaʿ wa'l-ʿiṣyān*. Ed. Muḥammad Sitītū. Wajdah: Kullīyat al-Ādāb wa'l-ʿUlūm al-Insānīya, Jāmiʿat Muḥammad al-Awwal, 2001.
al-Suyūṭī, Jalāl al-Dīn. *al-Muzhir fī ʿulūm al-lugha wa-anwāʿihā*. Ed. Muḥammad Aḥmad Jād al-Mawlā et al. 2 vols. Cairo: ʿĪsā al-Bābī al-Ḥalabī wa-Shurakāʾuhu, n.d.
al-Suyūṭī, Muṣṭafā ibn Saʿd. *Maṭālib ūlī al-nuhā fī sharḥ Ghāyat al-muntahā*. 6 vols. [Damascus]: Manshūrāt al-Maktab al-Islāmī, 1380/1961.
al-Ṭabarānī, Sulaymān ibn Aḥmad. *al-Muʿjam al-awṣaṭ*. 10 vols. Cairo: Dār al-Ḥaramayn, 1415/1995.
al-Ṭabarī, Muḥammad ibn Jarīr. *Jāmiʿ al-bayān ʿan taʾwīl āy al-qurʾān*. 30 vols. in 15. Beirut: Dār al-Fikr, 1408/1988.
The History of al-Ṭabarī, vol. XII: The Battle of al-Qādisiyya and the Conquest of Syria and Palestine. Trans. Yohanan Friedman. Albany: SUNY Press, 1992.
Taʾrīkh al-Ṭabarī. Ed. Muḥammad Abū'l-Faḍl Ibrāhīm. 11 vols. Beirut: Dār al-Turāth, n.d.
al-Tirmidhī, Muḥammad ibn ʿAlī al-Ḥakīm. *Kitāb Ithbāt al-ʿilal*. Ed. Khālid Zahrī. Rabat: Jāmiʿat Muḥammad al-Khāmis, Kullīyat al-Ādāb wa'l-ʿUlūm al-Insānīya, 1998.
al-Ṭūsī, Muḥammad ibn al-Ḥasan. *Tahdhīb al-aḥkām*. Beirut: Dār al-Aḍwāʾ, 1406/1985.
al-Ubbī, Muḥammad ibn Khalīfa al-Washtānī. *Ikmāl Ikmāl al-muʿallim*, printed with Muslim ibn Ḥajjāj al-Qushayrī al-Naysābūrī, *Ṣaḥīḥ Muslim*. 9 vols. Beirut: Dār al-Kutub al-ʿIlmīya, 1415/1994.
Usama ibn Munqidh. *The Book of Contemplation*. Trans. Paul M. Cobb. London: Penguin Books, 2008.
ʿUthaymīn, Muḥammad ibn Ṣāliḥ. *Fatāwā arkān al-islām*. Riyadh: Dār al-Thurayyā li-l-Nashr, 1421/[2000–1].
Wānilī, Khayr al-Dīn. *al-Masjid fī'l-islām: risālatuhu, niẓām bināʾihi, aḥkāmuhu, ādābuhu, bidaʿuhu*. N.p., n.d.
al-Wansharīsī, Aḥmad ibn Yaḥyā. *al-Miʿyār al-muʿrib wa'l-jāmiʿ al-mughrib ʿan fatāwā ahl ifrīqīya wa'l-andalus wa'l-maghrib*. 13 vols. Rabat: Wizārat al-Awqāf wa'l-Shu'ūn al-Islāmīya bi'l-Mamlaka al-Maghribīya, 1401/1981.

Watt, W. Montgomery, trans. *The Faith and Practice of al-Ghazālī*. London: George Allen & Unwin Ltd., 1953.

Wehr, Hans. *Arabic–English Dictionary*. Ed. J. M. Cowan. Ithaca: Spoken Language Services, 1976.

al-Zabīdī, Murtaḍā. *Tāj al-ʿarūs min jawāhir al-Qāmūs*. 40 vols. in 20. Beirut: Dār al-Kutub al-ʿIlmīya, 1428/2007.

Zaghlūl, Muḥammad al-Saʿīd ibn Basyūnī. *Mawsūʿat aṭrāf al-ḥadīth al-nabawī al-sharīf*. 11 vols. Beirut: Dār al-Kutub al-ʿIlmīya, n.d.

al-Zamakhsharī, Mahmūd ibn ʿUmar. *al-Kashshāf ʿan ḥaqāʾiq al-tanzīl wa-ʿuyūn al-aqāwīl fī wujūd al-taʾwīl*. 4 vols. Cairo: Muṣṭafā al-Bābī al-Ḥalabī, 1388/1966.

al-Zarkashī, Badr al-Dīn Muḥammad ibn Bahādur. *al-Manthūr fī'l-qawāʿid*. 2 vols. Beirut: Dār al-Kutub al-ʿIlmīya, 1421/2000.

al-Zarkashī, Muḥammad ibn ʿAbd Allāh. *Sharḥ al-Zarkashī ʿalā Mukhtaṣar al-Khiraqī*, Ed. ʿAbd Allāh ibn ʿAbd al-Raḥmān al-Jabrīn. 7 vols. Riyadh: Maktabat al-ʿUbaykān, 1993.

al-Zaylaʿī, ʿUthmān ibn ʿAlī. *Tabyīn al-ḥaqāʾiq sharḥ Kanz al-daqāʾiq*. 6 vols. Būlāq: al-Maṭbaʿa al-Kubrā al-Amīrīya, 1313–15 [1895/6–97/8].

II. SECONDARY SOURCES

Abu-Rabiʿ, Ibrahim M. *Intellectual Origins of Islamic Resurgence in the Modern Arab World*. Albany: SUNY Press, 1996.

Abu-Zahra, Nadia. "The Rain Rituals as Rites of Spiritual Passage." *International Journal of Middle East Studies* 20 (1988), pp. 507–29.

Ali, Abdullah Yusuf. *The Holy Qur'an: English Translation of the Meanings with Notes*. Indianapolis: H&C International, 1992.

Ali, Mohamed Mohamed Yunis. *Medieval Islamic Pragmatics: Sunni Legal Theorists' Models of Textual Communication*. Richmond: Curzon Press, 2000.

Baron, Beth. *The Women's Awakening in Egypt: Culture, Society, and the Press*. New Haven: Yale University Press, 1994.

Bauer, Karen. "'Traditional' Exegeses of Q 4:34." *Comparative Islamic Studies* 2 (2006), pp. 129–42.

Becker, C. H. "On the History of Muslim Worship." In Gerald Hawting, ed., *The Development of Islamic Ritual*. Aldershot: Ashgate Publishing Limited, 2006, pp. 49–74.

Bell, Joseph Norment. *Love Theory in Late Hanbalite Islam*. Albany: SUNY Press, 1979.

Berkey, Jonathan. *The Formation of Islam*. Cambridge: Cambridge University Press, 2003.

Bowen, John R. *Muslims through Discourse*. Princeton: Princeton University Press, 1993.

"Salat in Indonesia: The Social Meanings of an Islamic Ritual." *Man* 24 (1989), pp. 600–19.

Bravmann, M. M. *The Spiritual Background of Early Islam: Studies in Ancient Arab Concepts*. Leiden and Boston: Brill, 2009.

Bringa, Tone. *Being Muslim the Bosnian Way: Identity and Community in a Central Bosnian Village*. Princeton: Princeton University Press, 1995.

Brink, Judy. "Lost Rituals: Sunni Muslim Women in Rural Egypt." In Judy Brink and Joan Mencher, eds. *Mixed Blessings: Gender and Religious Fundamentalism Cross Culturally*. New York: Routledge, 1997, pp. 199–208.

Brockopp, Jonathan. *Early Mālikī Law: Ibn ʿAbd al-Ḥakam and His Major Compendium of Jurisprudence*. Leiden: Brill, 2000.

Calder, Norman. "Friday Prayer and the Juristic Theory of the Caliphate: Sarakhsī, Shīrāzī, Māwardī." *Bulletin of the School of Oriental and African Studies* 49 (1986), pp. 35–47.

Studies in Early Muslim Jurisprudence. Oxford: Clarendon Press, 1993.

Calderini, Simonetta. "Contextualizing Arguments about Female Ritual Leadership (Women Imāms) in Classical Islamic Sources." *Comparative Islamic Studies* 5, 1 (2009), pp. 5–32.

Chittick, William C. *The Sufi Path of Knowledge: Ibn al-ʿArabi's Metaphysics of Imagination*. Albany: SUNY Press, 1989.

Chodkiewicz, Michel. *An Ocean without Shore: Ibn ʿArabî, the Book, and the Law*. Trans. from the French by David Streight. Albany: SUNY Press, 1993.

Choksy, Jamsheed K. *Purity and Pollution in Zoroastrianism: Triumph over Evil*. Austin: University of Texas Press, 1989.

Colby, Frederick S. *Narrating Muḥammad's Night Journey: Tracing the Development of the Ibn ʿAbbās Ascension Discourse*. Albany: SUNY Press, 2008.

Commins, David Dean. *Islamic Reform: Politics and Social Change in Late Ottoman Syria*. New York: Oxford University Press, 1990.

Cook, Michael. *Commanding Right and Forbidding Wrong in Islamic Thought*. Cambridge: Cambridge University Press, 2000.

Cooperson, Michael. *Classical Arabic Biography: The Heirs of the Prophets in the Age of al-Maʾmūn*. Cambridge: Cambridge University Press, 2000.

Courteille A. P. and Arnot, A. *Turkish Literature, Comprising Fables, Belles-Lettres, and Sacred Traditions*. Rev. ed. New York: Colonial Press, [1901].

Crone, Patricia. *God's Rule: Government and Islam*. New York: Columbia University Press, 2004.

Crone, Patricia and Cook, Michael. *Hagarism: The Making of the Islamic World*. Cambridge: Cambridge University Press, 1977.

Dannenfeldt, Karl H. *Leonhard Rauwolf, Sixteenth-Century Physician, Botanist, and Traveler*. Cambridge, Mass.: Harvard University Press, 1968.

de Callataÿ, Godefroid. *Ikhwan al-Safaʾ: A Brotherhood of Idealists on the Fringe of Orthodox Islam*. Oxford: Oneworld, 2005.

Deeb, Lara. *An Enchanted Modern: Gender and Public Piety in Shi'i Lebanon*. Princeton and Oxford: Princeton University Press, 2006.

Dols, Michael W. *The Black Death in the Middle East*. Princeton: Princeton University Press, 1977.

Donohue, John J. and Esposito, John L., eds. *Islam in Transition: Muslim Perspectives*. 2nd ed. New York: Oxford University Press, 2007.

Douglas, Mary. *Natural Symbols: Explorations in Cosmology*. New York: Pantheon Books, 1982.

Doumato, Eleanor Abdella. *Getting God's Ear: Women, Islam, and Healing in Saudi Arabia and the Gulf*. New York: Columbia University Press, 2000.

D'Souza, Diane. "Women's Presence in the Mosque: A Viewpoints" [*sic*], in Asghar Ali Engineer, ed., *Islam, Women and Gender Justice*. New Delhi: Gyan Publishing House, 2001, pp. 193–217.

Dutton, Yasin. "ʿAmal v. Ḥadīth in Islamic Law: The Case of Sadl al-Yadayn (Holding One's Hands by One's Sides) When Doing the Prayer." *Islamic Law and Society* 3 (1996), pp. 13–40.

Ehrlich, Uri. *The Nonverbal Language of Prayer: A New Approach to Jewish Liturgy.* Trans. Dena Ordan. Tübingen: Mohr Siebeck, 2004.

EI[2] = *Encyclopaedia of Islam*. 2nd ed. Ed P. Bearman, T. Bianquis, C. E. Bosworth, E. van Donzel, and W. P. Heinrichs. Leiden: Brill, 1954–2009.

El Cheikh, Nadia Maria. *Byzantium Viewed by the Arabs*. Cambridge, Mass.: Distributed for the Center for Middle Eastern Studies of Harvard University by Harvard University Press, 2004.

Elewa, Ahmed, and Silvers, Laury. "'I *Am* One of the People': A Survey and Analysis of Legal Arguments on Woman-Led Prayer in Islam." *Journal of Law and Religion* 26 (2010), pp. 141–71.

Encyclopaedia Iranica. Ed. Ehsan Yar-Shater. New York: Columbia University Center for Iranian Studies, 1997–.

Encyclopaedia of the Qurʾān. Ed. Jane Dammen McAuliffe. Leiden: Brill, 2001–6.

Fierro, Maribel. "Women as Prophets in Islam." In Manuela Marín and Randi Deguilhem, eds., *Writing the Feminine: Women in Arab Sources*. London: I. B. Tauris, 2002, pp. 183–98.

Fischer, Michael M. J. *Iran: From Religious Dispute to Revolution*. Madison: University of Wisconsin Press, 1980.

Fischer, Michael M. J. and Abedi, Mehdi. *Debating Muslims: Cultural Dialogues in Postmodernity and Tradition*. Madison: University of Wisconsin Press, 1990.

Frank, R. M. *al-Ghazālī and the Ashʿarite School*. Durham and London: Duke University Press, 1994.

Franke, Patrick. "Ritual Prayer and Madhhab Identity in Mecca at the Turn of the Seventeenth Century: Some Texts by the Hanafi Scholar Ali al-Qari." Unpublished conference paper delivered at the conference Performing Religion: Actors, Contexts, and Text, Orient-Institut Beirut, November 18, 2011.

Goldziher, Ignaz. *The Ẓāhirīs: Their Doctrine and Their History.* Trans. Wolfgang Behn. Leiden: E. J. Brill, 1971.

Gräf, Bettina and Skovgaard-Petersen, Jakob, eds. *Global Mufti: The Phenomenon of Yusuf al-Qaradawi*. New York: Columbia University Press, 2009.

Graham, William A. "Islam in the Mirror of Ritual." In Richard G. Hovanisian and Speros Vryonis, Jr., eds., *Islam's Understanding of Itself* (Malibu, Calif.: Undena Publications, 1983), pp. 53–71.

Haider, Najam. *The Origins of the Shīʿa: Identity, Ritual, and Sacred Space in Eighth-Century Kūfa*. Cambridge: Cambridge University Press, 2011.

Halevi, Leor. *Muhammad's Grave: Death Rites and the Making of Islamic Society.* New York: Columbia University Press, 2007.

Hallaq, Wael B. *Sharīʿa: Theory, Practice, Transformations*. Cambridge: Cambridge University Press, 2009.

Hamza, Feras and Rizvi, Sajjad, eds. *An Anthology of Qur'anic Commentaries*. Vol. 1: *On the Nature of the Divine*. Oxford: Oxford University Press, in association with the Institute of Ismaili Studies, London, 2008.

Harnischfeger, Johannes. *Democratization and Islamic Law.* Frankfurt and New York: Campus Verlag, 2008.

Hawting, G. R. *The Idea of Idolatry and the Emergence of Islam: From Polemic to History*. Cambridge: Cambridge University Press, 1999.

Heath, Peter. *Allegory and Philosophy in Avicenna (Ibn Sînâ)*. Philadelphia: University of Pennsylvania Press, 1992.

Henkel, Heiko. "'Between Belief and Unbelief Lies the Performance of Salāt': Meaning and Efficacy of a Muslim Ritual." *Journal of the Royal Anthropological Institute* 11 (2005), pp. 487–507.

Heyd, Uriel. *Studies in Old Ottoman Criminal Law*. Ed. V. L. Ménage. Oxford: Clarendon Press, 1973.

Holod, Renata and Khan, Hasan-Uddin. *The Contemporary Mosque: Architects, Clients and Designs since the 1950s*. New York: Rizzoli, 1997.

Izutsu, Toshihiko. *Ethico-Religious Concepts in the Qur'ān*. Montreal and Kingston: McGill–Queen's University Press, 2002.

Jeffery, Arthur. *The Foreign Vocabulary of the Qur'an*. Baroda: Oriental Institute, 1938.

Johansen, Baber. *Contingency in a Sacred Law: Legal and Ethical Norms in the Muslim Fiqh*. Leiden: Brill, 1999.

Katz, Marion H. *Body of Text: The Emergence of the Sunnī Law of Ritual Purity*. Albany: SUNY Press, 2002.

"The Hajj and the Study of Islamic Ritual." *Studia Islamica* 98/99 (2004), pp. 95–129.

"The Study of Islamic Ritual and the Meaning of *Wuḍū'*." *Der Islam* 82 (2005), pp. 106–45.

Khalidi, Tarif. *Arabic Historical Thought in the Classical Period*. Cambridge: Cambridge University Press, 1994.

Kister, M. J. "The Expedition of Bi'r Ma'ūna." In George Makdisi, ed., *Arabic and Islamic Studies in Honor of Hamilton A. R. Gibb*. Leiden: E. J. Brill, 1965, pp. 337–57.

"Some Reports Concerning al-Ṭā'if." *Jerusalem Studies in Arabic and Islam* 1 (1979), pp. 1–18.

Kraus, Paul. *Alchemie, Ketzerei, Apokryphen im frühen Islam: Gesammelte Aufsätze*. Hildesheim: Georg Olms Verlag, 1994.

Kugle, Scott. *Rebel between Spirit and Law: Ahmad Zarruq, Sainthood, and Authority in Islam*. Bloomington and Indianapolis: Indiana University Press, 2006.

Loeffler, Reinhold. *Islam in Practice: Religious Beliefs in a Persian Village*. Albany: SUNY Press, 1988.

Maghen, Ze'ev. "Much Ado about Wuḍū'." *Der Islam* 76 (1999), pp. 205–52.

Virtues of the Flesh: Passion and Purity in Early Islamic Jurisprudence. Leiden and Boston: Brill, 2005.

Mahdjoube, Abdolrahmane. "The Inner Revolution of a Khomeyni Activist." In Monique Gadant, ed., *Women of the Mediterranean*. London: Zed, 1986, pp. 60–71.

Mahmood, Saba. *Politics of Piety: The Islamic Revival and the Feminist Subject*. Princeton: Princeton University Press, 2005.

Makdisi, George. "Ibn Taymīya: A Ṣūfī of the Qādirīya Order." *American Journal of Arabic Studies* 1 (1973), pp. 118–29.

The Rise of Colleges: Institutions of Learning in Islam and the West. Edinburgh: Edinburgh University Press, 1981.

Marín, Manuela. *Mujeres en al-Ándalus*. Madrid: Consejo Superior de Investigaciones Científicas, 2000.

al-Mawsūʿa al-fiqhīya. 2nd printing. 45 vols. Kuwait: Wizārat al-Awqāf wa'l-Shu'ūn al-Islāmīya, 1404/1983–.
McGinnis, Jon. *Avicenna*. Oxford and New York: Oxford University Press, 2010.
Melchert, Christopher. "Whether to Keep Women Out of the Mosque: A Survey of Medieval Islamic Law." In B. Michalak-Pikulska and A. Pikulski, eds., *Authority, Privacy and Public Order in Islam: Proceedings of the 22nd Congress of L'Union Européenne des Arabisants et Islamisants, Cracow, Poland 2004*. Leuven: Peeters, 2006, pp. 59–69.
Mernissi, Fatima. *The Veil and the Male Elite: A Feminist Interpretation of Women's Rights in Islam*. Trans. Mary Jo Lakeland. Reading, Mass.: Addison-Wesley Publishing Company, Inc., 1991.
"Women, Saints, and Sanctuaries." *Signs* 3 (1977), pp. 101–12.
Messick, Brinkley. "Kissing Hands and Knees: Hegemony and Hierarchy in Shari'a Discourse." *Law & Society Review*, 22, 4, Special Issue: Law and Ideology (1988), pp. 637–60.
Morony, Michael. *Iraq after the Muslim Conquest*. Princeton: Princeton University Press, 1984.
al-Muḥārib, Ruqayya bint Muḥammad. *Kayfa takhshaʿīna fī'l-ṣalāt?* Riyadh: Dār al-Qāsim, 2000.
Murad, Abdal-Hakim. "Understanding the Four Madhhabs," www.al-fikr.name.my/understanding_the_four_madhabs.htm, accessed August 11, 2011.
Najmabadi, Afsaneh. "Crafting an Educated Housewife in Iran." In Lila Abu-Lughod, ed., *Remaking Women: Feminism and Modernity in the Middle East*. Princeton: Princeton University Press, 1998, pp. 91–125.
Nelson, Kristina. *The Art of Reciting the Qur'an*. Cairo and New York: American University in Cairo Press, 2001.
Neuwirth, Angelika. "Du texte de récitation au canon en passant par la liturgie." *Arabica* 47 (2000), pp. 174–209.
Newman, Andrew. "Fayd al-Kashani and the Rejection of the Clergy/State Alliance." In Linda S. Wallbridge, ed. *The Most Learned of the Shi'a*. Cary, N.C.: Oxford University Press, 2001, pp. 34–52.
Padwick, Constance E. *Muslim Devotions: A Study of Prayer Manuals in Common Use*. Oxford: Oneworld, 1996.
Perlmann, Moshe. "A Seventeenth Century Exhortation Concerning al-Aqṣā." *Israel Oriental Studies* 3 (1973), pp. 261–92.
Popenoe, Rebecca. *Feeding Desire: Fatness, Beauty, and Sexuality among a Saharan People*. London and New York: Routledge, 2004.
Powers, Paul R. *Intent in Islamic Law: Motive and Meaning in Medieval Sunnī Fiqh*. Leiden: Brill, 2006.
"Interiors, Intentions, and the 'Spirituality' of Islamic Ritual Practice." *Journal of the American Academy of Religion* 72 (2004), pp. 425–59.
Qureshi, Regula Burkhardt. "Transcending Space: Recitation and Community among South Asian Muslims in Canada." In Barbara Daly Metcalf, ed., *Making Muslim Space in North America and Europe*. Berkeley: University of California Press, 1996, pp. 46–64.
Rapoport, Yossef. *Marriage, Money and Divorce in Medieval Islamic Society*. Cambridge: Cambridge University Press, 2005.

Rapoport, Yossef, and Ahmed, Shahab, eds. *Ibn Taymiyya and His Times*. Oxford: Oxford University Press, 2010.

Reid, Megan. *Ritual and Piety in Medieval Islam*. Cambridge: Cambridge University Press, forthcoming.

Reinhart, A. Kevin. *Before Revelation: The Boundaries of Muslim Moral Thought*. Albany: SUNY Press, 1995.

"Impurity/No Danger." *History of Religions* 30 (1990), pp. 1–24.

Reuter, Bärbel. *Gelebte Religion: Religiöse Praxis junger Islamistinnen in Kairo*. Würzburg: ERGON Verlag, 1999.

Reynolds, Dwight F., ed. *Interpreting the Self: Autobiography in the Arabic Literary Tradition*. Berkeley: University of California Press, 2001.

Reynolds, Gabriel Said. *The Qur'ān in Its Historical Context*. London and New York: Routledge, 2008.

Rispler-Chaim, Vardit. *Disability in Islamic Law*. Dordrecht: Springer, 2007.

Rubin, Uri. "Morning and Evening Prayers in Early Islam." *Jerusalem Studies in Arabic and Islam* 10 (1987), pp. 40–64.

Sadeghi, Behnam. *The Logic of Law-Making in Islam: Women and Prayer in the Legal Tradition*. Cambridge: Cambridge University Press, 2012.

Sands, Kristin Zahra. *Ṣūfī Commentaries on the Qur'ān in Classical Islam*. London: Routledge, 2006.

Sayeed, Asma. "Early Sunni Discourse on Women's Mosque Attendance." *ISIM Newsletter* 7 (2001), p. 10.

Schacht, Joseph. *An Introduction to Islamic Law*. London: Oxford University Press, 1964.

Sezgin, Fuat. *Geschichte des arabischen Schrifttums*. 15 vols. Leiden: E. J. Brill, 1967.

Shoshan, Boaz. *Popular Culture in Medieval Cairo*. Cambridge: Cambridge University Press, 1993.

Starrett, Gregory. *Putting Islam to Work: Education, Politics, and Religious Transformation in Egypt*. Berkeley: University of California Press, 1998.

Stearns, Justin K. *Infectious Ideas: Contagion in Premodern Islamic and Christian Thought in the Western Mediterranean*. Baltimore: Johns Hopkins University Press, 2011.

Stewart, Devin. "Polemics and Patronage in Safavid Iran: The Debate on Friday Prayer During the Reign of Shah Tahmasb." *Bulletin of the School of Oriental and African Studies* 72 (2009), pp. 425–57.

Talmon-Heller, Daniella. *Islamic Piety in Medieval Syria: Mosques, Cemeteries and Sermons under the Zangids and Ayyubids (1146–1260)*. Leiden and Boston: Brill, 2007.

Targoff, Ramie. *Common Prayer: The Language of Public Devotion in Early Modern England*. Chicago: University of Chicago Press, 2001.

Taylor, Christopher Schurman. *In the Vicinity of the Righteous: Ziyāra and the Veneration of Saints in Late Medieval Egypt*. Leiden and Boston: Brill, 1999.

Thurfjell, David. *Living Shi'ism: Instances of Ritualisation Among Islamist Men in Contemporary Iran*. Leiden: Brill, 2006.

Torab, Azam. *Performing Islam: Gender and Ritual in Iran*. Leiden and Boston: Brill, 2007.

Tottoli, Roberto. "Muslim Attitudes towards Prostration (*sujūd*): I. Arabs and Prostration at the Beginning of Islam and in the Qur'ān." *Studia Islamica* 88 (1998), pp. 5–34.

"Muslim Attitudes towards Prostration (*sujūd*): II. The Prominence and Meaning of Prostration in Muslim Literature." *Le Muséon* 111 (1998), pp. 405–26.

Ukeles, Raquel Margalit. "Innovation or Deviation: Exploring the Boundaries of Islamic Devotional Law." Ph.D. dissertation, Harvard University, 2006.

Vishanoff, David R. *The Formation of Islamic Hermaneutics: How Sunni Legal Theorists Imagined a Revealed Law.* New Haven, Conn.: American Oriental Society, 2011.

von Schlegell, Barbara. "Sufism in the Ottoman Arab World: Shaykh ʿAbd al-Ghanī al-Nābulusī (d. 1143/1731)." Ph.D. dissertation, University of California, Berkeley, 1997.

Wadud, Amina. *Inside the Gender Jihad: Women's Reform in Islam.* Oxford: Oneworld, 2006.

Qur'an and Woman. New York and Oxford: Oxford University Press, 1999.

Wansbrough, John. *The Sectarian Milieu: Content and Composition of Islamic Salvation History.* Oxford: Oxford University Press, 1978.

Watenpaugh, Heghnar Zeitlian. "Deviant Dervishes: Space, Gender, and the Construction of Antinomian Piety in Ottoman Aleppo." *IJMES* 37 (2005), pp. 535–65.

Wensinck, A. J. *The Muslim Creed, its Genesis and Historical Development.* 2nd ed. New Delhi: Oriental Books Reprint Corporation, 1979 [Cambridge: Cambridge University Press, 1932].

Whittingham, Martin. *al-Ghazālī and the Qur'ān: One Book, Many Meanings.* London: Routledge, 2007.

al-Yūbī, Laḥsan. *al-Fatāwā al-fiqhīya fī ahamm al-qaḍāyā.* Rabat: al-Mamlaka al-Maghribīya, Wizārat al-Awqāf wa'l-Shu'ūn al-Islāmīya, 1419/1998.

Zaman, Muhammad Qasim. *The Ulama in Contemporary Islam.* Princeton and Oxford: Princeton University Press, 2002.

Zaydān, ʿAbd al-Karīm. *al-Mufaṣṣal fī aḥkām al-mar'a wa bayt al-muslim fī al-sharīʿa al-islāmīya.* 11 vols. Beirut: Mu'assasat al-Risāla, 1420/2000.

al-Zuḥaylī, Wahba. *al-Fiqh al-islāmī wa-adillatuhu.* 11 vols. Damascus: Dār al-Fikr, 1425/2005.

Index

Aaron (biblical figure), 175
ʿAbd Allāh, Sharīk ibn, 150
al-ʿĀbidīn, ʿAlī Zayn, 31
ablution, 87
Abraham (prophet), 10, 114
Abū Bakr (caliph), 68, 133, 163
Abū Dāwūd, 182, 190–191, 193
Abū Ḥanīfa
  on *duʿāʾ*, 33
  on *imāma*, 147
  on *nīya*, 49
  on *ṣalāt*, 27, 28
  on weeping, 69
  on women and prayer, 180, 195–196, 198, 199–200
Abūʾl-ʿĀliya, 150
Abū Shāma, 161
Abū Ṭālib, 17
Abū Thawr, 181, 186
Abū Yaʿlā ibn al-Farrāʾ, 133–134, 144, 156
Abū Yūsuf, 28, 69, 196, 199
acceptance and *duʿāʾ*, 34–35
Aceh province (Indonesia), 123
ʿadāla (probity), 142–143
Adam (prophet), 10, 16, 114
ʿAdīibn Zayd, 14
ʿĀʾisha (Prophet's wife)
  menstruation and, 178
  on prostration, 19
  on weeping, 68
  on women and prayer, 182, 184, 193, 200
al-Albānī, Nāṣir al-Dīn, 173–174
Algar, Hamid, 31, 135
Ali, Abdullah Yusuf, 95, 186
Ali, Mohamed Mohamed Yunis, 100
ʿAlī ibn Abī Ṭālib (Prophet's son-in-law), 24, 31, 56, 115, 131, 133, 135
al-ʿĀmilī, Muḥammad al-Makkī. *See* al-Shahīd al-Awwal
al-ʿĀmirī, Abūʾl-Ḥasan, 87
Aqṣā Mosque, 202–203
Arabic, *ṣalāt* performed in, 28–29
"Arab Spring," 176
Aristotelianism, 105–106
ascension of Prophet to heaven (*miʿrāj*), 96–98, 112
al-Aʿshā, 12, 13–14
al-Ashʿarī, Abū Mūsā, 133
Ashʿarī school
  duʿāʾ in, 40–42
  rational objectives in *ṣalāt* and, 78
  royal audience model of *ṣalāt* and, 92
Askia Muḥammad I, 170
al-ʿAsqalānī, Ibn Ḥajar, 36, 42–43, 202
ʿAtāʾ ibn Abī Rabāḥ, 133
atheism, 124
al-Athram, 143–144
ʿĀtika bint Zayd, 191–192
attentiveness *(ḥuḍūr al-qalb)*
  royal audience model of *ṣalāt* and, 89–91
  ṣalāt and, 58–62
al-ʿAynī, Badr al-Dīn, 95–96
Azawagh Arabs, 172
al-Azhar University (Cairo), 54, 175

al-Bahūtī, Manṣūr ibn Yūnūs, 149, 154
al-Bannā, Ḥasan, 122–123, 125, 173
al-Bāqillānī, Abū Bakr, 54–55
Becker, C. H., 140
Bell, Joseph, 65
Bilāl, 66, 67
Bin Bāz, ʿAbd al-ʿAzīz, 207–208
Bird, Mary R. S., 5
Bowen, John, 83, 84, 121
Böwering, Gerhard, 10
Brethren of Purity (Ikhwān al-Ṣafā), 105–109, 114
Bringa, Tone, 172
Brink, Judy, 214
al-Bukhārī, *Ṣaḥīḥ* of, 18–19, 94, 95–96, 177–178, 184, 190–191, 192, 193
al-Bukhārī, Ṭāhir ibn Aḥmad, 199–200
Burckhardt, John Lewis, 213–214

Friday prayers (*jumʿa*). See *jumʿa* (Friday prayers)

Gabriel (angel), 18, 20, 32–33
gender and prayer. *See* women and prayer
al-Ghazālī
  on *duʿā*ʾ, 30, 37, 39, 41
  on emotions in *ṣalāt*, 63, 64, 74
  on "Epistles of the Brethren of Purity," 109
  on failure to pray, 166–167
  on heart versus lower soul, 105
  on *ḥuḍūr al-qalb*, 58–62
  on instruction in and correction of prayer, 159
  on *munājāt*, 95
  on *nīya*, 52–53
  on political leaders, 93–94
  on *raghāʾib*, 160, 161
  on rational objectives of *ṣalāt*, 78–79
  on royal audience model of *ṣalāt*, 89, 92, 94
  on *ṣalāt* as communication, 98–100
  on *taʿabbud*, 82
  on women and prayer, 200
Graham, William, 83
grief, role of in *ṣalāt*, 68–70
Grunebaum, Gustave von, 6

ḥadīth (sayings of Prophet). *See specific topics*
Haider, Najam, 150
al-Ḥajjāj, 140
Ḥajjī Khalīfa, 161
Hallaq, Wael, 7
Ḥanafī school
  on congregational prayer, 128, 173
  on failure to pray, 163–164
  imāma in, 147–148
  jumʿa in, 130–131, 135
  khushūʿ and, 57
  nīya in, 45
  origins of, 24
  ṣalāt in, 28, 29
  on women and prayer, 183–185, 195–196, 199–201
Ḥanbalī school
  on congregational prayer, 128, 129, 173
  on failure to pray, 165
  imāma in, 143–146
  jumʿa in, 130
  nīya in, 45
  origins of, 24
  on women and prayer, 181–182, 183, 198
Harrison, Paul, 4
al-Ḥasan al-Baṣrī, 159–160
al-Ḥaṣkafī, Muḥammad, 50, 135
al-Haytamī, Ibn Ḥajar, 47–48, 164
Ḥayy ibn Yaqẓān (fictional character), 79
Henkel, Heiko, 83–84
heresy, 144
al-Hilali, Muḥammad Taqi-ud-Din, 186
al-Ḥiṣnī, Taqī al-Dīn, 200
historical background of *ṣalāt*, 10–11
al-Hītī, ʿAlī ibn ʿAṭīya, *see* Shaykh ʿAlwān
Holod, Renata, 208
honor in royal audience model of *ṣalāt*, 87–89, 91–92
ḥuḍūr al-qalb (attentiveness)
  royal audience model of *ṣalāt* and, 89–91
  ṣalāt and, 58–62
Husain, Ed, 215–216
Ḥusayn, Ṭāhā, 54
al-Ḥusayn ibn ʿAlī, 23, 135
hypocrisy, effect on *nīya*, 47–51

Ibn ʿAbbās, 133
Ibn ʿAbd al-Ghaffār, 202
Ibn ʿAbd al-Wahhāb, Muḥammad, 173
Ibn ʿĀbidīn, 45, 48–49, 135
Ibn Abī Shayba, 133, 140
Ibn ʿAjība, 211
Ibn al-Amyūṭī, 136
Ibn ʿArabī, Muḥyīal-Dīn, 96, 116–121, 183, 186–187
Ibn ʿArafa, 134
Ibn Baṭṭūṭa, 150–151, 155, 157, 203
Ibn Bazzāz, 48
Ibn Fāris, Abū'l-Ḥusayn Aḥmad, 12, 13
Ibn Ḥabīb, 141
Ibn al-Ḥājj, 129–130, 210, 212–213
Ibn Ḥanbal, Aḥmad
  on *duʿā*ʾ, 33–34
  on failure to pray, 163
  as founder of Ḥanbalī school, 24
  on *imāma*, 143–144, 145, 146
  on instruction in and correction of prayer, 157–158
  on *ṣalāt*, 17–18
  on weeping, 69–70
  on women and prayer, 182, 183, 192–193, 198, 211
Ibn Ḥazm, 187
Ibn al-Jazarī, 37
Ibn Jubayr, 171
Ibn Kathīr, 129
Ibn Khuzayma, 193
Ibn Māja, 18, 182
Ibn Manẓūr, 194–195
Ibn Masʿūd, 184
Ibn al-Munāṣif, 155–156, 166, 209–210
Ibn Nujaym, Zayn al-Dīn, 55, 57–58, 200
Ibn Qayyim al-Jawzīya
  on congregational prayer, 129

For EU product safety concerns, contact us at Calle de José Abascal, 56–1°,
28003 Madrid, Spain or eugpsr@cambridge.org.

www.ingramcontent.com/pod-product-compliance
Ingram Content Group UK Ltd.
Pitfield, Milton Keynes, MK11 3LW, UK
UKHW010040140625
459647UK00012BA/1511

* 9 7 8 0 5 2 1 7 1 6 2 9 1 *